1970

Setting the Course

Setting the Course
The First Year

•

Major Policy Statements by
President Richard Nixon

COMMENTARIES BY RICHARD WILSON

Washington Bureau Chief, Cowles Publications, Inc.

An RD Press Book

FUNK & WAGNALLS NEW YORK

Contents

Preface

Theodore Roosevelt called the Presidency a "bully pulpit." In modern times it is that and much more: a combined broadcasting center, research establishment, and information agency.

This function of the Presidency has become so paramount that no major political party would seriously consider nominating for President a candidate not regarded as a master or quick learner of the new techniques of public communication.

The President and the Vice President have the singular distinction in a nation of 200 million as the only public officials elected by all the people. It is the whole people from whom their power flows, and they must remain compatible with a majority of them.

Maintaining compatibility is a more complex art than when the written word, a few still photographs, or halting moving pictures created the image of a remote Presidency clothed in ceremonial and magisterial dignity. Woodrow Wilson or Franklin D. Roosevelt might catch the public's fleeting devotion with a few well-turned phrases, or lose it that way, too. The public's devotion might turn as much on what was written about them, and how, as upon what they did and said.

In 1970 no fourth estate need interpose itself between the Presidency and the public. The President's communication today can be direct, personal, constant, and visual in living color as a running documentary in daily episodes. The Presidential opera enters the homes of those who read little and think little about public affairs except as they are personally touched by war, taxes, inflation. Out of this constant contact has grown an intimacy with the Presidency unknown until the middle part of the twentieth century and growing with each new Presidential term.

Intimacy on this scale can breed contempt or respect. Lyndon B. Johnson recognized with regret his own inability to communicate to the public the persuasiveness of his private discussions. Richard Nixon,

after his defeat in 1960, gave the highest priority to direct public communication and perfected his skills for the campaign of 1968.

The substance of what a President proposes, explains, defends, or
denounces remains the province of those seriously concerned with the
study of public affairs. The student's least informed neighbor or associate, having listened to and watched the President deliver an address
on the state of the Union, may have a pronounced view based as much
on the Presidential manner as on the substance of the speech. This
impression becomes a public fact such as Nixon's "pledge" to end the
war in Vietnam, when a careful reading of all that he has said on this
subject reveals conditioning factors affecting his ability to carry out
the "pledge" as the public understands it.

Much less can the average man absorb the truly astonishing volume of Presidential statements, speeches, press conferences, analyses,
and studies which emerge from the White House in an age when the
President is concerned by such technical matters as the lead content of
gasoline.

In another day a writer or two might suffice. Engulfed by war
and turmoil, Lincoln and Wilson wrote their own speeches and
statements. A master politician, Roosevelt, relied on a brain trust whose
main function was policy-making rather than phrase-making—with
writers Stanley High and Robert Sherwood to polish the product. Harry
S Truman used Clark Clifford and Charles J. Murphy, policy-makers,
and a writer, William Hillman. Dwight Eisenhower relied on special
assistants Malcolm Moos, Bryce Harlow, Kevin McCann, Gabriel Hauge,
and, for a brief period, a journalist, Emmett Hughes, to provide the
flourishes.

Writers for John F. Kennedy abounded and included Theodore
Sorensen, Arthur Schlesinger, Jr., John Kenneth Galbraith, and Richard
Goodwin. They also claimed policy-making functions. Johnson fell back
on the Kennedy holdovers and then added journalist Douglass Cater,
Horace Busby, Joseph Califano, and Harry McPherson, with an occasional contribution from Jack Valenti. Some of these men, too, were
policy-makers.

In the modern Presidential communications age, which may be
said to have begun with Eisenhower's first televised press conference,
large staffs at the White House, the Defense Department, the National
Security Council, the State Department, and numerous other agencies
contribute their share to the torrent of words.

Somewhere it must all be brought together. Nixon has done so
with his special regard for system and order. He placed his battery of
writers in large and comfortable offices on a long corridor on the first

floor of the rococo building which a long time ago housed the entire Departments of State, War, and Navy and now is called the Executive Office Building (EOB).

In precincts familiar to Cordell Hull, Douglas MacArthur, and John J. Pershing, a group of writers, phrasemakers, wordsmiths, and research assistants hammers out much of the word structure of the doctrine Nixon formulates.

They do not create this doctrine except to the extent that their verbalizations may crystallize views which previously have been obscured by indecision or controversy. That function should not be minimized in the gray areas of public policy where the government so often operates.

Under Nixon the White House writing process has been systemized. The writing and research staff is headed by James Keogh, fifty-three, former executive editor of *Time* magazine with a twenty-year career in the special art of dramatic news presentation.

The other writers are Patrick J. Buchanan, thirty, a former editorial writer for the St. Louis *Globe-Democrat;* Raymond K. Price, Jr., forty, former magazine and newspaper writer and editor of the editorial page of the New York *Herald Tribune* in its final two years; William L. Safire, forty-one, former newspaper reporter and radio-TV producer and head of his own public relations firm; Lee W. Huebner, twenty-nine, former teaching fellow and debate coach at Harvard and former president of the Ripon Society, Inc., a progressive Republican organization.

On Writers Row at the White House Buchanan leans right, Price leans left, with Safire in the center. Huebner provides remarks for less formal occasions or Rose Garden ceremonies. Keogh acts as an editor, protector, and counsel for the writing staff as well as doing some writing himself. Writing assignments are based in part on the philosophical or political orientation of the writers. The spectrum from right to left is not broad but does represent that unique combination of conservative, liberal, and center which makes up the Nixon political character. Pride of authorship is banished from their precincts.

An important distinction needs to be made between messages to Congress and speeches by the President, whether broadcast or not. A message to Congress ordinarily deals with requests for legislation to implement policy. The problem may be outlined factually, the need for legislation argued, and the form of the legislation suggested. The Administration may also send a drafted bill to Congress through legislative channels.

This represents a decision by the President, with help from his advisers in the White House, Cabinet members, administrators, and affected groups outside the government. A tax bill or a budget message is not something that can much be helped by rhetoric save to the extent that rhetoric supports reason.

A Presidential speech or broadcast, on the other hand, is often a persuasive bid for public support, relying less on factual analysis than appeals to reason, sentiment, patriotism, and principle. Such speeches are explanatory and communicative. They attempt to respond to or guide public opinion. President Nixon is regarded in Congress and among journalists in Washington as having successfully used the medium of the television broadcast to gain time and acceptance for the execution of controversial policies.

It is in this area that President Nixon's ability as a speechwriter and expositor has come into its fullest play. One of his speechwriters says that he contributes more to his own speeches than any President since Wilson. This, of course, cannot be proved but it is plausible. Important speeches said to be wholly, or almost wholly, Nixon's own include his acceptance speech at the Republican National Convention in August, 1968, the crucial November 3, 1969, broadcast on Vietnam, the State-of-the-Union address in January, 1970, and his exposition of the Cambodian incursion on April 30, 1970.

In preparing the speeches on Vietnam and Cambodia he worked from research data ("points," as they are called) supplied by the staff of the National Security Council. The November speech was dictated and transcribed by his secretary, Miss Rose Mary Woods. He corrected and revised it while sitting in the sunshine in the Rose Garden adjacent to his oval office in the White House. He wrote and revised his Cambodian broadcast at the Presidential retreat in the Catoctin Mountains northwest of Washington.

The President sketches out speeches on yellow, lined foolscap often used by lawyers. He prepares notes in the same way and relied solely on such an outline in delivering extemporaneously his famous "Checkers" broadcast in the campaign of 1952 when he was under challenge as Dwight D. Eisenhower's Vice Presidential nominee.

Associated Press writer Richard E. Meyer has related in detail the preparation of Nixon's State-of-the-Union message in January, 1970. The President began formal work on the message in early December, 1969, in a conference with Keogh and other writers. Nixon asked for deep research on the general theme of the speech as a "gateway to the decade" of the 1970s.

"I don't want any laundry list," said Nixon, mindful of detailed legislative proposals outlined under similar circumstances by Johnson and Kennedy. The President admired Wilson's speeches as the most cogent in this century, and noted that one of his State-of-the-Union messages was only ten minutes long, according to Safire.

Heavy-laden with research on national goals and priorities, the environment, international security, inflation, the quality of life, Nixon went to the "western White House" at San Clemente, California, for a New Year's holiday. During afternoons of seclusion and between rounds of golf, he outlined his speech on yellow scratch pads under Roman numeral headings.

After his working holiday in California, Nixon returned to Washington and then took his volume of material with him to Camp David, Maryland, where, alone with his Irish setter, King Timahoe, he began to write the first draft. He was frequently on the telephone to his assistants in Washington for more information, asked for three new major research and information papers, and after three days emerged with his first draft in longhand. This version was typed, edited, rewritten, shortened, and finally typed for reading in Nixon's special style.

Systemization of writing Presidential utterances would scarcely be practical and certainly of doubtful utility if the Chief Executive himself were inarticulate or vague in what he wished to say.

Safire, in his 1968 book, *The New Language of Politics,* attaches importance to a 1942 quotation of Walter Lippmann: "A public man can and needs to be supplied with material and advice and criticism in preparing an important address. But no one can write an authentic speech for another man; it is as impossible as writing his love letters for him or saying his prayers for him. The truth is that anyone who knows what he thinks can say what he thinks. Those who cannot speak for themselves are, with very rare exceptions, not very sure of what they are doing and of what they mean. The sooner they are found out the better."

Safire comments: "Lippmann's view did not prevail; the public does not frown on a president having speechwriters, indeed has come to expect a president to work from others' drafts. The idea of a speechwriter's assignment, in most people's minds, is one gently sold by every top-level speechwriter: to discuss the speech ideas with the public figure, reflect his point of view clearly and in organized fashion, to submit extra phrases and slogans for the top man's consideration, and to rewrite according to the speaker's wishes."

With Nixon none of this is a problem. He excels at extemporaneous exposition, especially so in groups of fifty to a hundred people. He has written hundreds of his own speeches and is one of the few men in public life capable of organizing and delivering an hour-long television presentation with reference only to notes as if he were reading from text.

Few appreciate now what a radical departure this is from Presidential practice in the more distant past. With a Calvin Coolidge or Herbert Hoover, a Presidential word weighed a ton and was scarcely ever uttered for publication without prayerful premeditation. Wilson's press conference remarks could not be quoted, Roosevelt's and Truman's only in the third person. Eisenhower made the long jump into taped television with direct quotation, and Kennedy completed the evolution with live television.

Nixon reads from a manuscript in slightly larger than normal pica type, triple spaced, and set up like a classical Harvard outline. This makes a picture or diagram of a speech, which Miss Woods is adept in preparing, and protects the President from getting lost in subthemes by fixing his attention on the main points of emphasis. Nevertheless, during his broadcast on the Cambodian incursion, Nixon lost the thread of his narrative in the process of moving his lectern to point out places on a map, hesitated, and came close to skipping a passage. Two Nixon rules: Never rehearse; never watch a replay.

The President is a stickler for the accuracy of allusions and seemed slightly miffed when a writer questioned a quotation of Wilson's on "the war to end war." Wilson may have spoken the words, but historians cannot discover that he ever wrote them, the writer contended, and the phrase was not actually Wilson's but the title of a 1914 book by the English author H. G. Wells, *The War That Will End War*. Nixon changed his allusion to Wilson "spoke the words" rather than wrote them. A week later a history professor in Connecticut expressed his gratitude for the distinction between writing and saying.

Devices familiar to Nixon's writers include the "I see" formulation of his nomination acceptance speech and the contrapuntal variation that appeals to the President. Safire reports in his book that orator Robert G. Ingersoll, if he did not originate the "I see" technique, used it effectively: "I see our country filled with happy homes . . . I see a world . . . where thrones have crumbled . . . I see a world without a slave. . . ." Samuel Rosenman used a variation of this routine in Franklin D. Roosevelt's inaugural in 1937. He wrote for Roosevelt: "I see tens of millions of citizens" denied the "necessities of life. . . . I see millions denied education," etc. Adlai E. Stevenson added his version in 1952: "I see an America where no man fears to think as he pleases, or say what he thinks. I see an America where no man is another's master—where no man's mind is dark with fear."

Nixon's version was keyed to America's two-hundredth birthday in 1976: "I see a day when Americans are once again proud of their flag. . . . I see a day when the President of the United States is respected and his office is honored as the world's greatest symbol of liberty and justice. . . . I see a day when we can look back on massive break-throughs in solving the problems of slums and pollution and traffic which are choking our citizens to death. . . . I see a day when our nation is at peace and the world is at peace and everyone on earth —those who hope, those who aspire, those who crave liberty—will look to America as the shining example of hopes realized and dreams achieved. . . ."

In a 1966 speech, Nixon worried long over a contrapuntal effect which was the keystone of his remarks on academic freedom. Finally he wrote: "Woodrow Wilson's distinction between men of thought and men of action can no longer be made. The man of thought who will not act is ineffective; the man of action who will not think is dangerous."

A writer comes into his own when the President has an idea in his mind but cannot precisely and succinctly express it himself. This was the case when the President was called upon to eulogize the late Everett McKinley Dirksen. Nixon was dissatisfied with comments in the eastern press about Dirksen's great service in putting through civil rights legislation, which was cited to forgive transgressions of the Illinois senator in other matters.

Being a politician, as Dirksen was, could be a proud estate, Nixon said, and it was that which he wished to make the theme of his eulogy.

The words he received from his writers expressed what was in his mind and can be evaluated as the Nixon political credo pronounced in the Capitol Rotunda in the presence of men and women whose life was politics.

"A politician," Nixon said, "knows that more important than a bill that is proposed is the law that is passed.

"A politician knows that his friends are not always his allies, and that his adversaries are not his enemies.

"A politician knows how to make the process of democracy work, and loves the intricate workings of the democratic system.

"A politician knows not only how to count votes, but how to make his vote count.

"A politician knows that only if he leaves room for discussion and room for concession can he gain room for maneuver.

"A politician knows that the best way to be a winner is to make the other side feel it does not have to be a loser.

"And a politician—in the Dirksen tradition—knows both the name of the game and the rules of the game, and he seeks his ends through the time-honored democratic means."

In this language a professional politician in the best sense was probably defined better than Nixon, a professional politician himself, could have managed alone. There are many subtleties in the foregoing passage which illuminate how Nixon operates as President, and it is a valuable contribution to a better understanding of him.

After I interviewed the White House writers, the President talked to me at some length on his own part in writing speeches and statements and preparing for press conferences. This matter is of first concern to him, and it is my impression that he attaches more importance to it than any politician at the Presidential level since Adlai E. Stevenson. Stevenson took pride in his writing, and I had watched him many times as he scribbled on his manuscript, sometimes making large revisions, before rising to speak. Kennedy's battery of writers of high talent tended to obscure the fact that he, too, was greatly concerned by the style in which he expressed his thoughts, but I think no more than Nixon.

Nixon discusses his own writing process with relish, placing first emphasis on the necessity of cutting down the impressive amounts of material the President can command when he formulates his thoughts. Those who are accustomed to leisurely, haphazard, or even careless research would be amazed at the instantaneous supply of material available to a President on command. He needs only lift the phone to release an avalanche of current, historical, deep or shallow research on almost any conceivable subject. Research agencies in a half dozen different government departments, the Library of Congress, or scientific agencies go into action, and what the President asks for he gets promptly.

The President tends to become somewhat lyrical when discussing his processes of articulation. A speech is like a symphony, or like building a cathedral. There must be a creative plan. It amounts to much more than just stringing together a few memorable phrases.

"Rhythm—rhythm is everything," he said. The hardest parts are the beginning and the end; what comes between can be compartmentalized in sections, but all parts must blend together to produce a total impact greater than the sum of any series of phrases.

In the beginning the speaker has to introduce himself and his subject and "shake hands with the audience" in an easy fashion. The conclusion must contain emotion, idealism, hope, challenge.

Thus, on an important speech, the President spends many hours in many days making outlines on his yellow scratch pads. The main points must be outlined, and then each section must build toward the next with careful attention to transitional passages. The President devotes much time to the latter so that the speech will "flow" from beginning to end. After the final outline is chosen from several alternatives, the first draft is dictated or written in longhand, and further attention is given to the conclusion. All through this process writers are relied upon, either for research or for passages and in some cases complete drafts. But the collective process is subject at all times to Nixon's manner of thought and expression. The writers say they do not consciously attempt to simulate his style but admit they may be subconsciously influenced to do so.

Often when he is working on a major speech, the President said, ideas come to him in the middle of the night. He gets up or sits up in bed and sketches out his ideas on his ever-present yellow pads. For his November 3 speech on Vietnam—which the President agrees was the most important of his Presidency thus far if not of his entire career— he got the idea for the conclusion at 3 A.M. while in bed at Camp David and got up to work it out.

With the first raw draft written by hand and including contributions made by his writers, the President will then speak into a Dictaphone some of the "best sentences" and connective passages. He never dictates directly to a secretary as do some officials when preparing a speech.

The final draft emerges and is typed by Miss Woods. She also keeps an extensive file of his speech outlines and other data supporting the speech.

The President said the rule on neither rehearsing a speech nor watching himself on a television replay is a "fetish" with him. If he joins his family and they are watching television that may include tapes of him speaking, he turns off the set. The only presentation of himself he has ever seen, he said, was a government movie produced by the United States Information Agency on his first year in office for distribution abroad. Nixon did not say what he thought of it.

The reason for not rehearsing—"before a mirror, as some have done"—and for not watching replays is that he thinks this might cause him to react involuntarily, affect his style, and make him self-conscious in subsequent broadcasts and speeches. He noted the difference between the ranting and raving of politicians in the old days when they appeared only before live audiences. Now, and particularly on TV, understatement is important. TV is conversational. There are no "cheer lines."

Preparation for a press conference is somewhat different than for a speech. He receives numerous "briefing books" from his staff and government agencies on issues in the news. Staff members explore answers to questions that may be asked. The President prepares eight or ten pages of notes on how he would expect to answer anticipated questions. He does not take these notes into press conferences, but the outlining of them helps to fix in his mind what he wishes to say.

When he does respond to an anticipated question, he said, his answer is usually much shorter than the notes he had prepared and more to the unembellished point he wishes to make. The President said he succeeds in anticipating ten or fifteen of the twenty to thirty questions usually asked and in about the form in which they are asked. He does not memorize the answers he expects to give but has his reply well in mind.

The matter of "planted" questions is always high in the awareness of reporters who attend Presidential press conferences. Concrete examples of planted questions are missing so far in the Nixon Administration, but it is a part of the common wisdom of the White House press corps that questions have been inspired by White House staff members in the past and probably will be in the future. The practice is not actually frowned upon if the questioner presents a logical question in unfawning manner and phraseology. The President, of course, is not confined to a cross-examination at a press conference. He can and does volunteer any statement he wishes, and it is the general impression that a President is usually very much in control of press conferences, perhaps even more in Nixon's case than with some predecessors. He has found one method of control effective. By reacting neither in anger, irritation, nor contempt, he has imposed on his questioners the imperative of appearing reasonable and fair before the audience of many millions who are watching and listening to every nuance. It is a duel viewed by tens of millions in which the least among us newsmen may parry with the President, possibly at more risk to us than to him.

Nixon spoke of the help given to him on foreign policy speeches by Dr. Henry A. Kissinger, his adviser on national security affairs. Our discussion was not exhaustive on who contributes what to Presidential speeches, but it is evident that ideas, concepts, and phrases come from other high-ranking advisers and counselors, including Daniel Patrick Moynihan, H. R. Haldeman, John Ehrlichman, Bryce Harlow, and others.

One who comments continually on the Washington scene will have read and listened to most, if not all of the speeches and messages in this book as they were delivered. In some instances, such as the historic press conference on the island of Guam, excerpts of which are now printed in direct quotation for the first time, he will have been present. The atmosphere makes a difference.

It is not until these Presidential utterances are reread without the pressure of having to analyze them in a hurry that the general pattern, massive reform, emerges. The Nixon Administration has shape and direction. If in the beginning it was thought that he was doing too little, it may now be surmised that he is trying to do more than can be done, certainly in one term as President.

What the President is doing, as it is disclosed in this large package, is the product of a great many years of experience both in and out of office.

His years in the House and Senate, as Vice President, as a defeated candidate in 1960 cannot be discounted as formulating his basic views and programs. But it was perhaps those eight years between 1960 and 1968, with its tremendous disappointment when Nixon was defeated for governor of California, that were the most formative. That was a period of study and reconsideration, an opportunity for extensive world travels, for reflection and analysis.

Nixon drew together new advisers, made new contacts, considered new programs. He did not return to the conventional Republican ways, although it seemed that he might have, but advanced into different gradations of thought broader in some respects than the "modern Republicanism" or middle way of the Eisenhower Administration.

Nixon was seeking, and still is, a new majority position respectful of minority views but not controlled by them and impervious to the assault of a combination of minorities. This is difficult and contrary to the political experience of more than three decades during which a combination of minorities formed the hard core of Democratic political superiority.

The speeches and messages in this volume outline the main structure upon which Nixon rests his appeal for an enlightened new majority.

—Richard Wilson

I

The
Inaugural
Address

THE INAUGURAL ADDRESS

JANUARY 20, 1969

An inaugural address, particularly the first inaugural, is a severe test of any President. He exposes, often for the first time, his qualities of inspirational leadership. He is expected to be poet, preacher, and politician all in one.

This great ceremonial occasion of the Presidency is a constitutional renewal of our national life in the four-year rhythm of continuous change that distinguished the American system, when it was established, from all others.

Some Presidents excel in their inspirational role. Some do not. Few are remembered for more than a line or two. Franklin D. Roosevelt's "The only thing we have to fear is fear itself," John F. Kennedy's "Ask not what your country can do for you: Ask what you can do for your country" expressed a mood and survived time's test.

So, apparently, in this age of conflict and confrontation, has Richard Nixon's "To lower our voices would be a simple thing. . . . We cannot learn from one another until we stop shouting at one another."

The reaction of the time was positive. The Nixon Administration began on a note of restraint and understanding, not shared, however, by six thousand antiwar protestors who organized a counter-inaugural. Activists among a crowd of several hundred threw rocks and bottles and spouted obscenities at the President as his limousine traveled down the historic Pennsylvania Avenue route from the Capitol to the White House—the first time, it is believed, that a Chief Executive of the United States was ever exposed to such rude indignity on inaugural day.

Senator Dirksen, Mr. Chief Justice, Mr. Vice President, President Johnson, Vice President Humphrey, My Fellow Americans—and my fellow citizens of the world community:

I ask you to share with me today the majesty of this moment. In the orderly transfer of power we celebrate the unity that keeps us free.

Each moment in history is a fleeting time, precious and unique. But some stand out as moments of beginning, in which courses are set that shape decades or centuries.

This can be such a moment.

3

Forces now are converging that make possible, for the first time, the hope that many of man's deepest aspirations can at last be realized. The spiraling pace of change allows us to contemplate, within our own lifetime, advances that once would have taken centuries.

In throwing wide the horizons of space, we have discovered new horizons on earth.

For the first time, because the people of the world want peace, and the leaders of the world are afraid of war, the times are on the side of peace.

Eight years from now America will celebrate its two-hundredth anniversary as a nation. Within the lifetime of most people now living mankind will celebrate that great new year which comes only once in a thousand years—the beginning of the third millennium.

What kind of a nation we will be, what kind of a world we will live in, whether we shape the future in the image of our hopes, is ours to determine by our actions and our choices.

The greatest honor history can bestow is the title of peacemaker. This honor now beckons America—the chance to help lead the world at last out of the valley of turmoil and onto that high ground of peace that man has dreamed of since the dawn of civilization.

If we succeed, generations to come will say of us now living that we mastered our moment, that we helped make the world safe for mankind.

This is our summons to greatness.

I believe the American people are ready to answer this call.

The second third of this century has been a time of proud achievement. We have made enormous strides in science and industry and agriculture. We have shared our wealth more broadly than ever. We have learned at last to manage a modern economy to assure its continued growth.

We have given freedom new reach. We have begun to make its promise real for black as well as for white.

We see the hope of tomorrow in the youth of today. I know America's youth. I believe in them. We can be proud that they are better educated, more committed, more passionately driven by conscience than any generation in our history.

No people has ever been so close to the achievement of a just and abundant society, or so possessed of the will to achieve it. And because our strengths are so great, we can afford to appraise our weaknesses with candor and to approach them with hope.

Standing in this same place a third of a century ago, Franklin Delano Roosevelt addressed a nation ravaged by depression and gripped in fear. He could say in surveying the nation's troubles: "They concern, thank God, only material things."

Our crisis today is in reverse.

We have found ourselves rich in goods, but ragged in spirit, reaching with magnificent precision for the moon, but falling into raucous discord on earth.

We are caught in war, wanting peace. We are torn by division, wanting unity. We see around us empty lives, wanting fulfillment. We see tasks that need doing, waiting for hands to do them.

To a crisis of the spirit, we need an answer of the spirit.

And to find that answer, we need only look within ourselves.

When we listen to "the better angels of our nature," we find that they celebrate the simple things, the basic things—such as goodness, decency, love, kindness.

Greatness comes in simple trappings.

The simple things are the ones most needed today if we are to surmount what divides us, and cement what unites us.

To lower our voices would be a simple thing.

In these difficult years America has suffered from a fever of words; from inflated rhetoric that promises more than it can deliver; from angry rhetoric that fans discontents into hatreds; from bombastic rhetoric that postures instead of persuading.

We cannot learn from one another until we stop shouting at one another—until we speak quietly enough so that our words can be heard as well as our voices.

For its part, government will listen. We will strive to listen in new ways—to the voices of quiet anguish, the voices that speak without words, the voices of the heart—to the injured voices, the anxious voices, the voices that have despaired of being heard.

Those who have been left out, we will try to bring in.

Those left behind, we will help to catch up.

For all of our people, we will set as our goal the decent order that makes progress possible and our lives secure.

As we reach toward our hopes, our task is to build on what has gone before—not turning away from the old, but turning toward the new.

In this past third of a century government has passed more laws, spent more money, initiated more programs than in all our previous history.

In pursuing our goals of full employment, better housing, excellence in education; in rebuilding our cities and improving our rural areas; in protecting our environment and enhancing the quality of life; in all these and more, we will and must press urgently forward.

We shall plan now for the day when our wealth can be transferred from the destruction of war abroad to the urgent needs of our people at home.

The American dream does not come to those who fall asleep.

But we are approaching the limits of what government alone can do.

Our greatest need now is to reach beyond government, to enlist the legions of the concerned and the committed.

What has to be done, has to be done by government and people together or it will not be done at all. The lesson of past agony is that without the people we can do nothing: with the people we can do everything.

To match the magnitude of our tasks, we need the energies of our people—enlisted not only in grand enterprises, but more importantly in those small, splendid efforts that make headlines in the neighborhood newspaper instead of the national journal.

With these, we can build a great cathedral of the spirit—each of us raising it one stone at a time, as he reaches out to his neighbor, helping, caring, doing.

I do not offer a life of uninspiring ease. I do not call for a life of grim sacrifice. I ask you to join in a high adventure—one as rich as humanity itself and exciting as the times we live in.

The essence of freedom is that each of us shares in the shaping of his own destiny.

Until he has been part of a cause larger than himself, no man is truly whole.

The way to fulfillment is in the use of our talents. We achieve nobility in the spirit that inspires that use.

As we measure what can be done, we shall promise only what we know we can produce, but as we chart our goals, we shall be lifted by our dreams.

No man can be fully free while his neighbor is not. To go forward at all is to go forward together.

This means black and white together, as one nation, not two. The laws have caught up with our conscience. What remains is to give life to what is in the law: to ensure at last that as all are born equal in dignity before God, all are born equal in dignity before man.

As we learn to go forward together at home, let us also seek to go forward together with all mankind.

Let us take as our goal: where peace is unknown, make it welcome; where peace is fragile, make it strong; where peace is temporary, make it permanent.

After a period of confrontation, we are entering an era of negotiation.

Let all nations know that during this Administration our lines of communication will be open.

We seek an open world—open to ideas, open to the exchange of goods and people, a world in which no people, great or small, will live in angry isolation.

We cannot expect to make everyone our friend, but we can try to make no one our enemy.

Those who would be our adversaries, we invite to a peaceful competition—not in conquering territory or extending dominion, but in enriching the life of man.

As we explore the reaches of space, let us go to the new worlds together—not as new worlds to be conquered, but as a new adventure to be shared.

With those who are willing to join, let us cooperate to reduce the burden of arms, to strengthen the structure of peace, to lift up the poor and the hungry.

But to all those who would be tempted by weakness, let us leave no doubt that we will be as strong as we need to be for as long as we need to be.

Over the past twenty years, since I first came to this capital as a freshman congressman, I have visited most of the nations of the world. I have come to know the leaders of the world, and the great forces, the hatreds, the fears that divide the world.

I know that peace does not come through wishing for it—that there is no substitute for days and even years of patient and prolonged diplomacy.

I also know the people of the world.

I have seen the hunger of a homeless child, the pain of a man wounded in battle, the grief of a mother who has lost her son. I know these have no ideology, no race.

I know America. I know the heart of America is good.

I speak from my own heart, and the heart of my country, the deep concern we have for those who suffer, and those who sorrow.

I have taken an oath today in the presence of God and my countrymen to uphold and defend the Constitution of the United States. To that oath I now add this sacred commitment: I shall consecrate my office, my energies, and all the wisdom I can summon to the cause of peace among nations.

Let this message be heard by strong and weak alike:

The peace we seek—the peace we seek to win—is not victory over any other people, but the peace that comes "with healing in its wings"; with compassion for those who have suffered; with understanding for those who have opposed us; with the opportunity for all the peoples of this earth to choose their own destiny.

Only a few short weeks ago we shared the glory of man's first sight of the world as God sees it, as a single sphere reflecting light in the darkness.

As the Apollo astronauts flew over the moon's gray surface on Christmas Eve, they spoke to us of the beauty of earth—and in that voice so clear across the lunar distance, we heard them invoke God's blessing on its goodness.

In that moment their view from the moon moved poet Archibald MacLeish to write: "To see the Earth as it truly is, small and blue and beautiful in that eternal silence where it floats, is to see ourselves as riders on the Earth together, brothers in that bright loveliness in the eternal cold—brothers who know now they are truly brothers."

In that moment of surpassing technological triumph, men turned their thoughts toward home and humanity—seeing in that far perspective that man's destiny on earth is not divisible; telling us that however far we reach into the cosmos, our destiny lies not in the stars but on earth itself, in our own hands, in our own hearts.

We have endured a long night of the American spirit. But as our eyes catch the dimness of the first rays of dawn, let us not curse the remaining dark. Let us gather the light.

Our destiny offers not the cup of despair, but the chalice of opportunity. So let us seize it not in fear, but in gladness—and, "riders on the Earth together," let us go forward, firm in our faith, steadfast in our purpose, cautious of the dangers; but sustained by our confidence in the will of God and the promise of man.

2

The

Vietnam

War

"The war must be ended," Richard Nixon said in a radio broadcast in the closing weeks of the 1968 Presidential campaign, but he did not spell out a detailed plan for ending the war.

Instead, conflict arose between the Saigon government and the Johnson Administration on stalled negotiations with the communist side. Nixon became involved through charges that Saigon was gambling that he would be elected and take a harder line.

In fact, Nixon took neither a harder nor softer line. After his election he moved immediately for better relations with Saigon and made a secret offer of settlement that was rejected by the communist side. As the hopes of January faded in May, doubt rose that President Nixon had a plan any different from President Johnson's to end the Vietnam war.

On May 14 Nixon made his first definite public proposal to *"move off dead center"* and end the war. Aside from containing specific proposals for a settlement, this speech was intended to inform the American public and assure the enemy that conventional military victory was not Nixon's aim. In his view, he was offering peace on a more viable basis than had President Johnson. The response at the Paris peace negotiations and from Hanoi was wholly negative as it continued to be through successive Nixon actions intended to reduce the American military commitment by half before early 1971.

On June 8 President Nixon, following a meeting at Midway Island with President Thieu of the Republic of South Vietnam, announced the immediate redeployment from Vietnam of a division, the equivalent of approximately 25,000 men.

He said that during the month of August and at regular intervals thereafter troop deployments in Vietnam would be reviewed, having in mind three criteria: Progress of training and equipping of South Vietnamese forces, progress in the Paris peace talks, and the level of enemy activity.

"No actions will be taken which threaten the safety of our troops and the troops of our allies; and second, no action will be taken which endangers the attainment of our objective, the right of self-determination for the people of South Vietnam," the President said.

This formula defined the beginning of a new policy of military withdrawal from Vietnam on a phased basis without an announced future schedule. The steady expansion of

troop commitments first ordered by President Johnson in early
1965, and dating from the arrival of the Ninth Marine
Expeditionary Brigade at Danang on March 8 of that year,
was thus brought to an end. The homeward flow of U.S. troops
began under Nixon's program of "Vietnamization" of the war
by the replacement of American combat forces with combat
troops of the Army of the Republic of Vietnam.

THE TERMS OF PEACE
Nationwide Radio and Television Address
MAY 14, 1969

Good evening, my fellow Americans.

I have asked for this television time tonight to report to you on our most difficult and urgent problem—the war in Vietnam.

Since I took office four months ago, nothing has taken so much of my time and energy as the search for a way to bring lasting peace to Vietnam. I know that some believe I should have ended the war immediately after the inauguration by simply ordering our forces home from Vietnam.

This would have been the easy thing to do. It might have been a popular move. But if I had done so, I would have betrayed my solemn responsibility as President of the United States.

I want to end this war. The American people want to end this war. The people of South Vietnam want to end this war. But we want to end it permanently so that the younger brothers of our soldiers in Vietnam will not have to fight in the future in another Vietnam someplace else in the world.

The fact that there is no easy way to end the war does not mean that we have no choice but to let the war drag on with no end in sight.

For four years American boys have been fighting and dying in Vietnam. For twelve months our negotiators have been talking with the other side in Paris. And yet the fighting goes on. The destruction continues. Brave men still die.

The time has come for some new initiatives. Repeating the old formulas and the tired rhetoric of the past is not enough. When Americans are risking their lives in war, it is the responsibility of their leaders to take some risks for peace.

I would like to report to you tonight on some of the things we have been doing in the past four months to bring true peace, and then I would like to make some concrete proposals to speed that day.

Our first step began before inauguration. This was to launch an intensive review of every aspect of the Nation's Vietnam policy. We accepted nothing on faith, we challenged every assumption and every statistic. We made a systematic, serious examination of all the alternatives open to us. We carefully considered recommendations offered both by critics and supporters of past policies.

From the review it became clear at once that the new Administration faced a set of immediate operational problems:

—The other side was preparing for a new offensive.

—There was a wide gulf of distrust between Washington and Saigon.

—In eight months of talks in Paris there had been no negotiations directly concerned with a final settlement.

Therefore, we moved on several fronts at once.

We frustrated the attack which was launched in late February. As a result, the North Vietnamese and the Viet Cong failed to achieve their military objectives.

We restored a close working relationship with Saigon. In the resulting atmosphere of mutual confidence President Thieu and his government have taken important initiatives in the search for a settlement.

We speeded up the strengthening of the South Vietnamese forces. I am glad to report tonight that, as a result, General Abrams told me on Monday that progress in the training program had been excellent, and that apart from any developments that may occur in the negotiations in Paris, the time is approaching when South Vietnamese forces will be able to take over some of the fighting fronts now being manned by Americans.

In weighing alternate courses, we have had to recognize that the situation as it exists today is far different from what it was two years ago or four years ago or ten years ago.

One difference is that we no longer have the choice of not intervening. We have crossed that bridge. There are now more than a half million American troops in Vietnam, and thirty-five thousand Americans have lost their lives.

We can have honest debate about whether we should have entered the war in Vietnam. We can have honest debate about how the war has been conducted. But the urgent question today is what to do now that we are there.

Against that background let me discuss, first, what we have rejected, and, second, what we are prepared to accept.

We have ruled out attempting to impose a purely military solution on the battlefield.

We have also ruled out either a one-sided withdrawal from Vietnam
or the acceptance in Paris of terms that would amount to a disguised
American defeat.

When we assumed the burden of helping defend South Vietnam,
millions of South Vietnamese men, women, and children placed their
trust in us. To abandon them now would risk a massacre that would
shock and dismay everyone in the world who values human life.

Abandoning the South Vietnamese people, however, would jeopardize more than lives in South Vietnam. It would threaten our long-
term hopes for peace in the world. A great nation cannot renege on its
pledges. A great nation must be worthy of trust.

When it comes to maintaining peace, "prestige" is not an empty
word. I am not speaking of false pride or bravado—they should have no
place in our policies. I speak, rather, of the respect that one nation has
for another's integrity in defending its principles and meeting its obligations.

If we simply abandoned our effort in Vietnam, the cause of peace
might not survive the damage that would be done to other nations'
confidence in our reliability.

Another reason for not withdrawing unilaterally stems from debates within the communist world between those who argue for a policy
of containment or confrontation with the United States, and those who
argue against it.

If Hanoi were to succeed in taking over South Vietnam by force—
even after the power of the United States had been engaged—it would
greatly strengthen those leaders who scorn negotiation, who advocate
aggression, who minimize the risks of confrontation with the United
States. It would bring peace now but it would enormously increase the
danger of a bigger war later.

If we are to move successfully from an era of confrontation to an
era of negotiation, then we have to demonstrate—at the point at which
confrontation is being tested—that confrontation with the United States
is costly and unrewarding.

Almost without exception, the leaders of non-communist Asia have
told me that they would consider a one-sided American withdrawal from
Vietnam to be a threat to the security of their own nations.

In determining what choices would be acceptable, we have to
understand our essential objective in Vietnam: What we want is very
little, but very fundamental. We seek the opportunity for the South
Vietnamese people to determine their own political future without outside interference.

Let me put it plainly: What the United States wants for South

Vietnam is not the important thing. What North Vietnam wants for South Vietnam is not the important thing. What is important is what the people of South Vietnam want for South Vietnam.

The United States has suffered over a million casualties in four wars in this century. Whatever faults we may have as a nation, we have asked nothing for ourselves in return for those sacrifices. We have been generous toward those whom we have fought. We have helped our former foes as well as our friends in the task of reconstruction. We are proud of this record, and we bring the same attitude in our search for a settlement in Vietnam.

In this spirit, let me be explicit about several points:

—We seek no bases in Vietnam.

—We seek no military ties.

—We are willing to agree to neutrality for South Vietnam if that is what the South Vietnamese people freely choose.

—We believe there should be an opportunity for full participation in the political life of South Vietnam by all political elements that are prepared to do so without the use of force or intimidation.

—We are prepared to accept any government in South Vietnam that results from the free choice of the South Vietnamese people themselves.

—We have no intention of imposing any form of government upon the people of South Vietnam, nor will we be a party to such coercion.

—We have no objection to reunification, if that turns out to be what the people of North Vietnam and the people of South Vietnam want: we ask only that the decision reflect the free choice of the people concerned.

At this point, I would like to add a personal word based on many visits to South Vietnam over the past five years. This is the most difficult war in America's history, fought against a ruthless enemy. I am proud of our men who have carried the terrible burden of this war with dignity and courage, despite the division and opposition to the war in the United States. History will record that never have America's fighting men fought more bravely for more unselfish goals than our men in Vietnam. It is our responsibility to see that they have not fought in vain.

In pursuing our limited objective, we insist on no rigid diplomatic formula. Peace could be achieved by a formal negotiated settlement. Peace could be achieved by an informal understanding, provided that the understanding is clear, and that there were adequate assurances that it would be observed. Peace on paper is not as important as peace in fact.

This brings us to the matter of negotiations.

We must recognize that peace in Vietnam cannot be achieved over-night. A war that has raged for many years will require detailed negotiations and cannot be settled by a single stroke.

What kind of a settlement will permit the South Vietnamese people to determine freely their own political future? Such a settlement will require the withdrawal of all non-South Vietnamese forces, including our own, from South Vietnam, and procedures for political choice that give each significant group in South Vietnam a real opportunity to participate in the political life of the nation.

To implement these principles, I reaffirm now our willingness to withdraw our forces on a specified timetable. We ask only that North Vietnam withdraw its forces from South Vietnam, Cambodia, and Laos into North Vietnam, also in accordance with a timetable.

We include Cambodia and Laos to ensure that these countries would not be used as bases for a renewed war. Our offer provides for a simultaneous start on withdrawal by both sides; for agreement on a mutually acceptable timetable; and for the withdrawal to be accomplished quickly.

The North Vietnamese delegates have been saying in Paris that political issues should be discussed along with military issues, and there must be a political settlement in the South. We do not dispute this, but the military withdrawal involves outside forces, and can, therefore, be properly negotiated by North Vietnam and the United States, with the concurrence of its allies.

The political settlement is an internal matter which ought to be decided among the South Vietnamese themselves, and not imposed by outsiders. However, if our presence at these political negotiations would be helpful, and if the South Vietnamese concerned agreed, we would be willing to participate, along with the representatives of Hanoi, if that also were desired.

Recent statements by President Thieu have gone far toward opening the way to a political settlement. He has publicly declared his government's willingness to discuss a political solution with the National Liberation Front, and has offered free elections. This was a dramatic step forward, a reasonable offer that could lead to a settlement. The South Vietnamese government has offered to talk without preconditions. I believe the other side should also be willing to talk without pre-conditions.

The South Vietnamese government recognizes, as we do, that a settlement must permit all persons and groups that are prepared to renounce the use of force to participate freely in the political life of South Vietnam. To be effective, such a settlement would require two things: first, a process that would allow the South Vietnamese people to express their choice; and, second, a guarantee that this process would be a fair one.

We do not insist on a particular form of government. The important thing is that the guarantees should have the confidence of the South Vietnamese people, and that they should be broad enough and strong enough to protect the interests of all major South Vietnamese groups.

This, then, is the outline of the settlement that we seek to negotiate in Paris. Its basic terms are very simple: mutual withdrawal of non-South Vietnamese forces from South Vietnam, and free choice for the people of South Vietnam. I believe that the long-term interests of peace require that we insist on no less, and that the realities of the situation require that we seek no more.

And now, to make very concrete what I have said, I propose the following specific measures, which seem to me consistent with the principles of all parties. These proposals are made on the basis of full consultation with President Thieu.

—As soon as agreement can be reached, all non-South Vietnamese forces would begin withdrawals from South Vietnam.

—Over a period of twelve months, by agreed-upon stages, the major portions of all U.S., Allied, and other non-South Vietnamese forces would be withdrawn. At the end of this twelve-month period the remaining U.S., Allied, and other non-South Vietnamese forces would move into designated base areas and would not engage in combat operations.

—The remaining U.S. and Allied forces would complete their withdrawals as the remaining North Vietnamese forces were withdrawn and returned to North Vietnam.

—An international supervisory body, acceptable to both sides, would be created for the purpose of verifying withdrawals, and for any other purposes agreed upon between the two sides.

—This international body would begin operating in accordance with an agreed timetable and would participate in arranging supervised cease-fires in Vietnam.

—As soon as possible after the international body was functioning, elections would be held under agreed procedures and under the supervision of the international body.

—Arrangements would be made for the release of prisoners of war on both sides at the earliest possible time.

—All parties would agree to observe the Geneva Accords of 1954 regarding South Vietnam and Cambodia, and the Laos Accords of 1962.

I believe this proposal for peace is realistic, and takes account of the legitimate interests of all concerned. It is consistent with President

Thieu's Six Points. It can accommodate the various programs put forth by the other side. We and the government of South Vietnam are prepared to discuss its details with the other side.

Secretary Rogers is now in Saigon and he will be discussing with President Thieu how, together, we may put forward these proposed measures most usefully in Paris. He will, as well, be consulting with our other Asian allies on these measures while on his Asian trip. However, I would stress that these proposals are not offered on a take-it-or-leave-it basis. We are quite willing to consider other approaches consistent with our principles.

We are willing to talk about anybody's program—Hanoi's Four Points, the NLF's Ten Points—provided it can be made consistent with the very few basic principles I have set forth here.

Despite our disagreement with several of its points, we welcome the fact that the NLF has put forward its first comprehensive program. We are studying that program carefully. However, we cannot ignore the fact that immediately after the offer, the scale of enemy attacks stepped up and American casualties in Vietnam increased.

Let me make one point clear. If the enemy wants peace with the United States, that is not the way to get it.

I have set forth a peace program tonight which is generous in its terms. I have indicated our willingness to consider other proposals. But no greater mistake could be made than to confuse flexibility with weakness or of being reasonable with lack of resolution. I must also make clear, in all candor, that if the needless suffering continues, this will affect other decisions. Nobody has anything to gain by delay.

Reports from Hanoi indicate that the enemy has given up hope for a military victory in South Vietnam, but is counting on a collapse of American will in the United States. There could be no greater error in judgment.

Let me be quite blunt. Our fighting men are not going to be worn down; our mediators are not going to be talked down; and our allies are not going to be let down.

My fellow Americans, I have seen the ugly face of war in Vietnam. I have seen the wounded in field hospitals—American boys, South Vietnamese boys, North Vietnamese boys. They were different in many ways—the color of their skins, their religions, their races. Some were enemies; some were friends.

But the differences were small compared with how they were alike. They were brave men, and they were so young. Their lives—their dreams for the future—had been shattered by a war over which they had no control.

With all the moral authority of the office which I hold, I say that America could have no greater and prouder role than to help to end this war in a way which will bring nearer that day in which we can have a world order in which people can live together in peace and friendship.

I do not criticize those who disagree with me on the conduct of our peace negotiations. And I do not ask unlimited patience from a people whose hopes for peace have too often been raised and then cruelly dashed over the past four years.

I have tried to present the facts about Vietnam with complete honesty, and I shall continue to do so in my reports to the American people.

Tonight, all I ask is that you consider these facts, and, whatever our differences, that you support a program which can lead to a peace we can live with and a peace we can be proud of. Nothing could have a greater effect in convincing the enemy that he should negotiate in good faith than to see the American people united behind a generous and reasonable peace offer.

In my campaign for the Presidency, I pledged to end this war in a way that would increase our chances to win true and lasting peace in Vietnam, in the Pacific, and in the world. I am determined to keep that pledge. If I fail to do so, I expect the American people to hold me accountable for that failure.

But while I will never raise false expectations, my deepest hope, as I speak to you tonight, is that we shall be able to look back on this day, at this critical turning point when American initiative moved us off dead center and forward to the time when this war would be brought to an end and when we shall be able to devote the unlimited energies and dedication of the American people to the exciting challenges of peace.

Thank you, and good night.

TO THE GREAT SILENT MAJORITY
Nationwide Radio and Television Address
NOVEMBER 3, 1969

No more effective single speech ever was made by a President, certainly in this century, than Nixon's televised address of November 3, 1969. Opponents of the Vietnam war, dissatisfied with Nixon's peace efforts and the rate of troop withdrawals first

announced on June 8, organized a massive nationwide
demonstration that took place on October 15 in major cities.
  The effect of Nixon's speech on the rising crescendo of
protest was instantaneous. The Vietnam Moratorium movement
lost its bearings in the calming sea of Nixon's "great silent
majority." Congressional dissent was muted. Nixon won more
time for the Vietnamization of the war and his ultimate aim of
complete withdrawal of American ground combat forces.

Good evening, my fellow Americans:

Tonight I want to talk to you on a subject of deep concern to all Americans and to many people in all parts of the world—the war in Vietnam.

I believe that one of the reasons for the deep division about Vietnam is that many Americans have lost confidence in what their government has told them about our policy. The American people cannot and should not be asked to support a policy which involves the overriding issues of war and peace unless they know the truth about that policy.

Tonight, therefore, I would like to answer some of the questions that I know are on the minds of many of you listening to me.

How and why did America get involved in Vietnam in the first place?

How has this Administration changed the policy of the previous Administration?

What has really happened in the negotiations in Paris and on the battlefront in Vietnam?

What choices do we have if we are to end the war?

What are the prospects for peace?

Let me begin by describing the situation I found when I was inaugurated on January 20.

—The war had been going on for four years.

—31,000 Americans had been killed in action.

—The training program for the South Vietnamese was behind schedule.

—540,000 Americans were in Vietnam, with no plans to reduce the number.

—No progress had been made at the negotiations in Paris, and the United States had not put forth a comprehensive peace proposal.

—The war was causing deep division at home and criticism from many of our friends as well as our enemies abroad.

In view of these circumstances there were some who urged I end the war at once by ordering the immediate withdrawal of all American forces.

From a political standpoint this would have been a popular and easy course to follow. After all, we became involved in the war while my predecessor was in office. I could blame the defeat which would be the result of my action on him and come out as the peacemaker. Some put it quite bluntly: This was the only way to avoid allowing Johnson's war to become Nixon's war.

But I had a greater obligation than to think only of the years of my Administration and the next election. I had to think of the effect of my decision on the next generation and on the future of peace and freedom in America and in the world.

Let us all understand that the question before us is not whether some Americans are for peace and some Americans are against peace. The question at issue is not whether Johnson's war becomes Nixon's war.

The great question is: How can we win America's peace?

Let us turn now to the fundamental issue. Why and how did the United States become involved in Vietnam in the first place?

Fifteen years ago North Vietnam, with the logistical support of Communist China and the Soviet Union, launched a campaign to impose a communist government on South Vietnam by instigating and supporting a revolution.

In response to the request of the government of South Vietnam, President Eisenhower sent economic aid and military equipment to assist the people of South Vietnam in their efforts to prevent a communist takeover. Seven years ago President Kennedy sent sixteen thousand military personnel to Vietnam as combat advisers. Four years ago President Johnson sent American combat forces to South Vietnam.

Now, many believe that President Johnson's decision to send American combat forces to South Vietnam was wrong. And many others—I among them—have been strongly critical of the way the war has been conducted.

But the question facing us today is: Now that we are in the war, what is the best way to end it?

In January I could only conclude that the precipitate withdrawal of American forces from Vietnam would be a disaster not only for South Vietnam but for the United States and for the cause of peace.

For the South Vietnamese, our precipitate withdrawal would inevitably allow the communists to repeat the massacres which followed their takeover in the North fifteen years before.

—They then murdered more than fifty thousand people, and hundreds of thousands more died in slave labor camps.

—We saw a prelude of what would happen in South Vietnam when the communists entered the city of Hué last year. During their brief rule, there was a bloody reign of terror in which three thousand civilians were clubbed, shot to death, and buried in mass graves.

—With the sudden collapse of our support, these atrocities of Hué would become the nightmare of the entire nation—and particularly for the million and a half Catholic refugees who fled to South Vietnam when the communists took over in the North.

For the United States, this first defeat in our nation's history would result in a collapse of confidence in American leadership, not only in Asia but throughout the world.

Three American Presidents have recognized the great stakes involved in Vietnam and understood what had to be done.

—In 1963 President Kennedy, with his characteristic eloquence and clarity, said, "We want to see a stable government there carrying on the struggle to maintain its national independence. We believe strongly in that. We're not going to withdraw from that effort. In my opinion, for us to withdraw from that effort would mean a collapse not only of South Vietnam, but Southeast Asia, so we're going to stay there."

President Eisenhower and President Johnson expressed the same conclusion during their terms of office.

For the future of peace precipitate withdrawal would thus be a disaster of immense magnitude.

—A nation cannot remain great if it betrays its allies and lets down its friends.

—Our defeat and humiliation in South Vietnam would without question promote recklessness in the councils of those great powers who have not yet abandoned their goals of world conquest.

—This would spark violence wherever our commitments help maintain peace—in the Middle East, in Berlin, eventually even in the Western Hemisphere.

Ultimately, this would cost more lives.

It would not bring peace but more war.

For these reasons I rejected the recommendation that I should end the war by immediately withdrawing all our forces. I chose instead to change American policy on both the negotiating front and the battlefront.

In order to end a war fought on many fronts, I initiated a pursuit for peace on many fronts.

In a television speech on May 14, in a speech before the United

Nations, and on a number of other occasions I set forth our peace proposals in great detail.

—We have offered the complete withdrawal of all outside forces within one year.

—We have proposed a cease-fire under international supervision.

—We have offered free elections under international supervision with the communists participating in the organization and conduct of the elections as an organized political force. The Saigon government has pledged to accept the result of the elections.

We have not put forth our proposals on a take-it-or-leave-it basis. We have indicated that we are willing to discuss the proposals that have been put forth by the other side. We have declared that anything is negotiable except the right of the people of South Vietnam to determine their own future. At the Paris peace conference Ambassador Lodge has demonstrated our flexibility and good faith in forty public meetings.

Hanoi has refused even to discuss our proposals. They demand our unconditional acceptance of their terms, which are that we withdraw all American forces immediately and unconditionally, and that we overthrow the government of South Vietnam as we leave.

We have not limited our peace initiatives to public forums and public statements. I recognized, in January, that a long and bitter war like this usually cannot be settled in a public forum. That is why in addition to the public statements and negotiations I have explored every possible private avenue that might lead to a settlement.

Tonight I am taking the unprecedented step of disclosing to you some of our other initiatives for peace—initiatives we undertook privately and secretly because we thought that we thereby might open a door which publicly would be closed.

I did not wait for my inauguration to begin my quest for peace.

—Soon after my election, through an individual who is directly in contact on a personal basis with the leaders of North Vietnam, I made two private offers for a rapid, comprehensive settlement. Hanoi's replies called in effect for our surrender before negotiations.

—Since the Soviet Union furnishes most of the military equipment for North Vietnam, Secretary of State Rogers, my Assistant for National Security Affairs Dr. Kissinger, Ambassador Lodge, and I, personally, have met on a number of occasions with representatives of the Soviet government to enlist their assistance in getting meaningful negotiations started. In addition we have had extended discussions directed toward that same end with representatives of other governments which have diplomatic relations with North Vietnam. None of these initiatives have to date produced results.

—In mid-July, I became convinced that it was necessary to make a major move to break the deadlock in Paris talks. I spoke directly in this office, where I am now sitting, with an individual who had known Ho Chi Minh on a personal basis for twenty-five years. Through him I sent a letter to Ho Chi Minh.

I did this outside of the usual diplomatic channels with the hope that with the necessity of making statements for propaganda removed, there might be constructive progress toward bringing the war to an end. Let me read from that letter:

"Dear Mr. President:

"I release [sic] that it is difficult to communicate meaningfully across the gulf of four years of war. But precisely because of this gulf, I wanted to take this opportunity to reaffirm in all solemnity my desire to work for a just peace. I deeply believe that the war in Vietnam has gone on too long and delay in bringing it to an end can benefit no one —least of all the people of Vietnam. . . .

"The time has come to move forward at the conference table toward an early resolution of this tragic war. You will find us forthcoming and open-minded in a common effort to bring the blessing of peace to the brave people of Vietnam. Let history record that at this critical juncture, both sides turned their face toward peace rather than toward conflict and war."

I received Ho Chi Minh's reply on August 30, three days before his death. It simply reiterated the public position North Vietnam had taken in the Paris talks and flatly rejected my initiative.

The full text of both letters is being released to the press.

—In addition to the public meetings I referred to, Ambassador Lodge has met with Vietnam's chief negotiator in Paris in eleven private meetings.

—We have taken other significant initiatives which must remain secret to keep open some channels of communication which may still prove to be productive.

But the effect of all the public, private, and secret negotiations which have been undertaken since the bombing halt a year ago and since this Administration came into office on January 20, can be summed up in one sentence: No progress whatever has been made except agreement on the shape of the bargaining table. Now who is at fault?

It has become clear that the obstacle in negotiating an end to the war is not the President of the United States. And it is not the South Vietnamese.

The obstacle is the other side's absolute refusal to show the least willingness to join us in seeking a just peace. It will not do so while it is convinced that all it has to do is to wait for our next concession and the next, until it gets everything it wants.

No longer can there be any question that progress in negotiation depends only on Hanoi's deciding to negotiate, to negotiate seriously.

I realize that this report on our efforts on the diplomatic fronts is discouraging to the American people, but the American people are entitled to know the truth—the bad news as well as the good news, where the lives of our young men are involved.

Now let me turn, however, to a more encouraging report on another front.

At the time we launched our search for peace I recognized we might not succeed in bringing an end to the war through negotiation. I, therefore, put into effect another plan to bring peace—a plan which will bring the war to an end regardless of what happens on the negotiating front.

It is in line with a major shift in U.S. foreign policy which I described in my press conference at Guam on July 25. Let me briefly explain what has been described as the Nixon Doctrine—a policy which not only will help end the war in Vietnam, but which is an essential element of our program to prevent future Vietnams.

We Americans are a do-it-yourself people. We are an impatient people. Instead of teaching someone else to do a job, we like to do it ourselves. And this trait has been carried over into our foreign policy.

In Korea and again in Vietnam the United States furnished most of the money, most of the arms, and most of the men to help the people of those countries defend their freedom against the communist aggression.

Before any American troops were committed to Vietnam, a leader of another Asian country expressed this opinion to me when I was traveling in Asia as a private citizen. He said, "When you are trying to assist another nation defend its freedom, U.S. policy should be to help them fight the war but not to fight the war for them."

Well, in accordance with this wise counsel, I laid down in Guam three principles as guidelines for future American policy toward Asia:

First, the United States will keep all of its treaty commitments.

Second, we shall provide a shield if a nuclear power threatens the freedom of a nation allied with us or of a nation whose survival we consider vital to our security.

Third, in cases involving other types of aggression, we shall furnish military and economic assistance when requested in accordance with our treaty commitments. But we shall look to the nation directly threatened to assume the primary responsibility of providing the manpower for its defense.

After I announced this policy I found that the leaders of the Philippines, Thailand, Vietnam, South Korea, and other nations which might be threatened by communist aggression welcomed this new direction in American foreign policy.

The defense of freedom is everybody's business—not just America's business. And it is particularly the responsibility of the people whose freedom is threatened. In the previous Administration we Americanized the war in Vietnam. In this Administration we are Vietnamizing the search for peace.

The policy of the previous Administration not only resulted in our assuming the primary responsibility for fighting the war, but even more significantly did not adequately stress the goal of strengthening the South Vietnamese so that they could defend themselves when we left.

The Vietnamization Plan was launched following Secretary Laird's visit to Vietnam in March. Under the plan, I ordered first a substantial increase in the training and equipment of South Vietnamese forces.

In July, on my visit to Vietnam, I changed General Abrams' orders so that they were consistent with the objectives of our new policies. Under the new orders the primary mission of our troops is to enable the South Vietnamese forces to assume the full responsibility for the security of South Vietnam.

Our air operations have been reduced by over 20 percent.

And now we have begun to see the results of this long overdue change in American policy in Vietnam:

—After five years of Americans going into Vietnam, we are finally bringing American men home. By December 15 over sixty thousand men will have been withdrawn from South Vietnam—including 20 percent of all of our combat forces.

—The South Vietnamese have continued to gain in strength. As a result they have been able to take over combat responsibilities from our American troops.

Two other significant developments have occurred since this Administration took office:

—Enemy infiltration, infiltration which is essential if they are to launch a major attack, over the last three months is less than 20 percent of what it was over the same period last year.

—Most important, United States casualties have declined during the last two months to the lowest point in three years.

Let me now turn to our program for the future.

We have adopted a plan which we have worked out in cooperation with the South Vietnamese for the complete withdrawal of all U.S. combat ground forces, and their replacement by South Vietnamese forces on an orderly scheduled timetable. This withdrawal will be made from strength and not from weakness. As South Vietnamese forces become stronger, the rate of American withdrawal can become greater.

I have not and do not intend to announce the timetable for our program. There are obvious reasons for this decision which I am sure you will understand. As I have indicated on several occasions, the rate of withdrawal will depend on developments on three fronts.

—One of these is the progress which can be or might be made in the Paris talks. An announcement of a fixed timetable for our withdrawal would completely remove any incentive for the enemy to negotiate an agreement.

—They would simply wait until our forces had withdrawn and then move in.

The other two factors on which we will base our withdrawal decisions are the level of enemy activity and the progress of the training program of the South Vietnamese forces. I am glad to be able to report tonight progress on both of these fronts has been greater than we anticipated. As a result, our timetable for withdrawal is more optimistic now than when we made our first estimates in June. This clearly demonstrates why it is not wise to be frozen in on a fixed timetable.

We must retain the flexibility to base each withdrawal decision on the situation as it is at that time rather than on estimates that are no longer valid.

Along with this optimistic estimate, I must—in all candor—leave one note of caution.

If the level of enemy activity significantly increases, we might have to adjust our timetable accordingly.

However, I want the record to be completely clear on one point.

At the time of the bombing halt just a year ago, there was some confusion as to whether there was an understanding on the part of the enemy that if we stopped the bombing of North Vietnam, they would stop the shelling of cities in South Vietnam. I want to be sure that there is no misunderstanding on the part of the enemy with regard to our withdrawal program.

We have noted the reduced level of infiltration, the reduction of our casualties, and are basing our withdrawal decisions partially on those factors.

If the level of infiltration or our casualties increase while we are trying to scale down the fighting, it will be the result of a conscious decision by the enemy.

Hanoi could make no greater mistake than to assume that an increase in violence will be to its advantage. If I conclude that increased enemy action jeopardizes our remaining forces in Vietnam, I shall not hesitate to take strong and effective measures to deal with that situation.

This is not a threat. This is a statement of policy which as Commander-in-Chief of our Armed Forces I am making in meeting my responsibility for the protection of American fighting men wherever they may be.

My fellow Americans, I am sure you recognize from what I have said that we really only have two choices open to us if we want to end this war:

—I can order an immediate, precipitate withdrawal of all Americans from Vietnam without regard to the effects of that action.

—Or we can persist in our search for a just peace through a negotiated settlement if possible, or through continued implementation of our plan for Vietnamization if necessary—a plan in which we will withdraw all of our forces from Vietnam on a schedule in accordance with our program, as the South Vietnamese become strong enough to defend their own freedom.

I have chosen the second course.

It is not the easy way.

It is the right way.

It is a plan which will end the war and serve the cause of peace—not just in Vietnam but in the Pacific and in the world.

In speaking of the consequences of a precipitate withdrawal, I mentioned that our allies would lose confidence in America.

Far more dangerous, we would lose confidence in ourselves. The immediate reaction would be a sense of relief that our men were coming home. But as we saw the consequences of what we had done, inevitable remorse and divisive recrimination would scar our spirit as a people.

We have faced other crises in our history and have become stronger by rejecting the easy way out and taking the right way in meeting our challenges. Our greatness as a nation has been our capacity to do what had to be done when we knew our course was right.

I recognize that some of my fellow citizens disagree with the plan for peace I have chosen. Honest and patriotic Americans have reached different conclusions as to how peace should be achieved.

In San Francisco a few weeks ago, I saw demonstrators carrying signs reading: "Lose in Vietnam, bring the boys home."

Well, one of the strengths of our free society is that any American has a right to reach that conclusion and to advocate that point of view. But as President of the United States, I would be untrue to my oath of office if I allowed the policy of this nation to be dictated by the minority who hold that point of view and who try to impose it on the nation by mounting demonstrations in the street.

For almost two hundred years the policy of this nation has been made under our Constitution by those leaders in the Congress and in the White House selected by all of the people. If a vocal minority, however fervent its cause, prevails over reason and the will of the majority this nation has no future as a free society.

And now I would like to address a word if I may to the young people of this nation who are particularly concerned—and I understand why they are concerned—about this war.

I respect your idealism.

I share your concern for peace.

I want peace as much as you do.

There are powerful personal reasons I want to end this war. This week I will have to sign eighty-three letters to mothers, fathers, wives, and loved ones of men who have given their lives for America in Vietnam. It is very little satisfaction to me that this is only one third as many letters as I signed the first week in office. There is nothing I want more than to see the day come when I do not have to write any of those letters.

—I want to end the war to save the lives of those brave young men in Vietnam.

—But I want to end it in a way which will increase the chance that their younger brothers and their sons will not have to fight in some future Vietnam someplace in the world.

—And I want to end the war for another reason. I want to end it so that the energy and dedication of you, our young people, now too often directed into bitter hatred against those responsible for the war, can be turned to the great challenges of peace, a better life for all Americans, a better life for all people on this earth.

I have chosen a plan for peace. I believe it will succeed.

If it does not succeed, what the critics say now won't matter. Or, if it does succeed, what the critics say now won't matter. If it does not succeed, anything I say then won't matter.

I know it may not be fashionable to speak of patriotism or national destiny these days. But I feel it is appropriate to do so on this occasion.

Two hundred years ago this nation was weak and poor. But even then, America was the hope of millions in the world. Today we have become the strongest and richest nation in the world. The wheel of destiny has turned so that any hope the world has for the survival of peace and freedom will be determined by whether the American people have the moral stamina and the courage to meet the challenge of free world leadership.

Let historians not record that when America was the most powerful nation in the world we passed on the other side of the road and allowed the last hopes for peace and freedom of millions of people to be suffocated by the forces of totalitarianism.

And so tonight—to you, the great silent majority of my fellow Americans—I ask for your support.

I pledged in my campaign for the Presidency to end the war in a way that we could win the peace. I have initiated a plan of action which will enable me to keep that pledge.

The more support I can have from the American people, the sooner that pledge can be redeemed; for the more divided we are at home, the less likely the enemy is to negotiate at Paris.

Let us be united for peace. Let us also be united against defeat. Because let us understand: North Vietnam cannot defeat or humiliate the United States. Only Americans can do that.

Fifty years ago, in this room and at this very desk, President Woodrow Wilson spoke words which caught the imagination of a war-weary world. He said, "This is the war to end wars." His dream for peace after World War I was shattered on the hard realities of great power politics and Woodrow Wilson died a broken man.

Tonight I do not tell you that the war in Vietnam is the war to end wars. But I do say this:

I have initiated a plan which will end this war in a way that will bring us closer to that great goal to which Woodrow Wilson and every American President in our history has been dedicated—the goal of a just and lasting peace.

As President, I hold the responsibility for choosing the best path to that goal and then leading the nation along it.

I pledge to you tonight that I shall meet this responsibility with all of the strength and wisdom I can command in accordance with your hopes, mindful of your concerns, sustained by your prayers.

Thank you, and good night.

THE WITHDRAWAL PROGRAM
Nationwide Radio and Television Address
DECEMBER 15, 1969

By early December, 1969, questions continued to rise on the rate of troop withdrawals from Vietnam and Nixon's sincerity in "winding down" the war. Nixon answered on December 15 with the announcement of another fifty thousand increment in the withdrawal. In a radio-TV address he also gave the American public his first optimistic appraisal of military progress in Vietnam.

Good evening, my fellow Americans.

I have asked for this television time tonight to give you a progress report on our plan to bring a just peace in Vietnam, which I described in my television address on November 3.

As you will recall, I said then that we were proceeding in our pursuit for peace on two fronts—a peace settlement through negotiation or, if that fails, ending the war through Vietnamization, a plan we have developed with the South Vietnamese for the complete withdrawal, first of all U.S. combat ground forces and eventually of other forces and their replacement by South Vietnamese forces on an orderly scheduled timetable.

I must report to you tonight with regret that there has been no progress whatever on the negotiating front since November 3. The enemy still insists on a unilateral, precipitate withdrawal of American forces and on a political settlement which would mean the imposition of a communist government on the people of South Vietnam against their will, and defeat and humiliation for the United States.

This we cannot and will not accept.

Typical of their attitude is their absolute refusal to talk about the fate of the American prisoners they hold and their refusal even to supply their names so as to ease the anguish of their loved ones in the United States. This cruel, indefensible action is a shocking demonstration of the inflexible attitude they have taken on all issues at the negotiating table in Paris.

But despite their attitude, we shall continue to participate in the Paris talks and to seek a negotiated peace—one which is fair, fair to North Vietnam, fair to the United States, but most important, fair to the people of South Vietnam. Because as I have indicated, anything is negotiable except the right of the people of South Vietnam to determine their own fate.

As you know, Ambassador Lodge has had to leave his assignment in Paris because of personal reasons. I have designated Philip Habib, one of our most experienced Foreign Service officers who has been participating in the negotiations for over eighteen months, as the acting head of our delegation with the personal rank of Ambassador. He has been given full authority to discuss any proposal that will contribute to a just peace.

Let me turn now to the progress of our plan for Vietnamization and our troop withdrawal program.

When I announced this program in June, I said that the rate of withdrawal would depend on three criteria—progress in the Paris negotiations, progress in the training of South Vietnamese forces, and the level of enemy activity.

Now, while there has been no progress on the negotiating front, I have a much more favorable report to give to you tonight with regard to the training of South Vietnamese forces.

First, let me share with you how I reached this conclusion. In making decisions, I believe a President should listen not only to those who tell him what he wants to hear, but to those who tell him what he needs to hear. It is most important to get independent judgments from individuals who are expert on the factors to be considered but who are not directly involved in the operations themselves. This is particularly essential when the lives of American men are involved.

Several months ago I read a book by Sir Robert Thompson, a British expert who was one of the major architects of the victory over the communist guerrillas who attempted to take over Malaya in the 1950s. In his book which was published just as this Administration took office, he was very pessimistic about the conduct of the war in Vietnam. He particularly noted the failure to prepare the South Vietnamese to take over their responsibilities for their own defense.

On October 7 I met with Mr. Thompson and asked him to go to Vietnam and give me a firsthand, candid, and completely independent report on the situation there. After five weeks of intensive investigation he gave me his report on December 3.

His full report, which makes several very constructive recommendations, must remain confidential since it bears on the security of our men. But let me read to you from his summary of his findings.

"I was very impressed by the improvement in the military and political situation in Vietnam as compared with all previous visits and especially in the security situation, both in Saigon and the rural areas.

"A winning position in the sense of obtaining a just peace (whether negotiated or not) and of maintaining an independent, non-communist South Vietnam has been achieved, but we are not yet through. We are in a psychological period where the greatest need is confidence. A steady application of the 'do it yourself' concept, with continuing U.S. support in the background, will increase the confidence already shown by many South Vietnam leaders."

Mr. Thompson's report, which I would describe as cautiously optimistic, is in line with my own attitude and with reports I have received from other observers and from our own civilian and military leaders in Vietnam.

There is one disturbing new development, however, with regard to enemy activity. Enemy infiltration has increased substantially. It has not yet reached the point where our military leaders believe the enemy has developed the capability to mount a major offensive, but we are watching the situation closely to see whether it could develop to that extent.

Now for the decision: Taking all these developments into consideration, I am announcing tonight a reduction in our troop ceiling of 50,000 more U.S. troops by April 15 next year. This means that the ceiling which existed when I took office on January 20 has now been reduced by 115,500 men. This reduction has been made with approval of the government of South Vietnam, and in consultation with the other nations which have combat forces in Vietnam.

Now, there are some who believe that to continue our withdrawals at a time when enemy infiltration is increasing is a risk we should not take. However, I have consistently said we must take risks for peace.

And in that connection, let me remind the leaders in Hanoi that if their infiltration and the level of enemy activity increases while we are reducing our forces, they also will be running a risk. I repeat the statement I made in my speech on November 3.

"Hanoi could make no greater mistake than to assume that an increase in violence will be to its advantage. If I conclude that increased enemy action jeopardizes our remaining forces in Vietnam, I shall not hesitate to take strong and effective measures to deal with that situation."

This reduction in our forces is another orderly step in our plan for peace in Vietnam.

—It marks further progress toward turning over the defense of South Vietnam to the South Vietnamese.

—And it is another clear sign of our readiness to bring an end to the war and to achieve a just peace.

Before concluding this report, I wish to express my appreciation to the great number of people from all over the nation who have indicated their support for our program for a just peace since my speech on November 3.

This support was particularly underlined by the action of the House of Representatives and the Congress in which a majority of both Democrats and Republicans voted overwhelmingly, 334 to 55, for a resolution supporting the plan for peace which I announced on November 3.

The leaders in Hanoi have declared on a number of occasions that division in the United States would eventually bring them the victory they cannot win over our fighting men in Vietnam. This demonstration of support by the American people for our plan to bring a just peace has dashed those hopes.

Hanoi should abandon its dream of military victory.

It is time for them to join us in serious negotiations.

There is nothing to be gained by delay.

If Hanoi is willing to talk seriously, they will find us flexible and forthcoming.

I am glad that I was able to report tonight some progress in reaching our goal of a just peace in Vietnam. After five years of increasing the number of Americans in Vietnam, we are bringing American men home.

Our casualties continue to be at the lowest rate in three years.

But I want you to know that despite this progress, I shall not be satisfied until we achieve the goal we all want—an end to the war on a just and lasting basis.

This is the fifth Christmas when Americans will be fighting in a war far away from home.

I know that there is nothing the American people want more and there is nothing I want more than to see the day come when the Christmas message of "Peace on Earth, Good Will to Men" will be not just an eloquent ideal but a reality for Americans and for all others who cherish peace and freedom throughout the world.

Your continued support of our plan for peace will greatly strengthen our hopes that we can achieve that great goal.

Thank you, and good night.

3
The
Human
Equation

President Nixon's first year began quietly, so quietly that the general direction of his policies remained in doubt. He considered and then abandoned altogether making the usual Presidential State-of-the-Union address at the opening of each new session of Congress. Most new Presidents have appeared in person before joint sessions of Congress to state their general aims and have sometimes outlined specific legislation they intended to submit later for Congressional consideration.

Nixon decided to let his proposals speak for themselves as they were submitted, but this created the feeling in the beginning that there would be no central theme in the new Administration except to restore a sense of order and banish crisis in national affairs.

Not until the heavy weight of the President's messages began to accumulate was it realized that the central domestic theme of his Administration was reform. Nixon had not been thought of as a reformist. In fact, in the year prior to his nomination for the Presidency, throughout the campaign, and then in the crucial period between election and assumption of office, a large staff of specialists—most of them young—prepared thousands of pages of analyses and programs on national affairs for Nixon's consideration.

He came to the Presidency far better prepared in this respect than most of his predecessors, and it was his sense of timing and progressive impact that caused him to set initially a tone of calm restraint and then proceed in an orderly way with his reform proposals.

The result was a total social program for the poor, the jobless, and the elderly with some features that had long been regarded as purely visionary or so far in the future as to warrant little current discussion.

One of these was the idea of a guaranteed minimum income for all Americans, once ridiculed as the reductio ad absurdum *of the welfare state. In the Nixon scheme, a small initial floor under family income became a workfare plan as a substitute for welfare for those who would work, seek work, or train for work. He called it "a small initial floor under family income." Congressional opposition was forecast, but did not materialize in the beginning. Not until the spring of 1970 did underlying opposition begin to rise. It was based less on objection to the principle of guaranteed annual income than on imperfections in Nixon's plan said to place a premium, at some levels of income, on not working. The Nixon plan was sent back by a*

*Congressional committee to Robert Finch, then Secretary of
Health, Education, and Welfare, for restudy and revision. The
long-range outlook favored adoption of some form of the income
plan.*

*A second proposal, criticized as visionary or impractical, was
the sharing of Federal revenues with the states, also evidently
headed for ultimate Congressional approval.*

PEOPLE MUST BE GIVEN A CHANCE
Message to the Congress of the United States
FEBRUARY 19, 1969

The blight of poverty requires priority attention. It engages our
hearts and challenges our intelligence. It cannot and will not be treated
lightly or indifferently, or without the most searching examination of
how best to marshal the resources available to the Federal government
for combatting it.

At my direction the Urban Affairs Council has been conducting an
intensive study of the nation's antipoverty programs, of the way the
antipoverty effort is organized and administered, and of ways in which
it might be made more effective.

That study is continuing. However, I can now announce a number
of steps I intend to take, as well as spelling out some of the considerations that will guide my future recommendations.

The Economic Opportunity Act of 1964 is now scheduled to expire
on June 30, 1970. The present authorization for appropriations for the
Office of Economic Opportunity runs only until June 30, 1969. I will
ask Congress that this authorization for appropriations be extended for
another year. Prior to the end of the fiscal year I will send Congress a
comprehensive proposal for the future of the poverty program, including
recommendations for revising and extending the Act itself beyond its
scheduled 1970 expiration.

How the work begun by OEO can best be carried forward is a subject
on which many views deserve to be heard—both from within Congress
and among those many others who are interested or affected, including
especially the poor themselves. By sending my proposals well before the
Act's 1970 expiration, I intend to provide time for full debate and discussion.

In the maze of antipoverty efforts, precedents are weak and knowledge uncertain. These past years of increasing Federal involvement

have begun to make clear how vast is the range of what we do not yet know, and how fragile are projections based on partial understanding. But we have learned some lessons about what works and what does not. The changes I propose will be based on those lessons and those discoveries, and rooted in a determination to press ahead with antipoverty efforts even though individual experiments have ended in disappointment.

From the experience of OEO we have learned the value of having in the Federal government an agency whose special concern is the poor. We have learned the need for flexibility, responsiveness, and continuing innovation. We have learned the need for management effectiveness. Even those most thoroughly committed to the goals of the antipoverty effort recognize now that much that has been tried has not worked.

The OEO has been a valuable fount of ideas and enthusiasm, but it has suffered from a confusion of roles.

OEO's greatest value is as an initiating agency—devising new programs to help the poor, and serving as an "incubator" for these programs during their initial experimental phases. One of my aims is to free OEO itself to perform these functions more effectively, by providing for a greater concentration of its energies on its innovative role.

Last year Congress directed that special studies be made by the Executive Branch of whether Head Start and the Job Corps should continue to be administered directly by OEO, or whether responsibility should be otherwise assigned.

Section 309 of the Vocational Education Amendments of 1968 provides:

> The president shall make a special study of whether the responsibility for administering the Head Start program established under the Economic Opportunity Act of 1964 should continue to be vested in the Director of the Office of Economic Opportunity, should be transferred to another agency of the Government, or should be delegated to another such agency pursuant to the provisions of section 602(d) of the aforementioned Economic Opportunity Act of 1964, and shall submit the findings of this study to the Congress not later than March 1, 1969.

I have today submitted this study to the Congress. Meanwhile, *under the Executive authority provided by the Economic Opportunity Act,* I have directed that preparations be made for the delegation of Head Start to the Department of Health, Education and Welfare. Whether it should be actually transferred is a question I will take up in my later, comprehensive message, along with my proposals for a permanent status and organizational structure for OEO. Pending a final decision by the Secretary of HEW on where within the department responsibility for Head Start would be lodged, it will be located directly within the Office of the Secretary.

In order to provide for orderly preparation, and to ensure that there is no interruption of programs, I have directed that this delegation be made effective July 1, 1969. By then the summer programs for 1969 will all have been funded, and a new cycle will be beginning.

I see this delegation as an important element in a new national commitment to the crucial early years of life.

Head Start is still experimental. Its effects are simply not known— save of course where medical care and similar services are involved. The results of a major national evaluation of the program will be available this spring. It must be said, however, that preliminary reports on this study confirm what many have feared: the long-term effect of Head Start appears to be extremely weak. This must not discourage us. To the contrary, it only demonstrates the immense contribution the Head Start program has made simply by having raised to prominence on the national agenda the fact—known for some time, but never widely recognized—that the children of the poor mostly arrive at school age seriously deficient in the ability to profit from formal education, and already significantly behind their contemporaries. It also has been made abundantly clear that our schools as they now exist are unable to overcome this deficiency.

In this context the Head Start Follow-Through Program already delegated to HEW by OEO assumes an even greater importance.

In recent years enormous advances have been made in the understanding of human development. We have learned that intelligence is not fixed at birth, but is largely formed by the environmental influences of the early formative years. It develops rapidly at first, and then more slowly; as much of that development takes place in the first four years as in the next thirteen. We have learned further that environment has its greatest impact on the development of intelligence when that development is proceeding most rapidly—that is, in those earliest years.

This means that many of the problems of poverty are traceable directly to early childhood experience—and that if we are to make genuine, long-range progress, we must focus our efforts much more than heretofore on those few years which may determine how far, throughout his later life, the child can reach.

Recent scientific developments have shown that this process of early childhood development poses more difficult problems than had earlier been recognized—but they also promise a real possibility of major breakthroughs soon in our understanding of this process. By placing Head Start in the Department of HEW, it will be possible to strengthen it by association with a wide range of other early development programs within the department, and also with the research programs of the National Institute of Health, the National Institute of Mental Health, and the National Institute of Child Health and Human Development.

Much of our knowledge is new. But we are not on that ground absolved from the responsibility to respond to it. So crucial is the matter of early growth that we must make a national commitment to providing all American children an opportunity for healthful and stimulating development during the first five years of life. In delegating Head Start to the Department of HEW, I pledge myself to that commitment.

The Vocational Education Amendments of 1968 directed the Commissioner of Education to study the Job Corps in relation to state vocational education programs. I have directed the Secretaries of Labor and Health, Education and Welfare, and the Assistant Secretary of Labor for Manpower to work with the Acting Commissioner of Education in preparing such a report for submission to Congress at the earliest opportunity.

One of the priority aims of the new Administration is the development by the Department of Labor of a comprehensive manpower program, designed to make centrally available to the unemployed and the underemployed a full range of Federal job-training and placement services. Toward this end, it is essential that the many Federal manpower programs be integrated and coordinated.

Therefore, as a first step toward better program management, the Job Corps will be delegated to the Department of Labor.

For the Department, this will add another important manpower service component. For the Job Corpsmen, it will make available additional training and service opportunities. From the standpoint of program management, it makes it possible to coordinate the Job Corps with other manpower services, especially vocational education, at the point of delivery.

The Department of Labor already is deeply involved in the recruitment, counseling, and placement of Job Corpsmen. It refers 80 percent of all male and 45 percent of all female enrollees; it provides job market information and helps locate Job Corpsmen in the areas of greatest opportunity.

This delegation will also be made effective on July 1, 1969; and the

Departments of Interior and Agriculture will continue to have operating responsibility for the Job Corps centers concerned primarily with conservation.

I have directed that preparations be made for the transfer of two other programs from OEO to the Department of Health, Education and Welfare: Comprehensive Health Centers, which provide health service to the residents of poor neighborhoods, and Foster Grandparents program. In my judgment these can be better administered at present, or in the near future, within the structure of the Department.

In making these changes, I recognize that innovation costs money —and that if OEO is to continue its effectiveness as an innovating agency, adequate funds must be made available on a continuing basis. Moreover, it is my intent that Community Action Agencies can continue to be involved in the operation of programs such as Head Start at the local level, even though an agency other than OEO has received such programs, by delegation, at the national level. It also is my intent that the vital Community Action Programs wil be pressed forward, and that in the area of economic development OEO will have an important role to play, in cooperation with other agencies, in fostering community-based business development.

One of the principal aims of the Administration's continuing study of the antipoverty effort will be to improve its management effectiveness. When poverty-fund monies are stolen, those hurt most again are the poor. The public generally, and the poor especially, have a right to demand effective and efficient management. I intend to provide it.

I expect that important economies will result from the delegation of the Job Corps to the Department of Labor, and we shall continue to strive for greater efficiency, and especially for greater effectiveness in Head Start.

A Concentrated Management Improvement Program initiated in OEO will be intensified. Under this program selected Community Action Agencies will be required to take steps to devise improvements in such areas as organizational structure, financial and accounting systems, personnel training, and work scheduling. Standards will be applied under the "management improvement program" to evaluate the operations of Community Action Agencies. We intend to monitor these programs actively in order to ensure that they are achieving high-level effectiveness and that they are being administered on an orderly basis.

In the past problems have often arisen over the relationship of state, county, and local governments to programs administered by OEO. This has particularly been the case where the state and local officials have wanted to assume greater responsibility for the implementation

of the programs but for various reasons have been prevented from
doing so.

I have assigned special responsibility for working out these problems to the newly created office of Intergovernmental Relations, under
the supervision of the Vice President.

I have directed the Urban Affairs Council to keep the antipoverty
effort under constant review and evaluation, seeking new ways in which
the various departments can help and better ways in which their efforts
can be coordinated.

My comprehensive recommendations for the future of the poverty
program will be made after the Urban Affairs Council's own initial study
is completed, and after I have reviewed the Comptroller General's study
of OEO ordered by Congress in 1967 and due for submission next month.

Meanwhile, I would stress this final thought: if we are to make the
most of experimental programs, we must frankly recognize their experimental nature and frankly acknowledge whatever shortcomings they
develop. To do so is not to belittle the experiment, but to advance its
essential purpose: that of finding new ways, better ways, of making
progress in areas still inadequately understood.

We often can learn more from a program that fails to achieve its
purpose than from one that succeeds. If we apply those lessons, then
even the "failure" will have made a significant contribution to our
larger purposes.

I urge all those involved in these experimental programs to bear
this in mind—and to remember that one of the primary goals of this
Administration is to expand our knowledge of how best to make real
progress against those social ills that have so stubbornly defied solution.
We do not pretend to have all the answers. We are determined to find
as many as we can.

The men and women who will be valued most in this Administration will be those who understand that not every experiment succeeds,
who do not cover up failures but rather lay open problems, frankly and
constructively, so that next time we will know how to do better.

In this spirit, I am confident that we can place our antipoverty efforts on a secure footing—and that as we continue to gain in understanding of how to master the difficulties, we can move forward at an
accelerating pace.

FOOD AND HEALTH
Message to the Congress of the United States
MAY 6, 1969

*Hunger was, and remains, a keen issue in the Nixon
Administration. The contradiction of hunger in the midst of
plenty cannot be disentangled from a complex of political
factors. Chief among these has been a basic difference on the
purpose of Federal food programs. For decades agricultural
commodities have been given, under restrictions, to the needy as
an outlet for surpluses produced under the Federal farm control
programs. As such, this distribution was a function of economic
measures under the control of the established farm leadership
in Congress. The differing concept is that the prevention of hunger
and malnutrition is a humanitarian imperative that must be
separated from the political control of the Congressional farm bloc.*

*Nixon was caught between those two pressures and proposed
programs which the humanitarian-minded thought too stingy
and restrictive, and the farm bloc thought too generous. The
issue remains essentially unresolved, but Nixon has succeeded in
increasing the distribution of food to the needy.*

We have long thought of America as the most bounteous of nations.
In our conquest of the most elemental of human needs, we have set a
standard that is a wonder and aspiration for the rest of the world. Our
agricultural system produces more food than we can consume, and our
private food market is the most effective food-distribution system ever
developed. So accustomed are most of us to a full and balanced diet that,
until recently, we have thought of hunger and malnutrition as problems
only in far less fortunate countries.

But in the past few years we have awakened to the distressing fact
that despite our material abundance and agricultural wealth, many
Americans suffer from malnutrition. Precise factual descriptions of its
extent are not presently available, but there can be no doubt that
hunger and malnutrition exist in America, and that some millions may
be affected.

That hunger and malnutrition should persist in a land such as ours
is embarrassing and intolerable. But it is an exceedingly complex problem, not at all susceptible to fast or easy solutions. Millions of Americans
are simply too poor to feed their families properly. For them, there must

be first sufficient food income. But this alone would only begin to address the problem, for what matters finally is what people buy with the money they have. People must be educated in the choosing of proper foods. All of us, poor and non-poor alike, must be reminded that a proper diet is a basic determinant of good health. Our private food industry has made great advances in food processing and packaging, and has served the great majority of us very well. But these advances have placed great burdens on those who are less well off and less sophisticated in the ways of the modern marketplace. We must therefore work to make the private food market serve these citizens as well, by making nutritious foods widely available in popular forms. And for those caught in the most abject poverty, special efforts must be made to see that the benefits of proper foods are not lost amidst poor health and bad sanitary conditions.

The Council for Urban Affairs has for the past three months been studying the problem of malnutrition in America, and has assessed the capacities of our present food and nutrition programs. As a result of the Council's deliberations, I am today prepared to take the following actions:

1. Family Food Assistance Programs

The Federal government presently provides food assistance to nearly 7 million needy Americans through the Food Stamp and Direct Distribution programs. Though these programs have provided welcome and needed assistance to these persons, both programs are clearly in need of revision.

The present Food Stamp Program can be greatly improved. I shall in a short period of time submit to the Congress legislation which will revise the Food Stamp Program to:

—Provide poor families enough food stamps to purchase a nutritionally complete diet. The Department of Agriculture estimates this to be $100 a month for a typical family of four.

—Provide food stamps at no cost to those in the very low income brackets.

—Provide food stamps to others at a cost of no greater than 30 percent of income.

—Ensure that the Food Stamp Program is complementary to a revised welfare program, which I shall propose to the Congress this year.

—Give the Secretary of Agriculture the authority to operate both the Food Stamp and Direct Distribution programs concurrently in individual counties, at the request and expense of local officials. This will permit the Secretary to assist counties wishing to change from Direct Distribution to Food Stamps, and to meet extraordinary or emergency situations.

It will not be possible for the revised program to go into effect until sometime after the beginning of the calendar year 1970—that is to say, after the necessary legislative approval and administrative arrangements have been made. The requested appropriations will then permit the establishment of the revised program in all current Food Stamp counties before the end of the fiscal year, as well as a modest expansion into Direct Distribution counties, and some counties with no current programs.

This program, on a full-year basis, will cost something in excess of $1 billion per year. (Precise estimates will become available only over a period of time.) This will be in addition to the $1.5 billion for food for the hungry which I have requested for the forthcoming fiscal year, making a total program of $2.5 billion. In the meantime, $270 million is being reprogrammed within the forthcoming budget to permit the program to begin as soon as legislative and administrative arrangements can be made and other necessary measures taken.

While our long-range goal should be to replace direct food distribution with the revised Food Stamp Program, the Direct Distribution Program can fill many short-range needs. Today there are still over 440 counties without any Family Food Assistance program, and this Administration shall establish programs in each of these counties before July 1970. The Direct Distribution Program will be used in most of these counties. In these and other Direct Distribution counties, the most serious criticism of the program will be met by ensuring that all counties offer the full range of available foods.

To strengthen both current Family Food Assistance programs, efforts will proceed on a high priority basis to establish more distribution points, prompter and simpler certification, financing arrangements, mailing of food stamps, and appeal mechanisms.

2. *Special Supplemental Food Program*

Serious malnutrition during pregnancy and infancy can impair normal physical and mental development in children. Special effort must be made to protect this vulnerable group from malnutrition.

The Special Package Program, which provided needy women and mothers with packages of especially nutritious foods, was designed to meet this need. But the program has encountered logistical problems which have severely limited its success. I am therefore directing that a substantial portion of the fiscal year 1970 budget for this program be used to establish pilot programs that make use of the private food market. Under these programs, needy pregnant women and mothers of infants will be issued vouchers, redeemable at food and drug stores for infant formulas and other highly nutritious special foods. If such a program seems workable, and the administrative problems are resolved, the program will be expanded later on the basis of that experience.

3. Administration of Food Programs

I am directing the Urban Affairs Council to consider the establishment of a new agency, the Food and Nutrition Service, whose exclusive concern will be the administration of the Federal Food programs. Presently the food programs are operated in conjunction with numerous other unrelated programs. The creation of a new agency will permit greater specialization and concentration on the effective administration of the food programs.

4. Private Sector Involvement

I shall shortly announce a White House Conference on Food and Nutrition, involving executives from the nation's leading food-processing and food-distribution companies and trade unions. I shall ask these men to advise me on how the private food market might be used to improve the nutritional status of all Americans, and how the government food programs could be improved. I shall also call on these men to work with the advertising industry and the Advertising Council to develop an educational advertising and packaging campaign to publicize the importance of good food habits.

5. Inter-Agency Efforts

Although most of the current food and nutrition programs are administered by the Department of Agriculture, other agencies are critically involved. I am therefore establishing a sub-Cabinet working committee of the Urban Affairs Council to promote coordination between the food and nutrition programs and other health, educational, and antipoverty programs.

At the present time I am directing the Secretary of Health, Education and Welfare and the Director of the Office of Economic Opportunity to take a number of immediate steps.

I am asking the Secretary of HEW to:

—Work with state agencies to ensure that the Medicaid program is fully coordinated with the Special Package and pilot voucher programs for pregnant women and infants, so that vitamin and mineral products can be made available to those diagnosed as suffering from nutrient deficiencies.

—Expand the National Nutrition Survey, presently being conducted by the Public Health Service, to provide us with our first detailed description of the extent of hunger and malnutrition in our country.

—Initiate detailed research into the relationship between malnutrition and mental retardation.

—Encourage emphasis by medical schools on training for diagnosis and treatment of malnutrition and malnutrition-related diseases.

The Office of Economic Opportunity, with its exclusive commitment to the problems of poverty and its unique "outreach" among the poor themselves, has an especial role to play. I am asking the Director of OEO to:

—Work with the Secretaries of Agriculture and HEW to establish a greatly expanded role for the Community Action Agencies in delivering food stamps and commodity packages. Volunteers working in the VISTA program will also aid in the delivery and outreach process, supplementing the efforts of the Agricultural Extension Service.

—Redirect OEO funds into the Emergency Food and Health Service program to increase its food, health, and sanitation services for our most depressed areas. Presently, health and sanitary conditions in many of our most depressed counties are so poor that improved food services alone would have little impact on the nutritional health of the population. The Emergency Food and Health Service has provided invaluable services in aiding these areas, and its good work should be substantially expanded.

More is at stake here than the health and well-being of 16 million American citizens who will be aided by these programs and the current Child Food Assistance programs. Something very like the honor of American democracy is at issue. It was half a century ago that the "fruitful plains" of this bounteous land were first called on to do a great work of humanity, that of feeding a Europe exhausted and bleeding from the First World War. Since then on one occasion after another, in a succession of acts of true generosity, America has come to the aid of one starving people after another. But the moment is at hand to put an end to hunger in America itself for all time. I ask this of a Congress that has already splendidly demonstrated its own disposition to act. It is a moment to act with vigor; it is a moment to be recalled with pride.

WE MUST HAVE A NEW WELFARE PLAN
Nationwide Radio and Television Address
AUGUST 8, 1969

Good evening, my fellow Americans.

As you know, I returned last Sunday night from a trip around the world—a trip that took me to eight countries in nine days.

The purpose of this trip was to help lay the basis for a lasting peace, once the war in Vietnam is ended. In the course of it, I also saw once again the vigorous efforts so many new nations are making to leap the centuries into the modern world.

Every time I return to the United States after such a trip, I realize how fortunate we are to live in this rich land. We have the world's most advanced industrial economy, the greatest wealth ever known to man, the fullest measure of freedom ever enjoyed by any people anywhere.

Yet we, too, have an urgent need to modernize our institutions—and our need is no less than theirs.

We face an urban crisis, a social crisis—and at the same time, a crisis of confidence in the capacity of government to do its job.

A third of a century of centralizing power and responsibility in Washington has produced a bureaucratic monstrosity, cumbersome, unresponsive, ineffective.

A third of a century of social experiment has left us a legacy of entrenched programs that have outlived their time or outgrown their purposes.

A third of a century of unprecedented growth and change has strained our institutions and raised serious questions about whether they are still adequate to the times.

It is no accident, therefore, that we find increasing skepticism—and not only among our young people, but among citizens everywhere—about the continuing capacity of government to master the challenges we face.

Nowhere has the failure of government been more tragically apparent than in its efforts to help the poor and especially in its system of public welfare.

Since taking office, one of my first priorities has been to repair the machinery of government, and to put it in shape for the 1970s. I have made many changes designed to improve the functioning of the Executive Branch. I have asked Congress for a number of important structural reforms; among others, a wide-ranging postal reform, a comprehensive reform of the draft, a reform of unemployment insurance, a reform of our hunger programs, and reform of the present confusing hodgepodge of Federal grants-in-aid.

Last April 21 I sent Congress a message asking for a package of major tax reforms, including both the closing of loopholes and the removal of more than 2 million low-income families from the tax rolls altogether. I am glad Congress is now acting on tax reform, and I hope the Congress will begin to act on the other reforms that I have requested.

The purpose of all these reforms is to eliminate unfairness; to make government more effective as well as more efficient; and to bring an end to its chronic failure to deliver the service that it promises.

My purpose tonight, however, is not to review the past record, but to present a new set of reforms—a new set of proposals—a new and drastically different approach to the way in which government cares for those in need, and to the way the responsibilities are shared between the state and the Federal governments.

I have chosen to do so in a direct report to the people because these proposals call for public decisions of the first importance; because they represent a fundamental change in the nation's approach to one of its most pressing social problems; and because, quite deliberately, they also represent the first major reversal of the trend toward ever more centralization of government in Washington, D.C. After a third of a century of power flowing from the people and the states to Washington it is time for a New Federalism in which power, funds, and responsibility will flow from Washington to the states and to the people.

During last year's election campaign, I often made a point that touched a responsive chord wherever I traveled.

I said that this nation became great not because of what government did for people, but because of what people did for themselves.

This new approach aims at helping the American people do more for themselves. It aims at getting everyone able to work off welfare rolls and onto payrolls.

It aims at ending the unfairness in a system that has become unfair to the welfare recipient, unfair to the working poor, and unfair to the taxpayer.

This new approach aims to make it possible for people—wherever in America they live—to receive their fair share of opportunity. It aims to ensure that people receiving aid, and who are able to work, contribute their fair share of productivity.

This new approach is embodied in a package of four measures: first, a complete replacement of the present welfare system; second, a comprehensive new job-training and placement program; third, a revamping of the Office of Economic Opportunity; and fourth, a start on the sharing of Federal tax revenues with the states.

Next week—in three messages to the Congress and one statement —I will spell out in detail what these measures contain. Tonight I want to explain what they mean, what they are intended to achieve, and how they are related.

Whether measured by the anguish of the poor themselves, or by the drastically mounting burden on the taxpayer, the present welfare system has to be judged a colossal failure.

Our states and cities find themselves sinking in Federal quagmire, as caseloads increase, as costs escalate, and as the welfare system stagnates enterprise and perpetuates dependency.

What began on a small scale in the depression '30s has become a huge monster in the prosperous '60s. And the tragedy is not only that it is bringing states and cities to the brink of financial disaster, but also that it is failing to meet the elementary human, social, and financial needs of the poor.

It breaks up homes. It often penalizes work. It robs recipients of dignity. And it grows.

Benefit levels are grossly unequal—for a mother with three children they range from an average of $263 a month in one state, down to an average of $39 in another state. Now such an inequality as this is wrong; no child is "worth" more in one state than in another state. One result of this inequality is to lure thousands more into already overcrowded inner cities, as unprepared for city life as they are for city jobs.

The present system creates an incentive for desertion. In most states a family is denied welfare payments if a father is present—even though he is unable to support his family. Now, in practice, this is what often happens: A father is unable to find a job at all or one that will support his children. So, to make the children eligible for welfare, he leaves home—and the children are denied the authority, the discipline, and the love that come with having a father in the home. This is wrong.

The present system often makes it possible to receive more money on welfare than on a low-paying job. This creates an incentive not to work; and it also is unfair to the working poor. It is moraly wrong for a family that is working to try to make ends meet to receive less than the family across the street on welfare. This has been bitterly resented by the man who works, and rightly so—the rewards are just the opposite of what they should be. Its effect is to draw people off payrolls and onto welfare rolls—just the opposite of what government should be doing. To put it bluntly and simply—any system which makes it more profitable for a man not to work than to work, or which encourages a man to desert his family rather than to stay with his family, is wrong and indefensible.

We cannot simply ignore the failures of welfare, or expect them to go away. In the past eight years 3 million more people have been added to the welfare rolls—and this in a period of low unemployment. If the present trend continues, another 4 million will join the welfare rolls by 1975. The financial cost will be crushing, and the human cost will be suffocating.

That is why tonight I therefore propose that we will abolish the present welfare system and that we adopt in its place a new family assistance system. Initially, this new system will cost more than welfare. But unlike welfare, it is designed to correct the condition it deals with and thus to lessen the long-range burden and cost.

Under this plan, the so-called "adult categories" of aid—aid to the aged, the blind, and disabled—would be continued and a national minimum standard for benefits would be set, with the Federal government contributing to its cost and also sharing the cost of additional state payments above that amount.

But the program now called "Aid to Families with Dependent Children"—the program we all normally think of when we think of "welfare"—would be done away with completely. The new family assistance system I propose in its place rests essentially on these three principles: equality of treatment across the nation, a work requirement, and a work incentive.

Its benefits would go to the working poor, as well as the non-working; to families with dependent children headed by a father, as well as to those headed by a mother; and a basic Federal minimum would be provided, the same in every state.

What I am proposing is that the Federal government build a foundation under the income of every American family with dependent children that cannot care for itself—wherever in America that family may live.

For a family of four now on welfare, with no outside income, the basic Federal payment would be $1,600 a year. States could add to that amount and most states would add to it. In no case would anyone's present level of benefits be lowered.

At the same time, this foundation would be one on which the family itself could build. Outside earnings would be encouraged, not discouraged. The new worker could keep the first $60 a month of outside earnings with no reduction in his benefits; then beyond that, his benefits would be reduced by only fifty cents for each dollar earned.

By the same token, a family head already employed at low wages could get a family assistance supplement; those who work would no longer be discriminated against. For example, a family of five in which the father earns $2,000 a year—which is the hard fact of life for many families in America today—would get family assistance payments of $1,260, so that they would have a total income of $3,260. A family of seven earning $3,000 a year would have its income raised to $4,360.

Thus, for the first time, the government would recognize that it has no less an obligation to the working poor than to the non-working poor; and for the first time, benefits would be scaled in such a way that it would always pay to work.

With such incentives most recipients who can work will want to work. This is part of the American character.

But what of the others—those who can work but choose not to?

The answer is very simple.

Under this proposal, everyone who accepts benefits must also accept work or training, provided suitable jobs are available either locally or at some distance if transportation is provided. The only exceptions would be those unable to work and mothers of preschool children.

Even mothers of preschool children, however, would have the opportunity to work—because I am also proposing along with this a major expansion of day-care centers to make it possible for mothers to take jobs by which they can support themselves and their children.

This national floor under incomes for working or dependent families is not a "guaranteed income." Under the guaranteed income proposal, everyone would be assured a minimum income, regardless of how much he was capable of earning, regardless of what his need was, regardless of whether or not he was willing to work.

During the Presidential campaign last year, I opposed such a plan. I oppose it now and I will continue to oppose it, and this is the reason: A guaranteed income would undermine the incentive to work; the family assistance plan that I propose increases the incentive to work.

A guaranteed income establishes a right without any responsibilities; family assistance recognizes a need and establishes a responsibility. It provides help to those in need and, in turn, requires that those who receive help work to the extent of their capabilities. There is no reason why one person should be taxed so that another can choose to live idly.

In states that now have benefit levels above the Federal floor, family assistance would help ease the state's financial burdens. But in twenty states—those in which poverty is most widespread—the new Federal floor would be above present average benefits and would mean a leap upward for many thousands of families that cannot care for themselves.

Now I would like to turn to the job-training proposals that are part of our full opportunity concept. America prides itself on being the "land of opportunity." I deeply believe in this ideal, as I am sure everyone listening to me also believes in this ideal.

Full opportunity means the chance for upward mobility on every rung of the economic ladder—and for every American, no matter what the handicaps of birth.

The cold hard truth is that a child born to a poor family has far less chance to make a good living than a child born to a middle-income family.

He is born poor, fed poorly; and if his family is on welfare, he starts life in an atmosphere of handout and dependency; often he receives little preparation for work and less inspiration. The wonder of the American character is that so many have the spark and the drive to fight their way up. But for millions of others the burden of poverty in early life snuffs out that spark.

The new family assistance would provide aid for needy families; it would establish a work requirement and a work incentive; but these in turn require effective programs of job training and job placement— including a chance to qualify not just for any jobs, but for good jobs that provide both additional self-respect and full self-support.

Therefore, I am also sending a message to Congress calling for a complete overhaul of the nation's manpower training services.

The Federal government's job-training programs have been a terrible tangle of confusion and waste.

To remedy the confusion, arbitrariness, and rigidity of the present system, the new manpower training act would basically do three things:

—It would pull together the jumble of programs that presently exist, and equalize standards of eligibility.

—It would provide flexible funding—so that Federal money would follow the demands of labor and industry and flow into those programs that people most want and most need.

—It would decentralize administration, gradually moving it away from the Washington bureaucracy and turning it over to states and localities.

In terms of its symbolic importance, I can hardly overemphasize this last point. For the first time, applying the principles of the New Federalism, administration of a major established Federal program would be turned over to the states and local governments, recognizing that they are in a position to do the job better.

For years thoughtful Americans have talked of the need to decentralize government. The time has come to begin.

Federal job-training programs have grown to vast proportions, costing more than $1 billion a year. Yet they are essentially local in character. As long as the Federal government continues to bear the cost, they can perfectly well be run by states and local governments, and that way they can be better adapted to specific state and local needs.

The Manpower Training Act will have other provisions specifically designed to help move people off welfare rolls and onto payrolls.

—A computerized job bank would be established, to match job seekers with job vacancies.

—For those on welfare a $30-a-month bonus would be offered as an incentive to go into job training.

—For heads of families now on welfare 150,000 new training slots would be opened.

—As I mentioned previously, greatly expanded day-care facilities would be provided for the children of welfare mothers who choose to work. However, these would be day-care centers with a difference. There is no single ideal to which this Administration is more firmly committed than to the enriching of a child's first five years of life, and, thus, helping lift the poor out of misery at a time when a lift can help the most. Therefore, these day-care centers would offer more than custodial care; they would also be devoted to the development of vigorous young minds and bodies. As a further dividend, the day-care centers would offer employment to many welfare mothers themselves.

One common theme running through my proposals tonight is that of providing full opportunity for every American. A second theme is that of trying to equip every American to play a productive role, and a third is to the need to make government itself workable—which means reshaping, reforming, innovating.

The Office of Economic Opportunity is basically an innovative agency—and thus it has a vital place in our efforts to develop and test new programs and apply new knowledge. But in order to do so effectively what it can do best, OEO itself needs reorganization.

This Administration has completed a thorough study of OEO. We have assigned it a leading role in the effort to develop and test new approaches to the solving of social problems. OEO is to be a laboratory agency where new ideas for helping people are tried on a pilot basis. When they prove successful, they can be spun off to operating departments or agencies—just as the space agency, for example, spun off the weather satellite and the communciations satellite when these proved successful—then OEO would be free to concentrate on breaking even newer ground.

The new OEO organization to be announced next week will stress this role. It also will stress accountability, a clear separation of functions, and a tighter, more effective organization of field operations.

We come now to a proposal which I consider profoundly important to the future of our Federal system of shared responsibilities. As when we speak of poverty or jobs or opportunity or making government more effective or getting it closer to the people, it brings us directly to the financial plight of our states and cities.

We can no longer have effective government at any level unless we have it at all levels. There is too much to be done for the cities to do it alone, or for Washington to do it alone, or for the states to do it alone.

For a third of a century power and responsibility have flowed toward Washington—and Washington has taken for its own the best sources of revenue.

We intend to reverse this tide and to turn back to the states a greater measure of responsibility—not as a way of avoiding problems, but as a better way of solving problems.

Along with this would go a share of Federal revenues. I shall propose to the Congress next week that a set portion of the revenues from Federal income taxes be remitted directly to the states—with a minimum of Federal restrictions on how those dollars are to be used, and with a requirement that a percentage of them be channeled through for the use of local governments.

The funds provided under this program will not be great in the first year. But the principle will have been established, and the amounts will increase as our budgetary situation improves.

This start on revenue sharing is a step toward what I call the New Federalism. It is a gesture of faith in America's state and local governments and in the principle of democratic self-government.

With this revenue-sharing proposal we follow through on the commitment I made in the last campaign. We follow through on a mandate which the electorate gave us last November.

In recent years we all have concentrated a great deal of attention on what we commonly call the "crisis of the cities." These proposals I have made are addressed in part to that, but they also are focused much more broadly.

They are addressed to the crisis of government—to adapting its structures and making it manageable.

They are addressed to the crisis of poverty and need—which is rural as well as urban. This Administration is committed to full opportunity on the farm as well as in the city; to a better life for rural America; to ensuring that government is responsive to the needs of rural America as well as urban America. These proposals will advance these goals.

I have discussed these four matters together because they make both a package and a pattern. They should be studied together, debated together, and seen in perspective.

These proposals are of course controversial, just as any new program is controversial. They also are expensive. Let us face that fact frankly and directly.

The first-year costs of the new family assistance program, including the child-care centers and job training, would be $4 billion. I deliberated long and hard over whether we could afford such an outlay. I decided in favor of it for two reasons: first, because the costs would not begin until fiscal 1971, when I expect the funds to be available within the budget; and second, because I concluded that this is a reform we cannot afford not to undertake. The cost of continuing the present system, in financial as well as human terms, is staggering if projected into the 1970s.

Revenue sharing would begin in the middle of fiscal 1971, at a half-year cost of a half billion dollars. This cuts into the Federal budget, but it represents relief for the equally hard-pressed states. It would help curb the rise in state and local taxes which are such a burden to millions of American families.

Overall, we would be spending more—in the short run—to help people who now are poor and who now are unready for work or unable to find work.

But I see it this way: Every businessman, every working man knows what "start-up costs" are. They are heavy investments made in early years in the expectation that they will more than pay for themselves in future years.

The investment in these proposals in a human investment; it also is a "start-up cost" in turning around our dangerous decline into welfarism in America. We cannot produce productive people with the antiquated, wheezing, overloaded machine we now call the welfare system.

If we fail to make this investment in work incentives now, if we merely try to patch up the system here and there, we will only be pouring good money after bad in ever increasing amounts.

If we do invest in this modernization, the heavy-burdened taxpayer at least will have the chance to see the end of the tunnel. And the man who only looks ahead to a lifetime of dependency will see hope—hope for a life of work and pride and dignity.

In the final analysis, we cannot talk our way out of poverty; we cannot legislate our way out of poverty, but this nation can work its way out of poverty. What America needs now is not more welfare, but more "workfare."

The task of this government, the great task of our people, is to provide the training for work, the incentive for work, the opportunity for work, and the reward for work. Together these measures are a first long step in this direction.

For those in the welfare system today who are struggling to fight their way out of poverty, these measures offer a way to independence through the dignity of work.

For those able to work these measures provide new opportunities to learn work, and to find work.

For the working poor—the forgotten poor—these measures offer a fair share in the assistance given to the poor.

This new system established a direct link between the government's willingness to help the needy and the willingness of the needy to help themselves.

It removes the present incentive not to work, and substitutes an incentive to work; it removes the present incentive for families to break apart and substitutes an incentive for families to stay together.

It removes the blatant inequities, injustices, and indignities of the welfare system.

It establishes a basic Federal floor so that children in any state can have at least the minimum essentials of life.

Together these measures cushion the impact of welfare costs on states and localities, many of which have found themselves in fiscal crisis as costs have spiraled.

They bring reason, order, and purpose into a tangle of overlapping programs, and show that government can be made to work.

Poverty will not be defeated by a stroke of a pen signing a check; and it will not be reduced to nothing overnight with slogans or ringing exhortations.

Poverty is not only a state of income. It is also a state of mind and a state of health. Poverty must be conquered without sacrificing the will to work, for if we take the route of the permanent handout, the American character will itself be impoverished.

In my recent trip around the world, I visited countries in all stages of economic development; countries with different social systems, different economic systems, different political systems.

In all of them, however, I found that one event caught the imagination of the people and lifted their spirits almost beyond measure: the trip of Apollo to the moon and back. On that historic day, when the astronauts set foot on the moon, the spirit of Apollo truly swept through this world—it was a spirit of peace and brotherhood and adventure, a spirit that thrilled to the knowledge that man had dreamed the impossible, dared the impossible, and done the impossible.

Abolishing poverty, putting an end to dependency—like reaching the moon a generation ago—may seem to be impossible. But in the spirit of Apollo we can lift our sights and marshal our best efforts. We can resolve to make this the year, not that we reached the goal, but that we turned the corner; turned the corner from a dismal cycle of dependency toward a new birth of independence; from despair toward hope; from an ominously mounting impotence of government to a new effectiveness of government, and toward a full opportunity for every American to share the bounty of this rich land.

Thank you.

PROPOSAL FOR A NEW WELFARE PLAN
Message to the Congress of the United States

AUGUST 11, 1969

A measure of the greatness of a powerful nation is the character of the life it creates for those who are powerless to make ends meet.

If we do not find the way to become a working nation that properly cares for the dependent, we shall become a welfare state that undermines the incentive of the working man.

The present welfare system has failed us—it has fostered family breakup, has provided very little help in many states, and has even deepened dependency by all too often making it more attractive to go on welfare than to go to work.

I propose a new approach that will make it more attractive to go to work than to go on welfare, and will establish a nationwide minimum payment to dependent families with children.

I propose that the Federal government pay a basic income to those American families who cannot care for themselves in whichever state they live.

I propose that dependent families receiving such income be given good reason to go to work *by making the first $60 a month they earn completely their own, with no deductions from their benefits.*

I propose that we *make available an addition to the incomes of the "working poor,"* to encourage them to go on working and to eliminate the possibility of making more from welfare than from wages.

I propose that these payments be made upon certification of income, with demeaning and costly investigations replaced by simplified reviews and spot checks and with *no eligibility requirement that the household be without a father.* That present requirement in many states has the effect of breaking up families and contributes to delinquency and violence.

I propose that all employable persons who choose to accept these payments be required to register for work or job training and *be required to accept that work or training,* provided suitable jobs are available either locally or if transportation is provided. Adequate and convenient day care would be provided children wherever necessary to enable a parent to train or work. The only exception to this work requirement would be mothers of preschool children.

I propose *a major expansion of job-training and day-care facilities,* so that current welfare recipients able to work can be set on the road to self-reliance.

I propose that we also *provide uniform Federal payment minimums for the present three categories of welfare aid to adults*—the aged, the blind, and the disabled.

This would be total welfare reform—the transformation of a system frozen in failure and frustration into a system that would work and would encourage people to work.

Accordingly, we have stopped considering human welfare in isolation. The new plan is part of an overall approach which includes a comprehensive new Manpower Training Act, and a plan for a system of revenue sharing with the states to help provide all of them with necessary budget relief. Messages on manpower training and revenue sharing will follow this message tomorrow and the next day, and the three should be considered as parts of a whole approach to what is clearly a national problem.

Need for New Departures

A welfare system is a success when it takes care of people who cannot take care of themselves and when it helps employable people climb toward independence.

A welfare system is a failure when it takes care of those who can take care of themselves, when it drastically varies payments in different areas, when it breaks up families, when it perpetuates a vicious cycle of dependency, when it strips human beings of their dignity.

America's welfare system is a failure that grows worse every day.

First, it fails the recipient: in many areas, benefits are so low that we have hardly begun to take care of the dependent. And there has been no light at the end of poverty's tunnel. After four years of inflation, the poor have generally become poorer.

Second, it fails the taxpayer: since 1960, welfare costs have doubled and the number on the rolls has risen from 5.8 million to over 9 million, all in a time when unemployment was low. The taxpayer is entitled to expect government to devise a system that will help people lift themselves out of poverty.

Finally, it fails American society: by breaking up homes, the present welfare system has added to social unrest and robbed millions of children of the joy of childhood; by widely varying payments among regions, it has helped to draw millions into the slums of our cities.

The situation has become intolerable. Let us examine the alternatives available:

—We could permit the welfare momentum to continue to gather speed by our inertia; by 1975 this would result in 4 million more Americans on welfare rolls at a cost of close to $11 billion a year, with both recipients and taxpayers shortchanged.

—We could tinker with the system as it is, adding to the patchwork of modifications and exceptions. That has been the approach of the past, and it has failed.

—We could adopt a "guaranteed minimum income for everyone," which would appear to wipe out poverty overnight. It would also wipe out the basic economic motivation for work, and place an enormous strain on the industrious to pay for the leisure of the lazy.

—Or we could adopt a totally new approach to welfare, designed to assist those left far behind the national norm, and provide all with the motivation to work and a fair share of the opportunity to train.

This Administration, after a careful analysis of all the alternatives, is committed to a new departure that will find a solution for the welfare problem. The time for denouncing the old is over; the time for devising the new is now.

Recognizing the Practicalities

People usually follow their self-interest.

This stark fact is distressing to many social planners who like to look at problems from the top down. Let us abandon the ivory tower and consider the real world in all we do.

In most states welfare is provided only when there is no father at home to provide support. If a man's children would be better off on welfare than with the low wage he is able to bring home, wouldn't he be tempted to leave home?

If a person spent a great deal of time and effort to get on the welfare rolls, wouldn't he think twice about risking his eligibility by taking a job that might not last long?

In each case, welfare policy was intended to limit the spread of dependency; in practice, however, the effect has been to increase dependency and remove the incentive to work.

We fully expect people to follow their self-interest in their business dealings; why should we be surprised when people follow their self-interest in their welfare dealings? That is why we propose a plan in which it is in the interest of every employable person to do his fair share of work.

The Operation of the New Approach

1. We would assure an income foundation throughout every section of America for all parents who cannot adequately support themselves and their children. For a family of four with less than $1,000 income, this payment would be $1,600 a year; for a family of four with $2,000 income, this payment would supplement that income by $960 a year.

Under the present welfare system each state provides "Aid to Families with Dependent Children," a program we propose to replace. The Federal government shares the cost, but each state establishes key eligibility rules and determines how much income support will be provided to poor families. The result has been an uneven and unequal system. The 1969 benefits average for a family of four is $171 a month across the nation, but individual state averages range from $263 down to $39 a month.

A new Federal minimum of $1,600 a year cannot claim to provide comfort to a family of four, but the present low of $468 a year cannot claim to provide even the basic necessities.

The new system would do away with the inequity of very low benefit levels in some states, and of state-by-state variations in eligibility tests, by establishing a Federally-financed income floor with a national definition of basic eligibility.

States will continue to carry an important responsibility. In thirty states the Federal basic payment will be less than the present levels of combined Federal and state payments. These states will be required to maintain the current level of benefits, but in no case will a state be required to spend more than 90 percent of its present welfare cost. The Federal government will not only provide the "floor," but it will assume 10 percent of the benefits now being paid by the states as their part of welfare costs.

In twenty states the new payment would exceed the present average benefit payments, in some cases by a wide margin. In these states, where benefits are lowest and poverty often the most severe, the payments will raise benefit levels substantially. For five years every state will be required to continue to spend at least half of what they are now spending on welfare, to supplement the Federal base.

For the *typical "welfare family"*—a mother with dependent children and no outside income—the new system would provide a basic national minimum payment. A mother with three small children would be assured an annual income of at least $1,600.

For the family headed by an employed father or working mother the same basic benefits would be received, but $60 per month of earnings would be "disregarded" in order to make up the costs of working and provide a strong advantage in holding a job. The wage earner could also keep 50 percent of his benefits as his earnings rise above that $60 per month. A family of four, in which the father earns $2,000 in a year, would receive payments of $960, for a total income of $2,960.

For the *aged, the blind, and the disabled* the present system varies benefit levels from $40 per month for an aged person in one state to $145 per month for the blind in another. The new system would establish a minimum payment of $65 per month for all three of these adult categories, with the Federal government contributing the first $50 and sharing in payments above that amount. This will raise the share of the financial burden borne by the Federal government for payments to these adults who cannot support themselves, and should pave the way for benefit increases in many states.

For the *single adult* who is not handicapped or aged or for the *married couple without children* the new system would not apply. Food stamps would continue to be available up to $300 per year per person, according to the plan I outlined last May in my message to the Congress on the food and nutrition needs of the population in poverty. For dependent families there will be an orderly substitution of food stamps by the new direct monetary payments.

2. *The new approach would end the blatant unfairness of the welfare system.* In over half the states families headed by unemployed men do not qualify for public assistance. In no state does a family headed by a father working full time receive help in the current welfare system, no matter how little he earns. As we have seen, this approach to dependency has itself been a cause of dependency. It results in a policy that tends to force the father out of the house.

The new plan rejects a policy that undermines family life. It would end the substantial financial incentives to desertion. It would extend eligibility to *all* dependent families with children, without regard to whether the family is headed by a man or a woman. The effects of these changes upon human behavior would be an increased will to work, the survival of more marriages, the greater stability of families. We are determined to stop passing the cycle of dependency from generation to generation.

The most glaring inequity in the old welfare system is the exclusion of families who are working to pull themselves out of poverty. Families headed by a non-worker often receive more from welfare than families headed by a husband working full-time at very low wages. This has been rightly resented by the working poor, for the rewards are just the opposite of what they should be.

3. *The new plan would create a much stronger incentive to work.* For people now on the welfare rolls the present system discourages the move from welfare to work by cutting benefits too fast and too much as earnings begin. *The new system would encourage work by allowing the new worker to retain the first $720 of his yearly earnings without any benefit reduction.*

For people already working, but at poverty wages, the present system often encourages nothing but resentment and an incentive to quit and go on relief where that would pay more than work. The new plan, on the contrary, would provide a supplement that will help a low-wage worker—struggling to make ends meet—achieve a higher standard of living.

For an employable person who just chooses not to work, neither the present system nor the one we propose would support him, though both would continue to support other dependent members in his family.

However, a welfare mother with preschool children should not face benefit reductions if she decides to stay home. It is not our intent that mothers of preschool children must accept work. Those who can work and desire to do so, however, should have the opportunity for jobs and job training and access to day-care centers for their children; this will enable them to support themselves after their children are grown.

A family with a member who gets a job would be permitted to retain all of the *first $60 monthly income,* amounting to $720 per year for a regular worker, *with no reduction of Federal payments.* The incentive to work in this provision is obvious. But there is another practical reason: going to work costs money. Expenses such as clothes, transportation, personal care, Social Security taxes, and loss of income from odd jobs amount to substantial costs for the average family. Since a family does not begin to *add* to its net income until it surpasses the cost of working, in fairness this amount should not be subtracted from the new payment.

After the first $720 of income the *rest* of the earnings will result in a systematic reduction in payments.

I believe the vast majority of poor people in the United States prefer to work rather than have the government support their families. In 1968 600,000 families left the welfare rolls out of an average caseload of 1.4 million during the year, showing a considerable turnover, much of it voluntary.

However, there may be some who fail to seek or accept work, even with the strong incentives and training opportunities that will be provided. It would not be fair to those who willingly work, or to all taxpayers, to allow others to choose idleness when opportunity is available. Thus, they must accept training opportunities and jobs when offered, or give up their right to the new payments for themselves. No able-bodied person will have a "free ride" in a nation that provides opportunity for training and work.

4. *The bridge from welfare to work should be buttressed by training and child-care programs.* For many the incentives to work in this plan would be all that is necessary. However, there are other situations where these incentives need to be supported by measures that will overcome other barriers to employment.

I propose that *funds be provided for expanded training and job development programs* so that an additional 150,000 welfare recipients can become jobworthy during the first year.

Manpower training is a basic bridge to work for poor people, especially people with limited education, low skills, and limited job experience. Manpower training programs can provide this bridge for many of our poor. In the new Manpower Training proposal to be sent to the Congress this week, the interrelationship with this new approach to welfare will be apparent.

I am also requesting authority, as a part of the new system, to provide child care for the 450,000 children of the 150,000 current welfare recipients to be trained.

The child care I propose is more than custodial. This Administration is committed to a new emphasis on child development in the first five years of life. The day care that would be part of this plan would be of a quality that will help in the development of the child and provide for its health and safety, and would break the poverty cycle for this new generation.

The expanded child-care program would bring new opportunities along several lines: opportunities for the further involvement of private enterprise in providing high-quality child-care service; opportunities for volunteers; and opportunities for *training and employment in child-care centers of many of the welfare mothers themselves.*

I am requesting a total of $600 million [in] addition to fund these expanded training programs and child-care centers.

5. *The new system will lessen welfare red tape and provide administrative cost savings.* To cut out the costly investigations so bitterly resented as "welfare snooping," the Federal payment will be based upon a certification of income, with spot checks sufficient to prevent abuses. The program will be administered on an automated basis, using the information and technical experience of the Social Security Administration, but, of course, will be entirely separate from the administration of the Social Security trust fund.

The states would be given the option of having the Federal government handle the payment of the state supplemental benefits on a reimbursable basis, so that they would be spared their present administrative burdens and so a single check could be sent to the recipient. These simplifications will save money and eliminate indignities; at the same time, welfare fraud will be detected and lawbreakers prosecuted.

6. *This new departure would require a substantial initial investment, but will yield future returns to the nation.* This transformation of the welfare system will set in motion forces that will lessen dependency rather than perpetuate and enlarge it. A more productive population adds to real economic growth without inflation. The initial investment is needed now to stop the momentum of work-to-welfare, and to start a new momentum in the opposite direction.

The costs of welfare benefits for families with dependent children have been rising alarmingly the past several years, increasing from $1 billion in 1960 to an estimated $3.3 billion in 1969, of which $1.8 billion is paid by the Federal government, and $1.5 billion is paid by the states. Based on current population and income data, the proposals I am making today will increase Federal costs during the first year by an estimated $4 billion, which includes $600 million for job-training and child-care centers.

The "start-up costs" of lifting many people out of dependency will ultimately cost the taxpayer far less than the chronic costs—in dollars and in national values—of creating a permanent underclass in America.

From Welfare to Work

Since this Administration took office, members of the Urban Affairs Council, including officials of the Department of Health, Education and

Welfare, the Department of Labor, the Office of Economic Opportunity, the Bureau of the Budget, and other key advisers, have been working to develop a coherent, fresh approach to welfare, manpower training, and revenue sharing.

I have outlined our conclusions about an important component of this approach in this message; the Secretary of HEW will transmit to the Congress the proposed legislation after the summer recess.

I urge the Congress to begin its study of these proposals promptly so that laws can be enacted and funds authorized to begin the new system as soon as possible. Sound budgetary policy must be maintained in order to put this plan into effect—especially the portion supplementing the wages of the working poor.

With the establishment of the new approach, the Office of Economic Opportunity will concentrate on the important task of finding new ways of opening economic opportunity for those who are able to work. Rather than focusing on income support activities, it must find means of providing opportunities for individuals to contribute to the full extent of their capabilities, and of developing and improving those capabilities.

This would be the effect of the transformation of welfare into "workfare," a new work-rewarding system:

—For the first time, all dependent families with children in America, regardless of where they live, would be assured of minimum standard payments based upon uniform and single eligibility standards.

—For the first time, the more than 2 million families who make up the "working poor" would be helped toward self-sufficiency and away from future welfare dependency.

—For the first time, training and work opportunity with effective incentives would be given millions of families who would otherwise be locked into a welfare system for generations.

—For the first time, the Federal government would make a strong contribution toward relieving the financial burden of welfare payments from state governments.

—For the first time, every dependent family in America would be encouraged to stay together, free from economic pressure to split apart.

These are far-reaching effects. They cannot be purchased cheaply, or by piecemeal efforts. This total reform looks in a new direction; it requires new thinking, a new spirit, and a fresh dedication to reverse the downhill course of welfare. In its first year, more than half the families participating in the program will have one member working or training.

We have it in our power to raise the standard of living and the realizable hopes of millions of our fellow citizens. By providing an equal chance at the starting line, we can reinforce the traditional American spirit of self-reliance and self-respect.

PROPOSED BENEFIT SCHEDULE
(Excluding all state benefits)

Earned Income	New Benefit	Total Income
$ 0	$1,600	$1,600
500	1,600	2,100
1,000	1,460	2,460
1,500	1,210	2,710
2,000	960	2,960
2,500	710	3,210
3,000	460	3,460
3,500	210	3,710
4,000	0	4,000

(For a four-person family, with a basic payment standard of $1,600 and an earned income disregard of $720.)

FULL OPPORTUNITY FOR ALL AMERICANS
A White House Statement by the President
AUGUST 11, 1969

We live in an exciting and difficult time. We possess great strength and skill; yet we are often unable to harness our strength in the service of our ideals. We sense new possibilities for unlocking the full potential of every individual; yet our institutions too often are unresponsive to our needs. We dream of what we might be able to make of our society; but we have not yet learned to achieve that dream.

Our nation will attain its social objectives, I believe, only if we develop a new spirit of adventure in their pursuit. We must become pioneers in reshaping our society even as we have become pioneers in space. We must show a new willingness to take risks for progress, a new readiness to try the untried.

Such an innovative spirit should characterize all of our institutions and all agencies of government. But it is in the Office of Economic Opportunity that social pioneering should be a specialty. It is the OEO that should act as the "R and D" arm for government's social programs.

When I sent a message to the Congress on OEO last February, I offered several preliminary comments about the agency. Since that time, the new Director of the Office has made a thorough review of its operations. On the basis of our discussions I have reached a number of further conclusions about the direction of OEO and the way it does its work.

The following are among the specific changes in OEO which I am announcing today:

—Creation of a new Office of Program Development.

—Revamping and strengthening the Office of Planning, Research, and Evaluation.

—Strengthening and upgrading the Office of Health Services and the Office of Legal Services.

—Creation of a new Office of Program Operations to improve the administration of activities in the field.

These and other specific changes, in turn, are based on a number of general principles which will help set new directions for OEO.

Setting New Directions

It has been said frequently in the past few weeks that if our country can marshal resources so effectively that we can travel to the moon, then we should also use our power and knowledge to better advantage in solving social problems on our own planet. I share this view. But if we are to make a better response to social challenges, then we will have to act with the same clear commitment to well-defined goals, the same freedom to undertake bold experiments, the same managerial discipline, and the same spirit of teamwork that has characterized our accomplishments in space.

A Clear Commitment. This Administration believes that every American should have the opportunity to participate in our nation's economic life to the full extent of his abilities. The Office of Economic Opportunity will make this objective its highest priority. It will address itself to unanswered and difficult questions: What determines an individual's capacity for growth and achievement? What can be done to awaken this capacity and develop it? How can we be sure that these capacities, when they are available, will be fully used and properly rewarded?

It is important that OEO concentrate its energies on causes rather than symptoms, that it help people become productive participants in the economy rather than focusing on the conduct of income support or other ameliorative activities. These latter functions should belong instead to efforts such as the new family assistance program, a revised unemployment compensation system, improved plans for food distribution, and various benefit payment programs.

We see today a healthy determination on the part of our people to continuously examine and update national priorities so that the energy and resources of our country can be properly allocated to solve domestic problems. But our people have also learned that the challenge of bringing unproductive people into active economic roles is more difficult than many had thought. We know now that the amount of money we spend in this effort will mean little unless the approach is right. The Office of Economic Opportunity will help us develop needed new approaches to this problem. It will translate our general commitment to provide full opportunity to all Americans into specific programs which will help us use our resources to the greatest effect.

Bold Experimentation. The freedom to try out a wide variety of ideas, to test them fully both in theory and in practice, to move boldly on several fronts, to thoroughly master and carefully apply the results of this experimental process—these are capacities which are as instrumental to social progress as they are to advances in science.

Since OEO is to be the cutting edge by means of which government moves into unexplored areas, the experimental temper will be vital to its success. The agency should marshal the most creative minds in the country, both to ask new questions and find new answers. It should be free to take creative risks. It should set up a variety of demonstration projects, carefully test their effectiveness, and systematically assess the results.

Just as NASA developed weather satellites and communication satellites and then spun them off, transferring them to the Department of Commerce and to COMSAT, so OEO should concentrate on the experimental stage of domestic programs. When a program has proven successful in the domestic area, it too may be transferred to other agencies or other levels of the government or even to the private sector if that seems desirable. This approach will leave OEO free to break still newer ground.

Managerial Discipline. Too often the lines of responsibility in OEO programs have been badly blurred; too often there has been no method for determining whether a program has succeeded or failed and what is responsible for failure and success. Too often the same individuals or groups, at both the national and local level, have found themselves wearing many hats: coordinating old programs, doing new research, setting up demonstration projects, evaluating results, and serving as advocates before the government on behalf of the poor. Precisely because each of these functions is important, each should be assigned to specific offices wherever that is possible, and they, in turn, should be held strictly accountable for the way in which their work is performed.

A Spirit of Teamwork. Finally, our social programs will require a greater sense of common endeavor among our people. Close cooperation between the private sector and government, for example, can be a key in assisting the economically disadvantaged as it has been a key to success in space. Moreover, we should be certain that the fears or suspicions which sometimes separate races or economic groups are diminished by our activities and not accentuated. We must avoid words and actions which drive people apart and emphasize instead the common stake of all Americans in extending economic opportunity.

These are some of the new directions which will define the scope of OEO and give new focus to its work. The specific organizational reforms we are making in the agency will help us move in these new directions; they will make OEO a stronger and more flexible instrument in the struggle for human dignity.

Specific Reforms

1. Office of Program Development. This new unit will be responsible for most of the experimental efforts which OEO will now emphasize and will include within it both totally new programs and some existing activities which previously were distributed throughout the agency. The Office of Program Development will seek new ways of bringing services to the poor, helping them to increase their skills, educate their children, improve their homes, protect their health, and develop their communities. It will try to find new methods of increasing their business and employment opportunities.

2. Office of Planning, Research, and Evaluation. The office of Planning, Research, and Evaluation will be reorganized and strengthened. Reporting straight to the Director, it will have responsibility for reviewing existing social programs, for comparing the results of projects with the objectives which have been set for them, for commenting on the adequacy with which both programs and objectives are formulated, and for recommending alterations in existing programs as well as new experiments. It will seek to establish more precise standards for measuring performance than OEO has used in the past. The Office of Planning, Research, and Evaluation will provide a regular source for that independent appraisal of Federal social programs which often is not available at present.

3. Office of Health Services. A strengthened Office of Health Services will also report directly to the Director of OEO. Many of the problems of the poor are the product of ill health and many have serious medical consequences. We have already begun to develop new mechanisms for helping the poor pay medical costs. But now we must further improve our methods for delivering health services so that all the poor will have ready access to doctors, diagnosis, treatment, and hospital care. The Neighborhood Health Center program is one experimental effort which is working in this direction; OEO will initiate other activities in this area. The 1970 budget will also show increases in food and nutrition programs, family planning services, and other health-related activities.

4. *Office of Legal Services.* The Office of Legal Services will also be strengthened and elevated so that it reports directly to the Director. It will take on central responsibility for programs which help provide advocates for the poor in their dealings with social institutions. The sluggishness of many institutions—at all levels of society—in responding to the needs of individual citizens is one of the central problems of our time. Disadvantaged persons in particular must be assisted so that they fully understand the lawful means of making their needs known and having those needs met. This goal will be better served by a separate Legal Services Program, one which can test new approaches to this important challenge.

5. *Office of Program Operations.* More attention must be given to the way in which OEO policies are carried out at the local, state, and regional level. A new Office of Program Operations will work to improve the quality of field operations; it will be able to define more clearly the purposes for which grants and contracts are given and to apply higher standards of effective management. Training and technical assistance funds for those who run OEO-supported programs will be increased. We also plan to raise allocations to State Economic Opportunity officers.

It is particularly important that the management of Community Action Agencies be improved. The goals of community action are desirable ones and the work of these agencies deserves our support. Unfortunately many of these local agencies have suffered from a proliferation of duties and from a confusion of roles. While some progress has been made in correcting these problems, the activities of community action agencies must be further clarified and such agencies must more clearly assign priorities among their various functions.

One of the important strengths of the Community Action Program has been its ability to involve local citizens in planning and carrying out its projects. This value should not be lost. Community organizations, close to the people, can play an important role in delivering government programs on a local and individual level.

Other Programs

Following the belief that the Office of Economic Opportunity should be an innovative agency, this Administration has already moved the Job Corps to the Department of Labor and the Head Start Program to the Department of Health, Education and Welfare. In addition, I am suggesting in my Manpower Training proposals that several OEO-funded manpower programs which have been administered by the Department of Labor be transferred to that Department. These are ongoing programs which have passed the trial stage and should now be seen as parts of our established manpower strategy.

Some proven programs which are national in scope should, however, remain in OEO because they can help us develop new experiments and because of the agency's special identification with the problems of the poor. The VISTA program is one example; it will make a greater effort to attract people with specific technical and professional skills to its ranks.

Mankind is presently entering a new era of exploration and fulfillment. We are able to move beyond the limits which once confined us, both in our travels beyond this planet and in our efforts to shape our life upon it. Now we must use this ability to explore on earth, as we have explored in space, with intelligence and courage, recognizing always how little we really know and how far we still must go.

I believe that the goal of full economic opportunity for every American can be realized. I expect the Office of Economic Opportunity to play a central role in that achievement. With new organizational structures, new operating procedures, and a new sense of precision and direction, OEO can be one of the most creative and productive offices in the government. For here much of our social pioneering will be done. Here will begin many of our new adventures.

BETTER TRAINING FOR THE JOBLESS
Message to the Congress of the United States
AUGUST 12, 1969

The "War on Poverty" had become, by the end of 1968, like the
Vietnam war, an exercise in frustration. Some of its noblest
projects like the "Head Start" training of poor children in their
preschool years and so-called compensatory education to teach
disadvantaged children how to read were baffling in their
frequent ineffectuality. Poverty funds went into schools teaching
black children to hate whites and financed revolutionary and
criminal elements. Job Corps camps aroused local fear and
hostility and fell short of their stated goals of training ghetto
youths for useful work. Speculation rose that Nixon would abolish
both the Poverty Program and the Job Corps. His final decision
was to reform both. Without using the word "poverty," he
reorganized the Office of Economic Opportunity, President
Johnson's name for the chief administrative agency of the
antipoverty program. He proposed a comprehensive Manpower
Training Act and reorganized the Manpower Administration of
the Department of Labor.

A job is one rung on the ladder of a lifelong career of work.

That is why we must look at manpower training with new eyes: as
a continuing process to help people to get started in a job and to *get*
ahead in a career.

"Manpower training" is one of those phrases with a fine ring and
an imprecise meaning. Before a fresh approach can be taken, a clear
definition is needed.

Manpower training means: (1) making it possible for those who
are unemployed or on the fringes of the labor force to become permanent full-time workers; (2) giving those who are now employed at low
incomes the training and the opportunity they need to become more productive and more successful; (3) discovering the potential in those
people who are now considered unemployable, removing many of the
barriers now blocking their way.

Manpower training, in order to work on all rungs of the ladder,
requires the efficient allocation by private enterprise and government of
these human resources. We must develop skills in a place, in a quantity,

and in a way to ensure that they are used effectively and constantly improved.

Today, government spends approximately $3 billion in a wide variety of manpower programs, with half directly devoted to job training; private enterprise spends much more on job training alone. The investment by private industry—given impetus by the profit motive as well as a sense of social responsibility—is the fundamental means of developing the nation's labor force. But the government's investment has failed to achieve its potential for many reasons, including duplication of effort, inflexible funding arrangements, and an endless ribbon of red tape. For example:

—*A jobless man* goes to the local skill-training center to seek help. He has the aptitudes for training in blue-collar mechanical work, but no suitable training opportunities are available. At the same time, vacancies exist in a white-collar New Careers project and in the Neighborhood Youth Corps. But the resources of these programs cannot be turned over to the training program that has the most local demand.

—*A seventeen-year-old boy wants to take job training.* The only manpower program available to him is the Job Corps, but its nearest camp is hundreds of miles away. With no other choice, he leaves home; within thirty days he has become homesick or feels his family needs him; he drops out of the Corps and has suffered "failure" which reinforces his self-image of defeat.

—*A big-city mayor* takes the lead in trying to put together a cohesive manpower program for the entire labor market area—tying together jobless workers in the inner city with job openings outside the "beltway." He finds it difficult to assemble a coherent picture of what's going on. Manpower programs funded by different agencies follow different reporting rules, so that the statistics cannot be added up. Moreover, there is no single agency which maintains an inventory of all currently operating manpower programs. He knows that help is available—but where does he turn?

—*An unemployed high school dropout* in a small town wants to learn a trade in the electronics field. His local employment office tells him that there is not enough demand in his town for qualified technicians to warrant setting up a special training class in a local public school. He is also told that "administrative procedures" do not lend themselves to the use of a local private technical institute which offers the very course he wants. This youngster walks the streets and wonders what happened to all those promises of "equal opportunity."

This confused state of affairs in the development of human resources can no longer be tolerated. Government exists to serve the needs of people, not the other way around. The idea of creating a set of "programs," and then expecting people to fit themselves into those programs, is contrary to the American spirit; we must redirect our efforts to tailor government aid to individual need.

This government has a major responsibility to make certain that the means to learn a job skill and improve that skill are available to those who need it.

Manpower training is central to our commitment to aid the disadvantaged and to help people off welfare rolls and onto payrolls. Intelligently organized, it will save tax dollars now spent on welfare, increase revenues by widening the base of the taxpaying public, and—most important—lift human beings into lives of greater dignity.

I propose a comprehensive new Manpower Training Act that would pull together much of the array of Federal training services and make it possible for state and local government to respond to the needs of the individual trainee.

The nation must have a manpower system that will enable each individual to take part in a sequence of activities—tailored to his unique needs—to prepare for and secure a good job. The various services people need are afforded in laws already on the books. The need today is to knit together all the appropriate services in one readily available system. By taking this step, we can better help the disadvantaged gain control and direction of their own lives.

A first step was taken in this direction in March when I announced the reorganization of the Manpower Administration of the U.S. Department of Labor. This reorganization consolidated the agencies that had fragmented responsibility for carrying out most of the nation's manpower training program. We must now complete the job by streamlining the statutory framework for our manpower training efforts.

In specific terms, the Act which I propose would:

1. *Consolidate major manpower development programs* administered by the Department of Labor—namely, the Manpower Development and Training Act and Title I-A (Job Corps) and I-B (Community Work and Training Program) of the Economic Opportunity Act. These programs, operated in conjunction with strengthened state manpower agencies, will provide training activities in a cohesive manpower services system. The Office of Economic Opportunity, without major manpower operational responsibilities, will continue its role in research work and program development working with the Department of Labor in pioneering new manpower training approaches.

2. *Provide flexible funding* of manpower training services so that

they can be sensitive to and focused on local needs; this will ensure the most efficient use of available resources.

3. *Decentralize administration of manpower services* to states and metropolitan areas, as governors and mayors evidence interest, build managerial capacity, and demonstrate effective performance. This process will take place in three stages. First, a state will administer 25 percent of the funds apportioned to it when it develops a comprehensive manpower planning capability; second, it will exercise discretion over 66⅔ percent when it establishes a comprehensive Manpower Training Agency to administer the unified programs; and, third, it will administer 100 percent when the state meets objective standards of exemplary performance in planning and carrying out its manpower service system.

The proposed Act will assure that equitable distribution of the manpower training dollars is made to the large metropolitan areas and to rural districts, working through a state grant system.

By placing greater reliance on state and local elected officials, the day-to-day planning and administration of manpower programs will become more responsive to individual job-training needs. A dozen states have already taken steps to reshape administrative agencies and to unify manpower and related programs.

To qualify for full participation under the proposed Act, each state and the major cities in a state would unify its manpower administration under state and local prime sponsors. These agencies would administer the programs funded by the Federal government; be responsible for other state and local activities to help people secure employment; help employers find manpower; and work in close liaison with state and local vocational education, vocational rehabilitation, and welfare programs, for which leadership will be provided at the national level by the Department of Health, Education and Welfare.

In addition, the state and local prime sponsors would establish advisory bodies, including employees, employers, and representatives of the local populations to be served, to assist in developing local policy. In this manner the units of government would be able to benefit continually from the experience and counsel of the private sector.

4. *Provide more equitable allowances for trainees,* simplifying the present schedule to provide an incentive for a trainee to choose the training best suited to his own future, and not the training that "pays" most.

As an incentive to move from welfare rolls to payrolls, the allowance to welfare recipients who go into training would be increased to $30 per month above their present welfare payments. These increased training allowances carefully dovetail into the work incentives outlined in my message to the Congress regarding the transformation of the welfare system. As the welfare recipient moves up the ladder from training to work, the first $60 per month of earnings would result in no deductions from Federally financed payments.

5. *Create a career development plan for trainees,* tailored to suit their individual capabilities and ambitions.

Eligible applicants— in general, those over sixteen who need training—would be provided a combination of services that would help them to train, to find work, and to move on up the ladder. These services will include counseling, basic vocational education, medical care, work experience, institutional and on-the-job training, and job referral. Manpower services will also be available for those who are presently employed but whose skill deficiencies hold them in low-income dead-end jobs.

6. *Establish a National Computerized Job Bank* to match job seekers with job vacancies. It would operate in each state, with regional and national activities undertaken by the Secretary of Labor, who would also set technical standards.

The computers of the Job Bank would be programmed with constantly changing data on available jobs. A job seeker would tell an employment counselor his training or employment background, his skills and career plans, which could be matched with a variety of available job options. This would expand the potential worker's freedom of choice and help him make best use of his particular talents.

7. *Authorize the use of the comprehensive manpower training system as an economic stabilizer.* If rising unemployment were ever to suggest the possibility of a serious economic downturn, a counter-cyclical automatic "trigger" would be provided. Appropriations for manpower services would be increased by 10 percent if the national unemployment rate equals or exceeds 4.5 percent for three consecutive months. People without the prospect of immediate employment could use this period to enhance their skills—and the productive capacity of the nation.

I proposed a similar measure in my message to the Congress on expansion of the unemployment insurance system.

The proposed comprehensive Manpower Training Act is a good example of a new direction in making Federalism work. Working together, we can bring order and efficiency to a tangle of Federal programs.

We can answer a national need by decentralizing power, setting national standards, and assigning administrative responsibility to the states and localities in touch with community needs.

We can relate substantial Federal-state manpower efforts to other efforts in welfare reform, tax sharing, and economic opportunity, marshaling the resources of the departments and agencies involved to accomplish a broad mission.

We can meet individual human needs without encroaching on personal freedom, which is perhaps the most exciting challenge to government today.

With these proposals, which I strongly urge the Congress to enact, we can enhance America's human resources. By opening up the opportunity for manpower training on a large scale, we build a person's will to work; in so doing, we build a bridge to human dignity.

SOCIAL SECURITY BENEFITS
Message to the Congress of the United States
SEPTEMBER 25, 1969

One of President Johnson's last acts in the Presidency was a proposal for a 10-percent increase of Social Security benefits. President Nixon presented his own comprehensive plan for a 10-percent increase along with other improvements seven months later.

A Democratic Congress, sensing the political implications, voted a 15-percent increase as part of the tax reduction bill of 1969 over the objections of the Nixon Administration. A Presidential veto of the tax reduction measure, along with its Social Security increase as inflationary, was considered. But Nixon signed the bill, which he called "unbalanced" with "both good and bad" provisions.

His message to Congress of September 25, 1969, remained his definitive position on Social Security reform.

This nation must not break faith with those Americans who have a right to expect that Social Security payments will protect them and their families.

The impact of an inflation now in its fourth year has undermined the value of every Social Security check and requires that we once again increase the benefits to help those among the most severely victimized by the rising cost of living.

I request that the Congress remedy the real losses to those who now receive Social Security benefits by increasing payments by 10 percent.

Beyond that step to set right today's inequity, I propose that the Congress make certain once and for all that the retired, the disabled, and the dependent never again bear the brunt of inflation. *The way to prevent future unfairness is to attach the benefit schedule to the cost of living.*

This will instill new security in Social Security. This will provide peace of mind to those concerned with their retirement years, and to their dependents.

By acting to raise benefits now to meet the rise in the cost of living, we keep faith with today's recipients. By acting to make future benefit raises automatic with rises in the cost of living, we remove questions about future years; we do much to remove this system from biennial politics; and we make fair treatment of beneficiaries a matter of certainty rather than a matter of hope.

In the thirty-four years since the Social Security program was first established, it has become a central part of life for a growing number of Americans. Today approximately 25 million people are receiving cash payments from this source. Three quarters of these are older Americans; the Social Security check generally represents the greater part of total income. Millions of younger people receive benefits under the disability or survivor provisions of Social Security.

Almost all Americans have a stake in the soundness of the Social Security system. Some 92 million workers are contributing to Social Security this year. About 80 percent of Americans of working age are protected by disability insurance and 95 percent of children and mothers have survivorship insurance protection. Because the Social Security program is an essential part of life for so many Americans, we must continually re-examine the program and be prepared to make improvements.

Aiding in this Administration's review and evaluation is the Advisory Council on Social Security which the Secretary of Health, Education and Welfare appointed in May. For example, I will look to this Council for recommendations in regard to working women; changing work patterns and the increased contributions of working women to the system may make present law unfair to them. The recommendations of this Council and of other advisers, both within the Government and outside of it, will be important to our planning. As I indicated in my message to the Congress on April 14, improvement in the Social Security program is a major objective of this Administration.

There are certain changes in the Social Security program, however, for which the need is so clear that they should be made without awaiting the findings of the Advisory Council. The purpose of this message is to recommend such changes.

I propose an across-the-board increase of 10 percent in Social Security benefits, effective with checks mailed in April, 1970, to make up for increases in the cost of living.

I propose that future benefits in the Social Security system be automatically adjusted to account for increases in the cost of living.

I propose an increase from $1,680 to $1,800 in the amount beneficiaries can earn annually without reduction of their benefits, effective January 1, 1971.

I propose to eliminate the one-dollar-for-one-dollar reduction in benefits for income earned in excess of $2,880 a year and replace it by a $1 reduction in benefits for every $2 earned, which now applies at earnings levels between $1,680 and $2,880, also effective January 1, 1971.

I propose to increase the contribution and benefit base from $7,800 to $9,000, beginning in 1972, to strengthen the system, to help keep future benefits to the individual related to the growth of his wages, and to meet part of the cost of the improved program. From then on the base will automatically be adjusted to reflect wage increases.

I propose a series of additional reforms to ensure more equitable treatment for widows, recipients above age seventy-two, veterans, for persons disabled in childhood, and for the dependent parents of disabled and retired workers.

I emphasize that the suggested changes are only first steps, and that further recommendations will come from our review process.

The Social Security system needs adjustment now so it will better serve people receiving benefits today, and those corrections are recommended in this message. The system is also in need of long-range reform, to make it better serve those who contribute now for benefits in future years, and that will be the subject of later recommendations.

The Benefit Increase

With the increase of 10 percent, the average family benefit for an aged couple, both receiving benefits, would rise from $170 to $188 a month. Further indication of the impact of a 10-percent increase on monthly benefits can be seen in the following table:

	Present Minimum	New Minimum	Present Maximum	New Maximum
Single Person (a man retiring at age 65 in 1970)	$55.00	$61.00	$165.00	$181.50
Married Couple (husband retiring at age 65 in 1970)	$82.50	$91.50	$247.50	$272.30

The proposed benefit increases will raise the income of more than 25 million persons who will be on the Social Security rolls in April, 1970. Total budget outlays for the first full calendar year in which the increase effective will be approximately $3 billion.

Automatic Adjustments

Benefits will be adjusted automatically to reflect increases in the cost of living. The uncertainty of adjustment under present laws and the delay often encountered when the needs are already apparent is unnecessarily harsh to those who must depend on Social Security benefits to live.

Benefits that automatically increase with rising living costs can be funded without increasing Social Security tax rates so long as the amount of earnings subject to tax reflects the rising level of wages. Therefore, I propose that the wage base be automatically adjusted so that it corresponds to increases in earnings levels.

These automatic adjustments are interrelated and should be enacted as a package. Taken together they will depoliticize, to a certain extent, the Social Security system and give a greater stability to what has become a cornerstone of our society's social insurance system.

Reforming the System

I propose a series of reforms in present Social Security law to achieve new standards of fairness. These would provide:

1. *An increase in benefits to a widow who begins receiving her benefit at age sixty-five or later.* The benefit would increase the current 82.5 percent of her husband's benefit to a full 100 percent. This increased benefit to widows would fulfill a pledge I made a year ago. It would provide *an average increase of $17 a month to almost 3 million widows.*

2. *Non-contributory earnings credits of about $100 a month for military service* from January, 1957 to December, 1967. During that period, individuals in military service were covered under Social Security but credit was not then given for "wages in kind"—room and board, etc. A law passed in 1967 corrected this for the future, but the men who served from 1957 (when coverage began for servicemen) to 1967 should not be overlooked.

3. *Benefits for the aged parents of retired and disabled workers.* Under present law benefits are payable only to the dependent parents

of a worker who has died; we would extend this to parents of workers who are disabled or who retire.

4. *Child's insurance benefits for life* if a child becomes permanently disabled before age twenty-two. Under present law a person must have become disabled before age eighteen to qualify for these benefits. The proposal would be consistent with the payment of child's benefit to age twenty-two so long as the child is in school.

5. *Benefits in full paid to persons over seventy-two,* regardless of the amount of his earnings in the year he attains that age. Under present law he is bound by often confusing tests which may limit his exemption.

6. *A fairer means of determining benefits payable on a man's earnings record.* At present, men who retire at age sixty-two must compute their average earnings through three years of no earnings up to age sixty-five, thus lowering the retirement benefit excessively. Under this proposal only the years up to age sixty-two would be counted, just as is now done for women, and three higher-earning years could be substituted for low-earning years.

Changes in the Retirement Test

A feature of the present Social Security law that has drawn much criticism is the so-called "retirement test," a provision which limits the amount that a beneficiary can earn and still receive full benefits. I have been much concerned about this provision, particularly about its effects on incentives to work. The present retirement test actually penalizes Social Security beneficiaries for doing additional work or taking a job at higher pay. This is wrong.

In my view, many older people should be encouraged to work. Not only are they provided with added income, but the country retains the benefit of their skills and wisdom; they, in turn, have the feeling of usefulness and participation which employment can provide.

This is why I am recommending changes in the retirement test. Raising the amount of money a person can earn in a year without affecting his Social Security payments—from the present $1,680 to $1,800—is an important first step. But under the approach used in the present retirement test, people who earned more than the exempt amount of $1,680 plus $1,200, would continue to have $1 in Social Security benefits withheld for every $1 they received in earnings. A necessary second step is to eliminate from present law the requirement that when earnings reach $1,200 above the exempt amount, Social Security benefits will be reduced by a full dollar for every dollar of added earnings until all his benefits are withheld; in effect, we impose a tax of more than 100 percent on these earnings.

To avoid this, I would eliminate this $1 reduction for each $1 earned and replace it with the same $1 reduction for each $2 earned above $3,000. This change will reduce a disincentive to increased employment that arises under the retirement test in its present form.

The amount a retired person can earn and still receive his benefits should also increase automatically with the earnings level. It is sound policy to keep the exempt amount related to changes in the general level of earnings.

These alterations in the retirement test would result in added benefit payments of some $300 million in the first full calendar year. Approximately 1 million people would receive this money—some who are now receiving no benefits at all and some who now receive benefits but who would get more under this new arrangement. These suggestions are not by any means the solution to all the problems of the retirement test, however, and I am asking the Advisory Council on Social Security to give particular attention to this matter.

Contribution and Benefit Base

The contribution and benefit base—the annual earnings on which Social Security contributions are paid and that can be counted toward Social Security benefits—has been increased several times since the Social Security program began. The further increase I am recommending—from its present level of $7,800 to $9,000 beginning January 1, 1972—will produce approximately the same relationship between the base and general earnings levels as that of the early 1950s. This is important since the goal of Social Security is the replacement, in part, of lost earnings; if the base on which contributions and benefits are figured does not rise with earnings increases, then the benefits deteriorate. The future benefit increases that will result from the higher base I am recommending today would help to prevent such deterioration. These increases would, of course, be in addition to those which result from the 10-percent across-the-board increase in benefits that is intended to bring them into line with the cost of living.

Financing

I recommend an acceleration of the tax rate scheduled for hospital insurance to bring the hospital insurance trust fund into actuarial balance. I also propose to decelerate the rate schedule of the old-age, survivors, and disability insurance trust funds in current law. These funds taken together have a long-range surplus of income over outgo which will meet much of the cost. The combined rate, known as the "social security contribution," already scheduled by statute, will be decreased from 1971 through 1976. Thus, in 1971 the currently scheduled rate of 5.2 percent to be paid by employees would become 5.1 percent and in 1973 the currently scheduled rate of 5.65 percent would become 5.1 percent. The actuarial integrity of the two funds will be maintained, and the ultimate tax rates will not be changed in the rate schedules which will be proposed.

The voluntary supplementary medical insurance (SMI) of title XVIII of the Social Security Act, often referred to as part B Medicare coverage, is not adequately financed with the current $4 premium. Our preliminary studies indicate that there will have to be a substantial increase in the premium. The Secretary of Health, Education and Welfare will set the premium rate in December for the fiscal year beginning July, 1970, as he is required to do by statute.

To meet the rising costs of health care in the United States, this Administration will soon forward a Health Cost Control proposal to the Congress. Other administrative measures are already being taken to hold down spiraling medical expenses.

In the coming months this Administration will give careful study to ways in which we can further improve the Social Security program. The program is an established and important American institution, a foundation on which millions are able to build a more comfortable life than would otherwise be possible—after their retirement or in the event of disability or death of the family earner.

The recommendations I propose today, which I urge the Congress to adopt, will move the cause of Social Security forward on a broad front.

We will bring benefit payments up to date.

We will make sure that benefit payments stay up to date, automatically tied to the cost of living.

We will begin making basic reforms in the system to remove inequities and bring a new standard of fairness in the treatment of all Americans in the system.

And we will lay the groundwork for further study and improvement of a system that has served the country well and must serve future generations more fairly and more responsively.

HUNGER MUST BE BANISHED
Remarks of the President at the White House Conference
on Food, Nutrition, and Health, Washington, D.C.
DECEMBER 2, 1969

Members of the Cabinet, Mr. Mayor, all of the distinguished guests
on the platform, and all the distinguished representatives to this
conference:

I very much appreciate the opportunity to be here, and before
speaking myself, I want to express my appreciation to those who are
arranging the conference, to Dr. Mayer and others, for the introductions
that have been arranged.

I understand that Ezra Ellis, who came from my home town of
Whittier, California, gave the invocation, and I am most grateful for
that, and I am most grateful, too, that the Mayor of my city, Washington,
D.C., Mayor Washington, is here today. I think he is doing a fine job
as Mayor of this city.

I am not going to talk about the problems of the District, except
indirectly, at this point, but as I speak about the legislative imperatives,
three of which I will mention in my address, I want you to know that
at the very top of the list of other imperatives are the programs for the
District of Columbia.

We have offered a number of programs that are new in this field
and some that are old, but we have talked about the District for years.
It is time to act about the District of Columbia, and under the Mayor's
leadership we do plan to act, and with your help we will do something.

As all of you are aware, this is an historic conference. It is particularly an historic conference for me because it is the first White
House Conference that I have had the opportunity to address as President of the United States. I have addressed others as Vice President.
And it is the first that we have had in this Administration.

This meeting marks a vital milestone. What it does is to set the
seal of urgency on our national commitment to put an end to hunger
and malnutrition due to poverty in America.

At the same time, it marks the beginning of a new, more determined, and more concerted drive than ever before to reduce the
malnutrition that derives from ignorance or inadvertence.

I recognize that many of you who are here and who have participated in the panel have been under enormous pressure, because you

have had a relatively short time for the vast amount of work that it took to put this conference together and to prepare for it.

However, that pressure reflects the priority of the subject we are here to discuss. It reflects the sense of urgency we all feel.

Until this moment in our history as a nation the central question has been whether we as a nation would accept the problem of malnourishment as a national responsibility.

That moment is past. On May 6 I asserted to the Congress that "the moment is at hand to put an end to hunger in America itself. For all time."

Speaking for this Administration, I not only accept the responsibility—I claim the responsibility.

Malnourishment is a national concern because we are a nation that cares about its people, how they feel, how they live. We care whether they are well and whether they are happy.

First of all there is a moral imperative: Our national conscience requires it. We must because we can. We are the world's richest nation. We are the best-educated nation. We have an agricultural abundance that ranks as a miracle of the modern world. This nation cannot long continue to live with its conscience if millions of its own people are unable to get an adequate diet.

Even in purely practical terms there are compelling considerations requiring this challenge to be met.

A child ill-fed is dulled in curiosity, lower in stamina, distracted from learning. A worker ill-fed is less productive, more often absent from work. The mounting cost of medical care for diet-related illnesses; remedial education required to overcome diet-related slowness in school; institutionalization and loss of full productive potential; all of these place a heavy economic burden on a society as a whole.

And for many of us this subject also evokes vivid personal memories. I grew up in the Great Depression. I shall never forget the hopelessness that I saw so starkly etched on so many faces—the silent gratitude of others lucky enough to enjoy three square meals a day, or sometimes even one.

I recall in my native state of California in the 1930s a family that I knew, that I went to school with, subsisted on bread and gravy, bread and milk, beans. And later in the 1930s, in North Carolina, families who knew nothing much more than black-eyed peas, turnip greens.

We have come a long way since then, but we still have a long way to go.

The question is: What will we do about it?

We begin with the troublesome complex of definitions and causes.

Experts can argue—and they do—and you will—about the magnitude of the problem: about how many are hungry, how many malnourished, and how severely they are malnourished. Precise statistical data remain elusive and often contradictory. However, Dr. Arnold Schaefer, the man in charge of the National Nutrition Survey, recently made this cautious but forceful observation. He said:

"We have been alerted by recent studies that our population who are 'malnutrition risks' is beyond anticipated findings, and also that in some of our vulnerable population groups—pre-school children, the aged, teenagers and the poor—malnutrition is indeed a serious medical problem."

We don't know just how many Americans are actually hungry and how many suffer from malnutrition, who eat enough and who don't eat the right things. But we do know there are too many Americans in both categories.

We can argue its extent. But hunger exists.

We can argue its severity, but malnutrition exists.

The plain fact is that a great many Americans are not eating well enough to sustain health.

We see, then, that the problem of hunger and malnutrition is, really, two separate problems. One is to ensure that everyone is able to obtain an adequate diet. The second is to ensure that people actually are properly fed, where they have the ability to obtain the adequate diet.

On the one hand, we are dealing with problems of income distribution. On the other hand, with problems of education, habit, taste, behavior, personal preferences—the whole complex of things that lead people to act the way they do, to make the choices they do.

The answers to many of these questions are difficult to come by. The very fact that the same question evokes so many different, conflicting answers is itself testimony as to how fragile is the basis of our knowledge.

Assuming we can agree on definitions, and the causes of malnourishment, how do we eradicate it?

Now some will answer that the magic ingredient is money, and money certainly is one ingredient, and a very important one. The more than $5 billion that I have proposed for new or expanded programs for food and family assistance next year would go a long way toward bringing the problem under control.

In this connection, I would urge each of you in this great conference to enlist yourself in an effort to win passage of three landmark pieces of legislation I have already recommended to Congress.

One of these is what many observers consider to be the most important piece of domestic legislation proposed in the past fifty years, the establishment of a floor under the income of every American family.

For the first time—Mr. Moynihan please notice—for the first time, this new family assistance plan would give every American family a basic income, wherever in America that family may live. For the first time, it would put cash into the hands of families because they are poor, rather than because they fit certain categories. When enacted, this measure alone will either supplement the incomes or provide the basis for the incomes of 25 million American men, women, and children.

Our basic policies for improvement of the living conditions of the poor are based on this proposition: That the best judge of each family's priorities is that family itself, that the best way to ameliorate the hardships of poverty is to provide the family with additional income—to be spent as that family sees fit.

Now, some will argue with this proposition. Some argue that the poor cannot be trusted to make their own decisions, and therefore the government should dole out food and clothing and medicines, according to a schedule of what the government thinks is needed.

Well, I disagree. I believe there are no experts present in this great gathering who know more about the realities of hunger and malnutrition than those among you who are here because you have suffered from it; or than those among you who are here who do suffer from it, from great cities, from worn-out farms, from barren reservations, from frozen tundra, and tiny islands half a world away.

The task of government is not to make decisions for you or for anyone. The task of government is to enable you to make decisions for yourselves. Not to see the truth of that statement is fundamentally to mistake the genius of democracy. We have made too many mistakes of this type—but no more. Our job is to get resources to people in need and then to let them run their own lives.

And now I would stress that all of you who have been so strong and effective in achieving a breakthrough on national awareness on hunger will become an equally strong citizen lobby for welfare reform. The needs of the poor range far beyond food, though that is often the most visible and heart-rending aspect of poverty. More basically, they need money with which they can meet the full range of their needs, from basic shelter, to medicine, to clothes for school, to transportation. And they need these resources in a program framework that builds incentives for self-support and family stability.

Let the reform of the bankrupt welfare system be the next great cause of those who come together here today.

Now the second measure that I would especially urge your support for is one that you will be considering in your deliberations. It is the reform and expansion of the Food Stamp Program. I requested this in my May 6 Message on Food and Health. This has been designed to complement the welfare program. While the welfare proposals may be subject to long debate, I hope and expect the Congress will act quickly on the expanded Food Stamp plan.

The nation's food programs have been shot through with inequities —notably, the fact that many counties have not participated, and the fact that because food stamps had to be bought with cash, many of the neediest were unable to participate.

We are pressing hard to bring every county into one or other of the food distribution programs, and the new Food Stamp Bill would provide stamps free to those most in need—while expanding the program to a level that would reach $2.5 billion a year when fully implemented.

In a related matter, we already are greatly expanding our school-lunch programs, with the target of reaching every needy school child with a free or reduced-cost lunch by the end of the current fiscal year.

Now, there is a third measure, a third measure which at first will seem unrelated, but which is directly related to this conference. I ask your support for the Commission on Population Growth and the American Future which I have proposed to Congress and which has been most favorably received, not only in the Congress, but by church and civic organizations throughout the nation.

America, I believe, has come to see how necessary it is to be responsibly concerned with this subject. In proposing the Commission, I also declared that it would be the goal of this Administration to provide "adequate family-planning services within the next five years to all those who want them but cannot afford them." There are some 5 million women in low-income families who are in exactly that situation. But I can report that the steps to meet that goal have already been taken within the Administration, and the program is under way.

Taken together, these three measures would virtually eliminate the problem of poverty as a cause of malnutrition.

Their dollar cost is high, but their practical benefits to the nation are immense.

I know that your panels have advanced proposals for massive efforts on many fronts. They demonstrate that the goal cannot be won by government alone.

It is for each to ask how he, individually, can respond to the questions being asked here. For example:

—Can foods be better labeled, be made more nutritious, and be fortified with available additives?

—Can industry, the schools, government, and citizens individually join effectively in a program of public education?

—Can school-lunch programs feasibly be improved?

—Can voluntary programs by citizens and community organizations teach people what to eat, to close the knowledge gap?

The fact that so many groups are represented here today is itself evidence of a new sense of community responsibility, of industry responsibility, of individual responsibility. The fact that so many women are represented here, especially, is evidence of an enormous resource, particularly in the volunteer field, a resource that can do so much to ensure our success.

I, of course, in my official capacity, have already indicated legislative programs that I shall be supporting. But speaking now as one who from time to time can act in a volunteer capacity, I know the power of simply dropping a word as to what a President or a potential President does in certain fields.

I recall in your field, about eighteen months ago I was being interviewed on a talk show. I was asked how I kept my weight down—that was my problem rather than the other way around. I answered—I thought rather low-key—that the doctor had told me to eat cottage cheese. The difficulty is that I don't like cottage cheese. I said I took his advice, but I put catsup on it.

You can't imagine how many letters I got. The dairy industry wrote and told me that I should like cottage cheese. The catsup industry wrote and told me to try it on my cereal. And others wrote and said catsup with cottage cheese had to be unhealthy. I pointed to the fact that my grandmother lived to be ninety-two and she ate it all her life, so that was the answer.

I use this facetious example only to indicate that the power of example, not just from a President, but from those in this room—in the whole field of not just how much, but how and what we eat—can be tremendous.

Now, I want to turn to—with Dr. Mayer's suggestion and his approval—to a very important procedural point, one I discussed with him when he took the position which he is filling and one I wish to speak directly to you about.

We have not attempted to program those in this room. We have not attempted to program you as to the questions you may ask or the answers and recommendations that you will make.

I expect to read that you had a lively difference of opinion during this conference. As a matter of fact, I have already read about one lively difference of opinion that you have had, and that is as it should be. From an airing of views of all sides, answers and ideas will appear, answers and ideas are what we seek in this process. Obviously, if we knew all the answers we would not have convened the conference in the first place. That is why you are here.

I will say this: I want to speak quite directly. I can imagine in this room are many people who have attended White House conferences before. For twenty-two years I have been watching White House conferences. I have attended them and I have seen the effort that went into them, an enormous voluntary dedicated effort. I have seen it too often wither away in futility as the reports gathered dust on government shelves.

Well, beginning with this conference, that is going to change. It will be the policy of this Administration to follow up each White House conference, beginning with this conference, with a second meeting one year later, bringing together the key participants of the original conference to re-examine its findings and to measure what has been done about implementing them. We believe that is the only proper procedure.

I know that you take your work seriously and we are going to take your report seriously. I expect the results of this conference to be not just words, but action.

This conference marks a coalescing of the national conscience; it marks a triumph of the American system.

I realize that there is a ready disposition, whenever we confront an ill that is still uncorrected in America, to cry that "the system" is corrupt, or "the system" has failed.

Our so-called "system" has been under heavy assault, not from one quarter but from many quarters.

But let us remember that that system is what has brought us here together today in this conference. It is a system that embraces compassion and practicality; it has given us the abundance that allows us to consider ending hunger and malnutrition.

Ours is the most productive and the most generous country the world has ever known. Less than 5 percent of our population—according to Secretary Hardin, Secretary of Agriculture—produces enough food to feed all the American people and to supply the needs of millions in other countries as well. In the years since World War II the United States has provided more than $30 billion in food, in the form of aid, to needy nations and peoples abroad.

I have traveled to most of the nations of the world, in Asia, Africa, and Latin America. Do you realize that in most of the world today a conference like this would be meaningless because those nations would lack the resources to produce the food to meet the objectives that this conference may decide should be met or lack the resources to purchase the food which they themselves would not be able to produce?

It is precisely because our system has succeeded so well that we are now able to address the goals of this conference, and the fact that we are gathered here is an example of one of the greatest strengths of that same system. It has a capacity for self-correction, for self-regeneration; its constant reaching out to identify new or additional needs and to meet those needs, the readiness of its citizens to join in that effort, volunteering their time and their talents, as you are volunteering your time and your talents today.

This nation has the capacity to provide an adequate diet for every American. The calling of this conference demonstrates that we have the will to achieve this goal. What we need is to find the most effective means for doing so consistent with maintaining the vitality of the system that makes it all possible.

And so I will review your recommendations with great care.

And I will ask you to go about drawing up those recommendations with equally great care.

My fellow Americans, as you begin this conference I commit to your concern the lives of millions of Americans, too young, too old, or too hurt by life to do without your help. I commit to your concern the not less serious task of helping to bring the rest of America to understand what we seek and to join us in adding this new dimension to the concept of American democracy. For at this very moment we are gathered at one of those great historical moments when it becomes possible for all of us to act a little better than we are, and in so doing, to leave this great and good nation a little better because we were there.

4

The

Frightening

Problem

of

Numbers

THE FRIGHTENING PROBLEM OF NUMBERS
A Comprehensive Message to the Congress of the United States on the Population Explosion
JULY 18, 1969

For fifty years and more, birth control has been a sensitive political issue, involving moral practice and religious conviction. The past few years witnessed a major breakthrough in public consideration and acceptance of methods of population control, largely in terms of the expanding masses in undeveloped areas of the world unable to sustain in health and dignity their growing numbers.

President Nixon took the additional unprecedented step of focusing the government's attention on the problem in the world's richest and most highly industrialized nation, the United States. An irreverent wit stated in Nixon's presence that he was the first President to come out against *motherhood.*

His comprehensive message to Congress on the problems of population growth was the most studious and profound of his first year in office. It won support in Congress on a nonpartisan basis to a degree that would have been impossible a decade ago. The President proposed creation of a "Commission on Population Growth and the American Future"; Congress expanded this to embrace problems of the environment as they are affected by population.

The President signed the first population control bill in American history on March 16, 1970. He established the Commission at the same time, appointing John D. Rockefeller III as chairman. The Commission will not, said the President, make arbitrary decisions on what the American population will or should be at any given time. "It approaches the problem," he said, "in terms of trying to find out what we can expect in the way of population growth, where that population will move, and then how we can properly deal with it."

In 1830 there were 1 billion people on the planet Earth. By 1930 there were 2 billion, and by 1960 there were 3 billion. Today the world population is 3.5 billion persons.

These statistics illustrate the dramatically increasing rate of population growth. It took many thousands of years to produce the first billion people; the next billion took a century; the third came after thirty years; the fourth will be produced in just fifteen.

If this rate of population growth continues, it is likely that the earth will contain over 7 billion human beings by the end of this century. Over the next thirty years, in other words, the world's population could double. And at the end of that time, each new addition of 1 billion persons would not come over the millennia nor over a century nor even over a decade. If present trends were to continue until the year 2000, the eighth billion would be added in only five years and each additional billion in an even shorter period.

While there are a variety of opinions as to precisely how fast population will grow in the coming decades, most informed observers have a similar response to all such projections. They agree that population growth is among the most important issues we face. They agree that it can be met only if there is a great deal of advance planning. And they agree that the time for such planning is growing very short. It is for all these reasons that I address myself to the population problem in this message, first to its international dimensions and then to its domestic implications.

In the Developing Nations

It is in the developing nations of the world that population is growing most rapidly today. In these areas we often find rates of natural increase higher than any which have been experienced in all of human history. With their birth rates remaining high and with death rates dropping sharply, many countries of Latin America, Asia, and Africa now grow ten times as fast as they did a century ago. At present rates many will double and some may even triple their present populations before the year 2000. This fact is in large measure a consequence of rising health standards and economic progress throughout the world, improvements which allow more people to live longer and more of their children to survive to maturity.

As a result, many already impoverished nations are struggling under a handicap of intense population increase which the industrialized nations never had to bear. Even though most of these countries have made rapid progress in total economic growth—faster in percentage terms than many of the more industrialized nations—their far greater rates of population growth have made development in per-capita terms very slow. Their standards of living are not rising quickly, and the gap between life in the rich nations and life in the poor nations is not closing.

There are some respects, in fact, in which economic development threatens to fall behind population growth, so that the quality of life actually worsens. For example, despite considerable improvements in agricultural technology and some dramatic increases in grain production, it is still difficult to feed these added people at adequate levels of nutrition. Protein malnutrition is widespread. It is estimated that every day some ten thousand people—most of them children—are dying from diseases of which malnutrition has been at least a partial cause. Moreover, the physical and mental potential of millions of youngsters is not realized because of a lack of proper food. The promise for increased production and better distribution of food is great, but not great enough to counter these bleak realities.

The burden of population growth is also felt in the field of social progress. In many countries, despite increases in the number of schools and teachers, there are more and more children for whom there is no schooling. Despite construction of new homes, more and more families are without adequate shelter. Unemployment and underemployment are increasing, and the situation could be aggravated as more young people grow up and seek to enter the work force.

Nor has development yet reached the stage where it brings with it diminished family size. Many parents in developing countries are still victimized by forces such as poverty and ignorance which make it difficult for them to exercise control over the size of their families. In sum, population growth is a world problem which no country can ignore, whether it is moved by the narrowest perception of national self-interest or the widest vision of a common humanity.

International Cooperation

It is our belief that the United Nations, its specialized agencies, and other international bodies should take the leadership in responding to world population growth. The United States will cooperate fully with their programs. I would note in this connection that I am most impressed by the scope and thrust of the recent report of the Panel of the United Nations Association, chaired by John D. Rockefeller III. The report stresses the need for expanded action and greater coordination, concerns which should be high on the agenda of the United Nations.

In addition to working with international organizations, the United States can help by supporting efforts which are initiated by other governments. Already we are doing a great deal in this field. For example, we provide assistance to countries which seek our help in reducing high birth rates—provided always that the services we help to make available can be freely accepted or rejected by the individuals who receive them.

Through our aid programs we have worked to improve agricultural production and bolster economic growth in developing nations.

As I pointed out in my recent message on foreign aid, we are making important efforts to improve these programs. In fact, I have asked the Secretary of State and the Administrator of the Agency for International Development to give population and family planning high priority for attention, personnel, research, and funding among our several aid programs. Similarly, I am asking the Secretaries of Commerce and Health, Education and Welfare and the Directors of the Peace Corps and the United States Information Agency to give close attention to population matters as they plan their overseas operations. I also call on the Department of Agriculture and the Agency for International Development to investigate ways of adapting and extending our agricultural experience and capabilities to improve food production and distribution in developing countries. In all of these international efforts, our programs should give further recognition to the important resources of private organizations and university research centers. As we increase our population and family planning efforts abroad, we also call upon other nations to enlarge their programs in this area.

Prompt action in all these areas is essential. For high rates of population growth, as the report of the Panel of the United Nations Association puts it, "impair individual rights, jeopardize national goals, and threaten international stability."

In the United States

For some time population growth has been seen as a problem for developing countries. Only recently has it come to be seen that pressing problems are also posed for advanced industrial countries when their populations increase at the rate that the United States, for example, must now anticipate. Food supplies may be ample in such nations, but social supplies—the capacity to educate youth, to provide privacy and living space, to maintain the processes of open, democratic government —may be grievously strained.

In the United States our rate of population growth is not as great as that of developing nations. In this country, in fact, the growth rate has generally declined since the eighteenth century. The present growth rate of about 1 percent per year is still significant, however. Moreover, current statistics indicate that the fertility rate may be approaching the end of its recent decline.

Several factors contribute to the yearly increase, including the large number of couples of childbearing age, the typical size of American families, and our increased longevity. We are rapidly reaching the point in this country where a family reunion, which has typically brought together children, parents, and grandparents, will instead gather family members from *four* generations. This is a development for which we are grateful and of which we can be proud. But we must also recognize that it will mean a far larger population if the number of children born to each set of parents remains the same.

In 1917 the total number of Americans passed 100 million, after three full centuries of steady growth. In 1967—just half a century later —the 200 million mark was passed. If the present rate of growth continues, the third 100 million persons will be added in roughly a thirty-year period. This means that by the year 2000, or shortly thereafter, there will be more than 300 million Americans.

This growth will produce serious challenges for our society. I believe that many of our present social problems may be related to the fact that we have had only fifty years in which to accommodate the second 100 million Americans. In fact, since 1945 alone some 90 million babies have been born in this country. We have thus had to accomplish in a very few decades an adjustment to population growth which was once spread over centuries. And it now appears that we will have to provide for a third 100 million Americans in a period of just thirty years.

The great majority of the next 100 million Americans will be born to families which looked forward to their birth and are prepared to love them and care for them as they grow up. The critical issue is whether social institutions will also plan for their arrival and be able to accommodate them in a humane and intelligent way. We can be sure that society will *not* be ready for this growth unless it begins its planning immediately. And adequate planning, in turn, requires that we ask ourselves a number of important questions.

Where, for example, will the next 100 million Americans live? If the patterns of the last few decades hold for the rest of the century, then at least three quarters of the next 100 million persons will locate in highly urbanized areas. Are our cities prepared for such an influx? The chaotic history of urban growth suggests that they are not and that many of their existing problems will be severely aggravated by a dramatic increase in numbers. Are there ways, then, of readying our cities? Alternatively, can the trend toward greater concentration of population be reversed? Is it a desirable thing, for example, that half of all the counties in the United States actually lost population in the 1950s, despite the growing number of inhabitants in the country as a whole? Are there ways of fostering a better distribution of the growing population?

Some have suggested that systems of satellite cities or completely new towns can accomplish this goal. The National Commission on Urban Growth has recently produced a stimulating report on this matter, one which recommends the creation of a hundred new communities averaging 100,000 people each, and ten new communities averaging at least 1 million persons. But the total number of people who would be accommodated if even this bold plan were implemented is only 20 million—a mere one fifth of the expected thirty-year increase. If we were to accommodate the full 100 million persons in new communities, we would have to build a new city of 250,000 persons each month from now until the end of the century. That means constructing a city the size of Tulsa, Dayton, or Jersey City every thirty days for over thirty years. Clearly, the problem is enormous, and we must examine the alternative solutions very carefully.

Other questions also confront us. How, for example, will we house the next 100 million Americans? Already economical and attractive housing is in very short supply. New architectural forms, construction techniques, and financing strategies must be aggressively pioneered if we are to provide the needed dwellings.

What of our natural resources and the quality of our environment? Pure air and water are fundamental to life itself. Parks, recreational facilities, and an attractive countryside are essential to our emotional well-being. Plant and animal and mineral resources are also vital. A growing population will increase the demand for such resources. But in many cases their supply will not be increased and may even be endangered. The ecological system upon which we now depend may seriously deteriorate if our efforts to conserve and enhance the environment do not match the growth of the population.

How will we educate and employ such a large number of people? Will our transportation systems move them about as quickly and economically as necessary? How will we provide adequate health care when our population reaches 300 million? Will our political structures have to be reordered, too, when our society grows to such proportions? Many of our institutions are already under tremendous strain as they try to respond to the demands of 1969. Will they be swamped by a growing flood of people in the next thirty years? How easily can they be replaced or altered?

Finally, we must ask: How can we better assist American families so that they will have no more children than they wish to have? In my first message to Congress on domestic affairs, I called for a national commitment to provide a healthful and stimulating environment for all children during their first five years of life. One of the ways in which we can promote that goal is to provide assistance for more parents in effectively planning their families. We know that involuntary child-bearing often results in poor physical and emotional health for all members of the family. It is one of the factors which contribute to our distressingly high infant mortality rate, the unacceptable level of malnutrition, and the disappointing performance of some children in our schools. Unwanted or untimely childbearing is one of several forces which are driving many families into poverty or keeping them in that condition. Its threat helps to produce the dangerous incidence of illegal abortion. And finally, of course, it needlessly adds to the burdens placed on all our resources by increasing population.

None of the questions I have raised here is new. But all of these questions must now be asked and answered with a new sense of urgency. The answers cannot be given by government alone, nor can government alone turn the answers into programs and policies. I believe, however, that the Federal government does have a special responsibility for defining these problems and for stimulating thoughtful responses.

Perhaps the most dangerous element in the present situation is the fact that so few people are examining these questions from the viewpoint of the whole society. Perceptive businessmen project the demand for their products many years into the future by studying population trends. Other private institutions develop sophisticated planning mechanisms which allow them to account for rapidly changing conditions. In the governmental sphere, however, there is virtually no machinery through which we can develop a detailed understanding of demographic changes and bring that understanding to bear on public policy. The Federal government makes only a minimal effort in this area. The efforts of state and local governments are also inadequate. Most importantly, the planning which does take place at some levels is poorly understood at others and is often based on unexamined assumptions.

In short, the questions I have posed in this message too often go unasked, and when they are asked, they seldom are adequately answered.

Commission on Population Growth and the American Future

It is for all these reasons that I today propose the creation by Congress of a Commission on Population Growth and the American Future.

The Congress should give the Commission responsibility for inquiry and recommendations in three specific areas.

First, the probable course of population growth, internal migration, and related demographic developments between now and the year 2000.

As much as possible, these projections should be made by regions, states, and metropolitan areas. Because there is an element of uncertainty in such projections, various alternative possibilities should be plotted.

It is of special importance to note that, beginning in August of 1970, population data by county will become available from the decennial census, which will have been taken in April of that year. By April, 1971, computer summaries of first-count data will be available by census tract and an important range of information on income, occupations, education, household composition, and other vital considerations will also be in hand. The Federal government can make better use of such demographic information than it has done in the past, and state governments and other political subdivisions can also use such data to better advantage. The Commission on Population Growth and the American Future will be an appropriate instrument for this important initiative.

Second, the resources in the public sector of the economy that will be required to deal with the anticipated growth in population.

The single greatest failure of foresight—at all levels of government—over the past generation has been in areas connected with expanding population. Government and legislatures have frequently failed to appreciate the demands which continued population growth would impose on the public sector. These demands are myriad: they will range from preschool classrooms to postdoctoral fellowships; from public works which carry water over thousands of miles to highways which carry people and products from region to region; from vest-pocket parks in crowded cities to forest preserves and quiet lakes in the countryside. Perhaps especially, such demands will assert themselves in forms that affect the quality of life. The time is at hand for a serious assessment of such needs.

Third, ways in which population growth may affect the activities of Federal, state, and local government.

In some respects, population growth affects everything that American government does. Yet only occasionally do our governmental units pay sufficient attention to population growth in their own planning. Only occasionally do they consider the serious implications of demographic trends for their present and future activities.

Yet some of the necessary information is at hand and can be made available to all levels of government. Much of the rest will be obtained by the Commission. For such information to be of greatest use, however, it should also be interpreted and analyzed and its implications should be made more evident. It is particularly in this connection that the work of the Commission on Population Growth and the American Future will be as much educational as investigative. The American public and its governing units are not as alert as they should be to these growing challenges. A responsible but insistent voice of reason and foresight is needed. The Commission can provide that voice in the years immediately before us.

The membership of the Commission should include two members from each house of the Congress, together with knowledgeable men and women who are broadly representative of our society. The majority should be citizens who have demonstrated a capacity to deal with important questions of public policy. The membership should also include specialists in the biological, social, and environmental sciences, in theology and law, in the arts and in engineering. The Commission should be empowered to create advisory panels to consider subdivisions of its broad subject area and to invite experts and leaders from all parts of the world to join these panels in their deliberations.

The Commission should be provided with an adequate staff and budget, under the supervision of an executive director of exceptional experience and understanding.

In order that the Commission will have time to utilize the initial data which results from the 1970 census, I ask that it be established for a period of two years. An interim report to the President and Congress should be required at the end of the first year.

Other Government Activities

I would take this opportunity to mention a number of additional government activities dealing with population growth which need not await the report of the Commission.

First, increased research is essential. It is clear, for example, that we need additional research on birth control methods of all types and the sociology of population growth. Utilizing its Center for Population Research, the Department of Health, Education and Welfare should take the lead in developing, with other Federal agencies, an expanded research effort, one which is carefully related to those of private organizations, university research centers, international organizations, and other countries.

Second, we need more trained people to work in population and family programs, both in this country and abroad. I am therefore asking the Secretaries of State, Labor, Health, Education and Welfare, and Interior along with the Administrator of the Agency for International Development and the Director of the Office of Economic Opportunity to participate in a comprehensive survey of our efforts to attract people to such programs and to train them properly. The same group—in consultation with appropriate state, local, and private officials—should develop recommendations for improvements in this area. I am asking the Assistant to the President for Urban Affairs to coordinate this project.

Third, the effects of population growth on our environment and on the world's food supply call for careful attention and immediate action. I am therefore asking the Environmental Quality Council to give careful attention to these matters in its deliberations. I am also asking the Secretaries of Interior, Agriculture, and Health, Education and Welfare to give the highest priority to research into new techniques and to other proposals that can help safeguard the environment and increase the world's supply of food.

Fourth, it is clear that the domestic family-planning services supported by the Federal government should be expanded and better integrated. Both the Department of Health, Education and Welfare and the Office of Economic Opportunity are now involved in this important work, yet their combined efforts are not adequate to provide information and services to all who want them. In particular, most of an estimated 5 million low-income women of childbearing age in this country do not now have adequate access to family-planning assistance, even though their wishes concerning family size are usually the same as those of parents of higher income groups.

It is my view that no American woman should be denied access to family-planning assistance because of her economic condition. I believe, therefore, that we should establish as a national goal the provision of adequate family-planning services within the next five years to all those who want them but cannot afford them. This we have the capacity to do.

Clearly, in no circumstances will the activities associated with our pursuit of this goal be allowed to infringe upon the religious convictions or personal wishes and freedom of any individual, nor will they be allowed to impair the absolute right of all individuals to have such matters of conscience respected by public authorities.

In order to achieve this national goal, we will have to increase the amount we are spending on population and family planning. But success in this endeavor will not result from higher expenditures alone. Because the life circumstances and family planning wishes of those who receive services vary considerably, an effective program must be more flexible in its design than are many present efforts. In addition, programs should be better coordinated and more effectively administered. Under current legislation, a comprehensive state or local project must assemble a patchwork of funds from many different sources—a time-consuming and confusing process. Moreover, under existing legislation, requests for funds for family-planning services must often compete with requests for other deserving health endeavors.

But these problems can be overcome. The Secretary of Health, Education and Welfare—whose department is responsible for the largest part of our domestic family-planning services—has developed plans to reorganize the major family-planning service activities of this agency. A separate unit for these services will be established within the Health Services and Mental Health Administration. The Secretary will send to Congress in the near future legislation which will help the department implement this important program by providing broader and more precise legislative authority and a clearer source of financial support.

The Office of Economic Opportunity can also contribute to progress in this area by strengthening its innovative programs and pilot projects in the delivery of family-planning services to the needy. The existing network of OEO-supported community groups should also be used more extensively to provide family-planning assistance and information. I am asking the Director of the Office of Economic Opportunity to determine the ways in which his agency can best structure and extend its programs in order to help achieve our national goal in the coming years.

As they develop their own plans, the Secretary of Health, Education and Welfare and the Director of the Office of Economic Opportunity should also determine the most effective means of coordinating all our domestic family-planning programs and should include in their deliberations representatives of the other agencies that share in this important work. It is my intention that such planning should also involve state and local governments and private agencies, for it is clear that the increased activity of the Federal government in this area must be matched by a sizable increase in effort at other levels. It would be unrealistic for the Federal government alone to shoulder the entire burden, but this Administration does accept a clear responsibility to provide essential leadership.

For the Future

One of the most serious challenges to human destiny in the last third of this century will be the growth of the population. Whether man's response to that challenge will be a cause for pride or for despair in the year 2000 will depend very much on what we do today. If we now begin our work in an appropriate manner, and if we continue to devote a considerable amount of attention and energy to this problem, then mankind will be able to surmount this challenge as it has surmounted so many during the long march of civilization.

When future generations evaluate the record of our time, one of the most important factors in their judgment will be the way in which we responded to population growth. Let us act in such a way that those who come after us—even as they lift their eyes beyond Earth's bounds —can do so with pride in the planet on which they live, with gratitude to those who lived on it in the past, and with continuing confidence in its future.

5
Money
Matters

A risky decision was made by President Nixon in the early weeks of his Administration. He resolved deliberately to slow down the economy after four successive years of inflation by reducing government expenditures and adopting fiscal policies holding back business expansion at the price of increasing unemployment.

This calculated restriction of what had been since World War II a generally ascending spiral of prosperity carried the risk that the Nixon Administration, like the Hoover Administration during the Depression, would run ashoal on bad times. Nixon chose between rigid economic control of prices and wages and the more subtle restraints of balanced budgets, high interest levels, and high taxes.

It was all the more unusual that a Republican President, so often in the past identified by the public with the interests of business, should adopt policies that would adversely affect some businesses, specifically those that would benefit from continuing price and wage inflation.

Nixon gambled on his ability to get the economy moving again after arresting economic growth and inflation, and even more importantly on the accurate timing of re-expansion. He then faced a seeming contradiction: the continuing rise of prices while the economic growth rate withered. The wisdom of his policies was to become a major issue in the Congressional elections of 1970.

OUR WORST ENEMY: INFLATION
Message to the Congress of the United States
MARCH 26, 1969

Early in his first year, and briefly, the President gave notice to Congress that he placed controlling inflation ahead of expansionary new Federal programs. He thus collided head-on with the growing pressures in Congress for new priorities for health, education, welfare, and environmental projects.

Clearly this nation must come to grips with the problem of an inflation that has been allowed to run into its fourth year. This is far too long, and it has already caused substantial distortions in our economy.

Inflation is a form of economic aggression against the very young and the very old, the poor and the thrifty. It is these Americans who are largely defenseless against the kind of price increases for food, clothing, medicine, housing, and education that have swept over the nation in the last few years.

Government has two major instruments for dealing with this problem. One is monetary policy, which should continue its program of restraint. The other is fiscal policy—the management of the Federal budget—which must turn away from budgets which have propelled the inflation, and turn instead to one with a strong surplus that will help to curb it.

The prospect of a thin budget surplus or a return to deficits would again nudge monetary policy off course. The result, as always, would be further increases in interest rates, a dangerously overheated economic engine, and the threat of accelerating the advance of the price level. Because the problem of inflation was neglected far too long, we cannot risk even a neutral budget policy of narrow balance.

Only a combined policy of a strong budget surplus and monetary restraint can now be effective in cooling inflation, and in ultimately reducing the restrictive interest rates forced on us by past policies. This is fundamental economics, and we intend to deal with fundamentals.

We are determined to keep faith with America's wage earners, farmers, and businessmen. We are committed to take every necessary action to protect every American's savings and real income from further loss to inflation.

The budget for the year beginning July 1, 1969, submitted in January, estimates the surplus at $3.4 billion. However, current examination of this budget reveals that some of its estimates of expenditures were low. For example, interest on the Federal debt will be far more than was estimated. This, along with such items as an underestimate of farm price support payments and a substantial overestimate of offshore oil lease receipts, means that a current analysis of the budget submitted in January shows a reduction in the surplus of $1.3 billion for this fiscal year and $1.7 billion for the fiscal year 1970.

Thus, half of the projected 1970 surplus has disappeared before the year begins. Similarly, more than half of this year's projected surplus of $2.4 billion will not be realized—and for the same reasons.

On the Matter of Cutting Expenditures

To produce a budget that will stop inflation, we must cut expenditures while maintaining revenues. This will not be easy. Dealing with fundamentals never is.

I intend to submit budget revisions which will reduce Federal spending in fiscal 1970 significantly below the amount recommended in January, even before those previous figures have been adjusted to reflect current conditions.

On the Matter of Maintaining Revenues

I am convinced that the path of responsibility requires that the income tax surcharge, which is expected to yield $9.5 billion, be extended for another year. As I have said before, the surcharge is a temporary tax that must be ended as soon as our commitments in Southeast Asia and economic conditions permit. Because of budget and economic conditions, I reaffirm my support of the recommendation President Johnson made last January that the surcharge be extended, and I am transmitting to the Congress a request that this be done.

In addition, the scheduled reductions in the telephone and passenger car excise taxes must be postponed, and user charges equal in revenue yield to those now in the budget should be enacted. Together, these will produce close to $1 billion in revenue next year.

On the question of tax reform, this Administration remains committed to a more equitable and more efficient tax structure. In the coming month, the first specific proposals of that reform will be coming up to the Congress from the Treasury Department.

Taken together, these actions to reduce spending and maintain revenues will produce the strong budget surplus urgently needed to meet the inflationary threat.

Moreover, by proving government's serious intent to counter the upward spiral of prices and wages, we will create conditions which will encourage the private sector to stop assuming a high rate of inflation in long-range planning.

Courageous government action will modify the inflationary psychology which now afflicts business, labor, and consumers generally. It is particularly hard on small business and those of modest means in the management of their incomes and savings.

This ordering of our economic house—distasteful as it is in many respects—will do much to slow down the rise in the cost of living, help our seriously weakened position in international trade, and restore the sound basis for our ongoing prosperity.

OVERHAULING OUR TAX STRUCTURE
Message to the Congress of the United States
APRIL 21, 1969

A classic struggle between a Democratic-controlled Congress and a Republican President formed on the issue of taxation. Congress moved under pressures for tax relief which had built up at the end of the Johnson Administration. The President moved under pressures for general tax reform consistent with an economic policy of restraint. Popular demands for relief from the 10-percent surtax imposed as a Vietnam war measure influenced both.

The essential difference between Republican and Democratic policy was thus dramatized, as it rarely is in the complex cross currents of political strife. The Democratic leadership fought for relief for small taxpayers, whatever the general effect on the economy. The Republican leadership fought for balancing the tax system while stabilizing the general revenues of the government. Sharper issues formed on such matters as the level of personal exemptions, the timing of surtax reduction. The difference is sometimes oversimplified as Democratic fiscal irresponsibility versus Republican fixation on budget balancing.

All this was complicated by a successful Democratic drive for a 15-percent boost in Social Security payments as part of a tax reduction bill.

A year-long contest ended with a tax bill Nixon said reduced tax revenues by $3 billion while Congress increased spending by $3 billion. He signed the bill under protest. His own views on tax policy and tax reform in a time of inflation were contained in his special message to Congress submitted in late April.

Reform of our Federal income tax system is long overdue. Special preferences in the law permit far too many Americans to pay less than their fair share of taxes. Too many other Americans bear too much of the tax burden.

This Administration, working with the Congress, is determined to bring equity to the Federal tax system. Our goal is to take important first steps in tax reform legislation during this session of the Congress.

The economic overheating which has brought inflation into its fourth year keeps us from moving immediately to reduce Federal tax revenues at this time. Inflation is itself a tax—a cruel and unjust tax that hits hardest those who can least afford it. In order to "repeal" the tax of inflation, we are cutting budget spending and have requested an extension of the income tax surcharge.

Although we must maintain total Federal revenues, there is no reason why we cannot lighten the burden on those who pay too much, and increase the taxes of those who pay too little. Treasury officials will present the Administration's initial group of tax reform proposals to the Congress this week. Additional recommendations will be made later in this session. The overall program will be equitable and essentially neutral in its revenue impact. There will be no substantial gain or loss in Federal revenue, but the American taxpayer who carries more than his share of the burden will gain some relief.

Much concern has been expressed because some citizens with incomes of more than $200,000 pay no Federal income taxes. These people are neither tax dodgers nor tax cheats. Many of them pay no taxes because they make large donations to worthy causes, donations which every taxpayer is authorized by existing law to deduct from his income in figuring his tax bill.

But where we can prevent it by law, we must not permit our wealthiest citizens to be 100-percent successful at tax avoidance. Nor should the government limit its tax reform only to apply to these relatively few extreme cases. Preferences built into the law in the past—some of which have either outlived their usefulness or were never appropriate—permit many thousands of individuals and corporate taxpayers to avoid their fair share of Federal taxation.

A number of present tax preferences will be scaled down in the Administration's proposals to be submitted this week. Utilizing the revenue gained from our present proposals, we suggest tax reductions for lower-income taxpayers. Further study will be necessary before we can propose changes in other preferences and as these are developed we will recommend them to the Congress.

Specifically, the Administration will recommend:

—*Enactment of what is in effect a "minimum income tax" for citizens with substantial incomes by setting a 50-percent limitation on the use of the principal tax preferences which are subject to change by law.*

This limit on tax preferences would be a major step toward assuring that all Americans bear their fair share of the Federal tax burden.

—*Enactment of a "low income allowance," which will remove more than 2 million of our low-income families from the Federal tax rolls and assure that persons or families in poverty pay no Federal income taxes.*

This provision will also benefit students and other young people. For example, the person who works in the summer or throughout the year and earns $1,700 in taxable income—and now pays $117 in Federal income taxes—would pay nothing.

The married couple—college students or otherwise—with an income of $2,300 and current taxes of $100 would pay nothing.

A family of four would pay no tax on income below $3,500—the cut-off now is $3,000.

The "low income allowance," if enacted by the Congress, will offer genuine tax relief to the young, the elderly, the disadvantaged, and the handicapped.

Other tax reform proposals would also help workers who change jobs by liberalizing deductions for moving expenses and would reduce specific preferences in a number of areas.

—Taxpayers who have certain nontaxable income or other preferences would have their non-business deductions reduced proportionately.

—Certain mineral transactions (so-called "carved out" mineral production payments and "ABC" transactions) would be treated in a way that would stop artificial creation of net operating losses in these industries.

—Exempt organizations, including private foundations, would come under much stricter surveillance.

—The rules affecting charitable deductions would be tightened—but only to screen out the unreasonable and not stop those which help legitimate charities and therefore the nation.

—The practice of using multiple subsidiaries and affiliated corporations to take undue advantage of the lower tax rate on the first $25,000 of corporate income would be curbed.

—Farm losses, to be included in the "limitation on tax preferences," would be subject to certain other restrictions in order to curb abuses in this area.

I also recommend that the Congress repeal the 7-percent investment tax credit effective today.

This subsidy to business investment no longer has priority over other pressing national needs.

In the early '60s America's productive capacity needed prompt modernization to enable it to compete with industry abroad. Accordingly, government gave high priority to providing tax incentives for this modernization.

Since that time, American business has invested close to $400 billion in new plant and equipment, bringing the American economy to new levels of productivity and efficiency. While a vigorous pace of capital formation will certainly continue to be needed, national priorities now require that we give attention to the need for general tax relief.

Repeal of the investment tax credit will permit relief to every taxpayer through relaxation of the surcharge earlier than I had contemplated.

The revenue effect of the repeal of the investment tax credit will begin to be significant during calendar year 1970. *Therefore, I recommend that investment tax credit repeal be accompanied by extension of the full surcharge only to January 1, 1970, with a reduction to 5 percent on January 1.* This is a reappraisal of my earlier recommendation for continuance of the surcharge until June 30, 1970 at a 10-percent rate. If economic and fiscal conditions permit, we can look forward to elimination of the remaining surtax on June 30, 1970.

I am convinced, however, that reduction of the surtax without repeal of the investment tax credit would be imprudent.

The gradual increase in Federal revenues resulting from repeal of the investment tax credit and the growth of the economy will also facilitate a start during fiscal 1971 in funding two high-priority programs to which this Administration is committed:

—Revenue sharing with state and local governments.

—Tax credits to encourage investment in poverty areas and hiring and training of the hard-core unemployed.

These proposals, now in preparation, will be transmitted to the Congress in the near future.

The tax reform measures outlined earlier in this message will be recommended to the House Ways and Means Committee by Treasury officials this week. This is a broad and necessary program for tax reform. I urge its prompt enactment.

But these measures, sweeping as they are, will not by themselves trasform the U.S. tax system into one adequate to the long-range future. Much of the current tax system was devised in depression and shaped further in war. Fairness calls for tax reform now; beyond that, the American people need and deserve a simplified Federal tax system, and one that is attuned to the 1970s.

We must reform our tax structure to make it more equitable and efficient; we must redirect our tax policy to make it more conducive to stable economic growth and responsive to urgent social needs.

That is a large order. Therefore, I am directing the Secretary of the Treasury to review thoroughly the entire Federal tax system and present to me recommendations for basic changes, along with a full analysis of the impact of those changes, no later than November 30, 1969.

Since taxation affects so many wallets and pocketbooks, reform, and in the even greater debate on redirection, the nation would best be served by an avoidance of stereotyped reactions. One man's "loophole" is another man's "incentive." Tax policy should not seek to "soak" any group or give a "break" to any other—it should aim to serve the nation as a whole.

Tax dollars the government deliberately waives should be viewed as a form of expenditure, and weighed against the priority of other expenditures. When the preference device provides more social benefit than government collection and spending, that "incentive" should be expanded; when the preference is inefficient or subject to abuse, it should be ended.

Taxes, often bewailed as inevitable as death, actually give life to the people's purpose in having a government: to provide protection, service, and stimulus to progress.

We shall never make taxation popular, but we can make taxation fair.

THE WORTH OF A DOLLAR
Nationwide Radio Address
OCTOBER 17, 1969

In the fall of 1969 Nixon adopted a technique of direct contact with the American people on the pattern of the "fireside chats" on radio by President Franklin D. Roosevelt thirty-five years earlier. He explained in an afternoon radio address intended to reach housewives and retired people what he was doing to control inflation.

Good afternoon, my fellow Americans.

Today I would like to share my thoughts with you about a problem that worries millions of Americans: high prices that just keep getting higher.

All across this land, hard-working men and women look at paychecks that say they have had a raise. But they wonder why those bigger checks just don't buy any more than their lower paychecks bought four years ago.

All across this land men and women in their retirement, who depend on insurance and on Social Security and on their life savings, look at their monthly checks and wonder why they just can't seem to make ends meet anymore.

And all across this land, housewives wonder why they have to pay sixty-six cents a pound, and in some areas more, for hamburger that cost fifty-three cents four years ago; people who are ill want to know why in those four years the cost of one day in a hospital has gone from $27 to $48; children who pay a nickel for a candy bar want to know why that bar is only half as big as it used to be.

When it comes to rising prices, it seems to most people that there is no end in sight. Many Americans are upset, and many are even angry about this, and they have a right to be—because the ever rising cost of food and clothing and rent robs them of their savings, cheats them of the vacations and those necessary extras that they thought they had been working for.

Now, why does everything cost so much? And what can we do to hold down the upward climb of prices?

For five long years, you have heard politicians and economists denouncing "the high cost of living." Back in 1966 and '67, when prices rose by 3 percent a year, everyone said how bad that was; and then in 1968, when prices speeded up by 4 percent, everyone agreed something ought to be done; and now, when momentum has carried the rise to nearly 6 percent, the same heads are shaking.

You might begin to wonder: If a rising cost of living has so many enemies, why has it been allowed to grow so fast? For years, in political speeches, the high cost of living has been as safe to denounce as the man-eating shark; but after the speeches were over, nobody seemed to do anything about it.

Now, there was a very simple reason why your cost of living got out of hand: The blame for the spiral of wages and prices falls fundamentally on the past policies of your government.

The Federal government spent a lot more than it raised in taxes. Some of that spending was on the war in Vietnam, some of the spending was on new social programs, but the total spending was very heavy.

Now we are paying for all that red ink—not only in higher taxes, but in higher prices for everything you buy. To put it bluntly, the frequent failure to balance the Federal budget over the past five years has been the primary cause for unbalancing the family budgets of millions of Americans.

So today I want to tell you what we have been doing to make it easier for you to balance your family budget. I want you to know what results we are beginning to see, to understand the meaning of the news about the economy you will be reading in the coming months. And finally, I want to suggest what the American people—what you—can do together to hold down the cost of living.

When this Administration took office nine months ago, we decided that we were going to stop talking about higher prices and we were going to start doing something about them. We knew that some sophisticated investors could make out fairly well in a time of skyrocketing prices, but that the average family bore the brunt of the high cost of living, and the family on a fixed income was being driven right up the wall.

And so, to meet the real needs of most Americans, we began a steady effort to take the upward pressure off your cost of living.

Of course, there was a faster way available to bring prices down— many people suggested that we slam on the brakes hard and fast, and bring about a recession. But that kind of shock treatment is harsh and unnecessary—we want to level things off, not shake them up and down.

Step by step we took those measures necessary to get our nation's house in order.

Step One was to cut Federal spending, which more than anything else was pushing your prices up. We cut proposed Federal spending by more than $7 billion. We have taken it out of defense, we are cutting back on construction, we are squeezing it out of many other departmental budgets.

Now, we have been selective in these cuts, recognizing urgent national and social needs, but hardly anything has escaped some reduction. One area that was not cut, and I am sure you will agree with this decision, was the Department of Justice, which has fallen far behind in the war against crime—a war we are determined to win.

Next, working with the Congress, we proposed to phase out the tax surcharge over the course of a year. We could not afford to let the surtax lapse in the middle of 1969, because that would have driven up the prices you pay for everything.

And, also, we have supported our central banking system in its policy of keeping money hard to borrow. When too much money is borrowed, this money is simply used to bid prices up higher.

Now, let's face it: Holding down government spending and holding up the tax rate, and making it harder for people to get credit, is not the kind of policy that makes friends for people in politics. We have asked the American people to take some bitter medicine. We believe that the American people are mature enough to understand the need for it.

Well, here we are, nine months later, and I can report to you that the medicine has begun to work. There will be no overnight cure, but we are on the road to recovery from the disease of runaway prices.

Let me be careful not to mislead anyone: Prices are still going up. They may continue to do so for a while—a five-year momentum is not easy to stop. But now prices are no longer increasing faster and faster— the increases not only have slackened, but the rates of increase are actually down. Without shock treatment we are curing the causes of the rising cost of living.

For some time to come you will be reading about how some business is not doing very well. Sales may be sluggish in department stores; new housing, which this nation needs, has declined; the production of our industry has edged down for the first time in a year.

Ordinarily, this is bad news. But today, these declines are evidence that our policy of curbing the rising cost of living is beginning to take hold.

We must be realistic; as we gently, but firmly, apply the brakes, we are going to experience some "slowing pains." Just like growing pains, these are a healthy development—but they are painful nevertheless.

My point very simply is this: We have undertaken a policy that is slowing down the rise in prices. Unfortunately, some industries and some individuals will feel this necessary adjustment more directly than others. But difficult though it may be, and unpopular though it may become when the water gets choppier, by curbing inflation, we do what is best for all the American people.

Just as we must be realistic, we must be compassionate; we must keep a close watch on the rate of unemployment. Now, there are some who say that a high rate of unemployment can't be avoided.

I don't agree. In our leveling-off process, we intend to do everything we can to resist increases in unemployment, to help train and place workers in new jobs, to cushion the effects of readjustment.

For example, we have overhauled and modernized our job-training programs. We have proposed reforms extending unemployment insurance to millions not now covered, with higher benefits paid over longer periods to those in the system. We have proposed a computer job bank to match workers with hundreds of thousands of vacant jobs which exist all over this country.

The nation must dedicate itself to the ideal of helping every man who is looking for a job to find a job. Today, about 96 percent of the work force is employed. We want it to be more. But we cannot effectively and fairly make it more by ignoring the widespread hardship that a runaway cost of living imposes on so many Americans.

Now that we have begun to detect the signs of success in slowing down, what can you expect your government to do next?

First, let me tell you what we are not going to do.

We are not going to change our game plan at the end of the first quarter of the game, particularly at a time that we feel that we are ahead. We are not going to turn away from treating basic causes to start treating symptoms alone.

In other words, we are not considering wage or price controls. My own first job in government was with the old Office of Price Administration at the beginning of World War II. And from personal experience, let me just say this: wage and price controls are bad for business, bad for the working man, and bad for the consumer. Rationing, black markets, regimentation—that is the wrong road for America, and I will not take the nation down that road.

Nor are we considering putting the government into the business of telling the working man how much he should charge for his services or how much the businessman should charge for his goods. Those are called "guidelines." They collapsed back in 1966 because they failed to get to the root of the problem.

What we are going to do is based on total realism.

This weekend, I am sending a letter to a cross-section of leaders in labor and business across America calling their attention to the latest facts of economic life.

I am asking them to take a hard look at what government has done in these nine months—not just our words, but our deeds. And I am asking them to make their own future plans on the basis of working and selling in a country that is not fooling about slowing down the rise in the cost of living.

Instead of relying on our jawbone, we have put some backbone in government's determination to hold the line for the consumer. We are going to continue to exercise that backbone in the face of criticism by a lot of powerful special interests. You can rely on that. And, most important, you can make your plans on the basis that price rises are going to be slowed down.

As working men and businessmen get that message—as they see that government is willing to live up to its responsibilities for doing what is needed to hold down prices—we can expect to see a new responsibility in the decisions of labor and management. By responding to the changed conditions, they will be following their self-interest and helping the national interest as well.

Today, I have laid out our strategy to take the pressure off the prices you pay. There is a good reason for spelling out the strategy right now, at the beginning of a turning point in the struggle.

You see, there is a secret weapon that we intend to use in the battle against rising prices. That secret weapon is the confidence of the American people.

In recent years, that confidence in our ability to slow down the upward spiral has been missing. More and more, a paralyzing fatalism has crept into our view of prices. Too many of us have made the mistake of accepting ever higher prices as inevitable and, as a result, we have planned on higher and higher prices. And what we expected—we got.

Only our secret weapon of American confidence in ourselves will get us out of that vicious circle.

More than a generation ago, in the depths of the Depression, an American President told you—over this medium of radio—that the only thing we had to fear was fear itself.

Today, in a prosperity endangered by a speed-up of prices, the only thing we have to fear is fatalism—that destructive habit of shrugging our shoulders and resigning ourselves to a hopeless future on a wage-price treadmill.

I say to my fellow Americans today: the runaway cost of living is not a cross we are obliged to bear. It can be brought under control. It is being slowed by firm and steady action that deals with its root causes.

And as you plan for your own future on the assumption that the rise in prices will indeed slow down, you will be bringing our secret weapon into play. Your confidence in the strength of our economy, your confidence in the determination of America to win this battle—that is what will turn the tide.

On that note of confidence, let me issue this call:

I call upon the Congress to extend the surtax at half rate, 5 percent, from January 1 to June 30 of next year. Also I call upon the Congress, when it passes tax reform legislation, which I have recommended, which is greatly needed, that it do so in a way that we not have a net tax reduction of a size that will help push up prices that the consumer has to pay.

I call upon Americans to urge their Congressmen to pass those measures of manpower training and unemployment insurance that I have proposed—measures that would help make it easier for people to adjust to change.

And I call for your support in our policy of holding down Federal spending so that we are able to continue setting an example with a responsible budget for the next year, fiscal 1971.

I call upon the American people to urge their state and local governments to cooperate in postponing spending that can appropriately be delayed.

I call upon labor's leadership and labor's rank and file to base their wage demands on the new prospect of a return toward price stability.

I call upon businessmen to base their investment and price decisions on that new economic climate, keeping in mind it is in their private interest to be realistic in their planning and to help build a strong economy.

I call upon all Americans to bear the burden of restraint in their personal credit and purchasing decisions, so as to reduce the pressures that help drive prices out of sight.

I am convinced that Americans will answer this call.

I am convinced that a new confidence will be felt in this country when we match the strength of our resources with the strength of our resolution.

The dollar you earn should stay worth a dollar. The dollar you save should stay worth a dollar. This is no impossible dream—this is something you are entitled to.

The cost of living affects the quality of life. Together we are going to improve the quality of life—and together we are going to succeed in slowing down the rise in your cost of living.

HOLDING THE LINE
Nationwide Radio and Television Address
JANUARY 26, 1970

The final collision with Congress which had been forecast in President Nixon's first fiscal policy message in March occurred at the year's end. Congress favored an appropriation bill for the Department of Labor and Department of Health, Education and Welfare which exceeded by more than $1 billion the President's recommendations. A fiscal impasse delayed Congressional approval of funds to operate the departments more than six months beyond the actual beginning of the fiscal year for which they were to be appropriated. Finally passed at the opening of a new session in January, 1970, President Nixon vetoed the appropriation with a flourish on nationwide television and later sent his veto message to Congress.

Compromise was not reached until March 3, 1970, on a $19-billion bill midway between what Congress and the President desired. The President signed it March 6, for a savings of $400 million under the sum Congress first appropriated. The contest came to involve school desegregation and in the end settled

nothing except that Nixon was in earnest in trying to stop inflation
and at odds with Congress on how to do it.

Good evening, my fellow Americans.

I would like to share with you tonight a decision that is one of the most difficult I have made since I assumed the office of the Presidency a year ago.

I have here on my desk a bill, a bill which has been passed by the Congress and sent to me for signature. For the first time, I am exercising tonight the Constitutional power of the President to veto a bill and send it back to the Congress for further consideration.

This decision is particularly difficult because this bill provides funds for the Department of Health, Education and Welfare.

Now let us clearly understand the issues. The issue is not whether some of us are for education and health and others are against it.

There are no goals which I consider more important for this nation than to improve education and to provide better health care for the American people.

The question is: How much can the Federal government afford to spend on these programs this year?

In April I asked the Congress to appropriate more for the Department of Health, Education and Welfare than it has ever appropriated before. This means that this year the Federal government will spend 13 percent more on programs for health, education, and welfare than it spent last year. For Federal programs that affect education, we will spend over $10 billion. Now in this bill that I have before me the Congress has increased the amount that I recommended by $1,260 million. Over $1 billion of this increase is in the field of education.

Now, why, in an election year, particularly, would a President hesitate for one moment to sign a bill providing for such politically popular causes as this one? For this reason: The President of the United States has an obligation to consider all the worthy causes that come before him, and he is to consider them having in mind only one principle: What is best for all the people of the United States?

I believe that the increase over the amount that I recommended, the increase which is contained in this bill passed by the Congress, is not in the best interests of all the American people, because it is in the wrong amount for the wrong purposes and at the wrong time.

Let me address myself first to the questions of the amount of spending involved.

This nation faces a crisis which directly affects every family in

America—the continuing rise in the cost of living. From 1960 to 1970 the cost of living went up 25 percent in this country. Now, for the average family of four in America that meant an increase of $2,400 a year in the items that go into your cost of living—your grocery bills, your housing, your transportation, your medical costs.

A major reason for this increase in the cost of living is that in that same ten-year period from 1960 to 1970, the Federal government spent $57 billion more than it took in in taxes.

I think this was wrong. That is why as your President I intend to do everything that I can to see that the Federal government spends less in Washington so that you can have more to spend at home. If we are to stop the rise in the cost of living which is putting such a strain on the family budgets of millions of Americans, we have to cut the Federal budget.

That is why I ordered cuts of $7 billion in Federal spending in 1970. That is why, for example, the budget I will submit to Congress for 1971 will call for a smaller percentage of Federal spending for defense than in any year since 1950.

For the first time in twenty years the budget will provide more funds for human resources than for defense.

Now, if I approved the increased spending contained in this bill, I would win the approval of many fine people who are demanding more spending by the Federal government for education and health. But I would be surrendering in the battle to stop the rise in the cost of living, a battle we must fight and win for the benefit of every family in this nation.

A second reason I am vetoing this bill is that I believe that it increases spending for the wrong purposes. The increased spending ordered by Congress for the most part simply provides more dollars for the same old programs without making the urgent new reforms that are needed if we are to improve the quality of education and health care in America.

I believe, when we consider how much we are putting into education in the United States, that we are entitled to get more out in terms of better quality of education. That is why in my education message which I shortly will be submitting to the Congress I will propose a new and searching look at our American school system. In this examination we will look at such basic questions as why millions of our children in school are unable to read adequately; we will put emphasis on improving the quality of education for every child in America.

An example of the unfairness of this bill is the Impacted Aid Program which is supposed to help areas which need assistance because of the presence of Federal installations. The bill provides $6 million for the one half million people who live in the richest county in the United States, and only $3 million for the three million people that live in the hundred poorest counties in the United States.

President Eisenhower, President Kennedy, President Johnson all criticized this program as being unfair. And yet the Congress in this bill not only perpetuates this unfair program, it adds money to it.

The third reason I am vetoing this bill is because it requires the money to be spent at the wrong time. We are now nearly three quarters of the way through the school year. This bill forces us to spend the money it appropriates—and we would have to spend it all before June 30.

When money is spent in a hurry, a great deal is wasted. There is no good time to waste the taxpayers' money, but there is no worse time to waste it than today.

The Congress will determine on Wednesday whether it will sustain or override my veto of this legislation. If the veto is sustained, I will immediately seek appropriations which will assure the funds necessary to provide for the needs of the nation in education and health.

You can be sure that no school will need to be closed. No schoolchild will be denied an education as result of the action I take tonight. I will work with the Congress in developing a law that will ease the transition to education reform and do so without inflation.

I realize that a number of congressmen and senators, as well as many who are members of what is called the education lobby, disagree with the views I have expressed tonight. I respect their different viewpoint. I deeply share the concerns of those who want more funds for education, and for health and for other worthy causes in this country.

But it is my duty to act on behalf of the millions of Americans, including teachers and students, as well as patients in our hospitals, who will pay far more in the rise in the cost of living than they will receive from the increased spending provided for in this bill.

We spend more for health and education than any nation in the world. We are able to do this, and I hope we can continue to do so in the future, because we have the great good fortune to be the richest nation by far in the whole history of the world.

But we can spend ourselves poor. That is why no matter how popular a spending program is, if I determine that its enactment will have the effect of raising your prices or raising your taxes, I will not approve that program.

Now, for these reasons, for the first time, tonight, instead of signing a bill which has been sent to me by the Congress, I am signing this veto message. My fellow Americans, I believe this action is in the long-range interests of better education and improved health care. But most important, I believe that this action that I have just taken is in the vital interests of all Americans in stopping the rise in the cost of living.

Thank you, and good night.

VETO EXPLAINED
Message to the House of Representatives
of the United States

JANUARY 27, 1970

I return herewith, without my approval, H.R. 13111, an Act, "Making Appropriations for the Departments of Labor, and Health, Education and Welfare and Related Agencies for the Fiscal Year Ending June 30, 1970, and for Other Purposes."

The issue is not whether some of us are for education and health programs and others against.

There are no goals which I consider more important for this nation than to improve education and to provide better health care for the American people.

The question is how much can the Federal government afford to spend on those programs this year?

The enrolled bill is $1.3 billion over my budget request for the Department of Health, Education and Welfare (HEW).

It is the largest increase over my budget recommendations of any appropriations bill for 1970.

It is the largest excess over a Presidential request ever provided by the Congress for the Department of Health, Education and Welfare.

I have taken this action for four reasons:

One, these increases are excessive in a period of serious inflationary pressures. We must draw the line and stick to it if we are to stabilize the economy.

Two, nearly nine tenths of these increases is for *mandatory* programs which leave the Executive Branch no discretion whatever either as to the level or the purpose of the added expenditures. This fact sharply differentiates this appropriation from other inflated measures that I have approved.

Three, the added funds are largely for lower priority programs.

Four, because of the lateness in the fiscal year, increases of this magnitude cannot be used effectively in many cases.

Deficits Feed Inflation

The inflation we have at the start of the '70s was caused by heavy deficit spending in the '60s. In the past decade the Federal government spent more than it took in—$57 billion more. These deficits caused prices to rise 25 percent in a decade.

That is why I ordered Federal spending cut this year.

In April, 1969, I reduced the 1970 budget proposed by President Johnson by $4 billion. In July I cut another $3.5 billion. Seventy-five percent of new direct Federal construction projects were deferred.

But Congress increased other spending by $3.5 billion.

Priorities Have Been Reassessed

Of the $7.5 billion reduction I proposed for 1970, $4.1 billion was in defense spending. We are reducing defense spending to the minimum consistent with our national security. Defense spending went *down* from 1969 to 1970. It will go *down again* in 1971.

HEW spending is rising. Outlays for the department are presently estimated to increase in fiscal 1970 by $6.1 billion above 1969, a 13-percent rise. They will increase further in 1971.

For the first time in twenty years next year's budget will provide more funds for human resources than for defense.

The Fiscal 1970 Budget

For the Congress and the nation to understand my decision on the HEW appropriations, I must report today on current budget estimates for fiscal year 1970.

There are essentially two kinds of Federal government spending:

—*uncontrollables*, which are already committed either because a program is automatic or because contracts were let before the fiscal year began and now payment is due; and

—*controllables*, where budget decisions can be made to have programs reduced or eliminated to hold spending down.

Although we made deep cuts in "controllables" in 1970, the over-runs in "uncontrollables" have fully absorbed these cuts and now *far* exceed them.

The original spending ceiling set by the Congress in July was $191.9 billion, plus $2 billion allowance for designated uncontrollables. Actions taken by the Congress since then, and those now anticipated, would increase the ceiling another $1.8 billion. The result is an automatically revised Congressional ceiling of *$195.7 billion.*

It is the "uncontrollable" outlays— driven upward by the very inflationary forces we were trying to contain—that have frustrated the efforts of both the Executive and the Congress to hold down spending.

Since I submitted my budget estimates in April, interest on the public debt has increased $1.5 billion. Spending for health insurance has increased $.7 billion, in large part because inflation requires us to pay higher hospital and doctor bills for the senior citizens entitled to care.

Taking into account all the changes which we can presently assess, we now estimate 1970 outlays at close to *$198 billion,* more than $2 billion in excess of the ceiling. All of this overrun is attributable to "uncontrollables."

We faced these difficult budgetary facts of life in preparing the 1971 budget which I will send to the Congress on February 2. I will submit a budget for fiscal 1971 which will sharply reduce "spending momentum," evidence of my determination to restore price stability.

The Decision on H.R. 13111

Confronted with these budget overruns in 1970, I reached my decision in December to veto the HEW appropriation unless it was reduced by the Congress, and publicly stated my position.

Over four fifths of the increase in H.R. 13111 is for education. Even without this large increase in education funds, the Federal government in 1970 will spend over $10 billion for education—the most in our history. We care deeply about the need to improve our nation's schools. But we must ask two questions:

First, will the $1.1 billion which the Congress added for education go to those who need it the most?

Second, will it increase the quality of American education? This is the appropriate role of the Federal government in a system in which Federal aid for public schools is 8 percent of the $40 billion total spent by state and local governments.

My answer is that these Congressional increases do not target the scarce resources of the Federal government in ways I can accept in this period of budget stringency. I must veto H.R. 13111.

Schools have as much at stake as anyone in our efforts to curb inflation. As an official of a major school system recently wrote: "the Cost-of-Education Index makes it abundantly clear that inflation itself is far more damaging than any of the attempts to bring it under control."

Another 6-percent rise in prices this year would add more than $2.25 billion to the costs of public schools without any improvements in either quality or quantity. Twice as much as the $1.1 billion in increases for education proposed by the Congress will be swept away if we do not hold firm in our resolve to curb inflation.

Impacted Areas Aid

Nearly $400 million of the HEW increase would be for grants to schools in Federally impacted areas. In 1968 this program paid $5.8 million to the nation's richest county (which had a population of 500,000) and a total of $3.2 million to the hundred poorest counties (with a combined population of over 3 million).

For many school districts these payments exceed the cost to local schools of educating the children of Federal employees. Often, the program enables wealthy districts to exert a lower tax effort than other districts in the same state.

Four successive Presidents have tried to reduce or reorient this program. Yet the Congress in this bill not only perpetuates this unfair program, it adds money to it. It is wrong to increase sharply the Impacted School Aid Program in the face of the need to make long overdue reforms in this law. The Administration will make recommendations for reform of this program based on a study requested by the Congress. I will submit these recommendations shortly.

Excessive Increases

The Conference Bill would increase the 1970 budget by $575 million for vocational education, equipment, and other categorical education grants, and for Title I of the Elementary and Secondary Education Act.

This is a 34-percent increase over the 1969 appropriations for these programs. In 1970 these increases—some for worthy programs—are just too large. Moreover, they come at a critical time in the development of education policy. The present system of Federal aid to education is much too inflexible; it frustrates planning by local officials and the development of creative new programs. Results—in terms of improved student performance—have fallen far short of our expectations.

That is why in my education message which I will shortly be submitting to the Congress I will propose a new and searching look at our American school system.

We are placing new and strong emphasis on experimentation and evaluation to learn about more effective approaches to education. We have undertaken a thorough review of the Title I program for disadvantaged children to repair its deficiencies. I have proposed consolidation of grant authorizations to give states and localities more flexibility and responsibility for action. I will recommend other actions in the coming weeks.

Inefficient Use of Limited Federal Resources

The Conference Bill provides $100 million in Federal appropriations for college construction grants and capital contributions for National Defense Student Loan funds above my request. For both construction and college student aid the Congress has already authorized Federal interest subsidies for loans by private lenders. This is a much more efficient method of financing, which takes advantage of the loan placement and collection machinery of private lending institutions, while reserving Federal appropriations for other purposes where loans cannot be used.

Failure to Recognize Priorities

At the same time that the Congress was adding large amounts to these existing education support programs, it refused to vote the $25 million I requested for innovation in elementary and secondary education. These funds would have been used to develop and test promising approaches for improving student achievement—such as new ways to teach reading and the use of older children to teach younger children.

The refusal to grant these modest research and development funds comes at a time when the nation is devoting less than one half of 1 percent of its total investment in education to research. We do not know enough about how to get more for our education dollars; we must intensify our efforts to find out.

The Problem of Congressional Delay

The lateness of Congressional action on the appropriations for HEW creates serious problems.

School budgets are prepared in the early months of a calendar year. Teachers are customarily employed in the spring and early summer before academic sessions begin in September. Large unplanned Federal grants coming only a few months before the close of the year will, if experience is a guide, be used disproportionately to substitute for other school revenues and to make hasty purchases not essential for school improvement.

The nation has had bitter experience with the waste of large amounts allocated to education late in the school year. This was particularly true in the first year of funding for Title I. Money to help educate poor children went, not for teachers and well-planned programs, but often for unneeded equipment. A pattern of spending was established that has plagued this program ever since, creating management and operational problems that are still unsolved.

Not only does late funding result in waste when a full year's appropriation is crammed into three or four months, it also creates a spending rate bulge. This is the kind of "on-again, off-again" relationship with states and localities that we are trying to avoid, because it hampers intelligent community planning.

Misdirected Health Funds

For HEW in 1970 the Congress also added $104 million above my request to the Hill-Burton appropriation for grants to build and modernize community hospitals. This increase was voted despite the growing awareness that a more pressing need is to fund ambulatory care facilities which offer an alternative to expensive hospital care. This is what was proposed to the Congress last April. While this point is recognized in the report of the Senate Appropriations Committee, the appropriation bill itself allocates most of the increased funds to grants for lower priority purposes rather than for needed out-patient facilities.

For hospital construction, the Administration has recommended legislation authorizing guaranteed loans, which would create a program much more responsive to today's needs. Combined with the reimbursement formulas for construction under Medicare and Medicaid, this approach is efficient and equitable, and avoids having the Federal government pay twice for hospital beds.

The amounts added by the Congress for health research represent less than one half of 1 percent of the total appropriation. Taken separately, I would not have vetoed these increases. On the contrary, when the budget for 1971 is submitted to the Congress, it will make a strongly increased commitment for health research, where advances can be made to serve the health needs of the nation—cancer, heart disease, population research, and environmental health.

Forced Spending

Nearly nine tenths of this Congressional increase—about $1.1 billion—is for *mandatory* programs. The Executive Branch would have no control over these appropriations once H.R. 13111 was signed into law.

Left without any latitude in these areas, we may be faced with the need to make offsetting and disproportionate reductions in high-priority programs. Because so much of the budget at this time of the year is already committed, the areas remaining where offsetting reductions can be made are limited. To a disturbing degree, they consist of health service programs, scientific research, manpower training, food and nutrition, and other programs that continue to be identified by the Administration and the Congress as vital to the nation's needs.

Office of Economic Opportunity Earmarking

One issue remains to be dealt with that has arisen since my decision of last December to veto H.R. 13111. I am very concerned about a provision which was struck from the bill last week. The effect of this action would be to require the Executive to allocate funds for the Office of Economic Opportunity (OEO) according to specific earmarks.

The amount available for OEO programs is *not* at issue. Rather, the issue is the effective use of resources.

To set requirements upon the use of OEO funds with less than five months of the fiscal year left will disrupt many of its programs. We will be forced to increase some programs well beyond planned spending levels and to make damaging reductions in others, particularly Head Start, Legal Services, VISTA, JOBS, and programs for migrants and senior citizens.

I ask the Congress to reconsider its action, and restore the flexibility necessary to enable OEO to use its funds to the best advantage of the poor. The Congress will shortly begin its review of my 1971 budget recommendations. This will provide an opportunity for a timely and orderly examination of the objectives of OEO, its performance and program levels.

What Next?

I have vetoed this bill because the increases for HEW voted by the Congress are mandatory, and because in the context of present efforts to curb inflation they are misdirected and excessive.

If the veto is sustained, I will immediately seek appropriations which will assure the funds necessary to provide for the needs of the nation in education and health. No school will need to be closed, no child need have his education interrupted or impaired as a result of this veto action.

Another approach to a solution would be for the Congress to remove the requirement in the law that all formula grant funds must be spent, leaving it to the Executive Branch to take the necessary action. (In its actions setting ceiling on obligations and expenditures for fiscal years 1968 and 1969, the Congress provided such flexibility.)

Provision must also be made so that impacted area aid funds are not cut off for hardship-case school districts. Until we come to agreement on a basic reform of this program, I believe we should work out a temporary solution which involves full funding for children whose parents live and work on Federal installations and partial funding for children whose parents do not live on Federal installations. In addition, I favor a specific "No Hardship Clause" which will guarantee that no school district will, as a result of these changes in the Impacted School Aid Program, have a school budget less than 95 percent of what it had in 1969.

In working together to resolve this appropriations problem, care must be taken to avoid the extreme rhetoric which freezes positions. All Americans are "for schools" and "against inflation." The suggestions which I have made will do much to meet both objectives.

I believe this action is in the long-range interests of better programs for education and health. Above all, it is in the vital interests of all Americans in stopping the rise in the cost of living.

6

The Central Government and the States

President Nixon borrowed an idea from the Johnson Administration, and under the phrase "New Federalism" made it into an active policy. He picked up where President Eisenhower had left off a decade before in a conscious effort to transfer power and responsibility back to the states.

Nixon implemented the policy by adopting a proposal that had been advanced for at least ten years by liberal economists and governmental experts—the sharing of Federal revenue with the states. The power of the Federal government to generate tax revenue had become so great in the post-World War II period, and the power of the states so impaired, that a kickback, so to speak, of tax money from Washington to the state capitols and city halls provided a ready remedy.

President Nixon proposed Federal tax sharing in a message to Congress and followed up with a more philosophical outline of his "New Federalism" in an address at the National Governors' Conference.

Congress was responsive but slow to act.

SHARING THE REVENUE
Message to the Congress of the United States
AUGUST 13, 1969

If there is a single phenomenon that has marked the recent history of nations, large and small, democratic and dictatorial, it has been rise of the central government.

In the United States revenues of the Federal government have increased ninetyfold in thirty-six years. The areas of our national life where the Federal government has become a dominant force have multiplied.

The flow of power from the cities and states to Washington accelerated in the Depression years, when economic life in America stagnated, and an energetic national government seemed the sole instrument of national revival. World War II brought another and necessary expansion of the Federal government to marshal the nation's energies to wage war on two sides of the world.

When the war ended, it looked as if the tide would be reversed. But the onset of the Cold War, the needs of a defeated and prostrate Europe, the growing danger and then the reality of a conflict in Asia, and later, the great social demands made upon the Federal government by millions of citizens, guaranteed the continued rapid growth and expansion of Federal power.

Today, however, a majority of Americans no longer supports the continued extension of Federal services. The momentum for Federal expansion has passed its peak; a process of deceleration is setting in.

The cause can be found in the record of the last half decade. In the last five years the Federal government enacted scores of new Federal programs; it added tens of thousands of new employees to the Federal payrolls; it spent tens of billions of dollars in new funds to heal the grave social ills of rural and urban America. No previous half decade had witnessed domestic Federal spending on such a scale. Yet despite the enormous Federal commitment in new men, new ideas, and new dollars from Washington, it was during this very period in our history that the problems of the cities deepened rapidly into crises.

The problems of the cities and the countryside stubbornly resisted the solutions of Washington; and the stature of the Federal government as America's great instrument of social progress has suffered accordingly —all the more so because the Federal government promised so much and delivered so little. This loss of faith in the power and efficacy of the Federal government has had at least one positive impact upon the American people. More and more, they are turning away from the central government to their local and state governments to deal with their local and state problems.

As the Federal government grew in size and power it became increasingly remote, not only from the problems it was supposed to solve, but from the people it was supposed to serve. For more than three decades, whenever a great social change was needed, a new national program was the automatic and inevitable response. Power and responsibility flowed in greater and greater measure from the state capitals to the national capital.

Furthermore, we have hampered the effectiveness of local government by constructing a Federal grant-in-aid system of staggering complexity and diversity. Many of us question the efficiency of this intergovernmental financial system which is based on the Federal categorical grant. Its growth since the end of 1962 has been near explosive. Then there were 53 formula grant and 107 project grant authorizations—a total of 160. Four years later, on January 1, 1967, there were 379 such grant authorizations.

While effective in many instances, this rapid growth in Federal grants has been accompanied by:

—Overlapping programs at the state and local level.

—Distortion of state and local budgets.

—Program delay and uncertainty.

—A decline in the authority and responsibility of chief executives, as grants have become tied to functional bureaucracies.

—Creation of new and frequently competitive state and local governmental institutions.

Another inevitable result of this proliferation of Federal programs has been a gathering of the reins of power in Washington. Experience has taught us that this is neither the most efficient nor effective way to govern; certainly it represents a radical departure from the vision of Federal-state relations the nation's founders had in mind.

This Administration brought into office both a commitment and a mandate to reverse the trend of the last three decades—a determination to test new engines of social progress. We are committed to enlist the full potential of the private sector and the full potential of the levels of government closer to the people.

This week I am sending to Congress for its approval for fiscal year 1971 legislation asking that a set amount of Federal revenues be returned annually to the states to be used as the states and their local governments see fit—without Federal strings.

Because of budget stringencies, the initial fund set aside to start the program will not be great—$500 million. The role of the Federal government will be redefined and redirected. But it is my intention to augment this fund annually in the coming years so that in the fiscal year beginning in mid-1975, $5 billion in Federal revenues will be returned to the states without Federal strings. Ultimately, it is our hope to use this mechanism to so strengthen state and local government that by the end of the coming decade the political landscape of America will be visibly altered, and states and cities will have a far greater share of power and responsibility for solving their own problems. The role of the Federal government will be redefined and redirected toward those functions where it proves itself the only or the most suitable instrument.

The fiscal case for Federal assistance to states and localities is a strong one. Under our current budget structure, Federal revenues are likely to increase faster than the national economy. At the local level, the reverse is true. State and local revenues, based heavily on sales and property taxes, do not keep pace with economic growth, while expenditures at the local level tend to exceed such growth. The result is a "fiscal mismatch," with potential Federal surpluses and local deficits.

The details of this revenue sharing program were developed after close consultation with members of the Congress, governors, mayors, and county officials. It represents a successful effort to combine the desirable features of simplicity and equity with a need to channel funds where they are most urgently needed and efficiently employable.

The program can best be described by reviewing its four major elements.

First, the size of the total fund to be shared will be a stated percentage of personal taxable income—the base on which Federal individual income taxes are levied. For the second half of fiscal year 1971 this will be one third of 1 percent of personal taxable income; for subsequent fiscal years this percentage will rise to a regular constant figure. In order to provide for the assured flow of Federal funds, a permanent appropriation will be authorized and established for the Treasury Department, from which will be automatically disbursed each year an amount corresponding to the stipulated percentage.

Second, the allocation of the total annual fund among the fifty states and the District of Columbia will be made on the basis of each state's share of national population, adjusted for the state's revenue effort.

The revenue effort adjustment is designed to provide the states with some incentive to maintain (and even expand) their efforts to use their own tax resources to meet their needs. A simple adjustment along these lines would provide a state whose revenue effort is above the national average with a bonus above its basic per-capita portion of revenue sharing.

Third, the allocation of a state's share among its general units of local government will be established by prescribed formula. The total amount a state will share with all its general political subdivisions is based on the relative roles of state and local financing in each state. The amount which an individual unit of general local government will receive is based on its share of total local government revenue raised in the state.

Several points should be noted about these provisions—distribution of a state's portion of revenue sharing.

—The distribution will be made by the state.

—The provisions make allowance for state-by-state variations and would tend to be neutral with respect to the current relative fiscal importance of state and local governments in each state.

—In order to provide local flexibility, each state is authorized to develop an alternative distribution plan, working with its local governments.

Fourth, administrative requirements are to be kept at a minimum. Each state will meet simple reporting and accounting requirements.

While it is not possible to specify for what functions these Federally shared funds will provide—the purpose of this program being to leave such allocation decisions up to the recipient units of government—an analysis of existing state and local budgets can provide substantial clues. Thus one can reasonably expect that education, which consistently takes over two fifths of all state and local general revenues, will be the major beneficiary of these new funds. Another possible area for employment of shared funds, one most consistent with the spirit of this program, would be for intergovernmental cooperation efforts.

This proposal marks a turning point in Federal-state relations, the beginning of decentralization of governmental power, the restoration of a rightful balance between the state capitals and the national capital.

Our ultimate purposes are many: to restore to the states their proper rights and roles in the Federal system with a new emphasis on and help for local responsiveness; to provide both the encouragement and the necessary resources for local and state officials to exercise leadership in solving their own problems; to narrow the distance between people and the government agencies dealing with their problems; to restore strength and vigor to local and state governments; to shift the balance of political power away from Washington and back to the country and the people.

This tax-sharing proposal was pledged in the campaign; it has long been a part of the platform of many men in my own political party— and men in the other party as well. It is integrally related to the national welfare reform. Through these twin approaches we hope to relieve the fiscal crisis of the hard-pressed state and local governments and to assist millions of Americans out of poverty and into productivity.

SHARING THE RESPONSIBILITY
Remarks of the President at the National Governors' Conference in Colorado Springs
SEPTEMBER 1, 1969

Vice President and Mrs. Agnew, Governor Ellington, Governor Love, all of the distinguished Governors and their First Ladies who are here, and all the distinguished members of this audience:

I first want to express my appreciation to Governor Ellington for his eloquent and generous introduction, and I hope that in my remarks tonight I can respond in the same spirit.

I also want to express my appreciation to the governors of the fifty states for their service to this nation, whether they be Republicans or Democrats, for inviting me to address them on this occasion.

I speak with a certain humility whenever I address a group of governors. If you will permit a personal reference at the outset, I might mention that I have run for many offices in my political career. Twenty-three years ago I ran for the House and four years later for the Senate, and then for Vice President and then for President, and then for Governor and then for President. The only office that I have sought and have never won is that of governor; so I have a particular respect for the governors who are here tonight. . . .

We are meeting here at a time of great and fundamental change in America—of changes more far-reaching than have ever been seen in the span of a single lifetime.

These changes summon all of us—the Federal government, the states, the counties, cities, and towns—each person everywhere—to a high adventure in human advancement.

We stand on the threshold of a time when the impossible becomes possible—a time when we can choose goals that, just a generation ago, would have seemed as unreachable as the moon seemed to be unreachable then. We can reach those goals.

The Spirit of Apollo gave us a brief, glittering glimpse of how far we can stretch. Thousands of minds, thousands of hands, all were marshaled in selfless dedication in achieving a great human dream—and the dream came true.

Today, we in America can afford to dream—but we have to put drive behind those dreams.

This requires that we turn—now—to a new strategy for the '70s—one that enables us to command our own future by commanding the forces of change.

Only seven years from now, in 1976, America will celebrate its two-hundredth birthday as a nation. So let us look ahead to that great anniversary in the Spirit of Apollo—and discover in ourselves a new Spirit of '76.

Let us resolve that what we can do, we will do.

When a great nation confronts its shortcomings, not angrily, but analytically; when it commits its resources, not wantonly, but wisely; when it calms its hatreds, masters its fears, and draws together in a spirit of common endeavor, then the forces of progress are on the march.

The central race in the world today is neither an arms race nor a space race. It is the race between man and change. The central question is whether we are to be the master of events or the pawn of events.

If we are to win this race, our first need is to make government governable.

When the new Administration took office last January, we confronted a set of hard and unpleasant facts. I cite these facts not in a partisan way; they are not the fault of any one Administration or of any one party. Rather, they are part of our common experience as a people, the result of an accumulating failure of government over the years to come to grips with a future that soon overtook it.

We confronted a legacy of Federal deficits that has added $58 billion to the burden of public debt in the past ten years.

We confronted the fact that state and local governments were being crushed in a fiscal vise, squeezed by rising costs, rising demands for services, exhaustion of revenue sources.

We confronted the fact that in the past five years the Federal government alone has spent more than a quarter of a trillion dollars on social programs—over $250 billion. Yet far from solving our problems, these expenditures had reaped a harvest of dissatisfaction, frustration and bitter division.

Never in human history has so much been spent by so many for such a negative result. The cost of the lesson has been high, but we have learned that it is not only what we spend that matters, but how we spend it.

Listen to Professor Peter Drucker analyze the problem of government today: "There is mounting evidence that government is big rather than strong; that it is fat and flabby rather than powerful; that it costs a great deal but does not achieve very much. Indeed, government is sick—and just at the time we need a strong, healthy, and vigorous government."

The problem has not been a lack of good intentions, and not merely a lack of money. Methods inherited from the '30s proved to be out of date in the '60s. Structures put together in the '30s broke down under the load of the '60s.

Overcentralized, overbureaucratized, the Federal government became unresponsive as well as inefficient.

In their struggle to keep up states and localities found the going increasingly difficult.

In the space of only ten years state and local expenditures rose by two and a half times—from $44 billion in 1958 to $108 billion in 1968.

States alone have had to seek more than two hundred tax increases in the past eight years.

You know—you as governors—and I know that simply piling tax on tax is not the long-range solution to the problems we face together.

We have to devise a new way to make our revenue system meet the needs of the '70s. We have to put the money where the problems are, and we have to get a dollar's worth of return for a dollar spent.

Our new strategy for the '70s begins with the reform of government:

—Overhauling its structure.

—Pruning out those programs that have failed, or that have outlived their time.

—Ensuring that its delivery systems actually deliver the intended services to the intended beneficiaries.

—Focusing its activities not only on tomorrow, but on the day after tomorrow.

This must be a cooperative venture among governments at all levels, because it centers on what I have called the "New Federalism"— in which power, funds, and authority are channeled increasingly to those governments that are closest to the people.

The essence of the New Federalism is to help regain control of our national destiny by returning a greater share of control to state and local governments and to the people.

This in turn requires constant attention in raising the quality of government at all levels.

The new strategy for the '70s also requires a strategy for peace— and I pledge to you tonight that we will have an effective strategy for peace.

Let me tell you what that strategy means and what it does not mean. It means maintaining defense forces strong enough to keep the peace, but not allowing wasteful expenditures to drain away expenditures we need for progress.

It means limiting our commitments abroad to those we can prudently and realistically keep. It means helping other free nations maintain their own security, but not rushing in to do for them what they can and should do for themselves.

It does not mean laying down our leadership. It does not mean abandoning our allies. It does mean forging a new structure of world stability in which the burdens as well as the benefits are fairly shared— a structure that does not rely on the strength of one nation, but that draws strength from all nations.

An effective strategy for peace abroad makes possible an effective strategy for meeting our domestic problems at home. To place this new domestic strategy in concrete terms, I would like to cite a few examples of changes we in the new Administration have made or proposed since taking office.

We have proposed, as all of you know, because you have discussed it in this conference, the first major reform of welfare in the history of welfare.

This would abolish the discredited Aid to Families with Dependent Children program, and launch in its place a new system that for the first time would ensure a minimum income for every family with dependent children—and at the same time provide a coordinated structure of work requirements, work incentives, and training designed to move people off the welfare rolls and onto payrolls in the United States.

Now I realize that some object to some of these proposals—understandably—as seeming to favor one region over another, or because they give the rich states more or less than they give to poorer states. I considered these arguments, rejected them, because as Buford Ellington indicated in his introduction, we are one country. We must think in terms of the people and their needs—whatever they are. We must meet our problems where the problems are. Because unless we act to meet the problems of human need in the places where they exist, the problems and troubles of rural America today will be the problems of urban America tomorrow.

Consider for a moment the name of this nation: the United States of America. We establish minimum national standards because we are united; we encourage local supplements because we are a federation of states; and we care for the unfortunate because this is America.

We have proposed the first major restructuring of food programs for the needy in the history of food programs.

Let's face it: for years, food programs were designed as much to get rid of surplus commodities as to feed hungry people, and now, for the first time, we propose that every American family shall have the resources, in food stamps, commodities, and other assistance, to obtain a minimum nutritious diet, with free food stamps for those with very low incomes.

We have declared the first five years of a child's life to be a period of special and specific Federal concern.

New knowledge recently acquired has shown that these earliest, formative years are crucial to a child's later development. Yet with only random exceptions, no provision has previously been made to ensure the welfare of children during these years. With an eye to the next generation, we have made it our business to fill this void.

We have proposed the first major reform of the income tax system in nearly twenty years, to remove millions of the poor from the tax rolls entirely, to close loopholes that have allowed many of the rich to escape any taxation at all, and to make the entire structure more balanced and more equitable.

We have proposed the most fundamental reform of the unemployment insurance system in the history of unemployment insurance.

We have proposed the first reform in the fiscal structure of Federalism since the 1930s.

In proposing to begin the sharing of Federal tax revenues with the states—to be spent as the states see fit—we are putting our money where our principles are. The power to tax is the power to destroy; but the sharing of tax revenues provides the power to build.

We have proposed, for the first time in history, a comprehensive and effective delegation of Federal programs to state and local management.

The Comprehensive Manpower Act would turn over to state and local direction a major Federal program which clearly has to be nationwide in scope, and Federally funded, but which can most effectively be managed at the state and local level.

We have begun the first overall reform of the organization of the Federal government since the Hoover Commission.

By establishing common headquarters and common regional boundaries for the various Federal agencies, we have made decentralized administration possible—and made it possible for governors and mayors to do their business with those agencies at one time and one place.

As I chatted with Governor Rhodes of Ohio this evening, he mentioned the fact that in his state, for some Federal programs, the welfare programs, approximately 40 percent of the payroll was for the purpose of filling out the Federally required forms.

Let me say that we would welcome from the governors your suggestions as to how we can reduce that kind of a load that has been imposed upon you by the Federal government.

For the first time machinery has been created to raise the problems of the cities and the problems of the environment to the level of formal, interdepartmental, Cabinet-level concern, with the creation of an Urban Affairs Council and the Council on Environment.

For the first time machinery has been created within the White House for a coordinated system of forward planning of needs and resources. With establishment of the National Goals Research Staff, we have built into the budgetary and program operations of the National government a systematic assessment of future needs and the resources available for meeting those needs.

Another reform I have asked for, and to which I attach special priority as a matter of the highest principle, is the reform of the draft.

Until peacetime conditions make a shift to an all-volunteer armed force possible—and while the draft remains necessary—it is imperative that we make it as nearly fair as possible, and that we reduce to a minimum the unnecessary long period of uncertainty that now hangs over the lives of millions of our young people. We shall have some directives that will be issued in the very near future that will accomplish some of those results.

In summary, the twenty-four legislative proposals—the major ones —that I have sent to Congress have also included proposals ranging from an overhaul of foreign aid to the most wide-ranging reform of the postal service in history; from a new program of mass transit aid to new measures for the combatting of narcotics, pornography, and organized crime.

Taken together, these measures are sweeping in their implications. I admit, too, they are controversial as any new programs are. They also represent fundamental new directions in national policy. But to those who say they are controversial, to those who criticize them for what they are, I make this one suggestion: We have been on a road for a long time that is leading us to disaster, and when you are on the wrong road, the thing to do is get off and get on to a new road and a new progress.

These programs represent a comprehensive, concerted effort to make government work; to make it work fairly; to make it responsive; and to gear it to the early anticipation of emerging needs, rather than belated response to crises that could have been avoided.

I would like for all of us to look at these measures in a larger framework.

Exactly four months from today, we will enter the decade of the '70s. We look ahead toward that two-hundredth anniversary of American independence in 1976; we have a target to shoot for.

What kind of a nation we will be on that momentous anniversary is ours to determine by what we do or fail to do now.

As conditions are changing, so we must change.

The reforms I have proposed in these legislative recommendations are not partisan changes. They are positive changes. They have no special constituency of region or class or interest group. Their constituency is tomorrow.

It already is painfully clear that many hard choices will have to be made. Dreams of unlimited billions of dollars being released once the war in Vietnam ends are just that—dreams. True, there will be additional money—but the claims on it already are enormous. There should be no illusion that what some call the "peace and growth dividend" will automatically solve our national problems or release us from the need to establish priorities.

There are hard budget and tax decisions ahead. These involve your interests as governors; they involve the interests of all of us as citizens.

In order to find the money for new programs, we are going to have to trim it out of old ones. This is one reason why I regard the reform I have proposed as essential. We can no longer afford the luxury of inefficiency in government. We cannot count on good money to bail us out of bad ideas.

Equally important, continued improvement of governments at the state and local levels is essential to make these new concepts work.

If the delegation of funds and authority to the state and local governments under the Comprehensive Manpower Act is successful, this can then be a model for more delegations in the future. But we can only toss the ball; the states and localities have to catch it and they have to carry it.

I am confident that you can.

For a long time the phrase "states' rights" was often used as an escape from responsibility—as a way of avoiding a problem, rather than of meeting a problem.

But that time has passed.

I can assure you of this: We are not simply going to tell you the states have a job to do; we are going to help you find the funds, the resources, to do that job well.

We are not simply going to lecture you on what you should do. We are going to examine what we can do together.

One of the key points I want to make tonight is, in a sense, very similar to one I made on my recent visits to our NATO partners and to our friends in Asia. Washington will no longer try to go it alone; Washington will no longer dictate without consulting. A new day has come, in which we recognize that partnership is a two-way street, and if the partnership is to thrive, that street has to be traveled—both ways.

This poses a new challenge to the states—not only to administer programs, but to devise programs; not only to employ resources, but to choose the things for which they should be used.

In my talks with many governors and other state officials, I have found them ready to rise to that challenge. And I have become convinced that states today are ready for a new role.

The New Federalism also recognizes the role of people—of individuals doing, and caring, and sharing. The concept of voluntary action, of community action, of people banding together in a spirit of neighborliness to do those things which they see must be done, is deeply rooted in America's character and tradition. As we have swept power and responsibility to Washington, we have undercut this tradition. Yet when it comes to helping one another, Washington can never bring to the task the heart that neighbors can. Washington can never bring the sensitivity to local conditions, or the new sense of self-importance that a person feels when he finds that some one person cares enough to help him individually.

In encouraging a new birth of voluntary action, I intend to look not only to the Federal government, but also to the states, for inspiration and encouragement. Each state has its own pattern of experience, its own examples of how people have successfully helped people. By sharing these examples, they can be multiplied.

As we look toward 1970 and beyond, our range of possible choices is truly breathtaking; how we manage our growing abundance, how we make real our ideals of full opportunity, how we clean up our air and our water, how we balance our systems of transportation, how we expand our systems of education and health care—the list could go on and on, indefinitely.

As only one dimension to the new tasks we face, the best estimates are that America's population will increase by 100 million between now and the year 2000—thirty years from now. This means that thirty years from now there will be half again as many people in America as there are today. It means that in this short span of time we have to build fifty cities the size of Philadelphia today.

Or to put it another way, the Committee on Urban Growth Policy has recommended that we should begin planning now for a hundred new cities of 100,000 each, and ten new cities of 1 million each—and yet even if we did this it would accommodate only 20 percent of the added population we have to plan for the year 2000.

Yet the other side of this coin of challenge is an enormous opportunity.

Growth on such an heroic scale offers an unprecedented opportunity to shape that growth so that our cities and communities enhance man himself.

More than anything else, it is these new tasks of the future—not the distant future, but the immediate future—that give urgency to the need to reform government today.

We can command the future only if we can manage the present. The reforms I have proposed are designed to make this possible.

Only if we stop fighting the battles of the '30s can we take on the necessary.

Only if we stop fighting the battles of the '30s can we take on the battles of the '70s.

These reforms represent a New Federalism; a new humanism, and I suggest also, a new realism.

They are based not on theoretical abstractions, but on the hard experience of the past third of a century.

They are addressed to the real problems of real people in a real world—and to the needs of the next third of a century.

They represent not an end, but a beginning—the beginning of a new era in which we confound the prophets of doom, and make government an instrument for casting the future in the image of our hopes.

That task requires the best efforts of all of us together.

It requires the best thinking of all of us together, as we choose our goals and devise the means of their achievement.

But the future that beckons us also holds greater promise than any man has ever known. These reforms are steps in the direction of that promise—and as we take them, let us do so confident in the strength of America, firm in our faith that we can chart our destiny to the abundant spirit of a great and resourceful people. This spirit has been our strength. Marshaled in a new Spirit of '76, giving force to our purposes and direction to our efforts, it can be our salvation.

As all of you know, I have had the opportunity of traveling both to Europe and to Asia during the first seven months of my term of office. I visited the leaders in the great countries of both Europe and Asia. I have seen great civilizations and great governments and great peoples.

Back in the United States, after meeting with these leaders, one truth always comes home to me, and it is this: This is the period of time in which the survival of peace and freedom in the world will depend upon what happens in the United States of America. And it depends not only on what a President will do, but on what we do in all areas, governmental and non-governmental. It depends not only on what we do on the Federal level, but on the state and local levels as well. If the United States is going to meet the challenge which is ours, if we are going to deserve the mantle of leadership which is ours—whether we want it or not—we must first demonstrate that we can handle our problems at home.

No men, no women, could have a more exciting challenge than this. Yes, the task is a great one, and at times it may seem frustrating. But I want to say to all of you that as we look toward the challenge of the last third of the century, as we look toward the decade of the '70s, I have great confidence in that future, confidence in it because I know that there are men and women in this country—in the field of politics, in the field of government—who are determined to make government work, who are determined that we will not fail.

Let me put it in historical perspective: This nation was founded in 1776—thirteen colonies, 3 million people, very weak militarily, poor economically. The men who founded this nation said: "We act not just for ourselves, but for the whole human race."

That was a presumptuous thing for them to say then. Yet somehow that spirit of '76 appealed to all the world.

Today the United States of America, because of its power, because of its wealth, because of what we stand for, does act for the whole human race. That is the challenge we face, the challenge I know we can meet.

I am proud to work with the governors of the fifty states, Republicans and Democrats alike, to see that America deals effectively with its problems at home. For it is thus that we can provide the example of leadership so urgently necessary to preserve peace and freedom abroad.

7
Freedom
and
Protests

Confronted in the fall of 1969 with what promised to be a massive outpouring of youthful war opposition, President Nixon said on September 26 at a press conference, "As far as this kind of activity is concerned, we expect it. However, under no circumstances will I be affected whatever by it."

Three months earlier, in speeches at General Beadle State College in Madison, South Dakota, and at the Air Force Academy at Colorado Springs, the President presented the broad philosophical outline of his attitude toward protest and revolt.

In the age of high technology a crisis of the national spirit compelled a President of the United States to probe those deep questions of man's place in the state which concerned the French and British philosophers of the eighteenth century. The ideas of Washington, Madison, and Jefferson grew from those early concepts, and now nearly three centuries later they were to be restated in terms related to modern life.

Nothing illustrated more clearly a requirement of the Presidency not heavily weighed by the Founding Fathers: moral, ethical, and spiritual leadership, providing a central focus in a pluralistic nation of differing races, religions, social status, ideology, and national origins.

FREEDOM DOES NOT INCLUDE THE RIGHT TO BE A BULLY

Remarks of the President at the Dedication of the Karl E. Mundt Library at General Beadle State College, Madison, South Dakota

JUNE 3, 1969

Senator and Mrs. Mundt, Governor and Mrs. Farrar, all of the distinguished guests on the platform, and all of the very gracious guests in the audience:

I first want to begin with a personal note, responding to the warm-hearted remarks that have been made to me and about me by the Governor and by Karl Mundt, and as I respond to them I want you to know that I feel very much at home here.

I feel at home here because I, too, grew up in a small town. I attended a small college, about the size of this one, and when I was in law school at a much larger university, one of the ways I helped support myself was to work in the law school library.

So I feel very much at home here before a great new library, on the campus of a small college which is growing larger, and in a small town in the heartland of America.

I would like to relate what I have said perhaps a little more closely to this state. I suppose the best thing I could say would be that I was born in South Dakota. I was not. I was born in California. I could also say, possibly, that Mrs. Nixon was born in South Dakota. She was not. She was born in Nevada.

But I can go very close to that, because my wife's mother and father, Mr. and Mrs. Thomas Ryan, were married and lived in their early years, before they moved to California, in Lee, South Dakota. So we have a South Dakota background.

I should also point out that in the small estate that my wife's father left was a mining claim in the Black Hills of South Dakota. We paid taxes on that in California for many, many years, so we were South Dakota taxpayers.

No gold was ever discovered there, but when I returned to South Dakota as a candidate in 1960, I was presented with some Black Hills gold cufflinks, and I am wearing them today to show my relationship to South Dakota.

Now an occasion like this does call for more than the usual informal remarks which, I think, are usually quite welcomed by an audience.

This is a solemn occasion. It is the beginning of a new institution as part of a larger institution.

I think as we dedicate this new library, this is the time and place to speak of some very basic things in American life. It is the time, because we find our fundamental values under bitter and even violent attack all over America. It is the place, because so much that is basic to America is represented right here where we stand.

Opportunity for all is represented here.

This is a small college: not rich and famous, like Yale and Harvard; not a vast state university, like Michigan and Berkeley. But for almost ninety years it has served the people of South Dakota, opening doors of opportunity for thousands of deserving young men and women. Like hundreds of other fine small colleges across this nation, General Beadle State College—soon to be known as Dakota State College—has offered a chance to people who might otherwise not have had a chance. As one who attended a small college, I know what that means.

The pioneer spirit is represented here, and the progress that has shaped our heritage.

Because here in South Dakota we still can sense the daring that converted a raw frontier into part of the vast heartland of America.

The vitality of thought is represented here.

A college library is a place of living ideas: a place where timeless truths are collected, to become the raw materials of discovery. In addition, the Karl E. Mundt Library will house the papers of a wise and dedicated man who for thirty years has been at the center of public events. Thus, more than most, this is a library of both thought and action, combining the wisdom of past ages with a uniquely personal record of the present time.

So today, as we dedicate this place of ideas, I think we should reflect on some of the values we have inherited which are now under challenge.

We live in a deeply troubled and profoundly unsettled time. Drugs, crime, campus revolts, racial discord, draft resistance—on every hand we find old standards violated, old values discarded, old precepts ignored. A vocal minority of our young people are opting out of the process by which a civilization maintains its continuity: the passing on of values from one generation to the next. Old and young across the nation shout across a chasm of misunderstanding—and the louder they shout, the broader the chasm becomes.

As a result of all this, our institutions in America today are undergoing what may be the severest challenge of our history. I do not speak of the physical challenge: the force and threats of force that have wracked our cities and now our colleges. Force can be contained. We have the power to strike back if need be, and we can prevail. The nation has survived other attempts at insurrection. We can survive this one. It has not been a lack of civil power, but the reluctance of a free people to employ it, that so often has stayed the hand of authorities faced with confrontation.

The challenge I speak of today is deeper: the challenge to our values and to the moral base of the authority that sustains those values.

At the outset let me draw a very clear distinction.

A great deal of today's debate about "values," or about "morality," centers on what essentially are private values and personal codes: patterns of dress and appearance; sexual mores; religious practices; the uses to which a person intends to put his own life.

Now these are immensely important, but they are not the values I mean to discuss here.

My concern and our concern today is not with the length of a person's hair, but with his conduct in relation to the community; not with what he wears, but with his impact on the process by which a free society governs itself.

I speak not of private morality, but of public morality—and of "morality" in its broadest sense, as a set of standards by which the community chooses to judge itself.

Some critics call ours an "immoral" society because they disagree with its policies, or they refuse to obey its laws because they claim that those laws have no moral basis. Yet the structure of our laws has rested from the beginning on a foundation of moral purpose. That moral purpose embodies what is, above all, a deeply humane set of values— rooted in a profound respect for the individual, for the integrity of his person and the dignity of his humanity.

At first glance, there is something homely and unexciting about basic values as we have long believed in them. We feel apologetic about espousing them; even the profoundest truths become clichés with repetition. But they can be like sleeping giants: slow to rouse, but magnificent in their strength.

So today let us look at some of those values—so familiar now, and yet once so revolutionary in America and in the world.

—Liberty: recognizing that liberties can only exist in balance, with the liberty of each stopping at that point at which it would infringe the liberty of another.

—Freedom of conscience: meaning that each person has the freedom of his own conscience, and therefore none has the right to dictate the conscience of his neighbor.

—Justice: recognizing that true justice is impartial, and that no man can be judge in his own cause.

—Human dignity: a dignity that inspires pride, is rooted in self-reliance, and provides the satisfaction of being a useful and respected member of the community.

—Concern: concern for the disadvantaged and dispossessed, but a concern that neither panders nor patronizes.

—The right to participate in public decisions: which carries with it the duty to abide by those decisions when reached, recognizing that no one can have his own way all the time.

—Human fulfillment: in the sense not of unlimited license, but of maximum opportunity.

—The right to grow, to reach upward, to be all that we can become, in a system that rewards enterprise, encourages innovation, and honors excellence.

In essence, these are all aspects of freedom. They inhere in the concept of freedom; they aim at extending freedom; they celebrate the uses of freedom. They are not new. But they are as timeless and as timely as the human spirit, because they are rooted in the human spirit.

Our basic values concern not only what we seek, but how we seek it.

Freedom is a condition; it is also a process. And the process is essential to the freedom itself.

We have a Constitution that sets certain limits on what government can do, but that allows wide discretion within those limits. We have a system of divided powers, of checks and balances, of periodic elections, all of which are designed to ensure that the majority has a chance to work its will—but not to override the rights of the minority or to infringe the rights of the individual.

What this adds up to is a democratic process, carefully constructed and stringently guarded. It is not perfect. No system could be. But it has served the nation well—and nearly two centuries of growth and change testify to its strength and adaptability.

They testify, also, to the fact that avenues of peaceful change do exist in America. Those who can make a persuasive case for changes they want can achieve them through this orderly process.

To challenge a particular policy is one thing; to challenge the government's right to set that policy is another—for this denies the process of freedom itself.

Lately, however, a great many people have become impatient with this democratic process. Some of the more extreme even argue, with a rather curious logic, that there is no majority, because the majority has no right to hold opinions that they disagree with. Scorning persuasion they prefer coercion. Awarding themselves what they call a higher morality, they try to bully authorities into yielding to their "demands." On college campuses they draw support from faculty members who should know better; in the larger communities they find the usual apologists ready to excuse any tactic in the name of "progress."

It should be self-evident that this sort of self-righteous moral arrogance has no place in a free community in America, because it denies the most fundamental of all the values we hold: respect for the rights of others. This principle of mutual respect is the keystone of the entire structure of ordered liberty that makes freedom possible.

The student who invades an administration building, roughs up the dean, rifles the files, and issues "non-negotiable demands" may have some of his demands met by a permissive university administration. But the greater his "victory," the more he will have undermined the security of his own rights. In a free society the rights of none are secure unless the rights of all are respected. It is precisely the structure of law and custom that he has chosen to violate—the process of freedom—by which the rights of all are protected.

We have long considered our colleges and universities citadels of freedom, where the rule of reason prevails. Now both the process of freedom and the rule of reason are under assault. At the same time, our colleges are under pressure to reduce our educational standards, in the misguided belief that this would promote "opportunity."

Instead of seeking to raise the lagging students up to meet the college standards, the cry now is to lower the standards to meet the students. This is the old, familiar, self-indulgent cry for the easy way. It debases the integrity of the educational process. There is no easy way to excellence, no shortcut to the truth, no magic wand that can produce a trained and disciplined mind without the hard discipline of learning. To yield to these demands would weaken the institution; more importantly, it would cheat the student of what he comes to college for: a good education.

No group, as a group, should be more zealous defenders of the integrity of academic standards and the rule of reason in academic life than the faculties of our great colleges and universities. But if the teachers simply follow the loudest voices, parrot the latest slogan, yield to unreasonable demands, they will have won not the respect but the contempt of their students and they will deserve that contempt. Students have some rights. They have a right to guidance, to leadership and direction; they also have a right to expect their teachers to listen, and to be reasonable, but also to stand for something—and most especially, to stand for the rule of reason against the rule of force.

Our colleges and universities have their weaknesses. Some have become too impersonal or too ingrown, and curricula have lagged. But let us never forget that with all its faults, the American system of higher education is the best in this whole imperfect world, and it provides in the United States today a better education for more students of all economic levels than ever before anywhere in the history of the world.

I submit this is no small achievement. We should be proud of it. We should defend it and we should never apologize for it.

Often the worst mischief is done in the name of the best cause. In our zeal for instant reform we should be careful not to destroy our educational standards and our educational system along with it; and not to undermine the process of freedom on which all else rests.

The process of freedom will be less threatened in America, however, if we pay more heed to one of the great cries of our young today. I speak now of their demand for honesty; intellectual honesty, personal honesty, public honesty. Much of what seems to be revolt is really little more than this: an attempt to strip away sham and pretense, to puncture illusion, and to get down to the basic nub of truth.

We should welcome this. We have seen too many patterns of deception in our lives:

—In political life, impossible promises.
—In advertising, extravagant claims.
—In business, shady deals.

In personal life, we have all witnessed deceits that ranked from the "little white lie" to moral hypocrisy; from cheating on income taxes to bilking the insurance companies.

In public life we have seen reputations destroyed by smear, and gimmicks paraded as panaceas. We have heard shrill voices of hate shouting lies and sly voices of malice twisting facts.

Even in intellectual life, we too often have seen logical gymnastics performed to justify a pet theory, and refusal to accept facts that fail to support it.

Of course, absolute honesty, on the other hand, would be ungenerous. Courtesy sometimes compels us to welcome the unwanted visitor and kindness leads us to compliment the homely girl on how pretty she looks. But in our public discussions we sorely need a kind of honesty that has too often been lacking: the honesty of straight talk; a doing-away with hyperbole; a careful concern with the gradations of truth, and a frank recognition of the limits of our knowledge about the problems we have to deal with. We have long demanded financial integrity in public life. We now need the most rigorous kind of intellectual integrity in public debate.

Unless we can find a way to speak plainly, truly unself-consciously, about the facts of public life, we may find that our grip on the forces of history is too loose to control our own destiny.

The honesty of straight talk leads us to the conclusion that some of our recent social experiments have worked, and some have failed, and that most have achieved something—but less than their advance billing promised. This same honesty is concerned not with assigning blame, but with discovering what lessons can be drawn from that experience in order to design better programs next time. Perhaps the goals were unattainable. Perhaps the means were inadequate; perhaps the program was based on an unrealistic assessment of human nature.

We can learn these lessons only to the extent that we can be candid with one another. We have and we must face enormously complex choices. In approaching these, confrontation is no substitute for consultation; and passionate concern gets us nowhere without dispassionate analysis. For fundamentally, our structure of values depends on mutual faith and faith depends on truth.

The values we cherish are sustained by a fabric of self-restraint, woven of ordinary civil decency, respect for the rights of others, respect for the laws of the community, and respect for the democratic process of orderly change. The purpose of these restraints is not to protect an "establishment," but to establish the protection of the liberty; not to prevent change, but to ensure that change reflects the public will and respects the rights of all.

This process is our most precious resource as a nation. But it depends on public acceptance, public understanding, and public faith.

Whether our values are maintained depends ultimately not on government, but on people.

A nation can only be as great as the people want it to be.

A nation can only be as free as the people insist that it be.

A nation's laws are only as strong as the people's will to see them enforced.

A nation's freedoms are only as secure as the people's determination to see them maintained.

A nation's values are only as lasting as the ability of each generation to pass them on to the next.

We often have a tendency to turn away from the familiar because it is familiar, and turn to the new because it is new.

To those intoxicated with the romance of violent revolution, the continuing revolution of democracy may sometimes seem quite unexciting. But no system has ever liberated the spirits of so many so fully. Nothing has ever "turned on" man's energies, his imagination, his unfettered creativity, the way that freedom has. We can be proud that we have that legacy.

Now there are some who see America's vast wealth and protest that this has made us materialistic. But we should not be apologetic about our abundance. We should not fall into the easy trap of confusing the production of things with the worship of things. We produce abundantly; but our values turn not on what we have but on what we believe.

What we believe very simply is this: We believe in liberty, in decency and the process of freedom. On these beliefs we rest our pride as a nation. In these beliefs we rest our hopes for the future and by our fidelity to the process of freedom we can assure to ourselves and our posterity the blessings of freedom.

I have spoken today of these basic values on this occasion because of the man we honor and also because of the place in which I stand. I know that many in this audience have shared the concern that I have shared in recent years: due to the fact that the spotlight has been turned on some public officials who have not reached the standard of integrity that we think they should have reached, we have tended to lose faith in the integrity of all of our institutions.

Let me, as one who for almost a quarter of a century has had the opportunity to meet governors, congressmen, senators, state legislators, judges, and public officials all over this land—as a matter of fact, I have probably met more than any living American—just let me say something based on my own observations.

There are men, some, who fail to meet the standards of integrity which should be met by a public servant, but I want this audience to know that as I look at the men who serve in public life during my own generation, the great majority of congressmen, senators, governors, state legislators, mayors, and judges are honest, dedicated, decent men. And Karl Mundt represents that kind of honesty, decency, and honor. His public life stands for these values about which I have spoken. I am proud to have known him for twenty-two years. I am proud to have had his friendship and support in victory and also in defeat. And I am proud today to join with you in honoring him by dedicating in his name a library which will preserve those values for which and about which he has spoken so eloquently in thirty years of public life.

OUR NATIONAL SECURITY IS NOT NEGOTIABLE
Remarks of the President at Commencement
Exercises at the Air Force Academy, Colorado Springs
JUNE 4, 1969

General Moorman, Governor Love, Senator Allott, Senator Dominick, General McConnell, Secretary Seamans, all the distinguished guests on the platform, members of the graduating class, and this great audience here in Falcon Stadium:

Before addressing the members of the graduating class, I would like to be permitted a personal word to the people of Colorado and to the people of this city. I want to thank you for the very warm and gracious welcome you gave to me and the members of our family.

I well remember the conversations that I had with General Eisenhower in the months before he died. He often reminisced about the past, and among his fondest memories were his visits to Colorado. These were some of the happiest days of his life.

Yesterday, when we arrived in Colorado Springs, we stepped out of the aircraft, we breathed this wonderful fresh air, we looked off across to the mountains fifty miles away; and as we stood there we knew what he meant when he spoke of Colorado, its people, and also the climate and everything that all of you who live here know and love so much.

I should like to give you just one impression that shows you there is some continuity in history. Dwight David Eisenhower II, the grandson of General Eisenhower, and his namesake, as he saw this beautiful country and looked to the mountains off to the distance, said, "Gee, this is great country." I want you to know that I agree and I congratulate the Air Force for having the good judgment to locate the Air Force Academy here in Colorado Springs.

One other personal note: I had the opportunity before coming to this stadium to take a tour of some of the campus facilities and particularly the chapel. There has been some controversy about that chapel. This is the first time that I have seen it. I am not an architectural expert, but I think it is magnificent, and I think you can be very proud of the chapel at the Air Force Academy.

Now, if I could address the members of the graduating class.

For each of you, and your parents, and your countrymen, this is a moment of quiet pride.

After years of study and training you have earned the right to be saluted.

But you are beginning your careers at a difficult time in military life.

On a fighting front, you are asked to be ready to make unlimited sacrifice in a limited war.

On the home front, you are under attack from those who question the need for a strong national defense, and indeed see a danger in the power of the defenders.

You are entering the military service of your country when the nation's potential adversaries abroad have never been stronger and when your critics at home have never been more numerous.

It is open season on the armed forces. Military programs are ridiculed as needless if not deliberate waste. The military profession is derided in some of the so-called best circles of America. Patriotism is considered by some to be a backward fetish of the uneducated and unsophisticated. Nationalism is hailed and applauded as a panacea for the ills of every nation—except the United States of America.

This paradox of military power is a symptom of something far deeper that is stirring in our body politic. It goes beyond the dissent about the war in Vietnam. It goes behind the fear of the "military-industrial complex."

The underlying questions are really these:

What is America's role in the world? What are the responsibilities of a great nation toward protecting freedom beyond its shores? Can we ever be left in peace if we do not actively assume the burden of keeping the peace?

When great questions are posed, fundamental differences of opinion come into focus. It serves no purpose to gloss over these differences or to try to pretend that they are mere matters of degree.

Because there is one school of thought that holds that the road to understanding with the Soviet Union and Communist China lies through a downgrading of our own alliances and what amounts to a unilateral reduction of our arms—in order to demonstrate our "good faith."

They believe that we can be conciliatory and accommodating only if we do not have the strength to be otherwise. They believe America will be able to deal with the possibility of peace only when we are unable to cope with the threat of war.

Those who think that way have grown weary of the weight of free world leadership that fell upon us in the wake of World War II. They argue that we, the United States, are as much responsible for the tensions in the world as the adversary we face.

They assert that the United States is blocking the road to peace by maintaining its military strength at home and its defenses abroad. If we would only reduce our forces, they contend, tensions would disappear and the chances for peace would brighten.

America's powerful military presence on the world scene, they believe, makes peace abroad improbable and peace at home impossible.

Now we should never underestimate the appeal of the isolationist school of thought. Their slogans are simplistic and powerful: "Charity begins at home. Let's first solve our problems at home and then we can deal with the problems of the world."

This simple formula touches a responsive chord with many an overburdened taxpayer. It would be easy, easy for the President of the United States to buy some popularity by going along with the new isolationists. But I submit to you that it would be disastrous for our nation and the world.

I hold a totally different view of the world, and I come to a different conclusion about the direction America must take.

Imagine for a moment, if you will, what would happen to this world if America were to become a dropout in assuming the responsibility for defending peace and freedom. As every world leader knows, and as even the most outspoken critics of America would admit, the rest of the world would live in terror.

Because if America were to turn its back on the world, there would be peace that would settle over this planet, but it would be the kind of peace that suffocated freedom in Czechoslovakia.

The danger to us has changed, but it has not vanished. We must revitalize our alliances, not abandon them.

We must rule out unilateral disarmament, because in the real world it wouldn't work. If we pursue arms control as an end in itself, we will not achieve our end. The adversaries in the world are not in conflict because they are armed. They are armed because they are in conflict and have not yet learned peaceful ways to resolve their conflicting national interests.

The aggressors of this world are not going to give the United States a period of grace in which to put our domestic house in order— just as the crises within our society cannot be put on a back burner until we resolve the problem of Vietnam.

The most successful solutions that we can possibly imagine for our domestic programs will be meaningless if we are not around to enjoy them. Nor can we conduct a successful peace policy abroad if our society is at war with itself at home.

There is no advancement for Americans at home in a retreat from the problems of the world. I say that America has a vital national interest in world stability, and no other nation can uphold that interest for us.

We stand at a crossroad in our history. We shall reaffirm our destiny for greatness or we shall choose instead to withdraw into ourselves. The choice will affect far more than our foreign policy; it will determine the quality of our lives.

A nation needs many qualities, but it needs faith and confidence above all. Skeptics do not build societies; the idealists are the builders. Only societies that believe in themselves can rise to their challenges. Let us not, then, post a false choice between meeting our responsibilities abroad and meeting the needs of our people at home. We shall meet both or we shall meet neither.

That is why my disagreement with the skeptics and the isolationists is fundamental. They have lost the vision indispensable to great leadership. They observe the problems that confront us; they measure our resources and then they despair. When the first vessels set out from Europe for the new world these men would have weighed the risks and they would have stayed behind. When the colonists on the Eastern seaboard started across the Appalachians to the unknown reaches of the Ohio Valley, these men would have counted the costs and they would have stayed behind.

Our current exploration of space makes the point vividly: here is testimony to man's vision and to man's courage. The journey of the astronauts is more than a technical achievement: it is a reaching-out of the human spirit. It lifts our sight; it demonstrates that magnificent conceptions can be made real.

They inspire us and at the same time they teach us true humility. What could bring home to us more the limitations of the human scale than the hauntingly beautiful picture of our earth seen from the moon?

When the first man stands on the moon next month, every American will stand taller because of what he has done, and we should be proud of this magnificent achievement.

We will know then that every man achieves his own greatness by reaching out beyond himself, and so it is with nations. When a nation believes in itself—as Athenians did in their golden age, as Italians did in the Renaissance—that nation can perform miracles. Only when a nation means something to itself can it mean something to others.

That is why I believe a resurgence of American idealism can bring about a modern miracle—and that modern miracle is a world order of peace and justice.

I know that every member of this graduating class is, in that sense, an idealist.

However, I must warn you that in the years to come you may hear your commitment to the American responsibility in the world derided as a form of militarism. It is important that you recognize that strawman issue for what it is, the outward sign of a desire by some to turn America inward and to have America turn away from greatness. I am not speaking about those responsible critics who reveal waste and inefficiency in our defense establishment, who demand clear answers on procurement policies, who want to make sure new weapons systems will truly add to our defense. On the contrary, you should be in the vanguard of that movement. Nor do I speak of those with sharp eyes and sharp pencils who are examining our post-Vietnam planning with other pressing national priorities in mind. I count myself as one of those.

But as your Commander-in-Chief, I want to relay to you as future officers in our armed forces some of my thoughts on some of those great issues of national moment.

I worked closely with President Eisenhower for eight years. I know what he meant when he said: ". . . we must guard against the acquisition of unwarranted influence, whether sought or unsought, by the military-industrial complex."

Many people conveniently forget that he followed that warning with another: "We must also be alert to the equal and opposite danger that public policy could itself become the captive of a scientific-technological elite."

We sometimes forget that in that same Farewell Address, President Eisenhower spoke of the need for national security. He said: "A vital element in keeping the peace is our military establishment. Our arms must be mighty, ready for instant action, so that no potential aggressor may be tempted to risk his own destruction."

I say to you, my fellow Americans, let us never forget those wise words of one of America's greatest leaders.

The American defense establishment should never be a sacred cow, but on the other hand, the American military should never be anybody's scapegoat.

America's wealth is enormous, but it is not limitless. Every dollar available in the Federal government has been taken from the American people in taxes. A responsible government has a duty to be prudent when it spends the people's money. There is no more justification for wasting money on unnecessary military hardware than there is for wasting it on unwarranted social programs.

There can be no question that we should not spend unnecessarily for defense. But we must also not confuse our priorities.

The question, I submit, in defense spending is a very simple one: "How much is necessary?" The President of the United States is the man charged with making that judgment. After a complete review of our foreign and defense policies I have submitted requests to the Congress for military appropriations—some of these are admittedly controversial. These requests represent the minimum I believe essential for the United States to meet its current and long-range obligations to itself and to the free world. I have asked only for those programs and those expenditures that I believe are necessary to guarantee the security of this country and to honor our obligations. I will bear the responsibility for those judgments. I do not consider my recommendations infallible. But if I have made a mistake, I pray that it is on the side of too much and not too little. If we do too much it will cost us our money. If we do too little, it may cost us our lives.

Mistakes in military policy today can be irretrievable. Time lost in this age of science can never be regained. America had months in order to prepare and to catch up in order to wage World War I. We had months and even years in order to catch up so we could play a role in winning World War II. When a war can be decided in twenty minutes, the nation that is behind will have no time to catch up.

I say: Let America never fall behind in maintaining the defenses necessary for the strength of this nation.

I have no choice in my decisions but to come down on the side of security because history has dealt harshly with those nations who have taken the other course.

So, in that spirit, to the members of this graduating class, let me offer this credo for the defenders of our nation:

I believe that we must balance our need for survival as a nation with our need for survival as a people. Americans, soldiers and civilians, must remember that defense is not an end in itself—it is a way of holding fast to the deepest values known to civilized men.

I believe that our defense establishment will remain the servants of our national policy of bringing about peace in the world and that those in any way connected with the military must scrupulously avoid even the appearance of becoming the master of that policy.

I believe that every man in uniform is a citizen first and a serviceman second, and that we must resist any attempt to isolate or separate the defenders from the defended. So you can see that, in this regard, those who agitate for the removal of the ROTC from college campuses contribute to an unwanted militarism.

I believe that the basis for decisions on defense spending must be "what do we do, what do we need for our security" and not "what will this mean for business and employment." The Defense Department must never be considered as a modern WPA. There are far better ways for government to help ensure a sound prosperity and high employment. I feel that moderation has a moral significance only in those who have another choice. The weak can only plead; magnanimity and restraint gain moral meaning coming from the strong.

I believe that defense decisions must be made on the hard realities of the offensive capabilities of our potential adversaries, and not on the fervent hopes about their intentions. With Thomas Jefferson, we can prefer "the flatteries of hope" to the gloom of despair, but we cannot survive in the real world if we plan our defense in a dream world.

I believe we must take risks for peace—but calculated risks, not foolish risks. We shall not trade our defenses for a disarming smile or charming words. We are prepared for new initiatives in the control of arms in the context of other specific moves to reduce tensions around the world.

I believe that America is not going to become a garrison state or a welfare state or a police state, simply because the American people will defend our values from those forces external or internal that would challenge or erode them.

And I believe this above all: that this nation shall continue to be a source of world leadership, a source of freedom's strength, in creating a just world order that will bring an end to war.

Members of the graduating class and your colleagues in the Academy, a President shares a special bond with the men and women in the nation's armed forces. He feels that bond strongly at moments like these, facing all of you who have pledged your lives, your fortunes, and your sacred honor to the service of your country. He feels that bond most strongly when he presents the Medal of Honor to an eight-year-old boy who will never see his father again. Because of that bond, let me say this to you:

In the past generation, since 1941, this nation has paid for fourteen years of peace with fourteen years of war. The American war dead of this generation have been far greater than of all the preceding generations in American history. In terms of human suffering, this has been the costliest generation in the two centuries of our history.

Perhaps this is why my generation is so determined to pass on a different legacy. We want to redeem that sacrifice. We want to be remembered, not as the generation that suffered in war, but as the generation that was tempered in its fire for a great purpose: to make the kind of peace that the next generation will be able to keep.

This is a challenge worthy of the idealism which I know motivates every man who will receive his diploma today.

I am proud to have served in the armed forces of this nation in a war which ended before the members of this class were born.

It is my deepest hope and my belief that each of you will be able to look back on your military career with pride, not because of the wars in which you have fought, but because of the peace and freedom which your service will make possible for America and the world.

8

The

War

Against

Crime

The rise in the incidence of statutory crime was less an issue than a common political concern in the 1968 election. This problem, however, became inextricably tangled with the broader issue of law and order and its overtones of racial conflict and political disorder.

In that broader scope the issue was affected by differences on the rights of the individual in conflict with the power of the state and the common good.

President Nixon and Attorney General John Mitchell submitted to Congress twenty-one measures to control crime, in 1969, some affecting the District of Columbia, where the crime rise shamed the nation. Deeply rooted issues included preventive detention, "no-knock" narcotics raids, bail reform, and electronic "bugging."

Congress, seemingly so avid for instant action against crime, moved slowly, and a year after submission none of the Nixon-sponsored anticrime measures had been adopted. Two measures, the District of Columbia crime "package" and a bill strengthening narcotics control, appeared headed for final passage.

THE DEEP ROOTS OF ORGANIZED CRIME
Message to the Congress of the United States
APRIL 23, 1969

Today, organized crime has deeply penetrated broad segments of American life. In our great cities, it is operating prosperous criminal cartels. In our suburban areas and smaller cities, it is expanding its corrosive influence. Its economic base is principally derived from its virtual monopoly of illegal gambling, the numbers racket, and the importation of narcotics.

To a large degree, it underwrites the loan-sharking business in the United States and actively participates in fraudulent bankruptcies. It encourages street crime by inducing narcotics addicts to mug and rob. It encourages housebreaking and burglary by providing efficient disposal methods for stolen goods. It quietly continues to infiltrate and corrupt organized labor. It is increasing its enormous holdings and influence in the world of legitimate business.

To achieve his end, the organized criminal relies on physical terror and psychological intimidation, on economic retaliation and political bribery, on citizen indifference and governmental acquiescence. He corrupts our governing institutions and subverts our democratic processes. For him, the moral and legal subversion of our society is a lifelong and lucrative profession.

Many decent Americans contribute regularly, voluntarily, and unwittingly to the coffers of organized crime: the suburban housewife and the city slum-dweller who place a twenty-five-cent numbers bet, the bricklayer and college student who buy a football card, the businessman and the secretary who bet illegally on a horse.

Estimates of the "take" from illegal gambling alone in the United States run anywhere from $20 billion, which is over 2 percent of the nation's gross national product, to $50 billion, a figure larger than the entire Federal administrative budget for fiscal year 1951. This wealth is but one yardstick of the economic and political power held by the leaders of organized crime who operate with little limitation or restriction within our society.

Organized crime's victims range all across the social spectrum: the middle-class businessman enticed into paying usurious loan rates, the small merchant required to pay protection money, the white suburbanite and the black city-dweller destroying themselves with drugs, the elderly pensioner and the young married couple forced to pay higher prices for goods. The most tragic victims, of course, are the poor whose lack of financial resources, education, and acceptable living standards frequently breed the kind of resentment and hopelessness that make illegal gambling and drugs an attractive escape from the bleakness of ghetto life.

Background

For two decades now, since the Attorney General's Conference on Organized Crime in 1950, the Federal effort has slowly increased. Many of the nation's most notorious racketeers have been imprisoned or deported and many local organized crime business operations have been eliminated. But these successes have not substantially impeded the growth and power of organized criminal syndicates. Not a single one of the twenty-four Cosa Nostra families has been destroyed. They are more firmly entrenched and more secure than ever before.

It is vitally important that Americans see this alien organization for what it really is: a totalitarian and closed society operating within an open and democratic one. It has succeeded so far because an apathetic public is not aware of the threat it poses to American life. This public apathy has permitted most organized criminals to escape prosecution by corrupting officials, by intimidating witnesses, and by terrorizing victims into silence.

As a matter of national "public policy," I must warn our citizens that the threat of organized crime cannot be ignored or tolerated any longer. It will not be eliminated by loud voices and good intentions. It will be eliminated by carefully conceived, well-funded, and well-executed action plans. Furthermore, our action plans against organized crime must be established on a long-term basis in order to relentlessly pursue the criminal syndicate. This goal will not be easily attained. Over many decades organized crime has extended its roots deep into American society and they will not be easily extracted. Our success will first depend on the support of our citizens, who must be informed of the dangers that organized crime poses. Success also will require the help of Congress and of the state and local governments.

This Administration is urgently aware of the need for extraordinary action and I have already taken several significant steps aimed at combatting organized crime. I have pledged an unstinting commitment, with an unprecedented amount of money, manpower, and other resources to back up my promise to attack organized crime. For example, I have authorized the Attorney General to engage in wiretapping of organized racketeers. I have authorized the Attorney General to establish twenty Federal racketeering field offices all across the nation. I have authorized the Attorney General to establish a unique Federal-State Racket Squad in New York City. I have asked all Federal agencies to cooperate with the Department of Justice in this effort and to give priority to the organized crime drive. I have asked the Congress to increase the fiscal 1970 budget by $25 million, which will roughly double present expenditures for the organized crime effort.

In addition, I have asked the Congress to approve a $300 million appropriation in the 1970 budget for the Law Enforcement Assistance Administration. Most of these funds will go in block grants to help state and local law enforcement programs, and a substantial portion of this assistance money will be utilized to fight organized crime. I have had discussions with the state attorneys general and I have authorized the Attorney General to cooperate fully with the states and local communities in this national effort, and to extend help to them with every means at his disposal. Finally, I have directed the Attorney General to mount our Federal anti-organized crime offensive and to coordinate the Federal effort with state and local efforts where possible.

Assistance to States and Local Governments

Through the Law Enforcement Assistance Administration and other units of the Department of Justice, the Attorney General has already taken some initial steps:

1. A program is being established so that state and local law enforcement people can exchange recent knowledge on the most effective tactics to use against organized crime at the local level.

2. The Justice Department is furnishing technical assistance and financial help in the training of investigators, prosecutors, intelligence analysts, accountants, statisticians—the professional people needed to combat a sophisticated form of criminal activity.

3. The Justice Department is encouraging municipalities and states to re-examine their own laws in the organized crime area. We are also encouraging and assisting in the formation of statewide organized crime investigating and prosecuting units.

4. A computerized organized crime intelligence system is being developed to house detailed information on the personalities and activities of organized crime nationally. This system will also serve as a model for state computer intelligence systems, which will be partially funded by the Federal government.

5. We are fostering cooperation and coordination between states and between communities to avoid a costly duplication of effort and expense.

6. We are providing Federal aid for both state and local public information programs designed to alert the people to the nature and scope of organized crime activity in their communities.

These actions are being taken now. But the current level of Federal activity must be dramatically increased, if we expect progress. More men and money, new administrative actions, and new legal authority are needed.

Expanded Budget

There is no old law or new law that will be useful without the necessary manpower for enforcement. I am therefore, as stated, asking Congress to increase the fiscal year 1970 budget for dealing with organized crime by $25 million. This will roughly double the amount spent in the fight against organized crime during fiscal year 1970, and will bring the total Federal expenditures for the campaign against organized crime to the unprecedented total of $61 million. I urge Congress to approve our request for these vital funds.

Reorganization of the Crime Effort

I have directed the newly appointed Advisory Council on Executive Organization to examine the effectiveness of the Executive Branch in combatting crime—in particular, organized crime.

Because many departments and agencies of the Executive Branch are involved in the organized crime effort, I believe we can make lasting improvement only if we view this matter in the full context of executive operations.

Federal Racketeering Field Offices

The focal center of the Federal effort against organized crime is the Department of Justice. It coordinates the efforts of all of the Federal agencies. To combine in one cohesive unit a cadre of experienced Federal investigators and prosecutors, to maintain a Federal presence in organized crime problem areas throughout the nation on a continuing basis, and to institutionalize and utilize the valuable experience that has been gained by the "Strike Forces" under the direction of the Department of Justice, the Attorney General has now established Federal Racketeering Field Offices in Boston, Brooklyn, Buffalo, Chicago, Detroit, Miami, Newark, and Philadelphia. These offices bring together, in cohesive single units, experienced prosecutors from the Justice Department, Special Agents of the FBI, investigators of the Bureau of Narcotics and Dangerous Drugs, the finest staff personnel from the Bureau of Customs, the Securities and Exchange Commission, the Internal Revenue Service, the Post Office, the Secret Service, and other Federal offices with expertise in diverse areas of organized crime.

The Racketeering Field Offices will be able to throw a tight net of Federal law around an organized crime concentration, and through large-scale target investigations, we believe we can obtain the prosecutions that will imprison the leaders, paralyze the administrators, frighten the street workers, and eventually paralyze the whole organized crime syndicate in any one particular city. The Attorney General plans to set up at least a dozen additional field offices within the next two years.

Federal-State Racket Squad

Investigations of the national crime syndicate, the Cosa Nostra, show its membership at some five thousand, divided into twenty-four "families" around the nation. In most cities organized crime activity is dominated by a single "family"; in New York City, however, the lucrative franchise is divided among five such "families."

To deal with this heavy concentration of criminal elements in the nation's largest city, a new Federal-State Racket Squad is being established in the Southern District of New York. It will include attorneys and investigators from the Justice Department as well as from New York State and City. This squad will be directed by the Department of Justice, in conjunction with a supervisory council of officials from state and local participating agencies, who will formulate policy, device strategy, and oversee tactical operations. Building on the experience of this special Federal-State Racket Squad, the Attorney General will be working with state and local authorities in other major problem areas to determine whether this concept of governmental partnership should be expanded to those areas through the formation of additional squads.

New Legislation

From his studies in recent weeks the Attorney General has concluded that new weapons and tools are needed to enable the Federal government to strike both at the Cosa Nostra hierarchy and the sources of revenue that feed the coffers of organized crime. Accordingly, the Attorney General will ask Congress for new laws, and I urge Congress to act swiftly and favorably on the Attorney General's request.

WITNESS IMMUNITY

First, we need a new broad general witness immunity law to cover all cases involving the violation of a Federal statute. I commend to the Congress for its consideration the recommendations of the National Commission on Reform of Federal Criminal Laws. Under the Commission's proposal, a witness could not be prosecuted on the basis of anything he said while testifying, but he would not be immune from prosecution based on other evidence of his offense. Furthermore, once the government has granted the witness such immunity, a refusal then to testify would bring a prison sentence for contempt. With this new law, government should be better able to gather evidence to strike at the leadership of organized crime and not just the rank and file. The Attorney General has also advised me that the Federal government will make special provisions for protecting witnesses who fear to testify due to intimidation.

WAGERING TAX AMENDMENTS

We shall ask for swift enactment of S. 1624 or its companion bill H.R. 322, sponsored by Senator Roman Hruska of Nebraska and Congressman Richard Poff of Virginia, respectively. These measures would amend the wagering tax laws and enable the Internal Revenue Service to play a more active and effective role in collecting the revenues owed on wagers; the bills would also increase the Federal operator's tax on gamblers from $50 annually to $1,000.

CORRUPTION

For most large-scale illegal gambling enterprises to continue operations over any extended period of time, the cooperation of corrupt police or local officials is necessary. This bribery and corruption of government closest to the people is a deprival of one of a citizen's most basic rights. We shall seek legislation to make this form of systematic corruption of community political leadership and law enforcement a Federal crime. This law would enable the Federal government to prosecute both the corruptor and the corrupted.

ILLEGAL GAMBLING BUSINESSES

We also shall request new legislation making it a Federal crime to engage in an illicit gambling operation from which five or more persons derive income, which has been in operation more than thirty days, or from which the daily "take" exceeds $2,000. The purpose of this legislation is to bring under Federal jurisdiction all large-scale illegal gambling operations which involve or affect interstate commerce. The effect of the law will be to give the Attorney General broad latitude to assist local and state government in cracking down on illegal gambling, the wellspring of organized crime's financial reservoir.

This Administration has concluded that the major thrust of its concerted anti-organized crime effort should be directed against gambling activities. While gambling may seem to most Americans to be the least reprehensible of all the activities of organized crime, it is gambling which provides the bulk of the revenues that eventually go into usurious loans, bribes of police and local officials, "campaign contributions" to politicians, the wholesale narcotics traffic, the infiltration of legitimate businesses, and to pay for the large stables of lawyers and accountants and assorted professional men who are in the hire of organized crime.

Gambling income is the lifeline of organized crime. If we can cut it or constrict it, we will be striking close to its heart.

PROCEDURAL LAWS

With regard to improving the procedural aspects of the criminal law as it relates to the prosecution of organized crime, the Attorney General has been working with the Senate Subcommittee on Criminal Laws and Procedures to develop and perfect S. 30, the "Organized Crime Control Act of 1969." As Attorney General Mitchell indicated in his testimony on that bill, we support its objectives. It is designed to improve the investigation and prosecution of organized crime cases, and to provide appropriate sentencing for convicted offenders. I feel confident that it will be a useful new tool.

DEVELOPMENT OF NEW LAWS

Finally, I want to mention an area where we are examining the need for new laws: the infiltration of organized crime into fields of legitimate business. The syndicate-owned business, financed by illegal revenues and operated outside the rules of fair competition of the American marketplace, cannot be tolerated in a system of free enterprise. Accordingly, the Attorney General is examining the potential application of the theories underlying our antitrust laws as a potential new weapon.

The injunction with its powers of contempt and seizure, monetary fines, and treble damage actions, and the powers of a forfeiture proceeding, suggest a new panoply of weapons to attach the property of organized crime—rather than the unimportant persons (the fronts) who technically head up syndicate-controlled businesses. The arrest, conviction, and imprisonment of a Mafia lieutenant can curtail operations, but does not put the syndicate out of business. As long as the property of organized crime remains, new leaders will step forward to take the place of those we jail. However, if we can levy fines on their real estate corporations, if we can seek treble damages against their trucking firms and banks, if we can seize the liquor in their warehouses, I think we can strike a critical blow at the organized crime conspiracy.

Clearly, the success or failure of any ambitious program such as I have outlined in this message depends on many factors. I am confident the Congress will supply the funds and the requested legislation, the states and communities across the country will take advantage of the Federal capability and desire to assist and participate with them, and the Federal personnel responsible for programs and actions will vigorously carry out their mission.

THE FLOOD OF SMUT
Message to the Congress of the United States
MAY 2, 1969

American homes are being bombarded with the largest volume of sex-oriented mail in history. Most of it is unsolicited, unwanted, and deeply offensive to those who receive it. Since 1964, the number of complaints to the Post Office about this salacious mail has almost doubled. One hundred and forty thousand letters of protest came in during the last nine months alone, and the volume is increasing. Mothers and fathers by the tens of thousands have written to the White House and the Congress. They resent these intrusions into their homes, and they are asking for Federal assistance to protect their children against exposure to erotic publications.

The problem has no simple solution. Many publications dealing with sex—in a way that is offensive to many people—are protected under the broad umbrella of the First Amendment prohibition against any law "abridging the freedom of speech, or of the press."

However, there are constitutional means available to assist parents seeking to protect their children from the flood of sex-oriented materials moving through the mails. The courts have not left society defenseless against the smut peddler; they have not ruled out reasonable government action.

Cognizant of the constitutional strictures, aware of recent Supreme Court decisions, this Administration has carefully studied the legal terrain of this problem.

We believe we have discovered some untried and hopeful approaches that will enable the Federal government to become a full partner with states and individual citizens in drying up a primary source of this social evil. I have asked the Attorney General and the Postmaster General to submit to Congress three new legislative proposals.

The first would prohibit outright the sending of offensive sex materials to any child or teenager under 18. The second would prohibit the sending of advertising designed to appeal to a prurient interest in sex. It would apply regardless of the age of the recipient. The third measure complements the second by providing added protection from the kind of smut advertising now being mailed, unsolicited, into so many homes.

Protecting Minors

Many states have moved ahead of the Federal government in drawing distinctions between materials considered obscene for adults and materials considered obscene for children. Some of these states, such as New York, have taken substantial strides toward protecting their youth from materials that may not be obscene by adult standards but which could be damaging to the healthy growth and development of a child. The United States Supreme Court has recognized, in repeated decisions, the unique status of minors and has upheld the New York statute. Building on judicial precedent, we hope to provide a new measure of Federal protection for the young.

I ask Congress to make it a Federal crime to use the mails or other facilities of commerce to deliver to anyone under eighteen years of age material dealing with a sexual subject in a manner unsuitable for young people.

The proposed legislation would not go into effect until the sixth month after passage. The delay would provide mailers of these materials time to remove from their mailing lists the names of all youngsters under eighteen. The Federal government would become a full partner with parents and states in protecting children from much of the interstate commerce in pornography. A first violation of this statute would be punishable by a maximum penalty of five years in prison and a $50,000 fine; subsequent violations carry greater penalties.

Prurient Advertising

Many complaints about salacious literature coming through the mails focus on advertisements. Many of these ads are designed by the advertiser to appeal exclusively to a prurient interest. This is clearly a form of pandering.

I ask the Congress to make it a Federal crime to use the mails, or other facilities of commerce, for the commercial exploitation of a prurient interest in sex through advertising.

This measure focuses on the intent of the dealer in sex-oriented materials and his methods of marketing his materials. Through the legislation we hope to impose restrictions on dealers who flood the mails with grossly offensive advertisements intended to produce a market for their smut materials by stimulating the prurient interest of the recipient. Under the new legislation, this form of pandering could bring a maximum penalty of five years' imprisonment and a fine of $50,000 for a first offense, and ten years and a fine of $100,000 for subsequent offenses.

Invasion of Privacy

There are other erotic, sex-oriented advertisements that may be constitutionally protected but which are, nonetheless, offensive to the citizen who receives them in his home. No American should be forced to accept this kind of advertising through the mails.

In 1967 Congress passed a law to help deal with this kind of pandering. The law permits an addressee to determine himself whether he considers the material offensive in that he finds it "erotically arousing or sexually provocative." If the recipient deems it so, he can obtain from the Postmaster General a judicially enforceable order prohibiting the sender from making any further mailings to him or his children, and requiring the mailer to delete them from all his mailing lists.

More than 170,000 persons have requested such orders. Many citizens, however, are still unaware of this legislation, or do not know how to utilize its provisions. Accordingly, I have directed the Postmaster General to provide every Congressional office with pamphlets explaining how each citizen can use this law to protect his home from offensive advertising. I urge Congress to assist our effort for the widest possible distribution of these pamphlets.

This pandering law was based on the principle that no citizen should be forced to receive advertisements for sex-oriented matter he finds offensive. I endorse that principle and believe its application should be broadened.

I therefore ask Congress to extend the existing law to enable a citizen to protect his home from any intrusion of sex-oriented advertising—regardless of whether or not a citizen has ever received such mailings.

This new stronger measure would require mailers and potential mailers to respect the expressed wishes of those citizens who do not wish to have sex-oriented advertising sent into their homes. These citizens will put smut-mailers on notice simply by filing their objections with a designated postal authority. To deliberately send such advertising to their homes would be an offense subject to both civil and criminal penalties.

As I have stated earlier, there is no simple solution to this problem. However, the measures I have proposed will go far toward protecting our youth from smut coming through the mails; they will place new restrictions upon the abuse of the postal service for pandering purposes; they will reinforce a man's right to privacy in his own home. These proposals, however, are not the whole answer.

The ultimate answer lies not with the government but with the people. What is required is a citizens' crusade against the obscene. When indecent books no longer find a market, when pornographic films can no longer draw an audience, when obscene plays open to empty houses, then the tide will turn. Government can maintain the dikes against obscenity, but only people can turn back the tide.

THE MENACE OF NARCOTICS
Message to the Congress of the United States
JULY 14, 1969

Within the last decade the abuse of drugs has grown from essentially a local police problem into a serious national threat to the personal health and safety of millions of Americans.

A national awareness of the gravity of the situation is needed; a new urgency and concerted national policy are needed at the Federal level to begin to cope with this growing menace to the general welfare of the United States.

Between the years 1960 and 1967 juvenile arrests involving the use of drugs rose by almost 800 percent; half of those now being arrested for the illicit use of narcotics are under twenty-one years of age. New York City alone has records of some forty thousand heroin addicts, and the number rises between seven thousand and nine thousand a year. These official statistics are only the tip of an iceberg whose dimensions we can only surmise.

The number of narcotics addicts across the United States is now estimated to be in the hundreds of thousands. Another estimate is that several million American college students have at least experimented with marijuana, hashish, LSD, amphetamines, or barbiturates. It is doubtful that an American parent can send a son or daughter to college today without exposing the young man or woman to drug abuse. Parents must also be concerned about the availability and use of such drugs in our high schools and junior high schools.

The habit of the narcotics addict is not only a danger to himself, but a threat to the community where he lives. Narcotics have been cited as a primary cause of the enormous increase in street crimes over the last decade.

As the addict's tolerance for drugs increases, his demand for drugs rises, and the cost of his habit grows. It can easily reach hundreds of dollars a day. Since an underworld "fence" will give him only a fraction of the value of goods he steals, an addict can be forced to commit two or three burglaries a day to maintain his habit. Street robberies, prostitution, even the enticing of others into addiction to drugs—an addict will reduce himself to any offense, any degradation in order to acquire the drugs he craves.

However far the addict himself may fall, his offenses against himself and society do not compare with the inhumanity of those who make a living exploiting the weakness and desperation of their fellow men. Society has few judgments too severe, few penalties too harsh for the men who make their livelihood in the narcotics traffic.

It has been a common oversimplification to consider narcotics addiction, or drug abuse, to be a law enforcement problem alone. Effective control of illicit drugs requires the cooperation of many agencies of the Federal and local and state governments; it is beyond the province of any one of them alone. At the Federal level the burden of the national effort must be carried by the Departments of Justice, Health, Education and Welfare, and the Treasury. I am proposing ten specific steps as this Administration's initial counter-moves against this growing national problem.

1. FEDERAL LEGISLATION

To more effectively meet the narcotics and dangerous drug problems at the Federal level, the Attorney General is forwarding to the Congress a comprehensive legislative proposal to control these drugs. This measure will place in a single statute, a revised and modern plan for control. Current laws in this field are inadequate and outdated.

I consider the legislative proposal a fair, rational, and necessary approach to the total drug problem. It will tighten the regulatory controls and protect the public against illicit diversion of many of these drugs from legitimate channels. It will ensure greater accountability and better recordkeeping. It will give law enforcement stronger and better tools that are sorely needed so that those charged with enforcing these laws can do so more effectively. Further, this proposal creates a more flexible mechanism which will allow quicker control of new dangerous drugs before their misuse and abuse reach epidemic proportions. I urge the Congress to take favorable action on this bill.

In mid-May the Supreme Court struck down segments of the marijuana laws and called into question some of the basic foundations for the other existing drug statutes. I have also asked the Attorney General to submit an interim measure to correct the constitutional deficiencies of the Marijuana Tax Act as pointed out in the Supreme Court's recent decision. I urge Congress to act swiftly and favorably on the proposal to close the gap now existing in the Federal law and thereby give the Congress time to carefully examine the comprehensive drug control proposal.

2. STATE LEGISLATION

The Department of Justice is developing a model State Narcotics and Dangerous Drugs Act. This model law will be made available to the fifty state governments. This legislation is designed to improve state laws in dealing with this serious problem and to complement the comprehensive drug legislation being proposed to Congress at the national level. Together these proposals will provide an interlocking trellis of laws which will enable government at all levels to control the problem more effectively.

3. INTERNATIONAL COOPERATION

Most of the illicit narcotics and high-potency marijuana consumed in the United States is produced abroad and clandestinely imported. I have directed the Secretary of State and the Attorney General to explore new avenues of cooperation with foreign governments to stop the production of this contraband at its sources. The United States will cooperate with foreign governments working to eradicate the production of illicit drugs within their own frontiers. I have further authorized these Cabinet officers to formulate plans that will lead to meetings at the law enforcement level between the United States and foreign countries now involved in the drug traffic, either as originators or avenues of transit.

4. SUPPRESSION OF ILLEGAL IMPORTATION

Our efforts to eliminate these drugs at their point of origin will be coupled with new efforts to intercept them at their point of illegal entry into the United States. The Department of the Treasury, through the Bureau of Customs, is charged with enforcing the nation's smuggling laws. I have directed the Secretary of the Treasury to initiate a major new effort to guard the nation's borders and ports against the growing volume of narcotics from abroad. There is a recognized need for more men and facilities in the Bureau of Customs to carry out this directive. At my request the Secretary of the Treasury has submitted a substantial program for increased manpower and facilities in the Bureau of Customs for this purpose which is under intensive review.

In the early days of this Administration, I requested that the Attorney General form an interdepartmental task force to conduct a comprehensive study of the problem of unlawful trafficking in narcotics and dangerous drugs. One purpose of the task force has been to examine the existing programs of law enforcement agencies concerned with the problem in an effort to improve their coordination and efficiency. I now want to report that this task force has completed its study and has a recommended plan of action, for immediate and long-term implementation, designed to reduce substantially the illicit trafficking in narcotics, marijuana, and dangerous drugs across United States borders.

To implement the recommended plan, I have directed the Attorney General to organize and place into immediate operation an "action task force" to undertake a frontal attack on the problem. There are high profits in the illicit market for those who smuggle narcotics and drugs into the United States; we intend to raise the risks and cost of engaging in this wretched traffic.

5. SUPPRESSION OF NATIONAL TRAFFICKING

Successful prosecution of an increased national effort against illicit drug trafficking will require not only new resources and men, but also a redeployment of existing personnel within the Department of Justice.

I have directed the Attorney General to create, within the Bureau of Narcotics and Dangerous Drugs, a number of special investigative units. These special forces will have the capacity to move quickly into any area in which intelligence indicates major criminal enterprises are engaged in the narcotics traffic. To carry out this directive, there will be a need for additional manpower within the Bureau of Narcotics and Dangerous Drugs. The budgetary request for fiscal year 1970 now pending before the Congress will initiate this program. Additional funds will be requested in fiscal year 1971 to fully deploy the necessary special investigative units.

6. EDUCATION

Proper evaluation and solution of the drug problem in this country has been severely handicapped by a dearth of scientific information on the subject—and the prevalence of ignorance and misinformation. Different "experts" deliver solemn judgments which are poles apart. As a result of these conflicting judgments Americans seem to have divided themselves on the issue, along generational lines.

There are reasons for this lack of knowledge. First, widespread drug use is a comparatively recent phenomenon in the United States. Second, it frequently involves chemical formulations which are novel or age-old drugs little used in this country until very recently. The volume of definitive medical data remains small—and what exists has not been broadly disseminated. This vacuum of knowledge—as was predictable—has been filled by rumors and rash judgments, often formed with a minimal experience with a particular drug, sometimes formed with no experience or knowledge at all.

The possible danger to the health or well-being of even a casual user of drugs is too serious to allow ignorance to prevail or for this information gap to remain open. The American people need to know what dangers and what risks are inherent in the use of the various kinds of drugs readily available in illegal markets today. I have therefore directed the Secretary of Health, Education and Welfare, assisted by the Attorney General through the Bureau of Narcotics and Dangerous Drugs, to gather all authoritative information on the subject and to compile a balanced and objective educational program to bring the facts to every American—especially our young people.

With this information in hand, the overwhelming majority of students and young people can be trusted to make a prudent judgment as to their personal course of conduct.

7. RESEARCH

In addition to gathering existing data, it is essential that we acquire new knowledge in the field. We must know more about both the short- and long-range effects of the use of drugs being taken in such quantities by so many of our people. We need more study as well to find the key to releasing men from the bonds of dependency forged by any continued drug abuse.

The National Institute of Mental Health has primary responsibility in this area, and I am further directing the Secretary of Health, Education and Welfare to expand existing efforts to acquire new knowledge and a broader understanding in this entire area.

8. REHABILITATION

Considering the risks involved, including those of arrests and prosecution, the casual experimenter with drugs of any kind must be considered at the very least rash and foolish. But the psychologically dependent regular users and the physically addicted are genuinely sick people. While this sickness cannot excuse the crimes they commit, it does help to explain them. Society has an obligation both to itself and to these people to help them break the chains of their dependency.

Currently, a number of Federal, state, and private programs of rehabilitation are being operated. These programs utilize separately and together psychiatry, psychology, and "substitute drug" therapy. At this time, however, we are without adequate data to evaluate their full benefit. We need more experience with them and more knowledge. Therefore, I am directing the Secretary of Health, Education and Welfare to provide every assistance to those pioneering in the field, and to sponsor and conduct research on the Federal level. This Department will act as a clearinghouse for the collection and dissemination of drug abuse data and experience in the area of rehabilitation.

I have further instructed the Attorney General to ensure that all

Federal prisoners who have been identified as dependent upon drugs be afforded the most up-to-date treatment available.

9. TRAINING PROGRAM

The enforcement of narcotics laws requires considerable expertise, and hence considerable training. The Bureau of Narcotics and Dangerous Drugs provides the bulk of this training in the Federal government. Its programs are extended to include not only its own personnel, but state and local police officers, forensic chemists, foreign nationals, college deans, campus security officers, and members of industry engaged in the legal distribution of drugs.

Last year special training in the field of narcotics and dangerous drug enforcement was provided for twenty-seven hundred state and local law enforcement officials. In fiscal year 1969 we expanded the program an estimated 300 percent in order to train some eleven thousand persons. During the current fiscal year we plan to redouble again that effort—to provide training to twenty-two thousand state and local officers. The training of these experts must keep pace with the rise in the abuse of drugs, if we are ever to control it.

10. LOCAL LAW ENFORCEMENT CONFERENCES

The Attorney General intends to begin a series of conferences with law enforcement executives from the various states and [with] concerned Federal officials. The purposes of these conferences will be several: first, to obtain firsthand information, more accurate data, on the scope of the drug problem at that level; second, to discuss the specific areas where Federal assistance and aid can best be most useful; third, to exchange ideas and evaluate mutual policies. The end result, we hope, will be a more coordinated effort that will bring us visible progress for the first time in an alarming decade.

These then are the first ten steps in the national effort against narcotics, marijuana, and other dangerous drug abuse. Many steps are already under way. Many will depend upon the support of the Congress. I am asking, with this message, that you act swiftly and favorably on the legislative proposals that will soon be forthcoming, along with the budgetary requests required if our efforts are to be successful. I am confident that Congress shares with me the grave concern over this critical problem, and that Congress will do all that is necessary to mount and continue a new and effective Federal program aimed at eradicating this rising sickness in our land.

9

Toward

a

Better

Postal

Service

Certain as death and taxes, deficits and increasing breakdowns in mail service brought the politically related U.S. postal system to its time of crisis in the first year of the Nixon Administration.

First, President Nixon proposed divorcing the service from politics and then he offered a broader proposal for a government-owned corporation to deliver the mail. He announced a policy of dispensing postmasterships on the basis of merit rather than as political patronage. The President tied passage of postal reform to proposals in Congress for postal pay increases.

Discontented postal workers would not wait. Over the heads of union leadership, illegal work stoppages caused Nixon to call out troops to keep large city post offices running. Postal reform followed behind pay increases—when the dispute was settled.

Nixon's proposals fell short of the privately owned public utility that many contended could operate the mails as efficiently as private telephone companies in another field of communications.

With a reformed postal service under control of a nonpolitical government corporation the problem would remain the same: how to operate the postal system without deficits and more efficiently.

NONPOLITICAL POSTMASTERS
Message to the Congress of the United States
FEBRUARY 25, 1969

Reform of the postal system is long overdue.

The postal service touches the lives of all Americans. Many of our citizens feel that today's service does not meet today's needs, much less the needs of tomorrow. I share this view.

In the months ahead, I expect to propose comprehensive legislation for postal reform.

If this long-range program is to succeed, I consider it essential, as a first step, that the Congress remove the last vestiges of political patronage in the Post Office Department.

Accordingly, I urge the Congress promptly to enact legislation that would:

—Eliminate the present statutory requirement for Presidential appointment and Senatorial confirmation of postmasters of first-, second-, and third-class post offices;

—Provide for appointment of all postmasters by the Postmaster General in the competitive civil service; and

195

—Prohibit political considerations in the selection or promotion of postal employees.

Such legislation would make it possible for future postmasters to be chosen in the same way that career employees have long been chosen in the other executive departments. It would not, however, affect the status of postmasters now in office.

Adoption of this proposal by the Congress would assure all of the American people—and particularly the more than 750,000 dedicated men and women who work in the postal service—that future appointments and promotions in this important department are going to be made on the basis of merit and fitness for the job, and not on the basis of political affiliations or political influence.

The tradition of political patronage in the Post Office Department extends back to the earliest days of the Republic. In a sparsely populated country, where postal officials faced few of the management problems so familiar to modern postmasters, the patronage system may have been a defensible method of selecting jobholders. As the operation of the postal service has become more complex, however, the patronage system has become an increasingly costly luxury. It is a luxury that the nation can no longer afford.

In the past two decades, there has been increasing agreement that postmaster appointments should be made on a nonpolitical basis. Both the first and second Hoover Commissions emphasized the need for such action. So did the recent President's Commission on Postal Organization, headed by Frederick R. Kappel. President Harry S Truman and many members of Congress from both political parties have proposed legislation designed to take politics out of postal appointments. In the 90th Congress, the Senate, by a vote of 75 to 9, passed a bill containing a provision that would have placed postal appointments on a merit basis. Forty-two such bills were introduced in the House of Representatives during the 90th Congress.

The overwhelmingly favorable public comment that followed my recent announcement of our intention to disregard political consideration in selecting postmasters and rural carriers suggests that the American people are more than ready for legislative action on this matter. The time for such action is now at hand.

The benefits to be derived from such legislation are, I believe, twofold.

First, the change would expand opportunities for advancement on the part of our present postal employees. These are hard-working and loyal men and women. In the past, many of them have not received adequate recognition or well-deserved promotions for reasons which have had nothing to do with their fitness for higher position or the quality of their work. For reasons of both efficiency and morale this situation must be changed.

Secondly, I believe that over a period of time the use of improved professional selection methods will improve the level of competence of those who take on these important postal responsibilities.

I would not request this legislation without also presenting a plan which ensures that the new selection process will be effectively and impartially administered. The Postmaster General has such a plan.

He is creating a high-level, impartial national board to assist him in the future selection of postmasters for the four hundred largest post offices in the country. Regional boards, also made up of exceptionally well-qualified citizens, will perform a similar task in connection with the selection of other postmasters. First consideration will be given to the promotion, on a competitive basis, of present postal employees.

The Postmaster General has also initiated action to improve the criteria by which postmasters are selected. The revised criteria will emphasize managerial competence, human relations sensitivity, responsiveness to customer concerns, an understanding of labor relations, and other important qualities.

Proposals for additional legislation dealing with the selection process will be included in the broad program for postal reform that the Postmaster General is now preparing.

Some of the needs of the Post Office clearly require extensive study before detailed solutions can be proposed. Other problems can and should be dealt with now. One objective which can be met promptly is that of taking politics out of the Post Office, and I strongly recommend the swift enactment of legislation that will allow us to achieve that goal. Such legislation will be an important first step "toward postal excellence."

A CORPORATION TO HANDLE OUR MAIL
Message to the Congress of the United States
MAY 27, 1969

Total reform of the nation's postal system is absolutely essential.

The American people want dependable, reasonably priced mail service, and postal employees want the kind of advantages enjoyed by workers in other major industries. Neither goal can be achieved within the postal system we have today.

The Post Office is not keeping pace with the needs of our expanding population or the rightful aspirations of our postal workers.

Encumbered by obsolete facilities, inadequate capital, and outdated operation practices, the Post Office Department is failing the postal worker in terms of truly rewarding employment. It is time for a change.

Two years ago Lawrence F. O'Brien, then Postmaster General, recognized that the Post Office was in "a race with catastrophe," and made the bold proposal that the postal system be converted into a government-owned corporation. As a result of Mr. O'Brien's recommendations, a Presidential Commission was established to make a searching study of our postal system. After considering all the alternatives, the Commission likewise recommended a government corporation. Last January, President Johnson endorsed that recommendation in his State of the Union message.

One of my first actions as President was to direct Postmaster General Winton M. Blount to review that proposal and others. He has made his own first-hand study of the problems besetting the postal service, and after a careful analysis has reported to me that only a complete reorganization of the postal system can avert the steady deterioration of this vital public service.

I am convinced that such a reorganization is essential. The arguments are overwhelming and the support is bipartisan. Postal Reform is not a partisan political issue, it is an urgent national requirement.

Career Opportunities and Working Conditions

For many years the postal worker walked a dead-end street. Promotions all too often were earned by the right political connections rather than by merit. This Administration has taken steps to eliminate political patronage in the selection of postal employees; but there is more—much more—that must be done.

Postal employees must be given a work environment comparable to that found in the finest American enterprises. Today, particularly in our larger cities, postal workers labor in crowded, dismal, old-fashioned buildings that are little short of disgraceful. Health services, employee facilities, training programs, and other benefits enjoyed by the worker in private industry and in other Federal agencies are all too often unavailable to the postal worker. In an age when machines do the heavy work for private companies, the postal worker still shoulders, literally, the burden of the nation's mail. That mail fills more than a billion sacks a year; and the men and women who move those sacks need help.

Postal employees must have a voice in determining their conditions of employment. They must be given a stake in the quality of the service the Department provides the public; they must be given a reason for pride in themselves and in the job they do. The time for action is now.

Higher Deficits and Increasing Rates

During all but seventeen years since 1838, when deficit financing became a way of life for the Post Office, the postal system has cost more than it has earned.

In this fiscal year the Department will drain over $1 billion from the national treasury to cover the deficit incurred in operating the Post Office. Over the last decade the tax money used to shore up the postal system has amounted to more than $8 billion. Almost twice that amount will be diverted from the Treasury in the next ten years if the practices of the past are continued. We must not let that happen.

The money to meet these huge postal deficits comes directly out of the taxpayer's pocket—regardless of how much he uses the mails. It is bad business, bad government, and bad politics to pour this kind of tax money into an inefficient postal service. Every taxpayer in the United States—as well as every user of the mails—has an important stake in seeing that the Federal government institutes the kind of reform that is needed to give the nation a modern and well-managed postal system. Without such a system Congress will either have to raise postage rates far above any level presently contemplated, or the taxpayers will have to shoulder the burden of paying postal deficits the like of which they have never seen before.

Neither alternative is acceptable. The nation simply cannot afford the cost of maintaining an inefficient postal system. The will of the Congress and the will of the people is clear. They want fast, dependable, and low-cost mail service. They want an end to the continuing cycle of higher deficits and increasing rates.

Quality Postal Service

The Post Office is a business that provides a vital service which its customers, like the customers of a private business, purchase directly. A well-managed business provides dependable service; but complaints about the quality of postal service under existing procedures are widespread. While most mail ultimately arrives at its destination, there is no assurance that important mail will arrive on time; and late mail—whether a birthday card or a proxy statement—is often no better than lost mail.

Delays and breakdowns constantly threaten the mails. A complete breakdown in service did in fact occur in 1966 in one of our largest cities, causing severe economic damage and personal hardship. Similar breakdowns could occur at any time in many of our major post offices. A major modernization program is essential to ensure against catastrophe in the Post Office.

A modern postal service will not mean fewer postal workers. Mail volume—tied as it is to economic activity—is growing at such a rate that there will be no cutback in postal jobs even with the most dramatic gains in postal efficiency. Without a modernized postal system, however, more than a quarter of a million new postal workers will be needed in the next decade simply to move the growing mountain of mail. The savings that can be realized by holding employment near present levels can and should mean more pay and increased benefits for the three quarters of a million men and women who will continue to work in the postal service.

Opportunity Through Reform

While the work of the Post Office is that of a business enterprise, its organization is that of a political department. Traditionally it has been run as a Cabinet agency of the United States government—one in which politics has been as important as efficient mail delivery. Under the present system those responsible for managing the postal service do not have the authority that the managers of any enterprise must have over prices, wages, location of facilities, transportation and procurement activities, and personnel policy.

Changes in our society have resulted in changes in the function of the Post Office Department. The postal system must be given a nonpolitical management structure consistent with the job it has to perform as a supplier of vital services to the public. Times change, and now is the time for change in the postal system.

I am, therefore, sending to the Congress reform legislation entitled the Postal Service Act of 1969.

Postal Service Act of 1969

The reform that I propose represents a basic and sweeping change in direction; the ills of the postal service cannot be cured by partial reform.

The Postal Service Act of 1969 provides for:

—Removal of the Post Office from the Cabinet.

—Creation of an independent Postal Service wholly owned by the Federal government.

—New and extensive collective bargaining rights for postal employees.

—Bond financing for major improvements.

—A fair and orderly procedure for changing postage rates, subject to Congressional review.

—Regular reports to Congress to facilitate Congressional oversight of the postal system.

—A self-supporting postal system.

The new government-owned corporation will be known as the United States Postal Service. It will be administered by a nine-member board of directors selected without regard to political affiliation. Seven members of the board, including the chairman, will be appointed by the President with the advice and consent of the Senate. These seven members will select a full-time chief executive officer, who will join with the seven others to select a second full-time executive who will also serve on· the board.

Employees will retain their Civil Service annuity rights, veterans' preference, and other benefits.

The Postal Service is unique in character. Therefore, there will be for the first time in history true collective bargaining in the postal system. Postal employees in every part of the United States will be given a statutory right to negotiate directly with management over wages and working conditions. A fair and impartial mechanism—with provision for binding arbitration—will be established to resolve negotiating impasses and disputes arising under labor agreements.

For the first time local management will have the authority to work with employees to improve local conditions. A modernization fund adequate to the needs of the service will be available. The postal worker will finally take his rightful place beside the worker in private industry.

The Postal Service will become entirely self-supporting, except for such subsidies as Congress may wish to provide for specific public service groups. The Postal Service, like the Tennessee Valley Authority and similar public authorities, will be able to issue bonds as a means of raising funds needed for expansion and modernization of postal facilities and other purposes.

Proposals for changes in classes of mail or postage rates will be heard by expert rate commissioners who will be completely independent of operating management. The Board of the Postal Service will review determinations made by the rate commissioners on rate and classification questions, and the Presidentially appointed members of the board will be empowered to modify such determinations if they consider it in the public interest to do so.

Congress will have express authority to veto decisions on rate and classification questions.

The activities of the Postal Service will be subject to Congressional oversight, and the Act provides for regular reports to Congress. The Postal Service and rules by which it operates can, of course, be changed by law at any time.

Toward Postal Excellence

Removing the postal system from politics and the Post Office Department from the Cabinet is a sweeping reform.

Traditions die hard and traditional institutions are difficult to abandon. But tradition is no substitute for performance, and if our postal system is to meet the expanding needs of the 1970s, we must act now.

Legislation, by itself, will not move the mail. This must be done by the three quarters of a million dedicated men and women who today wear the uniform of the Postal Service. They must be given the right tools—financial, managerial, and technological—to do the job. The legislation I propose today will provide those tools.

There is no Democratic or Republican way of delivering the mail. There is only the right way.

This legislation will let the Postal Service do its job the right way, and I strongly recommend that it be promptly considered and promptly enacted.

10

The

Future

of

Transportation

Congress responded generously to President Nixon's program for improvement of the nation's clogged transportation systems. The Senate approved $2 billion more than the President requested for general development of public transportation systems in local communities.

Under this measure the Federal government is moving into new fields of ground and air transportation development on a multibillion-dollar scale, encouraging novel methods, new vehicles, and modernized road and track ways in a long-term program.

The improvement of water transportation operated by the United States Merchant Marine is more controversial but no less critical. Justification for merchant marine subsidies in the past was found in the requirements of national defense. Merchant marine vessels became troop transports. Merchant ships carried the supplies of war to millions of troops overseas. They were needed on a standby basis. When war came, thousands more ships were built to carry incredible amounts of war matériel into the seven seas.

In the nuclear era of air transport the defense justification of ship subsidies, shipbuilding, and merchant marine operation has diminished. Some say the defense requirement has vanished altogether. In any case, the once proud U.S. Merchant Marine has come upon hard days. President Nixon is trying to revive it.

OF PLANES AND AIRPORTS
Message to the Congress of the United States
JUNE 16, 1969

Years of neglect have permitted the problems of air transportation in America to stack up like aircraft circling a congested airport.

The purpose of air transportation is to save time. This purpose is not served when passengers must wait interminably in terminals; when modern jet aircraft creep at five miles per hour in a long line waiting for takeoff; when it takes longer to land than it takes to travel between cities; or when it takes longer for the air traveler to get to an airport than it does to fly to his destination.

In the tenth year of the jet age, more intercity passenger miles were accounted for by air than by any other mode of common carriage. In 1968 scheduled airlines logged over 150 million passenger trips, triple that of a decade ago; at the same time, the non-airline aircraft fleet almost doubled and the use of air freight quintupled. That rate of increase is likely to continue for the next decade—but it can be accommodated only if we prepare for it now.

The growth in the next decade must be more orderly. It must be financed more fairly. It must be kept safe. And it must not permit congestion and inadequate facilities to defeat the basic purpose of air transportation: to save time.

Air travel is a convenience hundreds of thousands of people take for granted—a means of commerce that millions depend upon for their goods and services. In a nation as large as ours and in a world grown suddenly small, flight has become a powerful unifying force. The ability to transport people and products by air—safely, surely, and efficiently— is a national asset of great value and an international imperative for trade and travel.

That ability is being challenged today by insufficiencies in our nation's airports and airways. The demand for aviation services is threatening to exceed the capacity of our civil aviation system. Unless relieved, this situation will further compromise the convenience of air transportation, erode its efficiency, and ultimately require more regulation if the enviable safety record of the airplane as a means of public and private transportation is to be preserved.

The challenge confronting us is not one of quality or even of technology. Our air traffic control system is the best in the world; our airports among the finest anywhere. But we simply do not have the capacity in our airways and airports ample to our present needs or reflective of the future.

Accordingly, the Secretary of Transportation is submitting to the Congress today legislative proposals to provide the resources necessary to the air transportation challenges facing us. These proposals are responsive to the short-term as well as the long-range opportunities for civil aviation progress.

Improving Our Airways

To provide for the expansion and improvement of the airway system, and for a high standard of safety, this Administration proposes that *the program for construction of airways facilities and equipment be increased to about $250 million annually* for the next ten years. This is in sharp contrast to the average of $93 million appropriated in each of the past ten years, and is responsive to the *substantial expansion in the operation and maintenance of the air traffic system in the next decade.*

While this will provide for the needs of the '70s, development for the 1980s and beyond cannot be neglected. Technology is moving rapidly and its adaptation to provide future solutions must keep pace. Consequently, this program includes a provision for a doubling of development funds.

Building and Improving Airports

The proposed airport program consists of both an expanded planning effort and the provision of additional Federal aid for the construction and improvement of airports. The airport systems planning we contemplate at both the Federal and local level will begin a new era of Federal, state, and local cooperation in shaping airport development to meet national and local needs.

I propose Federal aid for airport development in fiscal 1970 of $180 million and in fiscal 1971 of $220 million, with continued expansion leading to a total of $2.5 billion in the next ten years. Together with matching grants on a fifty-fifty basis with state and local governments, this strongly increased program will permit financing of *$5 billion in new and expanded airfield facilities.*

The proposed fiscal year 1970 program of $180 million would help finance the development of airfield facilities, the conduct of airport systems planning, and airport planning and development activities carried on by states. Of the $180 million,

—$140 million would be available for grants to air carrier and general aviation airports, with a primary objective of alleviating congestion in the most heavily used air terminals.

—$25 million in grants would be available to aid in the development of airfields used solely by general aviation.

—$10 million would be available in grants to planning agencies to assist them in conducting airport systems planning.

—$5 million would be available for grants to states to carry on airport planning and development activities.

Airport terminal buildings are a responsibility of local airport authorities. The Administration's legislative proposal suggests ways in which those authorities can meet that responsibility.

Improving the Environment of Transportation

In all planning for airways and airports, it will be the policy of this Administration to consider the relation of air transportation to our total economic and social structure.

For example, existing jetports are adding to the noise and air pollution in our urban areas. New airports become a nucleus for metropolitan development. These important social and conservation considerations must be taken into greater account in future air systems development.

In addition, airport planners must carefully consider the opportunity for business growth and the availability of labor supply. The presence of airport facilities is both a follower of and a harbinger of business and job development.

Most important, government at all levels, working with industry and labor, must see to it that all aviation equipment and facilities are responsive to the needs of the traveler and the shipper and not the other way around. Transportation to airports, whether by public conveyance or private vehicle, is as much a part of a traveler's journey as the time he spends in the air, and must never be viewed as a separate subject. A plane travels from airport to airport, but a person travels from door to door. I have directed the Secretary of Transportation to give special attention to all the components of a journey in new plans for airways and airports improvements.

Financing Air Transportation Facilities

The Federal government must exert new leadership in the development of transportation, in the integration of the various modes, and in supporting programs of national urgency.

However, the added burden of financing future air transportation facilities should not be thrust upon the general taxpayer. The various users of the system, who will benefit from the developments, should assume the responsibility for the costs of the program. By apportioning the costs of airways and airports improvements among all the users, the progress of civil aviation should be supported on an equitable, pay-as-we-grow basis.

At present the Treasury obtains revenues, generally regarded as airways user charges, from airline passengers, who pay a 5-percent tax on the tickets they buy, and from the operators of aircraft, who pay a tax at the effective rate of two cents a gallon on aviation gasoline. The revenues obtained from these taxes are not applied directly to airways expenditures. They are either earmarked for other purposes or go into the general fund of the Treasury.

I propose that there be established a revised and expanded schedule of taxes as follows, the revenues from which would be placed in a Designated Account in the Treasury to be used only to defray costs incurred in the airport and airway programs:

—A tax of 8 percent on airline tickets for domestic flights.

—A tax of $3 on passenger tickets for most international flights beginning in the United States.

—A tax of 5 percent on air freight waybills.

—A tax of nine cents a gallon on all fuels used by general aviation.

This new tax schedule would generate about $569 million in revenues in fiscal year 1970, compared with the revenues of $295 million under existing taxes.

To sum up:

—For the airline passenger, the proposed legislation would save his time and add to his safety.

—For the air shipper, it would expedite the movement of his goods, thereby permitting him to improve his services.

—For the private aircraft owner, it would provide improved facilities and additional airports.

—For the airline, it would permit greater efficiencies and enable the carrier to expand its markets by providing greater passenger convenience.

In short, the airways and airports system which long ago came of age will come to maturity. Those who benefit most will be those who most bear its cost, and the nation as a whole will gain from aviation's proven impetus to economic growth.

The revenue and expenditure programs being proposed are mutually dependent and must be viewed together. We must act to increase revenues concurrently with any action to authorize expenditures; prudent fiscal management will not permit otherwise.

These proposals are necessary to the safety and convenience of a large portion of our mobile population, and I recommend their early enactment by the Congress.

OF TRAINS AND BUSES

Message to the Congress of the United States

AUGUST 7, 1969

Public transportation has suffered from years of neglect in America. In the last thirty years urban transportation systems have experienced a cycle of increasing costs, decreasing funds for replacements, cutbacks in service, and decrease in passengers.

Transit fares have almost tripled since 1945; the number of passengers has decreased to one third the level of that year. Transit industry profits before taxes have declined from $313 million in 1945 to $25 million in 1967. In recent years 235 bus and subway companies have gone out of business. The remaining transit companies have progressively deteriorated. Today they give their riders fewer runs, older cars, and less service.

Local governments, faced with demands for many pressing public services and with an inadequate financial base, have been unable to provide sufficient assistance.

This is not a problem peculiar to our largest cities alone. Indeed, many of our small and medium-sized communities have seen their bus transportation systems simply close down.

When the nation realized the importance and need for improved highways in the last decade, the Congress responded with the Highway Act of 1956. The result has been a magnificent Federally aided highway system. But highways are only one element in a national transportation policy. About a quarter of our population lack access to a car. For these people—especially the poor, the aged, the very young, and the handicapped—adequate public transportation is the only answer.

Moreover, until we make public transportation an attractive alternative to private car use, we will never be able to build highways fast enough to avoid congestion. As we survey the increasing congestion of our roads and strangulation of our central cities today, we can imagine what our plight will be when our urban population adds 100 million people by the year 2000.

We cannot meet future needs by concentrating development on just one means of transportation. We must have a truly balanced system. Only when automobile transportation is complemented by adequate public transportation can we meet those needs.

The Public Transportation Program

I propose that we provide $10 billion out of the general fund over a twelve-year period to help in developing and improving public transportation in local communities. To establish this program, I am requesting contract authorization totaling $3.1 billion for the first five years starting with a first-year authorization of $300 million and rising to $1 billion annually by 1975. Furthermore, I am asking for a renewal of this contract authorization every two years so that the outstanding contract authorization will never be for a shorter period than three years. Over the twelve-year period $9.5 billion is programmed for capital investments and $500 million for research and development.

The program which I am recommending would help to replace, improve, and expand local bus, rail, and subway systems. It would help to develop and modernize subway tracks, stations, and terminals; it would help to build and improve rail train tracks and stations, new bus terminals, and garages.

The program would authorize assistance to private as well as public transit systems so that private enterprise can continue to provide public services in urban transportation. It would give state governments an opportunity to comment on project applications in order to improve intergovernmetal coordination. It would require local public hearings before any major capital construction is undertaken. And it would permit localities to acquire rights-of-way in advance of system construction in order to reduce future dislocation and costs.

Fares alone cannot ordinarily finance the full cost of public transit systems, including the necessary capital investments. Higher fares usually result in fewer riders, taking much of the "mass" out of mass transit and defeating the social and economic purpose of the system.

One problem with most transit systems operating today is that they rely for revenues on people who *must* use them and make no appeal to those who have a choice of using them or not. Thus we have the self-defeating cycle of fewer riders, higher fares, lower revenues, worse facilities, and still fewer riders.

The way to break that cycle is to make public transit truly attractive and convenient. In this way, more riders will provide more revenues, and fare can be kept down while further efficiencies can be introduced.

In addition to assistance for capital improvements, I am proposing substantial research and technology efforts into new ways of making public transit an attractive choice for owners of private cars. These would include:

—Advanced bus and train design to permit easier boarding and dismounting.

—Improved interiors in bus and trains for increased convenience and security for riders.

—New traffic control systems to expedite the flow of buses over streets and highways.

—Tracked air-cushioned vehicles and automated transit.

—Flexible bus service based on computer-forecast demands.

—New bus propulsion systems which would reduce noise and air pollution as well as cost.

—Systems such as moving sidewalks and capsules to transport people for short distances within terminals, and other major activity.

In summary, this public transportation program I am recommending would give state and local governments the assurance of Federal commitment necessary both to carry out long-range planning and to raise their share of the costs. It would meet the challenge of providing resources that are adequate in amount and it would assure adequate duration of their availability.

The bus rider, train commuter, and subway user would have better service. The car driver would travel on less congested roads. The poor would be better able to get to work, to reach new job opportunities, and to use training and rehabilitation centers. The centers of big cities would avoid strangulation and the suburbs would have better access to urban jobs and shops.

Most important, we as a nation would benefit. The nation which has sent men to the moon would demonstrate that it can meet the transportation needs of the city as well.

OF SAILORS AND ANCIENT SHIPS
Message to the Congress of the United States
OCTOBER 23, 1969

The United States Merchant Marine—the fleet of commercial ships on which we rely for our economic strength in time of peace and our defense mobility in time of war—is in trouble.

While only one fourth of the world's merchant ships are more than twenty years old, approximately three fourths of American trading vessels are at least that antiquated. In the next four years, much of our merchant fleet will be scrapped. Yet we are now producing only a few new ships a year for use in our foreign trade. Building costs for American vessels are about twice those in foreign shipyards, and production delays are excessive. Operating expenses also are high by world standards, and labor-management conflicts have been costly and disruptive.

Both government and industry share responsibility for the recent decline in American shipping and shipbuilding. Both government and industry must now make a substantial effort to reverse that record. We must begin immediately to rebuild our merchant fleet and make it more competitive. Accordingly, I am announcing today a new maritime program for this nation, one which will replace the drift and neglect of recent years and restore this country to a proud position in the shipping lanes of the world.

Our program is one of challenge and opportunity. We will challenge the American shipbuilding industry to show that it can rebuild our Merchant Marine at reasonable expense. We will challenge American ship operators and seamen to move toward less dependence on government subsidy. And through a substantially revised and better administered government program, we will create the opportunity to meet that challenge.

The need for this new program is great since the old ways have not worked. However, as I have frequently pointed out, our budget constraints at this time are also significant. Our program, therefore, will be phased in such a way that it will not increase subsidy expenditures during the rest of fiscal year 1970 and will require only a modest increase for fiscal year 1971. We can thus begin to rebuild our fleet and at the same time meet our fiscal responsibilities.

The Shipbuilding Industry

Our shipbuilding program is designed to meet both of the problems which lie behind the recent decline in this field: low production rates and high production costs. Our proposals would make it possible for shipbuilders to build more ships and would encourage them to hold down the cost of each vessel. We believe that these two aspirations are closely related. For only as we plan a major long-range building program can we encourage builders to standardize ship design and introduce mass-production techniques which have kept other American products competitive in world markets. On the other hand, only if our builders are able to improve their efficiency and cut their costs can we afford to replace our obsolescent merchant fleet with American-built vessels. These cost reductions are essential if our ship operators are to make capital investments of several billion dollars over the next ten years to build new, high-technology ships.

Our new program will provide a substantially improved system of construction differential subsidies, payments which reimburse American shipbuilders for that part of their total cost which exceeds the cost of building in foreign shipyards. Such subsidies allow our shipbuilders—despite their higher costs—to sell their ships at world market prices for use in our foreign trade. The important features of our new subsidy system are as follows:

1. We should make it possible for industry to build more ships over the next ten years, moving from the present subsidy level of about ten ships a year to a new level of thirty ships a year.

2. We should reduce the percentage of total costs which are subsidized. The government presently subsidizes up to 55 percent of a builder's total expenses for a given vessel. Leaders of the shipbuilding industry have frequently said that subsidy requirements can be reduced

considerably if they are assured a long-term market. I am therefore asking that construction differential subsidies be limited to 45 percent of total costs in fiscal year 1971. That percentage should be reduced by 2 percent in each subsequent year until the maximum subsidy payment is down to 35 percent of total building expenses.

We are confident that the shipbuilding industry can meet this challenge. If the challenge is not met, however, then the Administration's commitment to this part of our program will not be continued.

3. Construction differential subsidies should be paid directly to shipbuilders rather than being channeled through shipowners as is the case under the present system. A direct-payment system is necessary if our program is to encourage builders to improve designs, reduce delays, and minimize costs. It will also help us to streamline subsidy administration.

4. The multiyear procurement system which is now used for other government programs should be extended to shipbuilding. Under this system the government makes a firm commitment to build a given number of ships over a specified and longer period of time, a practice which allows the industry to realize important economies of scale and to receive lower subsidies.

5. The increased level of ship construction will require a corresponding increase in the level of Federally insured mortgages. Accordingly, we should increase the ceiling on our present mortgage insurance programs from $1 billion to $3 billion.

6. We should extend construction differential subsidies to bulk carriers, ships which usually carry ore, grain, or oil and which are not covered by our present subsidy program.

7. A commission should be established to review the status of the American shipbuilding industry, its problems, and its progress toward meeting the challenge we have set forth. The commission should report on its findings within three years and recommend any changes in government policy which it believes are desirable.

The Ship-Operating Industry

My comments to this point have related to the building of merchant vessels. The other arm of our maritime policy is that which deals with the operation of these ships. Here, too, our new program offers several substantial improvements over the present system.

1. Operating differential subsidies should be continued only for the higher wage and insurance costs which American shipping lines experience. Subsidies for maintenance and repair and for subsistence should

be eliminated. Instead of paying the difference between the wages of foreign seamen and actual wages on American ships, however, the government should compare foreign wages with prevailing wage levels in several comparable sectors of the American economy. A policy which ties subsidies to this wage index will reduce subsidy costs and provide an incentive for further efficiencies. Under this system, the operator would no longer lose in subsidies what he saves in costs. Nor would he continue to be reimbursed through subsidies when his wage costs rise to higher levels.

2. At the same time that we are reducing operating subsidies, it is appropriate that we eliminate the "recapture" provisions of the Merchant Marine Act of 1936. These provisions require subsidized lines to pay back to the government a portion of profits. If the recapture provisions are removed, the purpose for which they were designed will be largely accomplished by corporate taxes, which were at much lower rates when these provisions were instituted. We will also save the cost of administering recapture provisions.

3. Many bulk carriers presently receive indirect operating subsidies from the government because of the statutory requirement that certain government cargoes must be shipped in United States vessels at premium rates. When the Department of Agriculture ships grain abroad, for example, it pays higher rates out of its budget than if it were allowed to ship at world market rates. We will propose a new, direct-subsidy system for such carriers, thus allowing us to phase out these premium freight rates and reduce the costs of several nonmaritime government programs.

4. Ship operators now receiving operating differential subsidies are permitted to defer Federal tax payments on reserve funds set aside for construction purposes. This provision should be extended to include all qualified ship operators in the foreign trade, but only for well-defined ship-replacement programs.

5. Past government policies and industry attitudes have not been conducive to cooperation between labor and management. Our program will help to improve this situation by ending the uncertainty that has characterized our past maritime policy. Labor and management must now use this opportunity to find ways of resolving their differences without halting operations. If the desired expansion of merchant shipping is to be achieved, the disruptive work stoppages of the past must not be repeated.

6. The larger capital investment necessary to construct a modern and efficient merchant fleet requires corresponding port development. I am therefore directing the Secretary of Commerce and the Secretary of

Transportation to work with related industries and local governments in improving our port operations. We must take full advantage of technological advances in this area and we should do all we can to encourage greater use of intermodal transportation systems, of which these high-technology ships are only a part.

Equal Employment Opportunities

The expansion of American merchant shipbuilding which this program makes possible will provide many new employment opportunities. All of our citizens must have equal access to these new jobs. I am therefore directing the Secretary of Commerce and the Secretary of Labor to work with industry and labor organizations to develop programs that will ensure all minority groups their rightful place in this expansion.

Research and Development

We will also enlarge and redirect the maritime research-and-development activities of the Federal government. Greater emphasis will be placed on practical applications of technological advances and on the coordination of Federal programs with those of industry.

The history of American commercial shipping is closely intertwined with the history of our country. From the time of the Colonial fishing sloops, down through the great days of the majestic clipper ships, and into the new era when steam replaced the sail, the venturesome spirit of maritime enterprise has contributed significantly to the strength of the nation.

Our shipping industry has come a long way over the last three centuries. Yet as one of the great historians of American seafaring, Samuel Eliot Morison, has written: "All her modern docks and terminals and dredged channels will avail nothing, if the spirit perish that led her founders to 'trye all ports.'" It is that spirit to which our program of challenge and opportunity appeals.

It is my hope and expectation that this program will introduce a new era in the maritime history of America, an era in which our shipbuilding and ship-operating industries take their place once again among the vigorous, competitive industries of this nation.

11

A Handful of Domestic Issues

ELECTORAL REFORM

Message to the Congress of the United States

FEBRUARY 20, 1969

Since the beginning of the Republic, the Electoral College system of choosing a President has been under challenge as unrepresentative.

The election of 1968 again aroused the fear that a minority President, unable to govern under modern conditions, would be chosen in the electoral system from the three major candidates, Richard Nixon, Hubert H. Humphrey, and George C. Wallace.

An inconclusive result in the Electoral College forcing the election into the House of Representatives, it was feared, could have given the balance of power to electors pledged to the third party candidate, Wallace.

Once elected by a scant half million votes in a three-way race, President Nixon's solution was a modification of proposals for direct election of a President. Congress moved anyway toward direct election with a second run-off election if any candidate failed to win 40 percent of the vote in the first election.

One hundred and sixty-five years ago Congress and the several states adopted the Twelfth Amendment to the United States Constitution in order to cure certain defects—underscored by the election of 1800— in the Electoral College method of choosing a President. Today our Presidential selection mechanism once again requires overhaul to repair defects spotlighted by the circumstances of 1968.

The reforms that I propose are basic in need and desirability. They are changes which I believe should be given the earliest attention by the Congress.

I have not abandoned my personal feeling, stated in October and November of 1968, that the candidate who wins the most popular votes should become President. However, practicality demands recognition that the electoral system is deeply rooted in American history and Federalism. Many citizens, especially in our smaller states, and their legislatures share the belief stated by President Johnson in 1965 that "our present system of computing and awarding electoral votes by states is an essential counterpart of our Federal system and the provisions of our Constitution which recognize and maintain our nation as a union of states." I doubt very much that any constitutional amendment proposing abolition or substantial modification of the electoral-vote system could win the required approval of three quarters of our fifty states by 1972.

For this reason, and because of the compelling specific weaknesses focused in 1968, I am urging Congress to concentrate its attention on formulating a system that can receive the requisite Congressional and state approval.

I realize that experts on constitutional law do not think alike on the subject of electoral reform. Different plans for reform have been responsibly advanced by Members of Congress and distinguished private groups and individuals. These plans have my respect and they merit serious consideration by the Congress.

I have in the past supported the proportional plan of electoral reform. Under this plan the electoral vote of a state would be distributed among the candidates for President in proportion to the popular vote cast. But I am not wedded to the details of this plan or any other specific plan. I will support any plan that moves toward the following objectives: first, the abolition of individual electors; second, allocation to Presidential candidates of the electoral vote of each state and the District of Columbia in a manner that may more closely approximate the popular vote than does the present system; third, making a 40-percent electoral-vote plurality sufficient to choose a President.

The adoption of these reforms would correct the principal defects in the present system. I believe the events of 1968 constitute the clearest proof that priority must be accorded to Electoral College reform.

Next, I consider it necessary to make specific provision for the eventuality that no Presidential slate recieves 40 percent or more of the electoral vote in the regular election. Such a situation, I believe, is best met by providing that a run-off election between the top two candidates shall be held within a specified time after the general election, victory going to the candidate who receives the larger popular vote.

We must also resolve some other uncertainties. First, by specifying that if a Presidential candidate who has received a clear electoral-vote plurality dies before the electoral votes are counted, the Vice President-elect should be chosen President. Second, by providing that in the event of the death of the Vice President-elect, the President-elect should, upon taking office, be required to follow the procedures otherwise provided in the Twenty-Fifth Amendment for filling the unexpired term of the Vice President. Third, by giving Congress responsibility, should both the President-elect and Vice President-elect die or become unable to serve during this interim, to provide for the selection—by a new election or some other means—of persons to serve as President and Vice President. And finally, we must clarify the situation presented by the death of a candidate for President or Vice President prior to the November general election.

Many of these reforms are noncontroversial. All are necessary. Favorable action by Congress will constitute a vital step in modernizing our electoral process and reaffirming the flexible strength of our constitutional system.

GREATER SAFETY FOR COAL MINERS
Message to the Congress of the United States
MARCH 3, 1969

The pressure of the times has required greater concern by the Federal government for the condition of the individual in industrialized society. Coal mine disasters and public indignation over the "black lung" disease caused President Nixon to propose new coal mine safety legislation early in his Administration.

Some of his proposals were included in the Federal Coal Mine Health and Safety Act of 1969 signed by him on December 30, 1969. Enforcement began March 30, 1970. The act gives the Secretary of Interior and the Secretary of Health, Education and Welfare power to set new health and safety standards "as the need is apparent." This grant of power enables Federal officials to deal with day-by-day accidents in the mines which in their total effect are more significant than the occasional disasters.

The workers in the coal mining industry and their families have too long endured the constant threat and often sudden reality of disaster, disease, and death. This great industry has strengthened our nation with the raw material of power. But it has also frequently saddened our nation with news of crippled men, grieving widows, and fatherless children.

Death in the mines can be as sudden as an explosion or a collapse of a roof and ribs, or it comes insidiously from pneumoconiosis or "black lung" disease. When a miner leaves his home for work, he and his family must live with the unspoken but always present fear that before the working day is over he may be crushed or burned to death or suffocated. This acceptance of the possibility of death in the mines has become almost as much a part of the job as the tools and the tunnels.

The time has come to replace this fatalism with hope by substituting action for words. Catastrophes in the coal mines are not inevitable. They can be prevented, and they must be prevented.

To these ends, I have ordered the following actions to advance the health and safety of the coal mine workers:

—Increase subtantially the number of inspectors, and improve coal mine inspections and the effectiveness of staff performance and requirements.

—Revise the instructions to the mine inspectors so as to reflect more stringent operating standards.

—Initiate an in-depth study to reorganize the agency charged with the primary responsibility for mine safety so that it can meet the new challenges and demands.

—Expand research activities with respect to pneumoconiosis and other mine health and safety hazards.

—Extend the recent advances in human engineering and motivational techniques, and enlarge and intensify education and training functions, for the improvement of health and safety in coal mines to the greatest degree possible.

—Establish cooperative programs between management and labor at the *mine level* which will implement health and safety efforts at the site of the mine hazards.

—Encourage the coordination of Federal and state inspections, in order to secure more effective enforcement of the present safety requirements.

—Initiate grant programs to the states, as authorized but not previously invoked, to assist the states in planning and advancing their respective programs for increased health and safety in the coal mines.

In addition to these immediate efforts under existing law, I am submitting to the Congress legislative proposals for a comprehensive new program to provide a vigorous and multifaceted attack on the health and safety dangers which prevail in the coal mining industry.

These proposals would:

—Modernize a wide range of mandatory health and safety standards, including new provisions for the control of dust, electrical equipment, roof support, ventilation, illumination, fire protection, and other operating practices in underground and surface coal mines engaged in commerce.

—Authorize the Secretary of the Interior to develop and promulgate any additional or revised standards which he deems necessary for the health and safety of the miners.

—Provide strict deterrents and enforcement measures and, at the same time, establish equitable appeal procedures to remedy any arbitrary and unlawful actions.

—Recruit and carefully train a highly motivated corps of coal mine inspectors to investigate the coal mines, and to enforce impartially and vigorously the broad new mandatory standards.

—Improve Federal-state inspection plans.

—Substantially increase, by direct action, grants and contracts, the necessary research, training, and education for the prevention and control of occupational diseases, the improvement of state workmen's compensation systems, and the reduction of mine accidents.

These legislative proposals, together with other steps already taken or to be taken, are essential to meet our obligation to the nation's coal miners, and to accomplish our mission of eliminating the tragedies which have occurred in the mines.

These proposals are not intended to replace the voluntary and enlightened efforts of management and labor to reduce coal mine hazards, which efforts are the touchstone to any successful health and safety program. Rather, these measures would expand and render uniform by enforceable authority the most advanced of the health and safety precautions undertaken and potentially available in the coal mining industry.

I urge the immediate adoption by Congress of this legislation.

BETTER GOVERNMENT FOR THE DISTRICT OF COLUMBIA
Message to the Congress of the United States
APRIL 28, 1969

As President and as a long-time resident of the District of Columbia, President Nixon took a greater interest in problems of the national capital than most Presidents. This interest also reflected the national mood about Washington as a poorly governed, crime-ridden city.

Carved out of swampland at our country's birth, the nation's capital city now sets a new test of national purpose. This was a city that men dared to plan—and build by plan—laying out avenues and monuments and housing in accordance with a common rational scheme. Now we are challenged once again to shape our environment: to renew our city by rational foresight and planning, rather than leaving it to grow, swamplike, without design.

At issue is whether the city will be enabled to take hold of its future: whether its institutions will be reformed so that its government can truly represent its citizens and act upon their needs.

Good government, in the case of a city, must be local government. The Federal government has a special responsibility for the District of Columbia. But it also bears toward the District the same responsibility it bears toward all other cities: to help local government work better, and to attempt to supplement local resources for programs that city officials judge most urgent.

My aim is to increase the responsibility and efficiency of the District of Columbia's new government, which has performed so ably during its first perilous years. Early in this Administration we recommended proposals that would increase the effectiveness of local law enforcement and provide the resources needed by local officials to begin revitalizing the areas damaged during the civil disturbance. Those proposals, however, cover only a part of the program which will be essential for the District government to respond to the wishes of its people.

I now present the second part of this program, worked out in close consultation with the District government, and based upon the needs articulated by the Mayor and the City Council.

This program will provide:

—An orderly mechanism for achieving self-government in the District of Columbia.

—Representation in Congress.

—Added municipal authority for the City Council and the Mayor.

—Additional top-management positions to bring new talents and leadership into the District government.

—A secure and equitable source of Federal funds for the District's budget.

—An expanded rapid rail transit system, linking the diverse segments of our Capital's metropolitan region.

The Federal government bears a major responsibility for the welfare of our Capital's citizens in general. It owns much of the District's land and employs many of its citizens. It depends on the services of local government. The condition of our capital city is a sign of the condition of our nation—and is certainly taken as such by visitors, from all the states of the Union, and from around the globe.

However, this Federal responsibility does not require Federal rule.

Besides the official Washington of monuments and offices, there is the Washington of 850,000 citizens with all the hopes and expectations of the people of any major city, striving and sacrificing for a better life— the eighth largest among the cities of our country.

Full citizenship through local self-government must be given to the people of this city: the District government cannot be truly responsible until it is made responsible to those who live under its rule. The District's citizens should not be expected to pay taxes for a government which they have no part in choosing—or to bear the full burdens of citizenship without the full rights of citizenship.

I therefore ask Congress to create a Commission on Self-Government for the District of Columbia, to be charged with submitting to Congress and the President a proposal for establishing meaningful self-government in the District.

In order for any government to be accountable to the people, responsibilities must be clearly pinpointed, and officials must have the powers they need to carry out their responsibilities. The Commission would recommend how best to augment and allocate the legislative and executive authorities with respect to governing the city.

The members of this Commission would be partly appointed by the President, partly designated by the Congress, and partly chosen in a citywide election by the citizens of the District. They would be given an adequate but strictly defined time period to formulate their plan. I would hope that the Commission would be established promptly, so that its reports could be submitted to Congress and the President in time for the 1970 legislative session. With adequate funding they would be able to draw on the wisdom of consultants throughout the country—men who know first hand the art of the possible, as well as those who study government—in addition to their own staff.

The Commission members must give thorough consideration to the many alternative plans for self-government which have been presented over the years. But they must also make use of new knowledge we have gained about the problems of existing local governments around the country— in finance, management, urban development, citizen participation, and many other areas. They must seek the sentiment of the District's citizens from the earliest stages of their work.

There also is a Federal interest that must be respected. The normal functions of the Federal agencies must be guaranteed and their vital operations protected. There must be continued Federal jurisdiction over public buildings and monuments and assurance of well-being for the men and women who work in them or come to visit. The rights of the national government must be protected at the same time as the rights of the city's residents are secured. There must be respect for the responsibilities with regard to the District which the Constitution places in the Congress.

To establish a new government in so diverse and active a city as the District is certainly no easy task. There are dangers in setting up new governments, as well as opportunities. Congress has been rightly concerned that the plan for self-government must ensure responsible elections, effective executive leadership, protection of individual liberty, and safeguards for District of Columbia employees. Self-government must be extended in a timely and orderly manner.

It is especially important that the Commission go beyond the issue of self-government as such, and concern itself with the effective functioning of government in the District of Columbia. Under the existing government structure the City Council finds itself without the power to deal with many crucial problems because of the conflicting and divided authorities that now reside in independent agencies.

But there is no cause for delay: self-government has remained an unfulfilled promise for far too long. It has been energetically supported by the past four Presidents—Harry S Truman, Dwight D. Eisenhower, John F. Kennedy, and Lyndon B. Johnson. The Senate approved measures to provide it during the 81st, 82nd, 84th, and 86th Congresses. We owe the present lack of local elections to the Reconstruction period, when Congress rescued the District from bankruptcy but suspended the voting franchise. Congress established the Commission form of government in 1874 as a temporary "receivership," but the Commissioners' government persisted for over ninety years—and today, even after reorganization in 1967, the District remains under Federal control.

The history of failure for self-government proposals shows the need for a new plan strong enough to stand up against the old questions or criticisms. Myriad different plans have been offered—and will be offered again this year. But each will have its own doubters as well as its supporters. A Commission must examine all of them, combining old and new ideas in a proposal that will at last win the broad-based respect necessary for final acceptance, and that will carry the authority of a disinterested group of men whose vocation is government—jurists, political leaders, and scholars, as well as other citizens, investing the wisdom of their life's work in a truly new government.

Recognizing both the solemn right of the District's citizens to self-government and the Federal interest, I ask Congress to act promptly on proposed legislation to establish a *Commission on Self-Government for the District of Columbia,* which will be transmitted shortly.

Congressional Representation

I also urge Congress to grant voting representation in Congress to the District of Columbia. It should offend the democratic senses of this nation that the 850,000 citizens of its Capital, comprising a population larger than eleven of its states, have no voice in the Congress.

I urge that Congress approve, and the states ratify, an Amendment to the Constitution granting to the District at least one representative in the House of Representatives, and such additional representatives in the House as the Congress shall approve, and to provide for the possibility of two Senators.

Until such an amendment is approved by Congress and ratified by the states, *I recommend that Congress enact legislation to provide for a non-voting House delegate from the District.*

Strengthening the City Council and Mayor

While working for self-government and congressional representation for the future, I recommend that Congress take certain measures this session to strengthen the present District government, in both authority and efficiency.

The reorganization plan which established the present government left to Congress many mundane municipal functions which are burdensome chores to it but important functions for good local government. At present Congress must allot a portion of its legislative calendar to setting ordinances for the District of Columbia, in effect performing the duties of a local city council for the Capital. It thus deals with matters which are of little or no importance to the nation as a whole—the setting of a fee, for example, to redeem a dog from the city pound. The concerns of the District are frequently shunted aside to allow for higher-priority legislative business. "No policy can be worse than to mingle great and small concerns," argued Augustus Woodward, one of the founders of our city, when Congress considered establishing a territorial form of government in 1800. "The latter become absorbed in the former; are neglected and forgotten."

Legislation will be proposed to transfer a number of specific authorities to the District government—including authority to change various fees for user charges now fixed by statute, waive license fees for new businesses, for persons whose businesses have been burnt out in a civil disturbance, and modernize the licensing of various businesses, occupations, and professions.

In addition, I recommend that the Mayor be given certain local responsibilities now exercised by Federal departments or agencies. Reorganization plans will be submitted in the coming weeks to transfer local functions now operated by the Federal government—and frequently paid for by the District—to the Executive Branch of the District government. Local services should be operated by local government. Such responsibilities are only an extra burden for the Federal departments, which should rightly devote their energies to the welfare of the entire nation.

I will also submit other reorganization plans to transfer certain independent or quasi-independent District agencies to the Mayor's jurisdiction. These actions will strengthen the executive direction of the City's administration and complement the continuing reorganization and strengthening of the District's administrative structure.

Granting new authority to the Mayor and City Council would in no way prejudice the ultimate form or degree of self-government. It would provide them with powers which any good local government, however chosen, should exercise. By initiating this process now, we thus build the strength of local institutions even as we make them more responsible, formally, to their citizens.

More High-Level Civil Servants

Good government is the product of able and dedicated people working together. The District government needs the very best urban managers and experts this nation has to direct the Capital's growth and apply its resources, and it must be able to attract such public servants at realistic salary rates.

Adding to the number of top-management positions is vital to the effective carrying out of District government reorganization—the creation of new departments recently announced by the Mayor, and other steps planned for the future. Such reorganization, streamlining the chain of command, is one of the most promising achievements of the Mayor's first years.

Accordingly, I urge Congress to enact legislation to increase the number of supergrade positions available to the District government.

The Federal Payment

The District of Columbia cannot achieve strong and efficient government unless it has ample and dependable sources of financing. Sound financing can be achieved only if the Federal government pays its appropriate share.

I therefore recommend that the Congress authorize a Federal payment formula, fixing the Federal contribution at 30 percent of local tax and other general fund revenues.

This formula would equitably reflect the Federal interest in the District of Columbia at this time with respect to:

—The 217,000 Federal employees who work in the District, about one third of the local work force.

—The more than 10 million Americans who visit their nation's Capital each year.

—The embassies and nationals of the foreign governments.

—The land and buildings owned by the Federal government which cannot be taxed but comprise more than 40 percent of the District's land value.

Enactment of a formula approach would be a significant step toward effective government in the District. It would tie the level of Federal aid to the burden of local taxes on the District's citizens. It would also provide the District with a predictable estimate for use in the annual budget process, thus allowing it to plan its expenditures more accurately and imaginatively for the growing needs of its population. A similar formula, dealing with District borrowing authorization, was enacted by the Congress more than a year ago—and has already proven its worth in improved budgetary planning.

The proposed Federal payment formula would not involve an automatic expenditure of Federal funds. The Federal payment would still have to be appropriated by Congress.

By authorizing the Federal payment at 30 percent of all District general fund revenues, the Congress would allow a payment of $120 million in fiscal 1970, an increase of $30 million above the present fixed authorization. This payment is incorporated in the District's 1970 budget request.

Balanced Transportation System

The national Capital needs and deserves a mass transit system that is truly metropolitan, unifying the central city with the surrounding suburbs. As a part of its responsibility for the National Capital Region, the Federal government should support deliberate action, based upon effective planning, to meet the future transportation needs of the region. The surrounding areas in Maryland and Virginia, as Congress rightly recognized, include the most rapidly growing areas of population and job opportunities, potentially of rich benefit to the inner city.

Mass transit must be part of a balanced transportation network. A subway will not relieve local governments of the duty to modernize and improve their highway systems and other forms of transportation, so that all citizens have an adequate choice as to how they travel. Clearly, the impasse that has arisen between proponents of road and rail transportation in the Washington metropolitan area has contributed little to the progress of either. There are, however, hopeful signs that a fair and effective settlement of these issues will be reached in the near future. It is in the interest of all those involved—central-city dwellers, suburbanites, shoppers, employees, and visitors alike—that this be done.

The Washington Metropolitan Area Transit Authority, in consultation with the District government and other local jurisdictions, has prepared legislation which would extend the presently authorized twenty-five-mile rapid rail transit system to a ninety-seven-mile regional system. The expanded system would provide rapid transit between the downtown and outlying areas. It would facilitate the free flow of resources and labor, and would benefit all eight jurisdictions involved in its planning and approval.

The proposed legislation fulfills the Congressional mandate in a 1966 Act, which directed the Washington Metropolitan Area Transportation Authority to plan, develop, finance, and provide for the operation of a full regional rapid rail system for the national capital area.

The ninety-seven-mile system would relieve downtown congestion; increase employment; make educational, cultural, and recreational facilities more accessible; reduce air pollution; stimulate business, industry, and tourism; broaden tax bases; and promote orderly urban development of the nation's Capital.

The cost of the expanded system is estimated to be some $2.5 billion. Farebox receipts would pay for $835 million. The remaining cost of $1.7 billion (the net project cost) would be divided equitably among all the governments concerned on a ⅔–⅓ sharing basis between Federal and local governments.

The local governments concerned have already passed bond referenda or taken other appropriate action to finance their contributions of $347 million. But action by Congress is needed to authorize grants sufficient to cover the $1.1 billion Federal (⅔) share of the net project cost and capital contributions of $216 million for the District's portion of the local (⅓) share.

I urge that Congress promptly enact the necessary authorizing legislation for the ninety-seven-mile system.

Pennsylvania Avenue

Finally, we come to the Washington that so many millions flock to visit; the Washington that stands as a proud physical symbol of our nation's liberties and its hopes.

Pennsylvania Avenue should be one of the great avenues of our Republic—as in the original vision of our capital city—and will be so if the Pennsylvania Avenue Commission presses forward with its present plans. Already, in accordance with the Commission's plans, construction of the Presidential Building at 13th Street has been completed; construction is continuing on the new Capital Reflecting Pool, as well as buildings for the Federal Bureau of Investigation and the Labor Department. Planning is going forward for the Federal Triangle, a new Municipal Center at Judiciary Square, and an extension of the National Gallery. Our ultimate goal must be the Avenue of L'Enfant's Plan, a *grande route* connecting the Congress and the President's House, the vital center of the city, monumental in importance but designed for the citizens of this nation to enjoy at all hours for work or pleasure. I will encourage the development of this plan and submit legislation at the appropriate time.

One of the most significant additions to Pennsylvania Avenue will be an international center for scholars, to be established as a living memorial to Woodrow Wilson in the area just north of the National Archives. There could hardly be a more appropriate memorial to a President who combined a devotion to scholarship with a passion for peace. The District has long sought, and long needed, a center for both men of letters and men of affairs. This should be, as it was first proposed, "an institution of learning that the twenty-second century will regard as having influenced the twenty-first."

The renewal of Pennsylvania Avenue is an enterprise which two Presidents have supported. Their vision was the great vision of Pierre L'Enfant, George Washington, and Thomas Jefferson, whose plans embodied the ageless ideal of a capital city. It is a vision which links Presidents, as it links the citizens of the District, in the love of this city. And I am proud to join them.

A Great Enterprise

It is a noble aim—this planning of a capital city. It encompasses a drive which must apply to areas of rebuilding beyond a single Avenue, and to areas of need beyond physical renovation. It infuses our knowledge of human want with a new urgency. It tests our vision of man, and of the future of his cities.

I ask the Congress, and the American people, to join in this great enterprise, knowing that if we govern with wisdom in this capital city, it will be a proud symbol of the quality of American life and the reach of America's aspirations.

REFORM OF OUR DRAFT PROCEDURES
Message to the Congress of the United States
MAY 13, 1969

President Nixon responded to a decade-long objection to the methods of the military draft with broad proposals for a reform of the Selective Service System. He also relieved as Draft Director Gen. Lewis B. Hershey, storm center of draft protest, after a distinguished career going back to World War II.

Congress adopted only one of Nixon's proposals, a single-sentence repeal of the 1967 prohibition against a lottery system. He then established the lottery system November 26, 1969, and the first drawing was held December 1.

Nixon proceeded with draft reform by Administrative order with the announced intention of ultimately creating a totally volunteer army, which he had announced as his aim during the Presidential campaign of 1968.

For almost 2 million young men who reach the age of military service each year—and for their families—the draft is one of the most important facts of life. It is my conviction that the disruptive impact of the military draft on individual lives should be minimized as much as possible, consistent with the national security. For this reason I am today asking the Congress for authority to implement important draft reforms.

Ideally, of course, minimum interference means no draft at all. I continue to believe that under more stable world conditions and with an armed force that is more attractive to volunteers, that ideal can be realized in practice. To this end, I appointed, on March 27, 1969, an Advisory Commission on an All-Volunteer Armed Force. I asked that group to develop a comprehensive plan which will attract more volunteers to military service, utilize military manpower in a more efficient way, and eliminate conscription as soon as that is feasible. I look forward to receiving the report of the Commission this coming November.

Under present conditions, however, some kind of draft will be needed for the immediate future. As long as that is the case, we must do everything we can to limit the disruption caused by the system and to make it as fair as possible. For one's vision of the eventual does not excuse his inattention to the immediate. A man may plan to sell his house in another year, but during that year he will do what is necessary to make it livable.

Accordingly, I will ask the Congress to amend the Military Selective Service Act of 1967, returning to the President the power which he had prior to June 30, 1967, to modify call-up procedures. I will describe below in some detail the new procedures which I will establish if Congress grants this authority. Essentially, I would make the following alterations:

1. Change from an oldest-first to a youngest-first order of call, so that a young man would become less vulnerable rather than more vulnerable to the draft as he grows older.

2. Reduce the period of prime draft vulnerability—and the uncertainty that accompanies it—from seven years to one year, so that a young man would normally enter that status during the time he was nineteen years old and leave it during the time he was twenty.

3. Select those who are actually drafted through a random system. A procedure of this sort would distribute the risk of call equally—by lot —among all who are vulnerable during a given year, rather than arbitrarily selecting those whose birthdays happen to fall at certain times of the year or the month.

4. Continue the undergraduate student deferment, with the understanding that the year of maximum vulnerability would come whenever the deferment expired.

5. Allow graduate students to complete, not just one term, but the full academic year during which they are first ordered for induction.

6. In addition, as a step toward a more consistent policy of deferments and exemptions, I will ask the National Security Council and the Director of Selective Service to review all guidelines, standards, and procedures in this area and to report to me their findings and recommendations.

I believe these reforms are essential. I hope they can be implemented quickly.

Any system which selects only some from a pool of many will inevitably have some elements of inequity. As its name implies, choice is the very purpose of the Selective Service System. Such choices cannot be avoided so long as the supply of men exceeds military requirements. In these circumstances, however, the government bears a moral obligation to spread the risk of induction equally among those who are eligible.

Moreover, a young man now begins his time of maximum vulnerability to the draft at age nineteen and leaves that status only when he is drafted or when he reaches his twenty-sixth birthday. Those who are *not* called up are nevertheless vulnerable to call for a seven-year period. For those who *are* called, the average age of induction can vary greatly. A few years ago, when calls were low, the average age of involuntary induction was nearly twenty-four. More recently it has dropped to just about twenty. What all of this means for the average young man is a prolonged time of great uncertainty.

The present draft arrangements make it extremely difficult for most young people to plan intelligently as they make some of the most important decisions of their lives, decisions concerning education, career, marriage, and family. Present policies extend a period during which young people come to look on government processes as particularly arbitrary.

For all of these reasons, the American people are unhappy about our present draft mechanisms. Various elements of the basic reforms which I here suggest have been endorsed by recent studies of the Selective Service System, including that of the Marshall Commission of 1967, the Clark panel of that same year, and the reports of both the Senate and the House Armed Services Committees. Reform of this sort is also sound from a military standpoint, since younger men are easier to train and have fewer family responsibilities.

My specific proposals, in greater detail, are as follows:

1. *A "youngest-first" order of call.* Under my proposal, the government would designate each year a "prime age group," a different pool of draft eligibles for each consecutive twelve-month period. (Since that period would not necessarily begin on January 1, it would be referred to as a "selective service year.") The prime age group for any given selective service year would contain those registrants who were nineteen years old when it began. Those who received deferments or exemptions would rejoin the prime age group at the time their deferment or exemption expired. During the first year that the new plan was in operation, the prime age group would include *all* eligible men from nineteen to twenty-six, not deferred or exempt, so that no one would escape vulnerability simply because of the transition.

2. *Limited vulnerability.* Each individual would experience maximum vulnerability to the draft only for the one selective service year in

which he is in the prime age group. At the end of the twelve-month period—which would normally come sometime during his twentieth year—he would move on to progressively less vulnerable categories and an entirely new set of registrants would become the new prime age group. Under this system, a young man would receive an earlier and more decisive answer to his question, "Where do I stand with the draft?" and he could plan his life accordingly.

3. *A random selection system.* Since more men are classified as available for service each year than are required to fill current or anticipated draft calls, Selective Service Boards must have some way of knowing whom to call first, whom to call second, and whom not to call at all. There must be some fair method of determining the sequence of induction for those available for service in the prime age group.

In my judgment a fair system is one which randomizes by lot the order of selection. Each person in the prime age group should have the same chance of appearing at the top of the draft list, at the bottom, or somewhere in the middle. I would therefore establish the following procedure:

At the beginning of the third month after Congress grants this authority, the first of a sequence of selective service years would begin. Prior to the start of each selective service year, the dates of the 365 days to follow would be placed in a sequence determined by a random method. Those who spend the following year in the pool would take their place in the draft sequence in the same order that their birthdays come up on this scrambled calendar. Those born on June 21st, for example, might be at the head of the list, followed by those born on January 12th, who in turn might be followed by those born on October 23rd. Each year, a new random order would be established for the next year's draft pool. In turn those who share the same birthday would be further distributed, this time by the first letter of their last names. But rather than systematically discriminating against those who come at the front of the alphabet, the alphabet would also be scrambled in a random manner.

Once a person's place in the sequence was determined, that assignment would never change. If he were granted a deferment or exemption at age nineteen or twenty, he would re-enter the prime age group at the time his deferment or exemption expires, taking the same place in the sequence that he was originally assigned.

While the random sequence of induction would be nationally established, it would be locally applied by each draft board to meet its local quota. In addition to distributing widely and evenly the risk of induction, the system would also aid many young men in assessing the likelihood of induction even before the classification procedure is completed. This would reduce uncertainty for the individual registrant and, particularly in times of low draft calls, simplify the task of the draft boards.

4. *Undergraduate student deferments.* I continue to believe in the wisdom of college deferments. Permitting the diligent student to complete his college education without interruption by the draft is a wise national investment. Under my proposal a college student who chooses to take a student deferment would still receive his draft sequence number at the time he first enters the prime age group. But he would not be subject to induction until his deferment ended and he re-entered a period of maximum vulnerability.

5. *Graduate Student Induction.* I believe that the induction of men engaged in graduate study should be postponed until the end of the full academic year during which they are first called to military service. I will ask the National Security Council to consider appropriate advice to the Director of the Selective Service to establish this policy. At present, graduate students are allowed to delay induction only to the end of a semester. This often means that they lose valuable time which has been invested in preparation for general examinations or other degree requirements. It can also jeopardize some of the financial arrangements which they made when they planned on a full year of schooling. Induction at the end of a full academic year will provide a less damaging interruption and will still be consistent with Congressional policy.

At the same time, however, the present policy against general graduate deferments should be continued, with exceptions only for students in medical and allied fields who are subject to a later special draft. We must prevent the pyramiding of student deferments—undergraduate and graduate—into a total exemption from military service. For this reason the postponement of induction should be possible only once for each graduate student.

6. *A review of guidelines.* The above measures will reduce the uncertainty of young men as to when and if they may be called for service. It is also important that we encourage a consistent administration of draft procedures by the more than four thousand local boards around the country. I am therefore requesting the National Security Council and the Director of Selective Service to conduct a thorough review of our guidelines, standards, and procedures for deferments and exemptions, and to report their findings to me by December 1, 1969. While the autonomy of local boards provides valuable flexibility and sensitivity, reasonable guidelines can help to limit geographic inequities and enhance the equity of the entire system. The twenty-five thousand con-

cerned citizens who serve their country so well on these local boards deserve the best possible framework for their decisions.

Ultimately we should end the draft. Except for brief periods during the Civil War and World War I, conscription was foreign to the American experience until the 1940s. Only in 1948 did a peacetime draft become a relatively permanent fact of life for this country. Now a full generation of Americans has grown up under a system of compulsory military service.

I am hopeful that we can soon restore the principle of no draft in peacetime. But until we do, let us be sure that the operation of the Selective Service System is as equitable and as reasonable as we can make it. By drafting the youngest first, by limiting the period of vulnerability, by randomizing the selection process, and by reviewing deferment policies, we can do much to achieve these important interim goals. We should do no less for the youth of our country.

TO STRENGTHEN UNEMPLOYMENT INSURANCE
Message to the Congress of the United States
JULY 28, 1969

President Nixon realized early that his economic stabilization policies required cushioning the effect of possible increases in unemployment. He proposed extensive changes in the existing system of unemployment insurance, substantially unrevised for some years.

Coverage expanded to include at least 4 million additional workers was agreed to in Congress with some modification of the President's program.

The best time to strengthen our unemployment insurance system is during a period of relatively full employment.

The Secretary of Labor is sending to the Congress today proposed legislation to extend unemployment insurance to 4.8 million workers not now covered; to end the shortsighted restrictions that stand in the way of needed retraining efforts; and to add a Federal program automatically extending the duration of benefits in periods of high employment.

There are three principles to be considered as we move to make the unemployment insurance system responsive to our times.

Unemployment insurance is an earned benefit. When a man covered by unemployment insurance is working, the employer pays a tax on his wages to insure against the day when the employee may be between jobs. That insurance is like a mandatory fringe benefit; it is insurance bought in the employee's behalf, and the worker therefore is entitled to the benefits he receives when he is unemployed. Accordingly, there is no demeaning of human dignity, no feeling of being "on the dole," when the insured worker receives benefits due.

Unemployment insurance is one of the foremost examples of creative Federal-state partnership. Although the system was created by Federal law, most decisions about the nature of the program are left to the states, which administer the system with state employees. This makes the system far more flexible and attuned to local needs and special circumstances of local economies.

Unemployment insurance is an economic stabilizer. If, for example, the economy were ever to slow and unemployment were to rise, this program automatically would act to sustain personal income. This would help prevent a downturn from gathering momentum resulting from declines in purchasing power. When employment is at a high level, and greater stimulation of consumer demand is unwanted, relatively little money flows into the economy from unemployment insurance.

With these principles in mind, I am making these recommendations for both Federal and state action:

1. We should act together to extend unemployment protection to more employees, including many highly vulnerable to layoffs who are not now covered.

2. The states should make certain that workers throughout the United States receive enough money for a long enough period of time to sustain them while they seek new jobs.

3. We should end the restrictions imposed by almost half the states on payments to unemployed workers undergoing retraining and, instead, follow the lead of those states which encourage retraining.

4. We should better protect the investment made on behalf of the insured by seeing to it that the funds are paid only to those who should receive them.

5. We should increase the responsiveness of the system to major changes in national economic conditions.

6. We should strengthen the financing of the system which presently discriminates against the low-wage worker and the steady employer.

1. *Protecting More Employees*

Over 57 million workers are protected by unemployment insurance. However, almost 17 million are not covered; more than half of these are employees of state and local governments. The last extension of coverage was enacted during the Eisenhower Administration, when 6 million additional workers were included; there is a clear social need today to cover as many more employees as we can.

I propose that an additional 4.8 million workers be covered by unemployment insurance. These include:

—1.6 million workers in *small firms* with less than four employees;

—400,000 on *large farms* employing four or more workers in each of twenty weeks;

—200,000 in *agricultural processing* activities;

—1.8 million in *non-profit organizations;*

—600,000 in *state hospitals* and *universities;*

—200,000 salesmen, delivery tradesmen, and others who are not currently defined as employees.

These 4.8 million workers are in real need of protection against unemployment. Many of them are low-wage workers with little job security and no prospect of termination pay if they are laid off.

The present gaps in coverage work a disproportionate hardship on minority workers, since a higher percentage of the 4.8 million are non-white, compared to the entire labor force.

To cushion the immediate impact of this extension on employers, I recommend that states be permitted to lower the tax rates on newly covered employers until such time as a record of employment experience can be compiled to determine what their true rate should be.

With the passage of this legislation, the majority of those remaining uncovered will be employees of state and local governments. I urge the states and localities to take action, in the light of their local circumstances, to include their own employees in unemployment insurance coverage.

2. *Making Benefits Adequate*

The basic purpose of the Unemployment Insurance Program is to pay weekly benefits high enough to prevent a severe cut in a worker's standard of living when he is between jobs. The principle is generally accepted that it takes at least 50 percent of the worker's wage to meet this purpose.

Almost every state subscribes to this general principle, but benefit ceilings in their legislation have in fact made this principle largely ineffective, especially for the family breadwinner. At least two out of five claimants currently fail to get a benefit equal to one half their wages.

In 1954 President Eisenhower recommended to states that they provide a maximum high enough to permit the great majority of covered workers to receive one half their wages. This means that at least 80 percent of insured workers should be able to receive a benefit of one half their wages if unemployed.

Men are most adversely affected by the limit on weekly benefits. In one large industrial state, for example, only 23 percent of the men receive benefits equal to as much as one half their weekly wages.

If the program is to fulfill its role, it is essential that the benefit maximum be raised. A maximum of two thirds of the average wage in the state would result in benefits of 50 percent in wages to at least 80 percent of insured workers.

Up to now the responsibility for determining benefit amounts has been the responsibility of the states. There are advantages in states having that freedom. However, the overriding consideration is that the objective of adequate benefits be achieved. I call upon the states to act within the next two years to meet this goal, thereby averting the need for Federal action.

3. Encouraging Retraining

During the present decade, many manpower programs were launched in the United States. We have seen how unemployed workers can be equipped with new skills and started on new careers. When the decade began, only three states permitted workers who enrolled in retraining programs to continue to receive benefit payments. All the rest disqualified them upon entry into training.

During the early 1960s, many states recognized the potential of training for employment rehabilitation, and by 1969 twenty-five states, plus Puerto Rico and the District of Columbia, had removed such restrictive requirements.

However, twenty-five states continue to discourage retraining by denying benefits to workers in such programs on the theory that they are not "available for work." On the contrary, the workers are trying to keep themselves available by learning new techniques and technologies, and government should certainly stop penalizing them for doing something that government, business, and labor all want to encourage.

I propose a requirement that the remaining states permit workers

to continue to receive benefits while enrolled in training programs de-
signed to increase their employability.

4. Protecting the Insurance System

We must also be sure that benefits are going only to those people
the system is designed to protect. The funds must not be dissipated.

Attachment to the Labor Force. The unemployment insurance system is designed to protect workers whose attachment to the labor force
is more than casual. A worker's attachment is measured by both his past
employment history and his present situation. He must be ready, willing,
and able to work and trying to find work while he is claiming benefits;
and he must have had at least a certain amount of employment in the
recent past. Generally, from fourteen to twenty weeks of work is required,
depending on the employment patterns of the state and the minimum
duration of benefits.

A few states, however, measure past employment by a flat dollar
amount. This discriminates against the low-wage worker, because it
means he must work for a longer period to be eligible. Also, it permits
other, high-wage workers to become eligible on the basis of very short
seasonal work. *I recommend that a standard based on a minimum period
of fifteen weeks' employment be required as a condition of benefit eligibility, and that no flat dollar amount be permitted as the only yardstick.*

Workers on Strike. The unemployment tax we require employers to
pay was never intended to supplement strike funds to be used against
them. A worker who chooses to exercise his right to strike is not involuntarily unemployed.

In two states workers on strike are paid unemployment insurance
benefits after a certain period. This is not the purpose of the unemployment insurance system.

*I propose a requirement that this practice of paying unemployment
insurance benefits to workers directly engaged in a strike be discon-
tinued.*

5. Improving Responsiveness to Economic Conditions

Difficult times are far less likely to occur in nations that take the
trouble to prepare for them. The presence of a strong, antirecessionary
arsenal will in itself help prevent the need for its ever being used.

In normal times, the duration of benefit payments may be adequate.
Most state programs now provide around twenty-six weeks of benefits;
for the great majority of claimants, this is enough to see them through

to another job. However, if the economy were ever to falter, the number of persons exhausting benefits would grow rapidly.

In each of the last two periods of high unemployment, the President proposed, and the Congress enacted, legislation to extend the duration of benefits temporarily. However, while this process was taking place, many workers were without income, and the economy was exposed to sharp declines in personal income due to unemployment.

I am proposing legislation that would automatically extend the length of time benefits are paid in all states when the national jobless rate of those covered by insurance equals or exceeds 4.5 percent for three consecutive months. If periods of high unemployment were ever to occur, individuals would receive benefits for an additional period up to thirteen weeks; this extension would end when the national unemployment rate of those in the system (currently 2.2 percent) fell back below 4.5 percent, and when the number exhausting their benefits in a three-month period dropped below 1 percent of those covered. These additional payments would be financed out of that portion of the unemployment tax that is now retained by the Federal government.

6. *Strengthening and Reforming Financing*

We must enable the Federal government to finance its share of the improvements proposed in this message, along with the costs of administering the Employment Security System. In addition, there will be a need to improve the ability of states to finance the higher benefit levels I am urging.

I propose that the taxable wage base be raised over a five-year period to $6,000 and thereafter be reviewed periodically to make certain the adequacy of financing.

In the majority of states the taxable wage base for the Unemployment Insurance Tax is the first $3,000 of wages—exactly what it was three decades ago. In that same period average wages in employment covered by the system have increased almost fivefold. The low tax base places obstacles in the way of hiring low-wage workers because a substantially higher proportion of their wage is taxed. In addition, the impact of the tax tends to encourage use of overtime rather than adding workers.

The higher base will have the desirable effect of allocating costs more equitably among employers. Particularly at the state level, overall benefit costs will represent a lower percent of taxable wages, and allow rates to reflect employer experience more accurately.

An Anchor to Windward. Unemployment insurance was begun as an answer to the human need for sustenance of the unemployed working-man seeking another job. It was designed to reduce the element of economic panic in job-hunting.

But as we move now to extend that insurance and meet that need more fully, we discover—not quite by accident—the bonus of serendipity. Here is insurance purchased through a tax on the employers of America in behalf of their employees that can be a potent counter to a downturn in the business cycle. This proves that well-conceived social legislation can be a great boon to business and to all Americans affected by the state of the economy.

The success of this system can be a great example in the relationship between the states and the Federal government.

The Federal government brought this unemployment insurance system into being—but the states have rightly adopted it as their own. The Federal government has traditionally established minimum coverage—but many states have expanded that coverage to fit their own needs.

Now the Federal-state system of unemployment insurance should move to provide adequate benefits in accordance with the goal that has been set and with full recognition of the diversity of economic conditions among states. Such action is most important to protect the individual and to achieve the antirecessionary potential of unemployment insurance.

The Federal and state actions recommended will help advance the economy of each state and in protecting the economy of the nation. In human terms the recommended changes will better enable a worker to weather the adversity of unemployment and to find a suitable job.

I urge that Congress and the states enact the legislation proposed to carry out these improvements.

SAFETY AND GOOD HEALTH FOR WORKERS
Message to the Congress of the United States
AUGUST 6, 1969

President Nixon decided to extend the increased protections provided in the Mine Safety Bill to other occupations. Legislation was submitted. Differences with Congress centered on methods of administration, but in the early months of 1970 the Occupational Safety and Health Bill moved toward passage.

Technological progress can be a mixed blessing. The same new method or new product which improves our lives can also be the source of unpleasantness and pain. For man's lively capacity to innovate is not always matched by his ability to understand his innovations fully, to use them properly, or to protect himself against the unforeseen consequences of the changes he creates.

The side effects of progress present special dangers in the work places of our country. For the working man and woman, the by-products of change constitute an especially serious threat. Some efforts to protect the safety and health of the American worker have been made in the past by private industry and by all levels of government. But new technologies have moved even faster to create newer dangers. Today we are asking our workers to perform far different tasks from those they performed five or fifteen or fifty years ago. It is only right that the protection we give them is also up-to-date.

There has been much discussion in recent months about the quality of the environment in which Americans live. It is important to note in this regard that during their working years most American workers spend nearly a quarter of their time at their jobs. For them, the quality of the work place is one of the most important of environmental questions. The protection of that quality is a critical matter for government attention.

Few people realize the extent of needless illness, needless injury, and needless death which results from unsafe or unhealthy working conditions. Every now and then a major disaster—in a factory or an office building or a mine—will dramatize certain occupational hazards. But most such dangers are realized under less dramatic circumstances. Often, for example, a threat to good health will build up slowly over a period of many years. To such situations the public gives very little attention. Yet the cumulative extent of such losses is great.

Consider these facts. Every year in this country some fourteen thousand deaths can be attributed to work-related injuries or illnesses. Because of accidents or diseases sustained on the job, some 250 million man-days of labor are lost annually. The most important consequence of these losses is the human tragedy which results when an employee— often the head of a family—is struck down. In addition, the economy loses millions of dollars in unrealized production and millions more must be used to pay workmen's compensation benefits and medical expenses. It is interesting to note that in the last five years the number of man-days lost because of work-related injuries has been ten times the number lost because of strikes.

What have we done about this problem? The record is haphazard and spotty. For many decades governmental responsibility for safe work places has rested with the states. But the scope and effectiveness of state laws and state administration varies widely, and discrepancies in the performances of state programs appear to be increasing. Moreover, some states are fearful that stricter standards will place them at a disadvantage with other states.

Many industries and businesses have made commendable progress in protecting worker health and safety on their own. Some, in fact, have managed to reduce the frequency of accidents by as much as 80 or 90 percent, demonstrating what can be accomplished with the proper effort. But such voluntary successes are not yet sufficiently widespread.

There are some other positive signs. Collective bargaining agreements often include safety and health provisions; many professional organizations have suggested voluntary standards; groups like the National Safety Council have worked to promote better working conditions. But the overall record is still uneven and unsettling.

The Federal role in occupational safety and health has thus far been limited. A few specific industries have been made subject to special Federal laws and limited regulations have been applied to workers in companies that hold certain government contracts. In my message to Congress last March on coal mine safety, I outlined an important area in which further specific Federal action is imperative. But something broader is also needed, I believe. I am therefore recommending a new mechanism through which safety and health standards for industry in general can be improved.

The comprehensive Occupational Safety and Health Act which the Secretary of Labor will soon transmit to the Congress will correct some of the important deficiencies of earlier approaches. It will go beyond the limited "accident" orientation of the past, giving greater attention to health considerations, which are often difficult to perceive and which have often been overlooked. It will separate the function of setting safety and health standards from the function of enforcing them. Appropriate procedures to guarantee due process of law and the right to appeal will be incorporated. The proposal will also provide a flexible mechanism which can react quickly to the new technologies of tomorrow.

Under the suggested legislation, maximum use will be made of standards established through a voluntary consensus of industry, labor, and other experts. No standard will be set until the views of all interested parties have been heard. This proposal would also encourage stronger efforts at the state level, sharing enforcement responsibility with states which have adequate programs. Greater emphasis will also be given to research and education, for the effects of modern technologies on the physical well-being of workers are complex and poorly understood. The Public Health Service has done some important groundwork in the field of occupational health, but we still need much more information and understanding.

Our specific recommendations are as follows:

1. Safety and health standards will be set by a new National Occupational Safety and Health Board. The five members of the Board will be appointed by the President with the advice and consent of the Senate to five-year terms; one member of the Board will change each year. At least three members of the Board must have technical competence in the field of occupational safety and health.

The Board will have the power to promulgate standards which have been established by nationally recognized public or private standard-setting organizations. Thousands of these standards have been carefully worked out over the years; the Board will adopt such a "national consensus standard" when the standard-setting organization possesses high technical competence and considers the views of all interested parties in making its decisions.

If the Secretary of Labor (in matters of safety) or the Secretary of Health, Education and Welfare (in matters of health) objects to any such "national consensus standard," he may bring that objection before the Board. The Board can then set a new standard after giving the matter a full public hearing. When national consensus standards do not exist, the Board will have the power to break new ground after full hearings. If the Secretary of Labor or the Secretary of Health, Education and Welfare object to the Board's action, he can delay its implementation until at least three of the Board members reconfirm their original decision.

2. The Secretary of Labor will have the initial role in enforcing the standards which the Board establishes. The Secretary will ask employers whom he believes to be in violation of the standards to comply with them voluntarily; if they fail to do so, he can bring a complaint before the Occupational Safety and Health Board which will hold a full hearing on the matter. If the Board determines that a violation exists, it shall issue appropriate orders which the Secretary of Labor can then enforce through the Court system. In emergency situations the Secretary can go directly to the courts and petition for temporary relief.

3. The state governments will be encouraged to submit plans for expanding and improving their own occupational safety and health programs. Federal grants will be available to pay up to 90 percent of the cost of developing such plans. When a state presents a plan which

provides at least as much protection to the worker as the Federal plan, then the Federal standard administration will give way to the state administration, with the Federal government assuming up to 50 percent of that state's costs.

4. The Secretary of Health, Education and Welfare will be given the specific assignment of developing and carrying out a broad program of study, experiment, demonstration, education, information, and technical assistance—and further means of promoting better safety and health practices in the work place. The Secretary will be required to submit a comprehensive report to the President and the Congress, including an evaluation of the program and further recommendations for its improvement.

5. A National Advisory Committee on Occupational Safety and Health will be established to advise the Secretary of Labor and the Secretary of Health, Education and Welfare in the administration of the Act.

Three years ago, following its study of traffic and highway safety, the Congress noted that modern technology had brought with it new driving hazards, and accordingly it enacted the National Traffic and Motor Vehicle Act and the Highway Safety Act. With the advent of a new work place technology, we must now give similar attention to work place safety and health.

The legislation which this Administration is proposing can do much to improve the environment of the American worker. But it will take much more than new government efforts if we are to achieve our objectives. Employers and employees alike must be committed to the prevention of accidents and disease and alert to every opportunity for promoting that end. Together the private and public sectors can do much that we cannot do separately.

PROTECTION FOR THE CONSUMER
Message to the Congress of the United States
OCTOBER 30, 1969

Consumerism, hailed by some, deplored by others, became an established trend in the Nixon Administration following a sputtering start. The President's first consumer consultant resigned in a furor over her desire to continue with a private consumer testing institute while advising President Nixon on consumer affairs.

In the autumn of his first year in office Nixon recognized growing pressure for consumer protection. He submitted a comprehensive message to Congress, by far the most extensive ever proposed on this subject. Four major bills were submitted: to create by statute a new Office of Consumer Affairs, to expand the powers of the Federal Trade Commission, to set up a system of consumer product testing, and to establish a new system of drug identification. A fifth bill originating in Congress on product warranties and guarantees attracted Administration support.

By initiating consumer legislation, the President pre-empted a field previously the preserve of Democratic Congressional pressure on the consumer product manufacturers, distributors, and advertisers.

Consumerism—Upton Sinclair and Rachel Carson would be glad to know—is a healthy development that is here to stay.

That does not mean that *caveat emptor*—"let the buyer beware"—has been replaced by an equally harsh *caveat venditor*—"let the seller beware." Nor does it mean that government should guide or dominate individual purchasing decisions.

Consumerism in the America of the '70s means that we have adopted the concept of "buyer's rights."

I believe that the buyer in America today has the right to make an intelligent choice among products and services.

The buyer has the right to accurate information on which to make his free choice.

The buyer has the right to expect that his health and safety is taken into account by those who seek his patronage.

The buyer has the right to register his dissatisfaction, and have his complaint heard and weighed, when his interests are badly served.

This "Buyer's Bill of Rights" will help provide greater personal freedom for individuals as well as better business for everyone engaged in trade.

The program I am outlining today represents the most significant set of Presidential recommendations concerning consumer interests in our history. Specifically, I propose:

—A new office of Consumer Affairs in the Executive Office of the President, with new legislative standing, an expanded budget, and greater responsibilities. This will give every American consumer a permanent voice in the White House.

—A new Division of Consumer Protection in the Department of

Justice, to act as a consumer advocate before Federal regulatory agencies in judicial proceedings and in government councils.

—A new consumer protection law which would be enforced by the Department of Justice and United States Attorneys across the land. Such a law would also better enable consumers either as individuals or as a class to go into court to obtain redress for the damages they suffer.

—Expanded powers for a revitalized Federal Trade Commission, to enable it to protect consumers promptly and effectively.

—A newly activated National Commission on Consumer Finance to investigate and report on the state of consumer credit.

—Expanded consumer education activities, including government review of product-testing processes, a new *Consumer Bulletin*, and the release of certain government information regarding consumer products.

—Stronger efforts in the field of food and drug safety, including a thorough re-examination of the Food and Drug Administration and a review of the products on the Generally Regarded As Safe list.

—Other reforms, including an expansion of consumer activities in the Office of Economic Opportunity and greater efforts to encourage the strengthening of state and local programs.

To their credit, producers and sellers have generally become far more responsible with the passing years, but even the limited abuses which occur now have greater impact. Products themselves are more complicated; there is more about them that can go wrong and less about them that can be readily understood by laymen. Mass production and mass distribution systems mean that a small error can have a wide effect; the carelessness of one producer can bring harm or disappointment to many. Moreover, the responsibility for a particular problem is far more difficult to trace than was once the case, and even when responsibility for an error can be assigned, it is often difficult to lodge an effective complaint against it.

All too often, the real advantages of mass production are accompanied by customer alienation; many an average buyer is intimidated by seemingly monolithic organizations, and frequently comes to feel alone and helpless in what he regards as a cruelly impersonal marketplace. In addition, many of the government's efforts to help the consumer are still geared to the problems of past decades; when it is able to act at all, government too often acts too slowly.

Fortunately, most businessmen in recent years have recognized that the confidence of the public over a long period of time is an important ingredient for their own success and have themselves made important voluntary progress in consumer protection. At the same time, buyers are making their voices heard more often, as individuals and through consumer organizations. These trends are to be encouraged and our governmental programs must emphasize their value. Government consumer programs, in fact, are a complement to these voluntary efforts. They are designed to help honest and conscientious businessmen by discouraging their dishonest or careless competitors.

New Office of Consumer Affairs

One of the central roles in present government efforts in the consumer rights field is performed by the President's Special Assistant for Consumer Affairs and those who work with her. This position has been created by Presidential order rather than by statute, however, and it is neither as visible nor as effective as it should be. It is important that both the prestige and the responsibility of this office be strengthened.

I am therefore asking the Congress to establish within the Executive Office of the President a new Office of Consumer Affairs to play a leading role in the crusade for consumer justice. This Office and its director would have central responsibility for coordinating all Federal activities in the consumer protection field, helping to establish priorities, to resolve conflicts, to initiate research, and to recommend improvements in a wide range of government programs. The Office would advise the President on consumer matters and would alert other government officials to the potential impact of their decisions on the consumers' interests. It would receive complaints from individual consumers and refer them to appropriate agencies or to the businesses concerned.

The new Office of Consumer Affairs would not work solely within the Executive Branch of the government, however; it would continue to carry out other assignments which the Special Assistant to the President for Consumer Affairs now performs. For example, when called upon, it would assist in the legislative process, testifying at Congressional hearings, and consulting with individual Congressmen. It would aid schools and media in educating the public in consumer skills. The new Office will continue the constructive interchange of information which the Special Assistant has established with businesses and industries, and carry forward its assistance to state and local consumer protection programs.

As I will explain in greater detail later in this message, I am also asking the Special Assistant for Consumer Affairs to undertake specific surveillance responsibilities in the area of product safety, to review the government's policy concerning the release of its own information on consumer products, and to publish a new *Consumer Bulletin* on a regular basis. When the new Office of Consumer Affairs is established, it would take over these and related duties.

A new Office of Consumer Affairs would be a focal point for a wide variety of government efforts to aid people who buy. I urge the Congress to grant it the legislative standing and the added resources necessary to do this work effectively.

A Division of Consumer Protection and a New Consumer Protection Law

A second important structural reform which I am recommending is the establishment by statute of a new Consumer Protection Division in the Department of Justice. This Division would be headed by an Assistant Attorney General and would be staffed by lawyers and economists. It would be adequately financed and given appropriate investigative power so that it could effectively ascertain consumer needs and advance consumer causes. The head of the new Division would act, in effect, as the consumers' lawyer, representing the consumer interest before Federal agencies, in judicial proceedings, and in government councils.

I also propose that Congress arm this new Consumer Protection Division with a new law—one which would prohibit a broad, but clearly defined, range of frauds and deceptions. The legislation I will propose will be of sufficient scope to provide substantial protection to consumers and of sufficient specificity to give the necessary advance notice to businessmen of the activities to be considered illegal.

The role of the new Assistant Attorney General for Consumer Protection would be similar to that of the Assistant Attorney General who heads the Antitrust Division in the Department of Justice. Just as the Antitrust Division enforces the antitrust laws and intervenes in various governmental proceedings to preserve competition, so the Consumer Protection Division would enforce consumer rights and intervene in agency proceedings to protect the consumer. In enforcing these rights, the Assistant Attorney General for Consumer Protection would also have the assistance of United States Attorneys throughout the country. Their power to take quick and effective action under the new statute would be particularly important for protecting low-income families who are frequently victimized by fraudulent and deceptive practices.

Effective representation of the consumer does not require the creation of a new Federal department or independent agency, but it does require that an appropriate arm of the government be given the tools to do an effective job. In the past a lone Justice Department lawyer—

the Consumer Counsel—has attempted to carry out a portion of this task. Our proposal asks that the new Division of Consumer Protection be adequately staffed and independently funded, as is the Antitrust Division, so that it can vigorously represent the interests of the consumer and enforce the newly proposed legislation.

The new Assistant Attorney General and his Division would, of course, work closely with the Office of Consumer Affairs, the Federal Trade Commission, and state and local law enforcement agencies.

Consumers in the Federal Courts— Individual and Class Suits

Present Federal law gives private citizens no standing to sue for fraudulent or deceptive practices, and state laws are often not adequate to their problems. Even if private citizens could sue, the damage suffered by any one consumer would not ordinarily be great enough to warrant costly, individual litigation. One would probably not go through a lengthy court proceeding, for example, merely to recover the cost of a household appliance.

To correct this situation, I will recommend legislation to give private citizens the right to bring action in a Federal court to recover damages, upon the successful termination of a government suit under the new consumer protection law.

This measure will, for the first time, give consumers access to the Federal courts for violation of a Federal law concerning fraudulent and deceptive practices, without regard to the amount in controversy. Under Federal court rules, consumers would have the right to sue as a class and not only as individuals. In other words, a group of people could come into court together if they could show that the act in question affected all of them. This is a significant consideration, for it would allow a number of citizens to divide among themselves the high costs of bringing a lawsuit. Although each person's individual damage might be small, the cumulative effect of a class complaint could be significant and in some circumstances could provide a significant deterrent to expensive fraud or deception. At the same time the fact that private action must follow in the wake of a successful government action will prevent harassment of legitimate businessmen by unlimited nuisance lawsuits.

The Federal Trade Commission

The problems of the American consumer first became a central matter of Federal concern in the late years of the nineteenth century and the early years of the twentieth. One of the important elements in the government's response at that time was the establishment in 1914 of the Federal Trade Commission, an independent body which was designed to play a leading role in the fight against unfair and deceptive trade practices. While new legislation has given the FTC additional and more specific duties, there has been increasing public concern over the Commission's ability to meet all of its many responsibilities. I believe the time has now come for the reactivation and revitalization of the FTC.

The chairman-designate of the FTC has assured me that he intends to initiate a new era of vigorous action as soon as he is confirmed by the Senate and takes office. A report prepared at my request by a commission of the American Bar Association should help considerably in this effort, for it presents a valuable description of the problems which face the FTC and the ways in which they can be remedied. I urge the FTC to give serious consideration to these recommendations. I have also asked the Bureau of the Budget to help with the revitalization process by supervising an even more detailed management study of this commission.

I am particularly hopeful that a number of specific improvements in the FTC can be quickly accomplished. For example, the Commission should immediately begin to process its business more rapidly so that it can reduce its unacceptably large backlog of cases. I also believe that it should seek out new information on consumer problems through more energetic field investigations, rather than waiting for complaints to come in through its mailrooms or from other government agencies. This initiative could begin with pilot field projects in a limited number of cities, as the ABA task force has suggested. Whatever the strategy, I would hope that it could be accomplished through a more efficient use of existing personnel and finances; if that proves impossible, added funds should later be appropriated for this purpose.

Administrative reforms will provide only part of the answer, however. I believe the Commission should also consider the extent to which Section 5 of the Federal Trade Commission Act, broadly interpreted, may be used more effectively to cope with contemporary consumer problems. This is the section which gives the Commission its legislative mandate to move against unfair or deceptive practices. The language of this section might well provide an appropriate instrument for policing more effectively some of the more prevalent abuses described by the ABA task force study.

Even if the Commission does apply Section 5 more broadly, however, there remains a question about its jurisdiction which the Congress should promptly resolve. Past FTC enforcement activities have been inhibited by a Supreme Court decision of some twenty-five years ago, holding that activities "affecting" interstate commerce were not subject to FTC jurisdiction since the language of the law was limited to activities "in" interstate commerce. This means that there is a doubt at present concerning the FTC's ability to consider many unfair and deceptive practices which have a nationwide impact but are local in terms of their actual operation.

I am therefore recommending that the Congress amend Section 5 so as to permit the FTC to take action concerning consumer abuses which "affect" interstate commerce, as well as those which are technically "in" interstate commerce. This amendment would make it clear that the FTC has a jurisdiction consistent with that of several other Federal agencies and commissions. The purpose of the amendment is to clarify FTC jurisdiction over cases which have true national significance; it should not be interpreted in a way which burdens the Commission with a large number of cases which are of only local importance.

One of the most important obstacles to the present effectiveness of the FTC is its inability to seek an injunction against an unfair or deceptive business practice. The result of this inability is an unacceptable delay between the time a harmful practice is discovered and the time it is ended. Often two years will pass between the time the FTC agrees to hear a complaint and the time it issues its final order, and another two years may pass while the order is reviewed by the courts.

I recommend that the Congress remedy this situation by giving to the Federal Trade Commission the power to seek and obtain from the Federal courts a preliminary injunction against consumer practices which are unfair or deceptive. The judicial process includes safeguards which will assure that this authority is fairly used. Courts will retain their usual discretion to grant or deny an injunction in the light of all the consequences for both the accused and the plaintiff. Parties will, of course, retain their right to a fair hearing before any injunction is issued.

National Commission on Consumer Finance

The buying public and businessmen alike have been concerned in recent years about the growth of consumer credit. Twenty-five years ago the total consumer credit outstanding was only $5.7 billion; today it is $110 billion. The arrangements by which that credit is provided are subject to government supervision and regulation, an assignment which has recently become increasingly complex and difficult. For this reason a National Commission on Consumer Finance was established by law in 1968. It was instructed to review the adequacy and the cost of consumer credit and to consider the effectiveness with which the public is protected against unfair credit practices.

The National Commission on Consumer Finance should begin its important work immediately. I will therefore announce shortly the names of three new members of the Commission, including a new chairman, and I will ask the Congress for a supplemental appropriation to finance the Commission's investigations during the current fiscal year. I look forward to receiving the report of the National Commission on Consumer Finance in January of 1971.

Consumer Education—Information on Product Testing

No matter how alert and resourceful a purchaser may be, he is relatively helpless unless he has adequate, trustworthy information about the product he is considering and *knows what to make of that information.* The fullest product description is useless if a consumer lacks the understanding or the will to utilize it.

This Administration believes that consumer education programs should be expanded. Our study of existing consumer education efforts in both the public schools and in adult education programs has been funded by the Office of Education and will report its results in the near future.

The Special Assistant to the President for Consumer Affairs is focusing many of the resources of her office on educational projects. One new project which I am asking that office to undertake is the preparation and publication, on a regular basis, of a new *Consumer Bulletin.* This publication will contain a selection of items which are of concern to consumers and which now appear in the daily government journal *The Federal Register.* The material it presents, which will include notices of hearings, proposed and final rules and orders, and other useful information, will be translated from its technical form into language which is readily understandable by the layman.

The government can help citizens do a better job of product evaluation in other ways as well. First, I recommend that Congress authorize the Federal government to review the standards for evaluation which are used by private testing laboratories and to publish its findings as to their adequacy, working through appropriate scientific agencies such as the National Bureau of Standards. Laboratories presently issue quality endorsements, of one kind or another, for a wide variety of products. Some of these endorsements have meaning, but others do not. It would be most helpful, I believe, if the testing procedures on which these endorsements were based were evaluated by government experts. Manufacturers whose products had been tested under government-evaluated testing standards would be allowed to advertise the fact. If no testing standard existed or if the standard in use was found to be inadequate, then the appropriate agency would be authorized to develop a new one.

Secondly, I propose that we help the consumer by sharing with him some of the knowledge which the government has accumulated in the process of purchasing consumer items for its own use. Government agencies, such as the General Services Administration and the Department of Defense, have developed their own extensive procedures for evaluating the products they buy—products which range from light bulbs and detergents to tires and electric drills. As a result of this process, they have developed considerable purchasing expertise; in short, they know what to look for when they are buying a given product. They know, for example, what general types of paint are appropriate for certain surfaces; they know what "checkpoints" to examine when a piece of machinery is being purchased. The release of such information could help all of our people become more skillful consumers. I am therefore asking my Special Assistant for Consumer Affairs to develop a program for disseminating general information of this sort and to carry on further studies as to how the skill and knowledge of government purchasers can be shared with the public in a fair and useful manner.

Food and Drugs

The surveillance responsibilities of the Food and Drug Administration extend not only to food and drugs themselves, but also to cosmetics, therapeutic devices, and other products. Both the structure and the procedures of the FDA must be fully adequate to this sizeable and sensitive assignment, which is why this Administration has made the FDA the subject of intensive study.

I have asked the Secretary of Health, Education and Welfare to undertake a thorough re-examination of the FDA, and I expect that this review will soon produce a number of important reforms in the agency's operations. This study is taking up several central questions: What further financial and personnel resources does the FDA require? Are laboratory findings communicated as promptly and fully as is desirable to high Administration officials and to the public? What should be the relationship of the FDA to other scientific arms of the government? What methods can bring the greatest possible talent to bear on the critical questions the FDA considers?

There are a number of actions relating to FDA matters which should be taken promptly, even while our study of that institution continues. For example, I have already asked the Secretary of Health, Education and Welfare to initiate a full review of food additives. This investigation should move as fast as our resources permit, re-examining the safety of substances which are now described by the phrase "Generally Recognized As Safe" (GRAS). Recent findings concerning the effects of cyclamate sweeteners on rats underscore the importance of continued vigilance in this field. The major suppliers and users of cyclamates have shown a sense of public responsibility during the recent difficulties, and I am confident that such cooperation from industry will continue to facilitate this investigation.

I also recommend that the Congress take action which would make possible, for the first time, the rapid identification of drugs and drug containers in a time of personal emergency. When overdosage or accidental ingestion of a drug presently occurs, a physician is often unable to identify that drug without elaborate laboratory analysis. Many manufacturers are already working to remedy this problem on a voluntary basis by imprinting an identification number on every drug capsule and container they produce. As many in the industry have urged, this simple process should now be required of all drug producers, provided they are given suitable time to adjust their production machinery.

Another important medical safety problem concerns medical devices—equipment ranging from contact lenses and hearing aids to artificial valves—which are implanted in the body. Certain minimum standards should be established for such devices; the government should be given additional authority to require premarketing clearance in certain cases. The scope and nature of any legislation in this area must be carefully considered, and the Department of Health, Education and Welfare is undertaking a thorough study of medical device regulation. I will receive the results of that study early in 1970.

Other Proposals

THE OFFICE OF ECONOMIC OPPORTUNITY

The problems which all American consumers encounter are experienced with particular intensity by the poor. With little purchasing experience to rely upon and no money to waste, poorer citizens are the most frequent and most tragic victims of commercial malpractices. The

Office of Economic Opportunity is therefore establishing its own Division of Consumer Affairs to help focus and improve its already extensive consumer activities for poorer Americans. The nationwide network of Community Action Agencies can be one instrument for extending consumer education into this area.

HELPING THE STATES AND LOCALITIES

An important segment of consumer abuses can be handled most effectively at the state and local level, we believe, provided that each state has a strong consumer protection statute and an effective mechanism for enforcing it. Several states set examples for the Federal government in this field; every state should be encouraged to explore the need for an adequately financed Division of Consumer Protection as a part of its State Attorney General's office. Both the Special Assistant for Consumer Affairs and the Federal Trade Commission can do much to help states and localities to improve their consumer protection activities. The codification of state consumer protection laws which the Special Assistant is now conducting promises to be a useful part of the states in this effort.

GUARANTEES AND WARRANTIES

Consumers are properly concerned about the adequacy of guarantees and warranties on the goods they buy. On January 8, 1969, a task force recommended that the household appliance industry disclose more fully the terms of the warranties it provides. It recommended that if at the end of one year voluntary progress had not occurred, then legislative action should be considered.

In order to evaluate the industry's recent progress, I am today reactivating that task force. It will be chaired by my Special Assistant for Consumer Affairs and will include representatives from the Department of Commerce, the Department of Labor, the Federal Trade Commission, the Department of Justice, and the Council of Economic Advisers. I am asking the task force to make its report by the end of this year and to comment on the need for guarantee and warranty legislation in the household appliance industries and in other fields.

PRODUCT SAFETY

The product safety area is one which requires further investigation and further legislation, as the hearings of the National Commission on Product Safety have already demonstrated. I am asking my Special Assistant for Consumer Affairs to provide continued surveillance in the area of product safety, particularly after June 30, 1970, when the

National Commission on Product Safety is scheduled to complete its work. And I am also instructing the appropriate agencies of the government to consult with the Commission and to prepare appropriate safety legislation for submission to Congress.

Finally, I am asking the Congress to require that any government agency, in any written decision substantially affecting the consumers' interest, give due consideration to that interest and express in its opinion the manner in which that interest was taken into account. I would also note that the major review which will be conducted this December by the White House Conference on Food, Nutrition, and Health will provide further welcome advances in the protection and education of the American consumer.

Interest in consumer protection has been an important part of American life for many decades. It was in the mid-1920s, in fact, that two of the leading consumer advocates of the day, Stuart Chase and F. J. Schlink, reached the following conclusion: "The time has gone— possibly forever—" they wrote, "when it is possible for each of us to become informed on all things we have to buy. Even the most expert today can have knowledge of only a negligible section of the field. What sense then in a specialized industrial society if each individual must learn by trial and error again and forever again?" It was clear at that time and it is clear today, that the consumer needs expert help. The consumer has received some of that needed help through the years, from a variety of sources, private and public.

Our program is a part of that tradition. Its goal is to turn the Buyer's Bill of Rights into a reality, to make life in a complex society more fair, more convenient, and more productive for all our citizens. Our program is fair to businessmen and good for business, since it encourages everyone who does business to do an even better job of providing quality goods and services. Our action is intended to foster a just marketplace—a marketplace which is fair both to those who sell and those who buy.

12
Our
NATO
Partners

One of the most significant events of the post-World War II period took place in the middle 1960s with the subsiding of Western European fears of Russia. The grand alliance of the North Atlantic Treaty Organization had been formed in 1949 under the American nuclear umbrella to protect the economic renaissance of Western Europe and assure its military security.

Under this protection and over a period of fifteen years Western Europe was stabilized, Russian policy ameliorated—with some exceptions—and the euphoria of security settled over the great European centers of Western culture.

This change rendered NATO less relevant to modern conditions than it had been in the days of Roosevelt, Churchill, and Stalin. President Nixon, recognizing the change, undertook to adjust the alliance to a world in which the Cold War had ended or was coming to an end and the alliance could direct its work toward common social objectives.

His chief proposals in an address in Washington marking the twentieth anniversary of the signing of the North Atlantic Treaty were adopted and are now operative. A committee on the challenges of modern society meets periodically in Brussels. The American representative is Presidential Adviser Daniel P. Moynihan. One of its first projects is sponsorship of an international conference in Detroit on auto safety. A special high-level planning group of NATO is in operation. Deputy foreign ministers have begun to meet to review long-range problems.

A BASTION OF PEACE
Remarks of the President to the NATO Council at Brussels, Belgium

FEBRUARY 24, 1969

Thank you very much, Mr. Secrètary General.

Mr. Chairman and Members of the North Atlantic Council:

I thank you for your very thoughtful and generous words of welcome to this Council and it is indeed a very great pleasure for me to be here.

This Council is both the symbol and the substance of the tie that has joined us as an Atlantic Alliance for nearly twenty years.

On this first trip abroad as President of the United States I find myself thinking back to my first visit to Europe. That was in 1947, in my first year in Congress—my first year, in fact, in public life. I came here then as a member of the Herter Committee, which studied Europe's postwar economic needs in order to help lay the foundations for the Marshall Plan. Although I have been back many times, those first impressions remain valid, for 1947 was the starting point of our journey together. What we have built in the past twenty-two years is a testimony to what can be achieved through common will and a spirit of partnership.

The years since I first visited Western Europe have further confirmed my commitment to the concept of Atlantic partnership.

I should like to take a few minutes today to share with you some of my thoughts about that partnership.

First, as all of us in this room know, partners are not expected always to agree. But they are expected to consult.

I know there have been rumblings of discontent in Europe—a feeling that too often the United States talked at its partners instead of with them, or merely informed them of decisions after they were made instead of consulting with them before deciding.

The United States is determined to listen with a new attentiveness to its NATO partners—not only because they have a right to be heard, but because we want their ideas. I believe we have a right to expect that consultation shall be a two-way street.

This point is at the heart of one of the vital problems facing the Alliance. Consultation, simply as a means of getting agreement for unilateral action, is demoralizing. What we need is genuine consultation, a new spirit of cooperation before the fact.

In the course of my campaign last fall, I said, "If our ideals of Atlantic interdependence are to mean anything in practice, it's time we began lecturing our European partners less and listening to them more. What we need is not more proclamations and declarations, but a greater attention to what our Allies think." This I deeply believe.

That is why I am here. My visits to some of your capitals—and I wish it could be all of them—and to this Council, are in the nature of a search. I have come for work, not for ceremony; to inquire, not to insist; to consult, not to convince; to listen and learn, and to begin what I hope will be a continuing interchange of ideas and insights.

After twenty years the Atlantic Alliance must adapt to the conditions brought on by its success.

It must pool not only its arms but also its brains.

One of the greatest values of having an alliance is the chance it provides to share ideas—to broaden the horizons of our thinking—to multiply the resources of experience and perspective we can bring to our problems, not only in our own immediate areas but throughout the world.

Surely one thing we have learned from these difficult years is that no one nation has a monopoly on wisdom.

We also have learned that no great nation, and no great group of nations, can view the problems of its own community in isolation.

We are all "riders on the Earth together"—fellow citizens of a world community.

In today's world what kind of an alliance shall we strive to build?

As I see it, an alliance is not the temporary pooling of selfish interests; it is a continuing process of cooperation—"a ship on its passage out, and not a voyage complete."

The purpose of this trip is to help encourage that process, to seek ways to keep the relationship between America and Europe in tune with the times.

A modern alliance must be a living thing, capable of growth, able to adapt to changing circumstances.

To keep the Alliance abreast of the times, we must, I believe, today, ask ourselves some hard questions.

NATO was brought into being by the threat from the Soviet Union. What is the nature of that threat today?

When NATO was founded, Europe's economies were still shattered by war. Now they are flourishing. How should this be reflected by changed relationships among the NATO partners?

We are all grappling with problems of a modern environment, which are the by-products of our advanced technologies—problems such as the pollution of air and water and the congestion in our cities. Together we can dramatically advance our mastery of these. By what means can we best cooperate to bring this about?

And most fundamental of all—the one thing certain about the next twenty years is that they will be different from the last twenty. What do we expect from our alliance in these next twenty years? How shall we adapt our structure to advance our purpose?

The answers to these great questions will not be decided in a week: they deal with the vast sweep of history, they need the most thorough deliberations. But the questions are with us; we cannot evade them; and the fact that we have begun this process of soul-searching is a good augury.

I have said before that we are ending a period of confrontation and entering an era of negotiation. In due course, and with proper preparation, the United States will enter into negotiations with the Soviet Union on a wide range of issues, some of which will affect our European allies.

We will do so on the basis of full consultation and cooperation with our allies, because we recognize that the chances for successful negotiations depend on our unity.

I realize that this course has not always been followed adequately in the past. But I pledge to you today, that in any negotiations affecting the interests of the NATO nations, there will be full and genuine consultation before and during those negotiations.

Beyond consulting on those negotiations, and beyond consulting on other policies that directly affect the NATO nations themselves, I intend to consult on a broad range of other matters. I shall not only welcome but actively seek the counsel of America's NATO partners on the questions that may affect the peace and stability of the world, whatever the part of the world in which they arise.

The nations of NATO are rich in physical resources—but they are even richer in their accumulated wisdom, and their experience of the world today. In fashioning America's policies, we need the benefit of that wisdom and that experience.

As NATO enters its third decade I see for it an opportunity to be more than it ever has been before: a bulwark of peace, the architect of new means of partnership, and an invigorated forum for new ideas and new technologies to enrich the lives of our peoples.

In creating new policy-making machinery in Washington, one of my principal aims has been to shift the focus of American policy from crisis management to crisis prevention. That is one of the reasons why I value NATO so highly. NATO was established as a preventive force— and NATO can be credited with the fact that while Europe has endured its share of crises in these past twenty years, the ultimate crisis that would have provoked a nuclear war has been prevented. Those nations that were free twenty years ago are still free today.

Thus, in its original purpose, NATO has been a resounding success: Europe and America, the Old World and the New, working together have proved that the dream of collective security can be made a reality.

But we cannot rest on our laurels; there is no real security in stagnation. The successful strategies of the past two decades are inadequate to the decades ahead.

The tie that binds Europe and America is not the contemplation of danger, to be stretched or tightened by the fluctuations of fear.

The ties that bind our continents are the common tradition of freedom; the common desire for progress; the common passion for peace.

In that more constructive spirit, let us look at new situations with new eyes, and in so doing, set an example for the world.

A NEW JOB FOR NATO
Remarks of the President at the Commemorative Session
of the North Atlantic Council in Washington, D.C.
APRIL 10, 1969

Mr. Secretary, Mr. President, Mr. Secretary General, Your Excellencies, and our distinguished guests:

As we gather here today, we celebrate a mementous anniversary. We celebrate one of the great successes of the postwar world.

Twenty years ago, as has already been mentioned, a few dedicated men gathered in Washington to cement an Atlantic partnership between the older nations of Europe and their offspring in the New World—and in this very room the North Atlantic Treaty was signed. Some of the men who were here then are here today—and I would like to suggest that those who were here then and who are here today stand for a moment. (*Applause.*)

Gentlemen, with our hindsight, we now have saluted your foresight at that time. In referring to that event, I thought I should share with you the conversation that I had with some of the founders in the room prior to coming to this meeting.

Secretary Acheson recalled that before the signing of the Treaty the Marine Band played "We Have Plenty of Nothing" [*sic*] and "It Ain't Necessarily So."

Certainly, what has happened in those twenty years proved that so far as the music was concerned, it was not prophetic.

As we sit here today we think, as the previous speakers have indicated, of all of those who have contributed to the Alliance—and particularly to the one who commanded the armies that liberated Europe, the first Supreme Commander of NATO, the American President who did so much to bring NATO to its strength and to give life to its principles, Dwight David Eisenhower.

His life demonstrated that there is a moral force in the world which can move men and nations. There *is* a spiritual force, lodged in the very roots of man's being.

As for NATO, it is precisely because it has always been more than a military alliance that its strength has been greater than the strength of arms. This Alliance represents a moral force which, if we marshal it, will ennoble our efforts.

Dwight Eisenhower was a great humanist. He was also a great

realist. If he were with us today, he would have recognized that together, as men of the Old World and of the New World, we must find ways of living in the real world.

As we know too well, that real world today includes men driven by suspicion, who would take advantage of their neighbors, men who confuse the pursuit of happiness with the pursuit of power.

It also is peopled with men of good will, with men of peace, with men of hope, and with men of vision.

No nation, and no community of nations, is made up entirely of one group of men or another. No part of the world has a monopoly on wisdom or virtue.

Those who think simply in terms of "good" nations and "bad" nations—of a world of staunch allies and sworn enemies—live in a world of their own. Imprisoned by stereotypes, they do not live in the real world.

On the other hand, those who believe that all it takes to submerge national self-interest is a little better communication; those who think that all that stands in the way of international brotherhood is stubborn leadership—they, too, live in a world of their own. Misled by wishful thinking, they do not live in the real world.

Two decades ago the men who founded NATO faced the truth of their times; as a result the Western world prospers today in freedom. We must follow their example by once again facing the truth—not of earlier times, but of our own times.

Living in the real world of today means recognizing the sometimes differing interests of the Western nations while never losing sight of our great common purposes.

Living in the real world of today means understanding old concepts of East versus West, understanding and unfreezing those concepts, but never losing sight of great ideological differences that still remain.

We can afford neither to blind our eyes with hatred, nor to distort our vision with rose-colored glasses. The real world is too much with us to permit either stereotyped reacting or wishful thinking to lay waste our powers.

Let us then count ourselves today among the hopeful realists.

In this same spirit of hopeful realism let us look at NATO today.

We find it strong but we find it challenged. We find disputes about its structure, political divisions among its members, and reluctance to meet prescribed force quotas. Many people on both sides of the Atlantic find NATO anachronistic, something quaint and familiar and a bit old-fashioned.

As the Alliance begins its third decade, therefore, there are certain fundamentals to be reaffirmed:

First, NATO is needed; and the American commitment to NATO will remain in force and it will remain strong. We in America continue to consider Europe's security to be our own.

Second, having succeeded in its original purpose, the Alliance must adapt to the conditions of success. With less of the original cement of fear, we must forge new bonds to maintain our unity.

Third, when NATO was founded, the mere fact of cooperation among the Western nations was of tremendous significance, both symbolically and substantively. Now the symbol is not enough; we need substance. The Alliance today will be judged by the content of its cooperation, not merely by its form.

Fourth, the allies have learned to harmonize their military forces; now, in the light of the vast military, economic, and political changes of two decades, we must devise better means of harmonizing our policies.

Fifth, by its nature, ours is more than a military alliance; and the time has come to turn a part of our attention to those non-military areas in which we all could benefit from increased collaboration.

Now, what does it all mean for the future of the Western Alliance?

To deal with the real world, we cannot respond to changing conditions merely by changing our words. We have to adapt our actions.

It is not enough to talk of flexible response, if at the same time we reduce our flexibility by cutting back on conventional forces.

It is not enough to talk of relaxing tension, unless we keep in mind the fact that twenty years of tension were not caused by superficial misunderstandings. A change of mood is useful only if it reflects some change of mind about political purpose.

It is not enough to talk of European security in the abstract. We must know the elements of insecurity and how to remove them. Conferences are useful if they deal with concrete issues, which means they must, of course, be carefully prepared.

It is not enough to talk of détente, unless at the same time we anticipate the need for giving it the genuine political content that would prevent détente from becoming delusion.

To take one example, a number of America's Western partners have actively supported the idea of strategic arms control talks with the Soviet Union. I support that idea. When such talks are held, we shall work diligently for their success.

But within our Alliance we must recognize that this would imply a military relationship far different from the one that existed when NATO was founded. Let's put it in plain words. The West does not today have the massive nuclear predominance that it once had, and any sort of broad-based arms agreement with the Soviet would codify the present balance.

How would progress toward arms control affect the nature of consultation within our Alliance?

Up to now our discussions have mainly had to do with tactics—ways and means of carrying out the provisions of a treaty drawn a generation ago. We have discussion clauses in proposed treaties; in the negotiations to come we must go beyond these to the processes which these future treaties will set in motion. We must shake off our preoccupation with formal structure to bring into focus a common world view.

Of course, there is a diversity of policies and interests among the Western nations; and of course those differences must be respected. But in shaping the strategies of peace, these differences need not block the way—not if we break through to a new and deeper form of political consultation.

To be specific, the forthcoming arms talks will be a test of the ability of the Western nations to shape a common strategy.

The United States fully intends to undertake deep and genuine consultation with its allies, both before and during any negotiations directly affecting their interests. That is a pledge I shall honor—and I expect to consult at length on the implications of anything that might affect the pattern of East-West relations.

In passing that test together, this Alliance will give new meaning to the principle of mutual consultation.

To seize the moment that this opportunity presents, we would be well to create new machinery for Western political consultation, as well as to make greater use of the machinery that we have.

First, I suggest that deputy foreign ministers meet periodically for a high-level review of major long-range problems before the Alliance.

Second, I suggest creation of a special political planning group, not to duplicate the work now being done by the Council or by the senior political advisers, but to address itself specifically and continually to the longer-range problems we face.

This would by no means preclude efforts to develop a fuller European cooperation. On the contrary, we in the United States would welcome that cooperation. What ties us to Europe is not weakness or division among our partners, but community of interest with them.

Third, I strongly urge that we create a committee on the challenges of modern society, responsible to the deputy ministers, to explore ways in which the experience and resources of the Western nations could most effectively be marshaled toward improving the quality of life of our peoples.

That new goal is provided for in Article II of our Treaty, but it has never been the center of our concern. Let me put my proposal in concrete terms and in personal terms. On my recent trip to Europe I met with world leaders and private citizens alike. I was struck by the fact that our discussions were not limited to military or political matters. More often than not our talks turned to those matters deeply relevant to our society; the legitimate unrest of young people, the frustration of the gap between generations, the need for a new sense of idealism and purpose in coping with an automated world.

These were not subjects apart from the concerns of NATO; indeed they went to the very heart of the real world we live in. We are not allies because we are bound by treaty; we bind ourselves by treaty because we are allied in meeting common purposes and common concerns.

For twenty years, our nations have provided for the military defense of Western Europe. For twenty years we have held political consultations.

Now the alliance of the West needs a third dimension.

It needs not only a strong military dimension to provide for the common defense; and not only a more profound political dimension to shape a strategy of peace; but it also needs a social dimension, to deal with our concern for the quality of life in this last third of the twentieth century.

This concern is manifested in many ways: culturally, technologically, through the humanities and the sciences.

The Western nations share common ideals and a common heritage. We are all advanced societies, sharing the benefits and the gathering torments of a rapidly advancing industrial technology. The industrial nations share no challenge more urgent than that of bringing twentieth-century man and his environment to terms with one another—of making the world fit for man, and helping man to learn how to remain in harmony with the rapidly changing world.

We in the United States have much to learn from the experiences of our Atlantic allies in their handling of internal matters: for example, the care of infant children in West Germany, the new towns policy of Great Britain; the development of depressed areas programs in Italy; the great skill of the Dutch in dealing with high-density areas; the effectiveness of urban planning by local governments in Norway; the experience of the French in metropolitan planning.

Having forged a working partnership, we all have a unique opportunity to pool our skills, our intellects, and our inventiveness in finding new ways to use technology to enhance our environments, and not to destroy them.

The work of the new committee which I have suggested would not be competitive with any now being carried on with other international agencies. Neither would it be our purpose to limit this cooperation and the benefits that flow from it to our own countries. Quite the opposite: Our purpose would be to share both ideas and benefits, recognizing that these problems have no national or regional boundaries. This could become the most positive dimension of the Alliance, opening creative new channels to all the rest of the world.

When I visited the North Atlantic Council in Brussels, I posed the question, "In today's world, what kind of an alliance shall we strive to build?"

Today I have sketched out some of the approaches that I believe the Alliance should take.

I believe we must build an Alliance strong enough to deter those who might threaten war; close enough to provide for continuous and far-reaching consultation; trusting enough to accept the diversity of views; realistic enough to deal with the world as it is; and flexible enough to explore new channels of constructive cooperation.

Ten years ago, addressing the North Atlantic Council in this same room, President Eisenhower spoke of the need for untiy. Listen to his words: "There is not much strength in the finger of one hand," he said, "but when five fingers are balled into a fist, you have a considerable instrument of defense."

We need such an instrument of defense and the United States will bear its fair share in keeping NATO strong.

All of us are also ready, as conditions change, to turn that fist into a hand of friendship.

NATO means more than arms, troop levels, consultative bodies, and treaty commitments. All of these are necessary. But what make them relevant to the future is what the Alliance stands for. To discover what this Western Alliance means today, we have to reach back, not across two decades, but through the centuries to the very roots of the Western experience.

When we do, we find that we touch a set of elemental ideals, eloquent in their simplicity, majestic in their humanity; ideals of decency, and justice, and liberty, and respect for the rights of our fellow men. Simple, yes; and to us they seem obvious. But our forebears struggled for centuries to win them and in our own lifetimes we have had to fight to defend them.

These ideals are what NATO was created to protect. It is to these ideals, on this proud anniversary, that we are privileged to consecrate the Alliance anew. These ideals—and the firmness of our dedication to them—give NATO's concept its nobility and NATO's backbone its steel.

13

Our

American

Neighbors

The effort to define and implement an effective Latin American policy extends back to Franklin D. Roosevelt's "Good Neighbor" policy. Progress has been slow but the forms of international cooperation have been created. Presidents Eisenhower and Kennedy initiated programs for Latin American political cooperation and economic development. The Organization of American States is a framework for cooperation.

Practical results are not so easily identifiable. President Nixon sent Governor Nelson A. Rockefeller of New York, long associated with efforts for Latin American cooperation, on a survey and good will mission. Rockefeller was welcomed by governments but resented by dissident groups.

President Nixon then dealt with the problems involved in an exceptionally frank address at the annual meeting of the Inter-American Press Association. He upgraded Latin American affairs in the American scheme of things, but the essential problems remain: communist penetration, the ability of Latin American governments to use American aid for the common good, social and political systems incompatible with American concepts, domineering attitudes in the big nation to the north, and the cultural orientation of the little nations to the south toward Europe.

In probably no other area of international relations is the potential so great and performance so disappointing compared to what it might ideally be.

TIME FOR CONSULTATION

Remarks to the Assembly of the Organization of American States in Washington, D.C.

APRIL 14, 1969

Mr. President, Your Excellencies, my fellow Americans:

I can use that term, "my fellow Americans," and cover everybody in this room. And this is the only international group in which I can do so.

As I speak to my fellow Americans today, I first want to thank the President of this organization for his very warm and friendly comments. And in responding to those comments, I want to establish a personal bond of communication with all of you here—or should I say re-establish it with you?

As I came into this Pan-American Building this morning, I recalled those many occasions a few years ago when my wife and I were here and you were gracious enough to allow us to use your "home" as the Vice President's place to entertain distinguished visitors from abroad.

My memory went back not only to many visits to this building, but to visits in every one of the countries in this hemisphere. I am very fortunate to have had the opportunity to know personally each of the countries represented here. And I only hope that in the years I am in office I shall have the opportunity to return and to visit all of those countries again.

As I stand here today I want to speak from my heart with regard to the feeling that I have personally insofar as our American family is concerned.

I come from the State of California. I was born in a little town of Yorba Linda. It had, of course, not only a Spanish name but a great Spanish tradition and background.

My wife and I, in the year 1940—as you see her now she must have been a child bride—spent our honeymoon in Mexico. And twenty-five years later we returned with our two daughters for our anniversary trip to Mexico.

During the years that I have visited each of your countries, I have had some highly interesting experiences. I know that the international press has attempted to build up those experiences that have at times been difficult. But I can assure everyone in this room that my memories and the memories of my wife are not of those few neighbors who may have been unfriendly, but of the thousands of *friendly* faces we saw. It is the latter we shall always take with us and remember as we attempt to develop our new policies for the future.

But having spoken of my personal affection for the peoples represented in this room, I now want to speak very candidly and very honestly about some of the problems with which we are presently confronted.

I think there has been a tendency, in examining the relations of the United States with our friends to the South, to smother the problems that we have with fine slogans and beautiful rhetoric. I think there is a place for a fine slogan and always there is a place for eloquent language. And I would not underplay, certainly, the importance of that kind of relationship on a dignified basis between nations and the leaders of nations.

But the problems we face in this hemisphere are too serious to be glossed over simply by the fine words and gestures of the past. What we need is a new policy, new programs, new approaches.

I would like to define those policies today, not with a new slogan, because I have none—none that I think would be appropriate to the challenge that we face. But I would like to describe our approach in this way: Sometimes the new Administration has been called an open Administration. I hope we can live up to that description. And if I were to set forth the objectives for our approach to the problems of this hemisphere, it would be in these words: I want our policies to be ones which are derived from open eyes, open ears, open minds, and open hearts.

Let me be specific on each of those items. When I speak of open eyes, I mean that it is necessary for us to look at our common problems without any of the prejudices that we may have had in the past, without being imprisoned by the policies of the past or without perpetuating the mistakes of the past.

The President of this organization has referred to Governor Rockefeller and the trip that he will be taking—or several trips, I should say—to the countries of this hemisphere in the months ahead.

On that trip, as Governor Rockefeller will tell the Ambassadors assembled here today, he is going with open eyes and open ears. He is not going there to tell the people in the various countries what the United States wants them to do; he is going there to listen to them and to hear what they believe we can do together.

I think there has been too much of a tendency in the past for the discussion to get down to this point: What will the United States do for Latin America?

The question, I think, should be—and this is the approach of the Rockefeller mission, it is the approach of the new Secretary of State and the new Assistant Secretary of State, Charles Meyer—not what do we do *for* Latin America, but what do we do *with* Latin America. What do we do *together*?

We want, therefore, to have both open eyes and open ears. We want to hear from our friends in each of the countries represented—what you think is wrong with our policy and also what you think you can do *with* us to develop a better policy.

And we, fortunately, approach this problem with no preconceived notions as to the policies of the past.

One of the reasons we must also have open minds is that there is sometimes a tendency to become wedded to a program because it has a popular connotation. I speak of the Alliance for Progress, the great concept.

As I examined the achievements of the Alliance for Progress on my last trip to Latin America in 1967—a journey in which I covered most of the countries of that continent—I saw many areas where the Alliance had done much good. On the other hand, when I looked at the overall statistics as to what has happened to the rate of growth in Latin America during the period of the Alliance for Progress as compared with the period immediately preceding the Alliance; and when I compared that rate of growth with the rates of growth in other areas of the world, I found a very disappointing result.

It is simply this: The rate of growth is not fast enough. It has been approximately the same during the period of the Alliance as it was before the Alliance.

But even more significant, the rate of growth in Latin America, overall—and of course there are some individual countries that are far ahead—is less than the rate of growth in non-communist Asia, and it is less even than the rate of growth in communist Eastern Europe.

This is a result which we cannot tolerate. We must do better. We must find the ways and the means whereby we can move forward together in a more effective way.

And that is why I emphasize that we will have open eyes and open ears and open minds in attempting to find the answer.

But I emphasize the last and most important element: We shall have open hearts. The warm reception you have given my wife and me here today is typical and symbolic. No one can visit the countries of Latin America, as we have on so many occasions, without realizing how close our bonds are.

We are all part of the New World. We are all part of the American family. We come from the same traditions. We share the same concerns.

Simon Bolivar said a hundred and fifty years ago that the "freedom of the New World is the hope of the universe." That was true then. I believe it is even more true today.

But of course we have to make this freedom something which can be more meaningful to the millions of people in all the countries of this hemisphere; so that there will be hope where there is now despair; so that there will be opportunity for the millions who simply want a chance to make it on their own.

And as we think of this problem in that context, as we think how close our bonds are, I try to put it in the perspective of history. I think how long this organization has been in operation. I look ahead just thirty-two years to the end of this century, and I think of what this hemisphere, the New World, will be like then. And I realize that if the present rates of growth that we have in the United States and in the balance of the hemisphere are not changed, the per-capita income in the United States of America by that time will be fifteen times as high as the per-capita income of our friends, our neighbors, the members of our family in the rest of the hemisphere.

This is something we cannot allow to happen. But if the trend is to be changed, it will require the best minds, the best ideas, that all of us can produce together.

So, Mr. President, as I come here today, let me say I was tempted simply to respond to your very gracious remarks with the response that I had in my heart—to express my appreciation for your welcome.

But I want you to know that we do consider the problems of this hemisphere to be of the highest priority. We do consider that whatever progress we have made has not been enough, and for that reason we come here today asking your assistance in working with us, so that we can find better solutions for those problems that we all share throughout the hemisphere.

Again, to all of you, my fellow Americans, our gratefulness for your warm reception, and I hope that this meeting may mark the beginning of a new era of cooperation, of consultation, but most important, of progress for all the members of our great American family.

Thank you.

SOME PROPOSALS FOR A BETTER RELATIONSHIP
Remarks to the Inter-American Press Association in Washington, D.C.

OCTOBER 31, 1969

President Copley, President Edwards, Mr. Secretary of State, Governor Rockefeller, all of the distinguished guests here, Your Excellencies, the Ambassadors from the American States, and members and guests of the Inter-American Press Association:

As we stand here on this twenty-fifth anniversary meeting of the Inter-American Press Association, I should like to be permitted some personal comments before I then deliver my prepared remarks to you.

I have learned that this is the first occasion in which the remarks of the President of any one of the American nations has been carried and is being carried live by Telstar to all the nations in the hemisphere. We are proud that it is before the Inter-American Press Association. . . .

Also, I am very privileged to appear before this organization again. I was reminded it was fifteen years ago that I, as Vice President, addressed the organization in New Orleans. It is good to be with you tonight, and particularly as the outgoing President is an old friend, Mr. Edwards, from Santiago. The new President is also an old friend, Mr.

Copley, from San Diego—sister cities, one in the northern hemisphere of the Americas and the other in the southern hemisphere.

There is one other matter, brought eloquently to my attention by Mrs. Edwards as we heard that magnificent rendition of "America the Beautiful." She said, "That is for all of us. We are all Americans in this room."

It is in that spirit that I want to address my remarks tonight to our partnership in the Americas. In doing so, I wish to place before you some suggestions for reshaping and reinvigorating that partnership.

Often we in the United States have been charged with an overweening confidence in the rightness of our own prescriptions, and occasionally we have been guilty of the charge. I intend to correct that. Therefore, my words tonight are meant as an invitation by one partner for further interchange, for increased communication, and above all for new imagination in meeting our shared responsibilities.

For years we in the United States have pursued the illusion that we alone could remake continents. Conscious of our wealth and technology, seized by the force of good intentions, driven by habitual impatience, remembering the dramatic success of the Marshall Plan in postwar Europe, we have sometimes imagined that we knew what was best for everyone else and that we could and should make it happen. Well, experience has taught us better.

It has taught us that economic and social development is not an achievement of one nation's foreign policy, but something deeply rooted in each nation's own traditions.

It has taught us that aid that infringes on pride is no favor to any nation.

It has taught us that each nation, and each region, must be true to its own character.

What I hope we can achieve, therefore, is a more mature partnership in which all voices are heard and none is predominant—a partnership guided by a healthy awareness that give-and-take is better than take-it-or-leave-it.

My suggestions this evening for new directions toward a more balanced relationship come from many sources.

First, they are rooted in my personal convictions. I have seen the problems of this hemisphere. As those in this room know, I have visited every nation in this hemisphere. I have seen them at first hand. I have felt the surging spirit of those nations—determined to break the grip of outmoded structures, yet equally determined to avoid social disintegration. Freedom, justice, a chance for each of our peoples to live a better and more abundant life—these are goals to which I am unshakeably committed, because progress in our hemisphere is not only a practical necessity, it is a moral imperative.

Second, these new approaches have been substantially shaped by the report of Governor Rockefeller, who, at my request and at your invitation, listened perceptively to the voices of our neighbors and incorporated their thoughts into a set of foresighted proposals.

Third, they are consistent with thoughts expressed in the Consensus of Viña del Mar, which we have studied with great care.

Fourth, they have benefited from the counsel of many persons in government and out, in this country and throughout the hemisphere.

And finally, basically, they reflect the concern of the people of the United States for the development and progress of a hemisphere which is new in spirit, and which—through our efforts together—we can make new in accomplishment.

Tonight, I offer no grandiose promise and no panaceas.

I do offer action.

The actions I propose represent a new approach. They are based on five principles:

—First, a firm commitment to the inter-American system, to the compacts which bind us in that system—as exemplified by the Organization of American States and by the principles so nobly set forth in its charter.

—Second, respect for national identity and national dignity, in a partnership in which rights and responsibilities are shared by a community of independent states.

—Third, a firm commitment to continued United States assistance for hemispheric development.

—Fourth, a belief that the principal future pattern of this assistance must be U.S. support for Latin American initiatives, and that this can best be achieved on a multilateral basis within the inter-American system.

—Finally, a dedication to improving the quality of life in this new world of ours—to making people the center of our concerns, and to helping meet their economic, social, and human needs.

We have heard many voices from the Americas in these first months of our new Administration—voices of hope, voices of concern, and some voices of frustration.

We have listened.

These voices have told us they wanted fewer promises and more action. They have told us that the United States aid programs seemed to have helped the United States more than Latin America. They have told us that our trade policies were insensitive to the needs of other

American nations. They have told us that if our partnership is to thrive, or even to survive, we must recognize that the nations of the Americas must go forward in their own way, under their own leadership.

Now it is not my purpose here tonight to discuss the extent to which we consider the various charges that I have listed right or wrong. But I recognize the concerns. I share many of them. What I propose tonight is, I believe, responsive to those concerns.

The most pressing concerns center on economic development—and especially on the policies by which aid is administered and by which trade is regulated.

In proposing specific changes tonight, I mean these as examples of the actions I believe are possible in a new kind of partnership in the Americas.

Our partnership should be one in which the United States lectures less and listens more. It should be one in which clear, consistent procedures are established to ensure that the shaping of the future of the nations in the Americas reflects the will of those nations.

I believe this requires a number of changes.

To begin with, it requires a fundamental change in the way in which we manage development assistance in the hemisphere.

That is why I propose that a multilateral inter-American agency be given an increasing share of responsibility for development assistance decisions. CIAP—the Inter-American Committee for the Alliance for Progress—could be given this new function. Or an entirely new agency could be created within the system.

Whatever the form, the objective would be to evolve an effective multilateral framework for bilateral assistance, to provide the agency with an expert international staff and, over time, to give it major operational and decision-making responsibilities.

The other American nations themselves would thus jointly assume a primary role in setting priorities within the hemisphere, in developing realistic programs, in keeping their own performance under critical review.

One of the areas most urgently in need of new policies is the area of trade. In my various trips to the Latin American countries and other American countries, I have found that this has been uppermost on the minds of the leaders for many, many years. In order to finance their import needs and to achieve self-sustaining growth, the other American nations must expand their exports.

Most Latin American exports now are raw material and foodstuffs. We are attempting to help the other countries of the hemisphere to stabilize their earnings from these exports, to increase them as time goes on.

Increasingly, however, those countries will have to turn more toward manufactured and semimanufactured products for balanced development and major export growth. Thus they need to be assured of access to the expanding markets of the industrialized world. In order to help achieve this, I have determined to take the following major steps.

—First, to lead a vigorous effort to reduce the non-tariff barriers to trade maintained by nearly all industrialized countries against products of particular interest to Latin America and other developing countries.

—Second, to support increased technical and financial assistance to promote Latin American trade expansion.

—Third, to support the establishment, within the inter-American system, of regular procedures for advance consultation on trade matters. United States trade policies often have a very heavy impact on our neighbors. It seems only fair that in the more balanced relationship we seek, there should be full consultation within the hemisphere family before decisions affecting its members are taken, not after.

—Finally, and most important, in world trade forums, I believe it is time to press for a liberal system of generalized tariff preferences for all developing countries, including Latin America. We will seek adoption by all of the industrialized nations of a scheme with broad product coverage and with no ceilings on preferential imports. We will seek equal access to industrial markets for all developing countries, so as to eliminate the discrimination against Latin America that now exists in many countries. We will also urge that such a system eliminate the inequitable "reverse preferences" that now discriminate against Western Hemisphere countries.

There are three other important economic issues that directly involve the new partnership concept, and which a number of our partners have raised. They raised them with me and raised them with Governor Rockefeller, with the Secretary of State, and others in our Administration.

These are: "tied" loans, debt service, and regional economic integration.

For several years now, virtually all loans made under United States aid programs have been "tied"—that is, as you know, they have been encumbered with restrictions designed to maintain United States exports, including a requirement that the money be spent on purchases in the United States.

These restrictions have been burdensome for the borrowers. They have impaired the effectiveness of the aid. In June, I ordered the most cumbersome restrictions removed.

In addition I announce tonight that I am now ordering that, effective November 1, loan dollars sent to Latin America under AID be freed to allow purchases not only here, but anywhere in Latin America.

As a third step, I am also ordering that all other onerous conditions and restrictions on U.S. assistance loans be reviewed, with the objective of modifying or eliminating them.

If I might add a personal word, this decision on freeing AID loans is one of those things that people kept saying ought to be done but could not be done. In light of our own balance-of-payments problems, there were compelling arguments against it. I can assure you that within the Administration we had a very vigorous session on this subject. But I felt and the rest of my colleagues within the Administration felt, that the needs of the hemisphere had to come first, so I simply ordered it done, showing our commitment in actions rather than only in words. This will be our guiding principle in the future.

We have present many members of the House and Senate here tonight. I am sure they realize that there are not too many occasions that the President can accomplish something by just ordering it to be done.

The growing burden of external debt service has increasingly become a major problem of future development. Some countries find themselves making heavy payments in debt service which reduce the positive effects of development aid. Therefore, tonight I suggest that CIAP might appropriately urge the international financial organizations to recommend possible remedies.

We have seen a number of moves in the Americas toward regional economic integration, such as the establishment of the Central American Common Market, the Latin American and Caribbean Free Trade Areas, and the Andean Group. The decisions on how far and how fast this process of integration goes, of course, are not ours to make. But I do want to stress this: We in the United States stand ready to help in this effort if our help is requested and is needed.

On all of these matters we look forward to consulting further with our hemisphere neighbors and partners. In a major related move I am also directing our representatives to invite CIAP, as a regular procedure, to conduct a periodic review of U.S. economic policies as they affect the other nations of the hemisphere, and to consult with us about them.

Similar reviews are now made of the other hemisphere countries' policies, as you are aware, but the United States has not previously opened its policies to such consultation. I believe that true partnership requires that we should, and henceforth, if our partners so desire, as I gather from your applause you do, we shall.

I would like to turn now to a vital subject in connection with economic development in the hemisphere, namely, the role of private investment. Clearly, each government in the Americas must make its own decision about the place of private investment, domestic and foreign, in its development process. Each must decide for itself whether it wishes to accept or forego the benefits that private investment can bring.

For a developing country constructive foreign private investment has the special advantage of being a prime vehicle for the transfer of technology. And certainly, from no other source is so much investment capital available, because capital, from government to government on that basis, is not expansible. In fact, it tends to be more restricted, whereas private capital can be greatly expanded.

As we have seen, however, just as a capital-exporting nation cannot expect another country to accept investors against its will, so must a capital-importing country expect a serious impairment of its ability to attract investment funds when it acts against existing investments in a way which runs counter to commonly accepted norms of international law and behavior. Unfortunately, and perhaps unfairly, such acts in one of the Americas affect investors in the entire region.

We will not encourage U.S. private investment where it is not wanted or where local conditions confront it with unwarranted risks. But I must state my own strong belief, and it is this: I think that properly motivated private enterprise has a vitally important role to play in social as well as economic development in all of the nations. We have seen it work in our own country. We have seen it work in other countries, whether they are developing or developed, other countries that lately have been recording the world's most spectacular rates of economic growth.

Referring to a completely other area of the world, exciting stories of the greatest growth rates are those that have turned toward more private investment, rather than less. Japan we all know about, but the story is repeated in Korea, Taiwan, Malaysia, Singapore, and Thailand.

In line with this belief, we are examining ways to modify our direct investment controls in order to help meet the investment requirements of developing nations in the Americas and elsewhere. I have further directed that our aid programs place increasing emphasis on assistance to locally owned private enterprise. I am also directing that we expand our technical assistance for establishing national and regional capital markets.

As we all have seen, in this age of rapidly advancing science the challenge of development is only partly economic. Science and technology increasingly hold the key to our national futures. If the promise of this final third of the twentieth century is to be realized, the wonders of science must be turned to the service of man.

In the Consensus of Viña del Mar we were asked for an unprecedented effort to share our scientific and technical capabilities.

To that request we shall respond in a true spirit of partnership.

This I pledge to you tonight: The nation that went to the moon in peace for all mankind is ready, ready to share its technology in peace with its nearest neighbors.

Tonight I have discussed with you a new concept of partnership. I have made a commitment to act. I have been trying to give some examples of actions we are prepared to take.

But as anyone familiar with government knows, commitment alone is not enough. There has to be the machinery to ensure an effective follow-through.

Therefore, I am also directing a major reorganization and upgrading of the United States government structure for dealing with Western Hemisphere affairs.

As a key element of this—and this is one of those areas where the President cannot do it, and he needs the approval of the Congress—but as a key element of this, I have ordered preparation of a legislative request, which I will submit to the Congress, raising the rank of the Assistant Secretary of State for Inter-American Affairs to Under Secretary—thus giving the hemisphere special representation.

I know that many in this room fifteen years ago urged that upon me, and I see Mr. Pedro Beltran here particularly applauding. He urged it upon me just a few years ago, too.

I trust we will be able, through the new Under Secretary of State, to do a more effective job with regard to the problems of the hemisphere, and the new Under Secretary will be given authority to coordinate all United States government activities in the hemisphere, so that there will be one window for all of those activities.

And now, my friends in the American family, I turn to a sensitive subject. Debates have long raged, raged in the United States and elsewhere, as to what our attitude should be toward the various forms of government within the inter-American system.

Let me sum up my own views, very candidly.

First, my own country lives by a democratic system which has preserved its form for nearly two centuries. It has its problems. But we are proud of our system. We are jealous of our liberties. We hope that eventually most, perhaps all, of the world's people will share what we believe to be the blessings.

I would be less than honest if I did not express my concern over examples of liberty compromised, of justice denied or of rights infringed.

Nevertheless, we recognize that enormous, sometimes explosive, forces for change are operating in Latin America. These create instabilities, and bring changes in governments. On the diplomatic level, we must deal realistically with governments in the inter-American system as they are. We have, of course, we in this country, a preference for democratic procedures, and we hope that each government will help its own people to move forward toward a better, a fuller, and a freer life.

In this connection, however, I would stress one other point. We cannot have a peaceful community of nations if one nation sponsors armed subversion in another's territory. The Ninth Meeting of American Foreign Ministers clearly enunciated this principle. The "export" of revolution is an intervention which our system cannot condone, and a nation like Cuba which seeks to practice it can hardly expect to share in the benefits of this community.

And now, finally, a word about what all this can mean—not just for the Americas, but for the world.

Today the world's most fervent hope is for a lasting peace in which life is secure, progress is possible, and freedom can flourish. In each part of the world we can have lasting peace and progress only if the nations directly concerned take the lead themselves in achieving it, and in no part of the world can there be a true partnership if one partner dictates its direction.

I can think of no assembly of nations better suited than ours to point the way in developing such a partnership. A successfully progressing Western Hemisphere, here in this New World, demonstrating in action mutual help and mutual respect, will be an example for the world. Once again, by this example, we will stand for something larger than ourselves.

For three quarters of a century many of us have been linked together in the Organization of American States and its predecessors in a joint quest for a better future. Eleven years ago Operation Pan America was launched as a Brazilian initiative. More recently we have joined in a noble Alliance for Progress, whose principles still guide us. Now I suggest our goal for the '70s should be a decade of *action for progress* for the Americas.

As we seek to forge a new partnership, we must recognize that we are a community of widely diverse peoples. Our cultures are different. Our perceptions are often different. Our emotional reactions are often different. May it always be that way. What a dull world it would be if we were all alike. Partnership, mutuality—these do not flow naturally. We have to work at them.

Understandably, perhaps, a feeling has arisen in many Latin American countries that the United States really "no longer cares."

My answer to that is very simple.

We do care. I care. I have visited most of your countries, as I have said before. I have met most of your leaders. I have talked with your people. I have seen your great need as well as your great achievements.

And I know this, in my heart as well as in my mind: If peace and freedom are to endure in this world, there is no task more urgent than lifting up the hungry and the helpless, and putting flesh on the dreams of those who yearn for a better life.

Today we in this American community share an historic opportunity. As we look together down the closing decades of the century, we see tasks that summon the very best that is in us. But those tasks are difficult, precisely because they do mean the difference between despair and fulfillment for most of the 600 million people who will live in Latin America in the year 2000. Those lives are our challenge. Those lives are our hope. And we could ask no prouder reward than to have our efforts crowned by peace, prosperity, and dignity in the lives of those 600 million human beings.

14

Some

World

Problems

THE PURPOSES OF FOREIGN AID
Message to the Congress of the United States
MAY 28, 1969

*President Nixon is committed to reforming foreign aid as part
of a general world economic policy. This little realized facet of
the Nixon policy has probably prevented Congress from phasing
out foreign aid as lacking continued American public support.*

*Nixon succeeded in inducing a Congressional turn-around
on foreign aid in 1969. While granting the President $750
million less than the $2.2 billion he requested, Congress increased
foreign aid funds over the previous year.*

*Congress also created, at Nixon's request, the Overseas
Private Investment Corporation, intended as a fresh approach
to involve private enterprise in foreign economic development.
This innovation in foreign aid is now in operation. Congress
also agreed to earmark funds for controlling the world's population
explosion and gave added impetus to technical assistance
programs.*

Americans have for many years debated the issues of foreign aid
largely in terms of our own national self-interest.

Certainly our efforts to help nations feed millions of their poor help
avert violence and upheaval that would be dangerous to peace.

Certainly our military assistance to allies helps maintain a world in
which we ourselves are more secure.

Certainly our economic aid to developing nations helps develop our
own potential markets overseas.

And certainly our technical assistance puts down roots of respect
and friendship for the United States in the court of world opinion.

These are all sound, practical reasons for our foreign aid programs.

But they do not do justice to our fundamental character and purpose. There is a moral quality in this nation that will not permit us to
close our eyes to the want in this world, or to remain indifferent when the
freedom and security of others are in danger.

We should not be self-conscious about this. Our record of generosity
and concern for our fellow men, expressed in concrete terms unparalleled in the world's history, has helped make the American experience
unique. We have shown the world that a great nation must also be a
good nation. We are doing what is right to do.

A Fresh Approach

This Administration has intensively examined our programs of foreign aid. We have measured them against the goals of our policy and the goad of our conscience. Our review is continuing, but we have come to this central conclusion:

U.S. assistance is essential to express and achieve our national goals in the international community—a world order of peace and justice.

But no single government, no matter how wealthy or well-intentioned, can by itself hope to cope with the challenge of raising the standard of living of two thirds of the world's people. This reality must not cause us to retreat into helpless, sullen isolation. On the contrary, this reality must cause us to redirect our efforts in four main ways:

We must enlist the energies of private enterprise, here and abroad, in the cause of economic development. We must do so by stimulating additional investment through businesslike channels, rather than offering ringing exhortations.

We must emphasize innovative technical assistance, to ensure that our dollars for all forms of aid go further, and to plant the seeds that will enable other nations to grow their own capabilities for the future.

We must induce other advanced nations to join in bearing their fair share—by contributing jointly to multilateral banks and the United Nations, by consultation and by the force of our example, and by effective coordination of national and multilateral programs in individual countries.

We must build on recent successes in furthering food production and family planning.

To accomplish these goals, this Administration's foreign aid proposals will be submitted to the Congress today. In essence, these are the new approaches:

1. ENLISTING PRIVATE ENTERPRISE

I propose the establishment of the Overseas Private Investment Corporation.

The purpose of the Corporation is to provide businesslike management of investment incentives now in our laws so as to contribute to the economic and social progress of developing nations.

The majority of the Board of Directors, including its President, will be drawn from private life and have business experience.

Venture capital seeks profit, not adventure. To guide this capital to higher-risk areas, the Federal government presently offers a system of insurance and guarantees. Like the Federal Housing Administration in the housing field here at home, the Overseas Private Investment Corporation will be able to place the credit of the United States government behind the insurance and guarantees which the Corporation would sell to U.S. private investors.

The Corporation will also have a small direct lending program for private developmental projects. It will carry out investment survey and development activities. And it will undertake for AID some of the technical assistance required to strengthen private enterprise abroad. The financial performance of OPIC will be measurable: It is expected to break even or to show a small profit.

The Overseas Private Investment Corporation will give new direction to U.S. private investment abroad. As such, it wil provide new focus to our foreign assistance effort.

Simultaneously, I propose a mandate for the Agency for International Development to direct a growing part of its capital, technical, and advisory assistance to improving opportunities for local private enterprise in developing countries—on farms as well as in commerce and industry.

We do not insist that developing countries imitate the American system. Each nation must fashion its own institutions to its own needs. But progress has been greatest where governments have encouraged private enterprise, released bureaucratic controls, stimulated competition, and allowed maximum opportunity for individual initiative. AID's mandate will be directed to this end.

2. EXPANDING TECHNICAL ASSISTANCE

I propose a strong new emphasis on technical assistance.

Over one fifth of the funds requested for fiscal year 1970 are for technical assistance activities. Imaginative use of these funds at the points where change is beginning can have a gradual but pervasive impact on the economic growth of developing nations. It can make our dollars for all forms of aid go further.

Technical assistance takes many forms. It includes the adaptation of U.S. technical knowledge to the special needs of poor countries, the training of their people in modern skills, and the strengthening of institutions which will have lives and influence of their own. The main emphases of technical assistance must be in agriculture, education, and in family planning. But needs must also be met in health, public administration, community action, public safety, and other areas. In all of these fields our aim must be to raise the quality of our advisory, training, and research services.

Technical assistance is an important way for private U.S. organizations to participate in development. U.S. technical assistance personnel serving abroad must increasingly come from private firms, universities and colleges, and non-profit service groups. We will seek to expand this broad use of the best of our American talent.

AID is preparing plans to reorganize and revitalize U.S. technical assistance activities. A new Technical Assistance Bureau headed by an Assistant Administrator will be created within AID to focus on technical assistance needs and ensure effective administration of these activities. The bureau will devise new techniques, evaluate effectiveness of programs, and seek out the best-qualified people in our universities and other private groups.

To make it possible to carry through these plans most effectively, I am requesting a two-year funding authorization for this part of the AID program.

3. SHARING THE ASSISTANCE EFFORT

I propose that we channel more of our assistance in ways that encourage other advanced nations to share fairly the burden of international development.

This can be done by:

—Increasing jointly our contributions to international development banks.

—Increasing jointly our contributions to the United Nations technical assistance program.

—Acting in concert with other advanced countries to share the cost of aid to individual developing countries.

Most development assistance—from other advanced nations as well as the United States—is provided directly from one country to another. That is understandable. Such bilateral programs provide assistance in accordance with each country's own standards, make the source more visible to the recipient's people, and can reflect historical political ties.

But assistance through international development banks and the United Nations is approaching a fifth of total worldwide aid for development and should be expanded. Multilateral programs cushion political frictions between donors and recipients and bring the experience of many nations to bear on the development problem. Moreover, they explicitly require shared contributions among the advanced nations. This calls for funds in addition to those which I am proposing today.

I appreciate the prompt response by the Congress to my earlier proposal authorizing the United States to join with others in the second replenishment of the International Development Association. I urge early passage of appropriations for this contribution so that we may meet our pledge.

I reaffirm my request for appropriations in fiscal 1970 of $20 million for the ordinary capital of the Asian Development Bank, and $300 million for our scheduled contribution to the Fund for Special Operations of the Inter-American Development Bank.

In separate legislation I will submit a new proposal for a U.S. contribution of $25 million to the Special Fund of the Asian Development Bank in fiscal year 1970. I am convinced that a fairly shared Special Fund, to enable the Bank to provide concessional financing for priority needs, is a necessary supplement to the Bank's ordinary lending facilities. The United States should join with other donor countries in establishing this Special Fund, and strengthen the Bank so that it can better deal with Asia's current development problems and future needs.

The United States will consult with the management of the African Development Bank and with other potential donors, to identify the most appropriate way we can support the objectives of African development and assist in meeting the needs of that continent.

Today's proposed legislation includes a 43-percent increase in the U.S. contribution to multilateral technical assistance through the United Nations Development Program. Our contribution will be on the same sharing basis as in the past.

4. FURTHERING FOOD PRODUCTION AND FAMILY PLANNING

This Administration, while moving in the new directions I have outlined, will apply the lessons of experience in our foreign aid programs.

One basic lesson is the critical importance of releasing the brakes on development caused by low agricultural productivity. A few years ago mass starvation within a decade seemed clearly possible in many poor nations. Today they stand at least on the threshold of a dramatic breakthrough in food production. The combination of the new "miracle" seeds for wheat and rice, aid-financed fertilizer, improved cultivation practices, and constructive agricultural policies shows what is possible. They also demonstrate the potential for success when foreign aid, foreign private investment, and domestic resources in developing countries join together in a concerted attack on poverty.

The experience of this decade has also shown that lower rates of population growth can be critical for speeding up economic development and social progress. An increasing number of countries have adopted national family-planning programs to attack the problem. At least another decade of sustained hard work will be needed if we are to win the battle between economic development and population. But our assistance to voluntary family-planning programs and support for the work of the United Nations and other international organizations in this field must continue to have high priority, as will our support of efforts to increase food production.

Another important lesson is that our aid programs need better means of continuous management inspection. We are creating a new position of Auditor-General in the Agency for International Development. His job will be to make sure that AID's funds are used for their intended purpose and that AID's operations are managed as tightly and efficiently as possible. He will report directly to the AID Administrator.

Legislative and Budget Requests

The proposed legislation revises that part of the present Foreign Assistance Act which deals with economic aid, to reflect the priorities of this Administration. The proposals are designed to accomplish the following:

—Create the Overseas Private Investment Corporation and authorize its programs for an initial five years.

—Strengthen AID's mandate to use official aid to stimulate private initiative in development.

—Expand the role of technical assistance under consolidated legislation and a two-year authorization.

The proposed budget includes a new appropriation of $2,210 million for AID, $138 million below the January budget request of the previous Administration. In addition, the budget includes $75 million to augment existing reserves for guarantees to be issued by the proposed Overseas Private Investment Corporation.

The appropriation request for economic assistance will support these regional programs:

—For Latin America, $605 million.

—For the Near East and South Asia, $625 million.

—For Africa, $186 million.

—For East Asia, $234 million.

—And for Vietnam, $440 million.

In order to protect the U.S. balance of payments at the same time we are providing assistance abroad, goods and services will be purchased in the United States wherever practicable. Over 90 percent of all AID expenditures and virtually all purchases of goods will be made in the United States. The remaining funds that are spent abroad are mainly for living expenses of U.S. personnel and for other local expenditures in support of technical assistance programs.

For military assistance, the proposed budget includes $375 million, the same as in the January budget. Maintenance of a climate of international security still calls for military strength sufficient to deter aggression. Seventy-seven percent of the total amount available for the military assistance program will be allocated to four of our longstanding allies—Korea, the Republic of China, Turkey, and Greece. The balance of the request will be used to provide modest amounts of training and equipment to forty-four other countries where our security and foreign policy interests are partially met by this form of assistance. We are negotiating a renewal of our base agreement with Spain. If these negotiations succeed, we shall then need to request an amendment to this authorization asking for additional funds to cover our year's needs for Spain.

The United States will continue to provide military assistance from the U.S. Armed Services budget to Vietnam, Laos, and Thailand.

I am also asking in separate legislation for $275 million for credit necessary to facilitate the purchase of essential military equipment by countries now able to buy all or a growing part of their defense requirements. These funds will be returned to the United States during the next few years as the purchasing countries meet their repayment obligations.

Planning for the '70s

I believe these proposals for fiscal year 1970 are sound—and necessary to make clearly desirable improvements in our foreign aid program.

But we need to learn more about the role which foreign assistance can play in the development process, and the relationship between development and overall U.S. foreign policy.

I am therefore establishing a task force of private citizens to make a comprehensive review of the entire range of U.S. aid activities, to consider proposals of the United Nations bodies and international commissions, and to help me determine what our national policies should be toward the developing countries in the decade of the 1970s. I will look to the task force's report in developing the program next year, in my response to the Javits Amendment to the Foreign Assistance Act, and in considering the recommendations of the internationally sponsored Pearson Commission report to be published in the fall.

Toward a World of Order

Foreign aid cannot be viewed in isolation. That is a statement with a double meaning, each side of which is true.

If we turn inward, if we adopt an attitude of letting the under-developed nations shift for themselves, we would soon see them shift away from the values so necessary to international stability. Moreover, we would lose the traditional concern for humanity which is so vital a part of the American spirit.

In another sense, foreign aid must be viewed as an integral part of our overall effort to achieve a world order of peace and justice. That order combines our sense of responsibility for helping those determined to defend their freedom; our sensible understanding of the mutual bene-fits that flow from cooperation between nations; and our sensitivity to the desires of our fellow men to improve their lot in the world.

In this time of stringent budgetary restraint, we must stimulate private investment and the cooperation of other governments to share with us in meeting the most urgent needs of those just beginning to climb the economic ladder. And we must continue to minimize the im-mediate impact on our balance of payments.

This request for foreign economic and military assistance is the lowest proposed since the program began. But it is about $900 million more than was appropriated last year. I consider it necessary to meet essential requirements now, and to maintain a base for future action.

The support by the Congress of these programs will help enable us to press forward in new ways toward the building of respect for the United States, security for our people, and dignity for human beings in every corner of the globe.

THE NIXON DOCTRINE
Edited Excerpts from an Informal Background Briefing and Press Conference on the Island of Guam
JULY 25, 1969

President Nixon sojourned for a night on the island of Guam after an exhausting trip by plane, helicopter, and ship to watch the Pacific splashdown of the first men to land on the moon.

Sustained by the inspiration of this event, Nixon outlined to accompanying newsmen in a background briefing in the Navy officers' club the elements of what was called the Guam Doctrine. He later spoke of his policy outline as the Nixon Doctrine and expanded its application to the entire world.

The President spoke extemporaneously for fifty minutes, without reference to notes, in defining a central principle of his

*foreign policy. News reports of his discussion were given
maximum prominence and were couched in the third person under
the limitation that his statements could be attributed to him
but not quoted directly.*

*Background information supplied to newsmen led to the
characterization of his policy as a "lowered profile" in Asia. His
statement was timed to be foremost in the news prior to his
visits to the heads of state of the Philippines, Indonesia, Thailand,
South Vietnam, India, and Pakistan, and in this way set the
tone of his Asian journey. The President said afterward that his
statement of policy had found common acceptance among the
Asian leaders.*

*The policy statement as it applied to both Asia and the world
had its origins in broad references Nixon had made in the same
vein during the Presidential campaign but not articulated so
precisely until after be became President. The Guam press
conference was one of the rare occasions when a major Presidential
policy was stated extemporaneously.*

*It had been carefully thought out and its essence was outlined
to newsmen at the White House in a lengthy official briefing
before Nixon left Washington for the Pacific. As read today, the
statement may seem to lay its heaviest emphasis on the U.S.
remaining a Pacific power. At the time, however, White House
sources said the new element the President was introducing was a
lowered U.S. profile in Asia while remaining a power in the Pacific.*

THE PRESIDENT: Before we go to your questions, I think a matter
of interest to you would be my perspective as to Asia and America's role
in Asia. . . .

The United States is going to be facing, we hope before too long, a
major decision: What will be its role in Asia and in the Pacific after the
end of the war in Vietnam? Not only will we be facing that decision, but
the Asian nations will be wondering what it is to be.

When I talked with Prime Minister Gorton [of Australia], for example, he indicated that, in the conversations he had had with a number
of Asian leaders, they all wondered whether the United States—because
of its frustration over the war in Vietnam and its earlier frustration over
the war in Korea—would continue to play a significant role in Asia. Or
would we, like the French and then the British, and of course the Dutch,
withdraw from the Pacific and hereafter play only a minor role?

This is a decision that will have to be made, of course, as the war
comes to an end. But the time to develop the thinking which will go into

that decision is now. I think one of the weaknesses in American foreign policy is that too often we react rather precipitately to events as they occur. We fail to have the perspective and the long-range view which are essential for a policy that will be viable. . . .

Even though the war in Vietnam has been terribly frustrating, and there is a tendency for Americans to say, "After we are through with this one, let's not become involved again in Asia," I am convinced that *the way to avoid becoming involved in another Asiatic war is for the United States to continue to play a significant role [in this part of the world].*

I think the way we could become involved [in another war] would be to attempt withdrawal [from Asia], because whether we like it or not, geography makes us a Pacific power. Consider, for example, that Indonesia at its closest point is only fourteen miles from the Philippines; that Guam, where we are presently standing, is of course in the heart of Asia; that the interests of the whole Pacific as they relate to Alaska and Hawaii must be taken into account.

Also, as we look over the historical perspective, while World War II began in Europe, for the United States it began in the Pacific. It came from Asia. The Korean war came from Asia. The Vietnamese war came from Asia. . . .

As we look around us today, we see that the major world power which adopts a very aggressive attitude, a belligerent attitude in its foreign policy, Communist China, is of course in Asia. We also find that the two minor world powers—minor in size but with significant strength, as we have learned—which most greatly threaten the peace of the world, North Korea and North Vietnam, are in Asia.

I think we should realize that if we are thinking down the road, the long road—not just four years or five years but ten, fifteen, or twenty —the greatest threat to peace will be in the Pacific. I do not mean to suggest that the Middle East is not a potential danger spot, and that there are not problems in Latin America which concern us, or in Africa; and, of course, over it all, we see the great potential conflict between the two superpowers, the United States and the Soviet Union. But as far as those other areas are concerned, the possibility of finding some kind of solution, I think, is potentially greater than it is in the Asian area.

Pursuing that line of reasoning a bit further, then, I would like to put it in a more positive sense. When we look at the problems of Asia, the threat to peace that is presented by the growing power of Communist China, the belligerence of North Korea and North Vietnam, we should not let that outlook obscure the great promise that is there.

As I have often pointed out, the fastest rate of growth in the world is occurring in non-communist Asia. Japan, in the last ten years, has tripled its gross national product; South Korea has doubled its GNP; Taiwan has doubled its GNP; Thailand has doubled its GNP. The same is true of Singapore and Malaysia.

The record in some of the other countries is less impressive. But consider the Philippines, where there are very grave problems—as you will learn when you are there—political problems and others. One of the brighter spots is that when I visited the Philippines in 1953, it was a major importer of rice; but today, as the result of the new "miracle rice," it no longer has to import [this staple]. Some progress is being made in areas like that.

When we look at India and Pakistan and the terribly traumatic experience they have had because of their conflict with each other— more than with the problems they have had from the outside—that picture tends to be rather black.

Yet India's rate of economic growth as the result of two good crop years and another reasonably good one this year, has been 6 percent. If they can get their population problem under better control, the promise for the future is rather bright. As far as Pakistan is concerned, it is emphasizing growth in manufacturing—its rate of increase in this field is around 10 percent a year. Also, Pakistan's agricultural production will have risen 21 percent from 1965 to 1970.

When you see those two countries, even in the brief visits we will make, and the poverty strikes you in the face with a tremendous impact —particularly if you have not seen it before—you will wonder whether there is a great deal to hope for. Yet I can say, having seen these areas in 1953 and again in 1957, that the amount of progress that is taking place is a very, very formidable thing.

So what I am trying to suggest is this: As we look at Asia, it poses, in my view, over the long haul, looking down to the end of the century, the greatest threat to the peace of the world; and, for that reason, the United States should continue to play a significant role. It also poses, it seems to me, the greatest hope for progress in the world, because of the available resources and the ability of the people; and I think we need policies that will enable us to play a part, a part that is appropriate to the conditions we will find.

One other point I wish to make, briefly, is that there are two great new factors which we must recognize and which you will see in the countries we visit. One is the very great growth of nationalism—nationalism even in the Philippines, vis-à-vis the United States, as well as in other countries of the world.

The second factor is one that I believe is going to have a major impact on the future of Asia, and it is something that we must take into account. Asians will say in every country we visit that they do not want to be dictated to from the outside. *Asia is for the Asians. And that is what we want, and that is the role we should play. We should assist, but we should not dictate.*

The political and economic plans that they [these countries] are gradually developing are very hopeful. We will give assistance to those plans. We of course will keep the treaty commitments that we have. *But so far as our role is concerned, we must avoid the kind of policy that will make countries in Asia so dependent upon us that we are dragged into conflicts such as the one we have in Vietnam.*

This is going to be a difficult line to follow. It is one, however, that I think, with proper planning, we can develop.

QUESTION: Mr. President, sir, on the question of U.S. military relationships in Asia, if I may ask a hypothetical question: Suppose a leader of one of the countries with which we have close military relationships, either through SEATO or in Vietnam, should say, "Well, you are pulling out of Vietnam with your troops; we can read the newspapers. So how can we know you will remain to play a significant role in Asia, as you say you wish to do?" What kind of approach can you take to that question?

THE PRESIDENT: I have already indicated that the answer to that question is not an easy one—not easy because we will be greatly tempted, when the question is put to us, to indicate that if any nation desires the assistance of the United States militarily in order to meet an internal or external threat, we will provide it.

However, I believe the time has come when the United States, in our relations with all our Asian friends, should be quite emphatic on two points: one, that we will keep our treaty commitments—our treaty commitments, for example, with Thailand under SEATO; and two, that as far as the problems of internal security are concerned—except for the threat of a major power involving nuclear weapons—the United States is going to encourage, and has a right to expect, that this problem will be increasingly handled by, and the responsibility for it taken by, the Asian nations themselves.

I believe, incidentally, from my preliminary conversations with several Asian leaders over the past few months, that they are going to be willing to undertake this responsibility. It will not be easy. But if the United States just continues down the road of responding to requests for assistance, of assuming the primary responsibility for defending these countries when they have internal problems or external problems, they are never going to take care of themselves.

I should add to that, too, that when we talk about collective security for Asia, at this time it looks like a weak reed. It actually is. But looking down the road—I am speaking of five years from now, ten years from now—I think collective security is an objective which free Asian nations can see and which the United States can support.

QUESTION: Mr. President, when you speak of internal threats, do you include threats internally assisted by a country from the outside, such as we have in Vietnam?

THE PRESIDENT: Generally speaking, that is the kind of internal threat that we do have in Asian countries. For example, in Thailand the threat is one that is indigenous to a certain extent to the northeast and the north, but that would not be too serious if it were not getting the assistance that it is from the outside. The same is true in several of the other Asian countries.

QUESTION: Mr. President, do you anticipate that during your talks with the Asian leaders, you are going to have to spend any significant amount of time convincing them that your plan for withdrawal of American forces from Vietnam will pose no threat to their security?

THE PRESIDENT: One of the reasons for this trip is to leave no doubt in the minds of the leaders of non-communist Asia that the United States is committed to a policy in the Pacific—a policy not of intervention but one which certainly rules out withdrawal from this region; and regardless of what happens in Vietnam that we intend to continue to play a role in Asia to the extent that Asian nations, bilaterally and collectively, desire us to play a role.

I think that some reassurance is needed because Vietnam is on the minds of all the Asian leaders. . . . I think I can provide some reassuring comments to those Asian leaders who might raise the question.

QUESTION: Mr. President, you mentioned that you felt that perhaps five years or ten years from now the Asian countries could collectively take care of their regional security problems. What is our policy to be in the meantime if a Vietnam-type situation does occur?

THE PRESIDENT: Well, I would rather not speculate about one occurring. Each of these countries, as you know, poses an entirely different question. I would say simply we are going to handle each country on a case-by-case basis, attempting to avoid that creeping involvement which eventually simply submerges you. . . . We can learn from past experience, and we must avoid that kind of involvement in the future.

Let me put it this way: I recall in 1964 some advice that I got from Ayub Khan, who was then the President of Pakistan. This was before the United States had any significant troop commitment in Vietnam. I asked him for his view as to what our role should be. He said, "Well, the role of the United States in Vietnam or the Philippines or Thailand, or in any of those countries which have internal subversion, is to help them fight the war but not fight the war for them." That, of course, is a good general principle, one which we would hope would be our policy generally throughout the world.

QUESTION: Mr. President, there are really two parts to this assistance problem—the economic part and the military part. I was wondering whether you see us as having a greater expenditure and a greater involvement in those respects or a lessened involvement as we look down the road.

THE PRESIDENT: What I would see would be that the military involvement, the military assistance, the military aid programs and the rest, and particularly the commitments of military personnel—that this type of program would recede.

However, as far as economic programs are concerned, and particularly those of multilateral character—and here we have some new ideas that we will be expanding on in the months ahead—I would say that the level of U.S. activity would be adequate to meet the challenge as it develops. It is very much in our interest, in terms of economic assistance through loans and other programs, to help build the economies of free Asia.

Let us consider, for example, what has happened to South Korea, what has happened to Taiwan, what has happened to Thailand, what has happened to Japan, all of whom we have assisted enormously economically. All of them now, or virtually all of them, are on their own feet, at least from an economic standpoint, and are very good customers of ours.

QUESTION: Mr. President, on the question of creeping involvement and the advice that Ayub Khan once gave you, could you tell us if there is any future in Asia for American counter-insurgency tactics as they have developed since 1960?

THE PRESIDENT: There is a future for American counter-insurgency tactics only in the sense that where one of our friends in Asia asks for advice or assistance, under proper circumstances, we will provide it. But where we must draw the line is in becoming involved heavily with our own personnel, doing the job for them, rather than helping them do the job for themselves.

There is an American trait which we saw in Korea, we have seen it in Vietnam, and we see it pretty much around the world: We do things, we think, rather well. And particularly in the military field, where we are pretty advanced, we think that we can do it better than to try to teach somebody else to do it.

That may be the easy answer at the outset, but it is the wrong answer in the long run. *I want to be sure that our policies in the future, all over the world— in Asia, Latin America, Africa, and the rest—reduce American involvement. One of assistance, yes, assistance in helping them solve some of their own problems, but not going in and just doing the job ourselves simply because that is the easier way to do it.*

PEACE MUST HAVE A SOLID BASE
Remarks to the General Assembly of the United Nations
SEPTEMBER 18, 1969

The Nixon Administration took office with a commitment to tailor America's commitments to its capabilities. So that none would assume this meant a return to isolationism, President Nixon has repeatedly defined the role he would expect America to play in the world of the present and the future.

Nowhere was it more essential that this distinction be made than in the world assembly of nations, for there had been doubt, particularly in European capitals, about the extent of continued American acceptance of world responsibilities.

The President's appearance before the United Nations was in this spirit and represents—along with his definitions of the Nixon Doctrine and his 1970 comprehensive statement on foreign policy—his basic approach to foreign affairs.

Madam President, Mr. Secretary General, Distinguished Foreign Ministers, Prime Ministers, Delegates, my fellow citizens of the world community:

I first wish to express my deep appreciation for the honor of addressing this organization for the first time and also to take this opportunity to welcome all of those from a hundred and twenty-six countries who are here at the United Nations General Assembly Session.

Particularly, on a personal note, I appreciate the opportunity to have been welcomed today by the Secretary General. It is hard to realize, as we were reminiscing, that just sixteen years ago he welcomed me to Burma when he was Chief of Protocol and I was Vice President.

Since then, we have both come up in the world to a certain extent.

I think we would all agree that there is no nobler destiny, nor any greater gift that one age could make to the ages that follow, than to forge the key to lasting peace.

In this great Assembly the desirability of peace needs no affirmation. The methods of achieving it are what so greatly challenge our courage, our intelligence, our discernment.

Surely if one lesson above all rings resoundingly among the many shattered hopes in this world, it is that good words are not a substitute for hard deeds, and noble rhetoric is no guarantee of noble results.

We might describe peace as a process embodied in a structure.

For centuries peace was the absence of war, stability was the absence of change.

But in today's world there can be no stability without change—so that peace becomes a continuing process of creating revolution. It is no longer enough to restrain war. Peace must also embrace progress—both in satisfying man's material needs and in fulfilling his spiritual needs.

The test of the structure of peace is that it ensure for the people of each nation the integrity of their borders, their right to develop in peace and safety, and their right to determine their own destiny without outside interference.

As long as we live with the threat of aggression, we need physical restraints to contain it.

But the truest peace is based on self-restraint—on the voluntary acceptance of those basic rules of behavior that are rooted in mutual respect and demonstrated in mutual forebearance.

The more closely the world community adheres to a single standard in judging international behavior, the less likely that standard is to be violated.

I am well aware that many nations have questions about the world role of the United States in the years ahead—about the nature and extent of our future contribution to the structure of peace.

Let me address those doubts and address them quite candidly before this organization.

In recent years there has been mounting criticism here in the United States of the scope and the results of our international commitments.

This trend, however, has not been confined to the United States alone. In many countries we find a tendency to withdraw from responsibilities; to leave the world's often frustrating problems to the other fellow and just to hope for the best.

As for the United States, I can state here today without qualification: We have not turned away from the world.

We know that with power goes responsibility.

We are neither boastful of our power nor apologetic about it. We recognize that it exists; and that as well as conferring certain advantages, it also imposes upon us certain obligations.

As the world changes, the pattern of those obligations and responsibilities changes.

At the end of World War II the United States for the first time in history assumed the major responsibility for world peace.

We were left in 1945 as the one nation with sufficient strength to contain the new threats of aggression, and with sufficient wealth to help the injured nations back to their feet.

For much of the world those first difficult postwar years were a time of dependency.

The next step was toward independence, as new nations were born and old nations revived.

Now we are maturing together into a new pattern of interdependence.

It is against this background that we have been urging other nations to assume a greater share of responsibility for their own security, both individually and together with their neighbors. The great challenge now is to enlist the cooperation of many nations in preserving peace and enriching life. This cannot be done by American edict, or by the edict of any other nation. It must reflect the concepts and the wishes of the people of those nations themselves.

The history of the postwar period teaches that nationalism can be dangerously disruptive—or powerfully creative.

Our aim is to encourage the creative forms of nationalism; to join as partners where our partnership is appropriate, and where it is wanted, but not to let a U.S. presence substitute for independent national effort or infringe on national dignity and national pride.

It is not my belief that the way to peace is by giving up our friends or letting down our allies. On the contrary, our aim is to place America's international commitments on a sustainable, long-term basis, to encourage local and regional initiatives, to foster national independence and self-sufficiency, and by so doing to strengthen the total fabric of peace.

It would be dishonest, particularly before this sophisticated audience, to pretend that the United States has no national interests of its own, or no special concern for its own interests.

However, our most fundamental national interest is in maintaining that structure of international stability on which peace depends, and which makes orderly progress possible.

Since I took office as President, no single question has occupied so much of my time and energy as the search for an end to the war in Vietnam—an end fair to the people of South Vietnam, fair to the people of North Vietnam, and fair to those others who would be affected by the outcome.

We in the United States want to end this war, and we are ready to take every reasonable step to achieve that goal. But let there be no question on this one fundamental point: In good conscience we cannot, in the long-term interests of peace we will not, accept a settlement that would arbitrarily dictate the political future of South Vietnam and deny to the people of South Vietnam the basic right to determine their own future free of outside interference.

As I put it in my address to the American people last May, "What the United States wants for South Vietnam is not the important thing. What North Vietnam wants for South Vietnam is not the important thing. What is important is what the people of South Vietnam want for South Vietnam."

To secure this right—and to secure this principle—is our one limited but fundamental objective.

Both in public and at the Paris talks we have offered a number of proposals which would bring peace and provide self-determination. We are ready to consider any other proposals that have the same objective. The missing ingredient so far has been the willingness of the other side to talk on any terms other than those that would predetermine the result and deny the right of self-determination to the people of South Vietnam. Once that willingness exists, and once there is a genuine willingness by the other side to reach agreement, the practical solutions can readily be found.

This makes it urgent that the UN members, those in this room, who have long taken an active interest in peace in Vietnam, now take an active hand in achieving it.

Many urged that if only we halted our bombing of the North, peace would follow. Nearly a year has passed since the bombing of the North was halted.

Three months have passed since we began the process of troop replacement, signaling both our own genuine desire for a settlement and the increased readiness of the South Vietnamese to manage their own defense.

As I announced on Tuesday, by December 15 our troop strength in Vietnam will have been reduced by a minimum of sixty thousand men.

On September 2, 1969, North Vietnam's chief negotiator in Paris said that if the United States committed itself to the principle of totally withdrawing its forces from South Vietnam, and if it withdrew a significant number of troops, Hanoi would take this into account.

I repeat here today what I said in my speech of May 14, that we are prepared to withdraw all of our forces from South Vietnam.

And the replacement of sixty thousand troops is a significant step.

The time has come for the other side to respond to these initiatives. The time has come for peace.

And in the name of peace I urge all of you here—representing a hundred and twenty-six nations—to use your best diplomatic efforts to persuade Hanoi to move seriously into the negotiations which could end this war. The steps we have taken have been responsive to views expressed in this room. And we hope that views from this organization may also be influential in Hanoi. If these efforts are successful, this war can end.

The people of Vietnam, North and South alike, have demonstrated heroism enough to last a century. And I speak from personal observation. I have been to North Vietnam, to Hanoi, in 1953, and all over South Vietnam. I have seen the people of the North and the people of the South. The people of Vietnam, North and South, have endured an unspeakable weight of suffering for a generation. And they deserve a better future.

When the war ends, the United States will stand ready to help the people of Vietnam—all of them—in their tasks of renewal and reconstruction. And when peace comes at last to Vietnam, it can truly come with healing in its wings.

In relations between the United States and the various communist powers, I have said that we move from an era of confrontation to an era of negotiation.

I believe our relations with the Soviet Union can be conducted in a spirit of mutual respect, recognizing our differences and also our right to differ; recognizing our divergent interests, and also our common interests; recognizing the interests of our respective allies, as well as our own.

Now, it would be idle to pretend that there are not major problems between us, and conflicting interests. The tensions of the past thirty years have not been caused by personal misunderstandings. This is why we have indicated the need for extended negotiations on a broad front of issues.

Already, as you know, we have had extensive consultations with the Soviet Union as well as with others about the Middle East, where events of the past few days point up anew the urgency of stable peace.

The United States continues to believe that the UN cease-fire resolu-

tions define the minimal conditions that must prevail on the ground if
settlement is to be achieved in the Middle East. We believe the Security
Council resolution of November, 1967, charts the way to that settlement.

A peace, to be lasting, must leave no seeds of a future war. It must
rest on a settlement which both sides have a vested interest in maintaining.

We seek a settlement based on respect for the sovereign right of
each nation in the area to exist within secure and recognized boundaries.
We are convinced that peace cannot be achieved on the basis of substantial alterations in the map of the Middle East. And we are equally
convinced that peace cannot be achieved on the basis of anything less
than a binding, irrevocable commitment by the parties to live together in
peace.

Failing a settlement, an agreement on the limitation of the shipment of arms to the Middle East might help to stabilize the situation. We
have indicated to the Soviet Union, without result, our willingness to
enter such discussions.

In addition to our talks on the Middle East, we hope soon to begin
talks with the Soviet Union on the limitation of strategic arms. There is
no more important task before us.

The date we proposed for the opening of talks has passed for lack of
response. We remain ready to enter negotiations.

Since the United States first proposed strategic talks three years
ago, the task of devising an effective agreement has become more
difficult.

The Soviet Union has been vigorously expanding its strategic forces;
weapons themselves have become more sophisticated, more destructive.
But as the difficulty of the talks increases, so too does their importance.

Though the issues are complex, we are prepared to deal with them
seriously, concretely, and purposefully—and to make a determined effort
not only to limit the buildup of strategic arms, but to reverse it.

Meanwhile, I want to affirm our support for arms control proposals
which we hope the Geneva Conference will place before this Assembly,
with regard to the seabed and the chemical and bacteriological warfare.
We hope also that the Nuclear Non-Proliferation Treaty will soon enter
into force.

We should be under no illusion, however, that arms control will
itself bring peace. Wars are fought by soldiers, but they are declared
by politicians. Peace also requires progress on those stubbornly per-
sistent political questions, questions that are considered in this room,
questions that still divide the world; and it requires other exchanges, not

only of words, but of deeds that can gradually weave a fabric of mutual trust among the nations and the peoples of the world.

We intend to conduct our negotiations with the Soviet Union soberly and seriously, neither encumbered by prejudices nor blinded by sentimentality, seeking to reach agreements rather than to make propaganda.

Whenever the leaders of Communist China choose to abandon their self-imposed isolation, we are ready to talk with them in the same frank and serious spirit.

For nearly a quarter of a century the UN has struggled with the often thankless task of peacekeeping.

As we look to the future, however, keeping the peace is only part of our task. We also must concentrate on building the peace.

Let us be candid. There are many differences among the great powers, and among others, which as realists, we know cannot be resolved quickly, cannot be resolved even by this organization. But we also know that there are at least five areas in particular of great concern to everyone here with regard to which there should be no national differences, in which our interests are common and on which there should be unanimity.

They are these:

—Securing the safety of international air travel.

—Encouraging international volunteer services.

—Fostering economic development and population control.

—Protecting our threatened environment.

—Exploring the frontiers of space.

By any standards, aircraft hijackings are morally, politically, and legally indefensible. The Tokyo Convention has now been brought into force, providing for prompt release of passengers, crews, and aircraft. Along with other nations, we also are working on a new convention for the punishment of hijackers. But neither of these conventions can be fully effective without cooperation. Sky piracy cannot be ended as long as the pirates receive asylum.

Consequently, I urge the United Nations to give high priority to this matter. This is an issue which transcends politics; there is no need for it to become the subject of polemics or a focus of political differences. It involves the interests of every nation, the safety of every air passenger, and the integrity of that structure of order on which a world community depends.

The creative, dynamic kind of peace I have spoken of, of course, requires more than such basic protections as the one I have just described.

To build this kind of peace, we must join together in building our societies—in raising a great cathedral of the spirit, which celebrates the infinite possibilities of man himself.

Such a peace requires a fuller enlistment, not only of government resources and of private enterprise resources, but also of the dedication and skill of those thousands of people all over the world who are ready to volunteer in the cause of human achievement. Our own Peace Corps has helped in many countries. And I especially welcome the consideration of the UN itself, which it is now giving to the establishment of an International Volunteer Corps. We stand ready to give this exciting new venture our full and enthusiastic cooperation.

As the UN looks toward the beginning of its second development decade, it faces a time of enormous challenge but enormous opportunity.

We can only guess at the new scientific discoveries that the '70s may bring. But we can see with chilling clarity the gap that already exists between the developed economies and the economies of the developing countries—and the urgent need for international cooperation in spurring economic development.

If, in the course of that second development decade, we can make both significant gains in food production and significant reductions in the rate of population growth, we shall have opened the way to a new era of splendid prosperity. If we do only one without the other, we shall be standing still, and if we fail in both, great areas of the world will face human disaster.

Increasingly, the task of protecting man's environment is a matter of international concern. Pollution of air and water, upsetting the balance of nature—these are not only local problems, and not only national problems, but matters that affect the basic relationships of man to his planet.

The United Nations already is planning a conference on the environment in 1972. I pledge the strongest support of the United States for that effort. I hope that even before then we can launch new national and international initiatives toward restoring the balance of nature, and maintaining our world as a healthy and hospitable place for man.

Of all of man's great enterprises, none lends itself more logically or more compellingly to international cooperation than the venture into space. Here, truly, mankind is one: as fellow creatures from the planet Earth, exploring the heavens that all of us enjoy.

The journey of Apollo 11 to the moon and back was not an end, but the beginning.

There will be new journeys of discovery. Beyond this, we are just beginning to comprehend the benefits that space technology can yield here on earth. And the potential is enormous.

For example, we now are developing earth resource survey satellites, with the first experimental satellite to be launched sometime early in the decade of the '70s.

Present indications are that these satellites should be capable of yielding data which would assist in as widely varied tasks as these: the location of schools of fish in the oceans, the location of mineral deposits on land, and the health of agricultural crops.

I feel it is only right that we should share both the adventures and the benefits of space. As an example of our plans, we have determined to take actions with regard to earth resource satellites, as this program proceeds and fulfills its promise.

The purpose of those actions is that this program will be dedicated to produce information not only for the United States, but also for the world community.

We shall be putting several proposals in this respect before the United Nations.

These are among the positive, concrete steps we intend to take toward internationalizing man's epic venture into space—an adventure that belongs not to one nation, but to all mankind, and one that should be marked not by rivalry, but by the same spirit of fraternal cooperation that has so long been the hallmark of the international community of science.

And now, Madam President, Mr. Secretary General, if I could speak a personal word to the representatives gathered in this room.

I recognize that those here are dedicating their lives to the cause of peace and that what is done here will have an enormous effect on the future of peace.

I have had the great privilege over the past twenty-three years to travel to most of the countries represented in this room. I have met most of the leaders of the nations represented in this room. And I have seen literally thousands of people in most of the countries represented in this room.

There are differences between the nations and differences between the leaders and differences between the peoples in this world. But based on my own experience, of this one thing I am sure: The people of the world, wherever they are, want peace. And those of us who have the responsibilities for leadership in the world have an overwhelming world mandate from the people of the nations we represent to bring peace, to keep the peace, and to build the peace.

Now, I realize that a survey of history might discourage those who seek to establish peace.

But we have entered a new age, different not only in degree, but in kind, from any that has ever gone before.

For the first time ever, we have truly become a single world community.

For the first time ever, we have seen the staggering fury of the power of the universe unleashed, and we know that we hold that power in a very precarious harness.

For the first time ever, technological advance has brought within reach what once was only a poignant dream for hundreds of millions— freedom from hunger and freedom from want; want and hunger that I have personally seen in nation after nation all over the world.

For the first time ever, we have seen changes in a single lifetime— in our lifetime—that dwarf the achievements of centuries before; and those changes continue to accelerate.

For the first time ever, man has stepped beyond his planet—and revealed us to ourselves as "riders on the Earth together," bound inseparably on this one bright, beautiful speck in the heavens, so tiny in the universe and so incomparably welcoming as a home for man.

In this new age of "firsts" even the goal of a just and lasting peace is a "first" we can dare to strive for. We must achieve it. And I believe we can achieve it.

In that spirit, then, let us press toward an open world—a world of open doors, open hearts, open minds—a world open to the exchange of ideas and of people, and open to the reach of the human spirit, a world open in the search for truth, and unconcerned with the fate of old dogmas and old isms; a world open at last to the light of justice, and the light of reason, and to the achievement of that true peace which the people of every land carry in their hearts and celebrate in their hopes.

WORLD TRADE AND TARIFFS
Message to the Congress of the United States
NOVEMBER 18, 1969

President Nixon submitted to Congress what he regarded as a modest and liberal revision of trade policies pending a more general review of longer-range policies for the '70s.

He has set up a "blue ribbon" commission on trade and investment policy for the more general study and recommendations that will probably be submitted to him in the next year or two.

At mid-year 1970 Congress took up the revisions recommended by the President in the fall of 1969. The principal points of controversy centered on import restrictions on chemicals (the so-called ASP, or American Selling Price, policy), the "escape clause" for tariff-affected domestic industries, and the usual effort to hang on Presidential trade proposals various protectionist amendments.

Trade and tariffs remain a basic controversy in which the general public takes little interest but which are a continuing reality of political conflict in Washington, and of vital importance in the economic health of a nation that has shifted from its historic creditor to a debtor position in world trade.

For the past thirty-five years the United States has steadfastly pursued a policy of freer world trade. As a nation we have recognized that competition cannot stop at the ocean's edge. We have determined that American trade policies must advance the national interest—which means they must respond to the whole of our interests, and not be a device to favor the narrow interest.

This Administration has reviewed that policy and we find that its continuation is in our national interest. At the same time, however, it is clear that the trade problems of the 1970s will differ significantly from those of the past. New developments in the rapidly evolving world economy will require new responses and new initiatives.

As we look at the changing patterns of world trade, three factors stand out that require us to continue modernizing our own trade policies:

First, world economic interdependence has become a fact. Reductions in tariffs and in transportation costs have internationalized the world economy just as satellites and global television have internationalized the world communications network. The growth of multinational corporations provides a dramatic example of this development.

Second, we must recognize that a number of foreign countries now compete fully with the United States in world markets.

We have always welcomed such competition. It promotes the economic development of the entire world to the mutual benefit of all, including our own consumers. It provides an additional stimulus to our own industry, agriculture, and labor force. At the same time, however, it requires us to insist on fair competition among all countries.

Third, the traditional surplus in the U.S. balance of trade has disappeared. This is largely due to our own internal inflation and is one more reason why we must bring that inflation under control.

The disappearance of the surplus has suggested to some that we should abandon our traditional approach toward freer trade. I reject this argument not only because I believe in the principle of freer trade, but also for a very simple and pragmatic reason: any reduction in our imports produced by U.S. restrictions not accepted by our trading partners would invite foreign reaction against our own exports—all quite legally. Reduced imports would thus be offset by reduced exports, and both sides would lose. In the longer term such a policy of trade restriction would add to domestic inflation and jeopardize our competitiveness in world markets at the very time when tougher competition throughout the world requires us to improve our competitive capabilities in every way possible.

In fact, the need to restore our trade surplus heightens the need for further movement toward freer trade. It requires us to persuade other nations to lower barriers which deny us fair access to their markets. An environment of freer trade will permit the widest possible scope for the genius of American industry and agriculture to respond to the competitive challenge of the 1970s.

Fourth, the less developed countries need improved access to the markets of the industrialized countries if their economic development is to proceed satisfactorily. Public aid will never be sufficient to meet their needs, nor should it be. I recently announced that, as one step toward improving their market access, the United States would press in world trade forums for a liberal system of tariff preferences for all developing countries. International discussions are now in progress on the matter and I will not deal with it in the trade bill I am submitting today. At the appropriate time, I will submit legislation to the Congress to seek authorization for the United States to extend preferences and to take any other steps toward improving the market access of the less-developed countries which might appear desirable and which would require legislation.

The Trade Act of 1969

The trade bill which I am submitting today addresses these new problems of the 1970s. It is modest in scope, but significant in its impact. It continues the general drive toward freer world trade. It also explicitly recognizes that while seeking to advance world interests, U.S. trade policies must also respect legitimate U.S. interests, and that to be fair to our trading partners does not require us to be unfair to our own people. Specifically:

—It restores the authority needed by the President to make limited tariff reductions.

—It takes concrete steps toward the increasingly urgent goal of lowering non-tariff barriers to trade.

—It recognizes the very real plight of particular industries, companies, and workers faced with import competition, and provides for readier relief in these special cases.

—It strengthens GATT—the General Agreement on Tariffs and Trade—by regularizing the funding of United States participation.

While asking enactment of these proposals now, the trade program I will outline in this message also includes getting preparations under way for the more ambitious initiatives that will later be needed for the long-term future.

TARIFF REDUCTION

I recommend that the President be given authority to make modest reductions in U.S. tariffs.

The President has been without such authority for over two years. This authority is not designed to be used for major tariff negotiations, but rather to make possible minor adjustments that individual circumstances from time to time require—as, for example, when it becomes necessary to raise the duty on an article as the result of an "escape clause" action or when a statutory change is made in tariff classification. Our trading partners are then entitled to reasonable compensation, just as we would be entitled to receive it from them in reverse circumstances. Lack of this authority exposes our exports to foreign retaliation. Therefore, the Bill would provide to the President, through June 30, 1973, the authority to reduce tariffs by limited amounts.

NON-TARIFF BARRIERS

The time has come for a serious and sustained effort to reduce non-tariff barriers to trade. These non-tariff barriers have become increasingly important with the decline in tariff protection and the growing interdependence of the world economy. Their elimination is vital to our efforts to increase U.S. exports.

As a first step in this direction I propose today that the United States eliminate the American Selling Price system of customs valuation.

Although this system applies only to a very few American products —mainly benzenoid chemicals—it is viewed by our principal trading partners as a major symbol of American protectionism. Its removal will bring reciprocal reductions in foreign tariffs on U.S. chemical exports, and a reduction in important foreign non-tariff barriers—including European road taxes, which discriminate against our larger automobiles, and the preferential treatment on tobacco extended by the United Kingdom to the countries of the Commonwealth. Beyond this, its removal will unlock the door to new negotiations on the entire range of non-tariff barriers. Because of the symbolic importance our trading partners attach to it, the American Selling Price system has itself become a major barrier to the removal of other barriers.

Essentially, the American Selling Price system is a device by which the value of imports for tariff purposes is set by the price of competitive American products instead of the actual price of the foreign product, which is the basis of tariff valuation for all other imports. The extraordinary protection it provides to these few products has outlived its original purposes. The special advantage it gives particular producers can no longer justify its heavy cost in terms of the obstacles it places in the way of opening foreign markets to American exports.

Reducing or eliminating other non-tariff barriers to world trade will require a great deal of detailed negotiating and hard bargaining.

Unlike tariffs, approaches to the reduction of non-tariff barriers are often difficult to embody in prior delegation of authority. Many— both here and abroad—have their roots in purely domestic concerns that are only indirectly related to foreign trade, and many arise from domestic laws.

Many would require specific legislative actions to accomplish their removal—but the nature of this action would not finally be clear until negotiation had shown what was possible.

This presents a special opportunity for Congress to be helpful in achieving international agreements in this vital area.

I would welcome a clear statement of Congressional intent with regard to non-tariff barriers to assist in our efforts to obtain reciprocal lowering of such barriers.

It is not my intention to use such a declaration as a "blank check." On the contrary, I pledge to maintain close consultation with the Congress during the course of any such negotiations, to keep the Congress fully informed on problems and progress, and to submit for Congressional consideration any agreements which would require new legislation. The purpose of seeking such an advance declaration is not to bypass Congress, but to strengthen our negotiating position.

In fact, it is precisely because ours is a system in which the Executive cannot commit the Legislative Branch that a general declaration of legislative intent would be important to those with whom we must negotiate.

At the same time, I urge private interests to work closely with the government in seeking the removal of these barriers. Close cooperation by the private sector is essential, because many non-tariff barriers are subtle, complex, and difficult to appraise.

AID FOR AFFECTED INDUSTRIES

Freer trade brings benefits to the entire community, but it can also cause hardship for parts of the community. The price of a trade policy from which we all receive benefits must not fall unfairly on the few— whether on particular industries, on individual firms, or on groups of workers. As we have long recognized there should be prompt and effective means of helping those faced with adversity because of increased imports.

The Trade Act of 1969 provides significant improvements in the means by which U.S. industry, firms, and workers can receive assistance from their government to meet injury truly caused by imports.

This relief falls into two broad categories: 1. the escape clause, which is industry-wide; and 2. adjustment assistance, which provides specific aid to particular firms or groups of workers.

These improvements are needed because the assistance programs provided in the Trade Expansion Act of 1962 have simply not worked.

ESCAPE CLAUSE

The escape clause provisions of the 1962 Act have proved so stringent, so rigid, and so technical that in not a single case has the Tariff Commission been able to justify a recommendation for relief. This must be remedied. We must be able to provide, on a case-by-case basis, careful and expedited consideration of petitions for relief, and such relief must be available on a fair and reasonable basis.

I recommend a liberalization of the escape clause to provide, for industries adversely affected by import competition, a test that will be simple and clear: relief should be available whenever increased imports are the primary cause of actual or potential serious injury. The increase in imports should not—as it now is—have to be related to a prior tariff reduction.

While making these escape clause adjustments more readily obtainable, however, we must ensure that they remain what they are intended to be: temporary relief measures, not permanent features of the tariff landscape. An industry provided with temporary escape clause relief must assume responsibility for improving its competitive position. The bill provides for regular reports on these efforts, to be taken into account in determining whether relief should be continued.

ADJUSTMENT ASSISTANCE

With regard to adjustment assistance for individual firms and groups of workers, the provisions of the Trade Expansion Act of 1962 again have not worked adequately.

The Act provides for loans, technical assistance, and tax relief for firms, and readjustment allowances, relocation, and training for workers. This direct aid to those individually injured should be more readily available than tariff relief for entire industries. It can be more closely targeted; it matches the relief to the damage; and it has no harmful side effects on overall trade policy.

I recommend that firms and workers be considered eligible for adjustment assistance when increased imports are found to be a substantial cause of actual or potential serious injury.

Again, the increase in imports would not have to be related to a prior tariff reduction. The "substantial cause" criterion for adjustment assistance would be less stringent than the "primary cause" criterion for tariff relief.

I also recommend two further changes in existing adjustment provisions:

—That the Tariff Commission continue to gather and supply the needed factual information, but that determinations of eligibility to apply for assistance be made by the President.

—That adjustment assistance be made available to separate units of multiplant companies and to groups of workers in them, when the injury is substantial to the unit but not to the entire parent firm.

With these modifications, plus improved administrative procedures, our program of assistance to import-injured firms and workers can and will be made to work. Taken together, they will remedy what has too long been a serious shortcoming in our trade programs.

These changes in our escape clause and adjustment assistance programs will provide an adequate basis for government help in cases where such help is justified in the overall national interest. They will thus help us move away from protectionist proposals, which would reverse the trend toward interdependence, and toward a constructive attack on the existing trade barriers of others.

The textile import problem, of course, is a special circumstance that requires special measures. We are now trying to persuade other countries to limit their textile shipments to the United States. In doing so, however, we are trying to work out with our trading partners a reasonable solution which will allow both domestic and foreign producers to share equitably in the development of the U.S. market.

Such measures should not be misconstrued, nor should they be allowed to turn us away from the basic direction of our progress toward freer exchange.

FAIR TREATMENT OF U.S. EXPORTS

By nature and by definition trade is a two-way street. We must make every effort to ensure that American products are allowed to compete in world markets on equitable terms. These efforts will be more successful if we have the means to take effective action when confronted with illegal or unjust restrictions on American exports.

Section 252 of the Trade Expansion Act of 1962 authorizes the President to impose duties or other import restrictions on the products of any nation that places unjustifiable restrictions on U.S. agricultural products. *I recommend that this authority be expanded in two ways:*

—By extending the existing authority to cover unfair actions against all U.S. products, rather than only against U.S. agricultural products.

—By providing new authority to take appropriate action against nations that practice what amounts to subsidized competition in third-country markets, when that subsidized competition unfairly affects U.S. exports.

Any weapon is most effective if its presence makes its use unnecessary. With these new weapons in our negotiating arsenal, we should be better able to negotiate relief from the unfair restrictions to which American exports still are subject.

STRENGTHENING GATT

Ever since its beginning in 1947, U.S. participation in GATT—the General Agreement on Tariffs and Trade—has been financed through general contingency funds rather than through a specific approporiation.

GATT has proved its worth. It is the international organization we depend on for the enforcement of our trading rights, and toward which we look as a forum for the important new negotiations on non-tariff barriers which must now be undertaken.

I recommend specific authorization for the funding of our participation in GATT, thus both demonstrating our support and regularizing our procedures.

For the Long-Term Future

The trade bill I have submitted today is a necessary beginning. It corrects deficiencies in present policies; it enables us to begin the 1970s with a program geared to the start of that decade.

As we look further into the '70s, it is clear that we must re-examine the entire range of our policies and objectives.

We must take into account the far-reaching changes which have occurred in investment abroad and in patterns of world trade. I have already outlined some of the problems which we will face in the 1970s. Many more will develop—and also new opportunities will emerge.

Intense international competition, new and growing markets, change in cost levels, technological developments in both agriculture and industry, and large-scale exports of capital are having profound and continuing effects on international production and trade patterns. We can no longer afford to think of our trade policies in the old, simple terms of liberalism vs. protectionism. Rather, we must learn to treat investment, production, employment, and trade as interrelated and interdependent.

We need a deeper understanding of the ways in which the major sectors of our economy are actually affected by international trade.

We have arrived at a point at which a careful review should also be made of our tariff structure itself—including such traditional aspects as its reliance upon specific duties, the relationships among tariff rates on various products, and adapting our system to conform more closely with that of the rest of the world.

To help prepare for these many future needs, I will appoint a Commission on World Trade to examine the entire range of our trade and related policies, to analyze the problems we are likely to face in the 1970s, and to prepare recommendations on what we should do about them. It will be empowered to call upon the Tariff Commission and the agencies of the Executive Branch for advice, support, and assistance, but its recommendations will be its own.

By expanding world markets, our trade policies have speeded the pace of our own economic progress and aided the development of others. As we look to the future we must seek a continued expansion of world trade, even as we also seek the dismantling of those other barriers— political, social, and ideological—that have stood in the way of a freer exchange of people and ideas, as well as of goods and technology.

Our goal is an open world. Trade is one of the doors to that open world. Its continued expansion requires that others move with us, and that we achieve reciprocity in fact as well as in spirit.

Armed with the recommendations and analyses of the new Commission on World Trade, we will work toward broad new policies for the 1970s that will encourage that reciprocity, and that will lead us, in growing and shared prosperity, toward a world both open and just.

15
We
Must Move
Now
Against
Pollution

Recognition of air and water pollution as a national problem with popular appeal came early in President Nixon's first year but his specific proposals were not formulated until the beginning of his second year in office.

Officials of his Administration sensed in the fall of 1969 the attraction of environmental improvement for young people looking for a cause. They were concerned that overstatement and emotionalism growing from ignorance or misinformation should not convert the crusade for environmental improvement into merely another assault on "the establishment."

President Nixon therefore sought a balanced program consistent with the analyses of his chief scientific adviser, Dr. Lee A. DuBridge, former President of the California Institute of Technology. Dr. DuBridge's approach accepts the existence of a technological society that produces pollution in the process of creating a higher standard of living for the majority. His approach gives little comfort to romantic concepts of a simpler and cleaner society by strangulation of the industrial process, but holds that technology can cleanse the waters and atmosphere. Dr. DuBridge also believes that the problem of pollution cannot be separated from that of growth in population.

As far as expenditures were concerned, Nixon's proposals were moderate in comparison with those advocated by Senator Edmund Muskie of Maine, the leading Democratic foe of pollution. The Nixon proposals implemented previous Congressional programs for sewage and waste disposal on a continuing and fairly large-scale basis.

Among his innovations were more stringent regulation of industrial pollution and hastening the time schedule for reducing or eliminating pollution of the atmosphere by automobiles, with the ultimate aim of producing an unconventionally powered, pollution-free automobile within five years. An entirely new proposal would build into the price of consumer products the cost of their ultimate disposal, an idea not explored in detail in Nixon's proposals.

The Congressional reaction has been generally favorable, and the President's proposals are eventually expected to grow into a large and comprehensive Federal program for environmental improvement.

WE MUST MOVE NOW AGAINST POLLUTION
A Comprehensive Message to the
Congress of the United States
FEBRUARY 10, 1970

Like those in the last century who tilled a plot of land to exhaustion and then moved on to another, we in this century have too casually and too long abused our natural environment. The time has come when we can wait no longer to repair the damage already done, and to establish new criteria to guide us in the future.

The fight against pollution, however, is not a search for villains. For the most part the damage done to our environment has not been the work of evil men, nor has it been the inevitable by-product either of advancing technology or of growing population. It results not so much from choices made, as from choices neglected; not from malign intention, but from failure to take into account the full consequences of our actions.

Quite inadvertently, by ignoring environmental costs, we have given an economic advantage to the careless polluter over his more conscientious rival. While adopting laws prohibiting injury to person or property, we have freely allowed injury to our shared surroundings. Conditioned by an expanding frontier, we came only late to a recognition of how precious and how vulnerable our resources of land, water, and air really are.

The tasks that need doing require money, resolve, and ingenuity— and they are too big to be done by government alone. They call for fundamentally new philosophies of land, air, and water use, for stricter regulation, for expanded government action, for greater citizen involvement, and for new programs to ensure that government, industry, and individuals all are called on to do their share of the job and to pay their share of the cost.

Because the many aspects of environmental quality are closely interwoven, to consider each in isolation would be unwise. Therefore, I am today outlining a comprehensive, thirty-seven-point program, embracing twenty-three major legislative proposals and fourteen new measures being taken by administrative action or Executive Order in five major categories:

—Water pollution control.
—Air pollution control.
—Solid waste management.

—Parklands and public recreation.

—Organizing for action.

As we deepen our understanding of complex ecological processes, as we improve our technologies and institutions and learn from experience, much more will be possible. But these thirty-seven measures represent actions we can take *now*, and that can move us dramatically forward toward what has become an urgent common goal of all Americans: the rescue of our natural habitat as a place both habitable and hospitable to man.

Water Pollution

Water pollution has three principal sources: municipal, industrial, and agricultural wastes. All three must eventually be controlled if we are to restore the purity of our lakes and rivers.

Of these three, the most troublesome to control are those from agricultural sources: animal wastes, eroded soil, fertilizers, and pesticides. Some of these are nature's own pollutions. The Missouri River was known as "Big Muddy" long before towns and industries were built on its banks. But many of the same techniques of pest control, livestock feeding, irrigation, and soil fertilization that have made American agriculture so abundantly productive have also caused serious water pollution.

Effective control will take time, and will require action on many fronts: modified agricultural practices, greater care in the disposal of animal wastes, better soil conservation methods, new kinds of fertilizers, new chemical pesticides, and more widespread use of natural pest-control techniques. A number of such actions are already under way. We have taken action to phase out the use of DDT and other hard pesticides. We have begun to place controls on wastes from concentrated animal feed-lots. We need programs of intensified research, both public and private, to develop new methods of reducing agricultural pollution while maintaining productivity. I have asked the Council on Environmental Quality to press forward in this area. Meanwhile, however, we have the technology and the resources to proceed now on a program of swift clean-up of pollution from the most acutely damaging sources: municipal and industrial waste.

MUNICIPAL WASTES

As long as we have the means to do something about it, there is no good reason why municipal pollution of our waters should be allowed to persist unchecked.

In the four years since the Clean Waters Restoration Act of 1966 was passed, we have failed to keep our promises to ourselves: Federal appropriations for constructing municipal treatment plants have totaled only about one third of authorizations. Municipalities themselves have faced increasing difficulty in selling bonds to finance their share of the construction costs. Given the saturated condition of today's municipal bond markets, if a clean-up program is to work it has to provide the means by which municipalities can finance their share of the cost even as we increase Federal expenditures.

The best current estimate is that it will take a total capital investment of about $10 billion over a five-year period to provide the municipal waste treatment plants and interceptor lines needed to meet our national water quality standards. This figure is based on a recently completed nationwide survey of the deficiencies of present facilities, plus projections of additional needs that will have developed by then— to accommodate the normal annual increase in the volume of wastes, and to replace equipment that can be expected to wear out or become obsolete in the interim.

This will provide every community that needs it with secondary waste treatment, and also special additional treatment in areas of special need, including communities on the Great Lakes. We have the industrial capacity to do the job in five years if we begin now.

To meet this construction schedule, I propose a two-part program of Federal assistance:

—I propose a Clean Waters Act with $4 billion to be authorized immediately, for fiscal 1971, to cover the full Federal share of the total $10 billion cost on a matching-fund basis. This would be allocated at a rate of $1 billion a year for the next four years, with a reassessment in 1973 of needs for 1975 and subsequent years.

By thus assuring communities of full Federal support, we can enable planning to begin *now* for all needed facilities and construction to proceed at an accelerated rate.

—I propose creation of a new Environmental Financing Authority, to ensure that every municipality in the country has an opportunity to sell its waste treatment plant construction bonds.

The condition of the municipal bond market is such that, in 1969, 509 issues totaling $2.9 billion proved unsalable. If a municipality cannot sell waste treatment plant construction bonds, EFA will buy them and will sell its own bonds on the taxable market. Thus construction of pollution control facilities will depend not on a community's credit rating, but on its waste disposal needs.

Providing money is important, but equally important is where and how the money is spent. A river cannot be polluted on its left bank and clean on its right. In a given waterway, abating *some* of the pollution is often little better than doing nothing at all, and money spent on such partial efforts is often largely wasted. Present grant allocation formulas —those in the 1966 Act—have prevented the spending of funds where they could produce the greatest results in terms of clean water. Too little attention has been given to seeing that investments in specific waste treatment plants have been matched by other municipalities and industries on the same waterway. Many plants have been poorly designed and inefficiently operated. Some municipalities have offered free treatment to local industries, then not treated their wastes sufficiently to prevent pollution.

To ensure that the new funds are well invested, five major reforms are needed. One requires legislation; the other four will be achieved by administrative action.

—*I propose that the present, rigid allocation formula be revised, so that special emphasis can be given to areas where facilities are most needed and where the greatest improvements in water quality will result.*

Under existing authority, the Secretary of the Interior will institute four major reforms:

—*Federally assisted treatment plants will be required to meet prescribed design, operation, and maintenance standards, and to be operated only by state-certified operators.*

—*Municipalities receiving Federal assistance in constructing plants will be required to impose reasonable users' fees on industrial users sufficient to meet the costs of treating industrial wastes.*

—*Development of comprehensive river basin plans will be required at an early date, to ensure that Federally assisted treatment plants will in fact contribute to effective clean-up of entire river basin systems. Collection of existing data on pollution sources and development of effluent inventories will permit systems approaches to pollution control.*

—*Wherever feasible, communities will be strongly encouraged to cooperate in the construction of large regional treatment facilities, which provide economies of scale and give more efficient and more thorough waste treatment.*

INDUSTRIAL POLLUTION

Some industries discharge their wastes into municipal systems; others discharge them directly into lakes and rivers. Obviously, unless we curb industrial as well as municipal pollution our waters will never be clean.

Industry itself has recognized the problem, and many industrial firms are making vigorous efforts to control their water-borne wastes.

But strict standards and strict enforcement are nevertheless necessary —not only to ensure compliance, but also in fairness to those who have voluntarily assumed the often costly burden while their competitors have not. Good neighbors should not be placed at a competitive disadvantage because of their good-neighborliness.

Under existing law standards for water pollution control often are established in only the most general and insufficient terms: for example, by requiring all affected industries to install secondary treatment facilities. This approach takes little account of such crucial variables as the volume and toxicity of the wastes actually being discharged, or the capacity of a particular body of water to absorb wastes without becoming polluted. Even more important, it provides a poor basis for enforcement: with no effluent standard by which to measure, it is difficult to prove in court that standards are being violated.

The present fragmenting of jurisdictions also has hindered comprehensive efforts. At present Federal jurisdiction generally extends only to interstate waters. One result has been that as stricter state-Federal standards have been imposed, pollution has actually increased in some other waters—in underground aquifers and the oceans. As controls over interstate waters are tightened, polluting industries will be increasingly tempted to locate on intrastate lakes and rivers—with a consequently increased threat to those waterways—unless they too are brought under the same strictures.

I propose that we take an entirely new approach, one which concerts Federal, state, and private efforts, which provides for effective nationwide enforcement, and which rests on a simple but profoundly significant principle: that the nation's waterways belong to us all, and that neither a municipality nor an industry should be allowed to discharge wastes into those waterways beyond their capacity to absorb the wastes without becoming polluted.

Specifically, I propose a seven-point program of measures we should adopt *now* to enforce control of water pollution from industrial and municipal wastes, and to give the states more effective backing in their own efforts.

    —*I propose that state-Federal water quality standards be amended to impose precise effluent requirements on all industrial and municipal sources. These should be imposed on an expeditious timetable, with the limit for each based on a fair allocation of the total capacity of the waterway to absorb the user's particular kind of waste without becoming polluted.*

    —*I propose that violation of established effluent requirements be considered sufficient cause for court action.*

—I propose that the Secretary of the Interior be allowed to proceed more swiftly in his enforcement actions, and that he be given new legal weapons including subpoena and discovery power.

—I propose that failure to meet established water quality standards or implementation schedules be made subject to court-imposed fines of up to $10,000 per day.

—I propose that the Secretary of the Interior be authorized to seek immediate injunctive relief in emergency situations in which severe water pollution constitutes an imminent danger to health or threatens irreversible damage to water quality.

—I propose that the Federal pollution-control program be extended to include all navigable waters, both inter- and intrastate, all interstate ground waters, the United States's portion of boundary waters, and waters of the Contiguous Zone.

—I propose that Federal operating grants to state pollution control enforcement agencies be tripled over the next five years—from $10 million now to $30 million in fiscal year 1975—to assist them in meeting the new responsibilities that stricter and expanded enforcement will place upon them.

Air Pollution Control

Air is our most vital resource, and its pollution is our most serious environmental problem. Existing technology for the control of air pollution is less advanced than that for controlling water pollution, but there is a great deal we can do within the limits of existing technology —and more we can do to spur technological advance.

Most air pollution is produced by the burning of fuels. About half is produced by motor vehicles.

MOTOR VEHICLES

The Federal government began regulating automobile emissions of carbon monoxide and hydrocarbons with the 1968 model year. Standards for 1970 model cars have been made significantly tighter. This year, for the first time, emissions from new buses and heavy-duty trucks have also been brought under Federal regulation.

In future years emission levels can and must be brought much lower.

The Secretary of Health, Education and Welfare is today publishing a notice of new, considerably more stringent motor vehicle emission standards he intends to issue for 1973 and 1975 models—including control of nitrogen oxides by 1973 and of particulate emissions by 1975.

These new standards represent our best present estimate of the lowest emission levels attainable by those years.

Effective control requires new legislation to correct two key deficiencies in the present law:

a. *Testing procedures.* Under present law, only manufacturers' prototype vehicles are tested for compliance with emission standards, and even this is voluntary rather than mandatory.

I propose legislation requiring that representative samples of actual production vehicles be tested throughout the model year.

b. *Fuel composition and additives.* What goes into a car's fuel has a major effect on what comes out of its exhaust, and also on what kinds of pollution-control devices can effectively be employed. Federal standards for what comes out of a car's engine should be accompanied by standards for what goes into it.

I propose legislation authorizing the Secretary of Health, Education and Welfare to regulate fuel composition and additives.

With these changes, we can drastically reduce pollution from motor vehicles in the years just ahead. But in making and keeping our peace with nature, to plan only one year ahead or even five is hardly to plan at all. Our responsibility now is also to look beyond the '70s, and the prospects then are uncertain. Based on present trends, it is quite possible that by 1980 the increase in the sheer number of cars in densely populated areas will begin outrunning the technological limits of our capacity to reduce pollution from the internal combustion engine. I hope this will not happen. I hope the automobile industry's present determined effort to make the internal combustion engine sufficiently pollution-free succeeds. But if it does not, then unless motor vehicles with an alternative, low-pollution power source are available, vehicle-caused pollution will once again begin an inexorable increase.

Therefore, prudence dictates that we move now to ensure that such a vehicle will be available if needed.

I am inaugurating a program to marshal both government and private research with the goal of producing an unconventionally powered, virtually pollution-free automobile within five years.

—*I have ordered the start of an extensive Federal research and development program in unconventional vehicles, to be conducted under the general direction of the Council on Environmental Quality.*

—*As an incentive to private developers, I have ordered that the Federal government should undertake the purchase of privately produced unconventional vehicles for testing and evaluation.*

A proposal currently before the Congress would provide a further incentive to private developers by authorizing the Federal government to offer premium prices for purchasing low-pollution cars for its own use. This could be a highly productive program once such automobiles are approaching development, although current estimates are that, initially, prices offered would have to be up to 200 percent of the cost of equivalent conventional vehicles rather than the 125 percent contemplated in the proposed legislation. The immediate task, however, is to see that an intensified program of research and development begins at once.

One encouraging aspect of the effort to curb motor vehicle pollution is the extent to which industry itself is taking the initiative. For example, the nation's principal automobile manufacturers are not only developing devices now to meet present and future Federal emission standards, but are also, on their own initiative, preparing to put on the market by 1972 automobiles which will not require and, indeed, must not use leaded gasoline. Such cars will not only discharge no lead into the atmosphere, but will also be equipped with still more effective devices for controlling emissions—devices made possible by the use of lead-free gasoline.

This is a great forward step taken by the manufacturers before any Federal regulation of lead additives or emissions has been imposed. I am confident that the petroleum industry will see to it that suitable non-leaded gasoline is made widely available for these new cars when they come on the market.

STATIONARY-SOURCE POLLUTION

Industries, power plants, furnaces, incinerators—these and other so-called "stationary sources" add enormously to the pollution of the air. In highly industrialized areas such pollution can quite literally make breathing hazardous to health, and can cause unforeseen atmospheric and meteorological problems as well.

Increasingly, industry itself has been adopting ambitious pollution-control programs, and state and local authorities have been setting and enforcing stricter anti-pollution standards. But they have not gone far enough or fast enough, nor, to be realistic about it, will they be able to without the strongest possible Federal backing. Without effective government standards, industrial firms that spend the necessary money for pollution control may find themselves at a serious economic disadvantage as against their less conscientious competitors. And without effective Federal standards, states and communities that require such controls find themselves at a similar disadvantage in attracting industry, against more permissive rivals. Air is no respecter of political boundaries: a community that sets and enforces strict standards may still find its air polluted from sources in another community or another state.

Under the Clean Air Act of 1967 the Federal government is establishing air quality control regions around the nation's major industrial and metropolitan areas. Within these regions, states are setting air quality standards—permissible levels of pollutants in the air—and developing plans for pollution abatement to achieve those air quality standards. All state air quality standards and implementation plans require Federal approval.

This program has been the first major Federal effort to control air pollution. It has been a useful beginning. But we have learned in the past two years that it has shortcomings. Federal designation of air quality control regions, while necessary in areas where emissions from one state are polluting the air in another, has been a time-consuming process. Adjoining states within the same region often have proposed inconsistent air quality standards, causing further delays for compromise and revision. There are no provisions for controlling pollution *outside* of established air quality control regions. This means that even with the designation of hundreds of such regions, some areas of the country with serious air pollution problems would remain outside of the program. This is unfair not only to the public but to many industries as well, since those within regions with strict requirements could be unfairly disadvantaged with respect to competitors that are not within regions. Finally, insufficient Federal enforcement powers have circumscribed the Federal government's ability to support the states in establishing and enforcing effective abatement programs.

It is time to build on what we have learned, and to begin a more ambitious national effort. I recommend that the Clean Air Act be revised to expand the scope of strict pollution abatement, to simplify the task of industry in pollution abatement through more nearly uniform standards, and to provide special controls against particularly dangerous pollutants.

—*I propose that the Federal government establish nationwide air quality standards, with the states to prepare within one year abatement plans for meeting those standards.*

This will provide a minimum standard for air quality for all areas of the nation, while permitting states to set more stringent standards for any or all sections within the state. National air quality standards will relieve the states of the lengthy process of standard-setting under Federal supervision, and allow them to concentrate on the immediate business of developing and implementing abatement plans.

These abatement plans would cover areas both inside and outside of Federally designated air quality control regions, and could be designed to achieve any higher levels of air quality which the states might choose to establish. They would include emission standards for stationary sources of air pollution.

—*I propose that designation of interstate air quality control regions continue at an accelerated rate, to provide a framework for establishing compatible abatement plans in interstate areas.*

—*I propose that the Federal government establish national emissions standards for facilities that emit pollutants extremely hazardous to health, and for selected classes of new facilities which could be major contributors to air pollution.*

In the first instance national standards are needed to guarantee the earliest possible elimination of certain air pollutants which are clear health hazards even in minute quantities. In the second instance national standards will ensure that advanced abatement technology is used in constructing the new facilities, and that levels of air quality are maintained in the face of industrial expansion. Before any emissions standards were established, public hearings would be required involving all interested parties. The states would be responsible for enforcing these standards in conjunction with their own programs.

—*I propose that Federal authority to seek court action be extended to include both inter- and intrastate air pollution situations in which, because of local non-enforcement, air quality is below national standards, or in which emissions standards or implementation timetables are being violated.*

—*I propose that failure to meet established air quality standards or implementation schedules be made subject to court-imposed fines of up to $10,000 per day.*

Solid Waste Management

"Solid wastes" are the discarded leftovers of our advanced consumer society. Increasing in volume, they litter the landscape and strain the facilities of municipal governments.

New packaging methods, using materials which do not degrade and cannot easily be burned, create difficult new disposal problems.

Though many wastes are potentially reusable, we often discard today what a generation ago we saved. Most bottles, for example, now are "non-returnable." We reprocess used paper less than we used to, not only adding to the burden on municipal sanitation services but also making wasteful use of scarce timberlands. Often the least expensive way to dispose of an old automobile is to abandon it—and millions of people do precisely that, creating eyesores for millions of others.

One way to meet the problem of solid wastes is simply to surrender to it: to continue pouring more and more public money into collection and disposal of whatever happens to be privately produced and discarded. This is the old way; it amounts to a public subsidy of waste pollution. If we are ever truly to gain control of the problem, our goal must be broader: to reduce the volume of wastes and the difficulty of their disposal, and to encourage their constructive reuse instead.

To accomplish this, we need incentives, regulations, and research directed especially at two major goals: a. making products more easily disposable—especially containers, which are designed for disposal; and b. reusing and recycling a far greaer proportion of waste materials.

As we look toward the long-range future—to 1980, 2000, and beyond—recycling of materials will become increasingly necessary not only for waste disposal but also to conserve resources. While our population grows, each one of us keeps using more of the earth's resources. In the case of many common minerals, more than half those extracted from the earth since time began have been extracted since 1910.

A great deal of our space research has been directed toward creating self-sustaining environments, in which people can live for long periods of time by reprocessing, recycling, and reusing the same materials. We need to apply this kind of thinking more consciously and more broadly to our patterns of use and disposal of materials here on earth.

Many currently used techniques of solid waste disposal remain crudely deficient. Research and development programs under the Solid Waste Disposal Act of 1965 have added significantly to our knowledge of more efficient techniques. The Act expires this year. I recommend its extension, and I have already moved to broaden its programs.

I have ordered a redirection of research under the Solid Waste Disposal Act to place greater emphasis on techniques for recycling materials, and on development and use of packaging and other materials which will degrade after use—that is, which will become temporary rather than permanent wastes.

Few of America's eyesores are so unsightly as its millions of junk automobiles.

Ordinarily, when a car is retired from use it goes first to a wrecker, who strips it of its valuable parts, and then to a scrap processor, who reduces the remainder to scrap for sale to steel mills. The prices paid by wreckers for junk cars often are less than the cost of transporting them to the wrecking yard. In the case of a severely damaged or "cannibalized" car, instead of paying for it the wrecker may even charge towing costs. Thus the final owner's economic incentive to deliver his car for processing is slight, nonexistent, or even negative.

The rate of abandonment is increasing. In New York City twenty-five hundred cars were towed away as abandoned on the streets in 1960. In 1964 twenty-five thousand were towed away as abandoned; in 1969 more than fifty thousand.

The way to provide the needed incentive is to apply to the automobile the principle that its price should include not only the cost of producing it, but also the cost of disposing of it.

—*I have asked the Council on Environmental Quality to take the lead in producing a recommendation for a bounty payment or other system to promote scrapping of all junk automobiles.*

The particular disposal problems presented by the automobile are unique. However, wherever appropriate we should also seek to establish incentives and regulations to encourage the reuse, recycling, or easier disposal of other commonly used goods.

—*I have asked the Chairman of the Council on Environmental Quality to work with the Cabinet Committee on the Environment, and with appropriate industry and consumer representatives, toward development of such incentives and regulations for submission to the Congress.*

Parks and Public Recreation

Increasing population, increasing mobility, increasing incomes, and increasing leisure will all combine in the years ahead to rank recreational facilities among the most vital of our public resources. Yet land suitable for such facilities, especially near heavily populated areas, is being rapidly swallowed up.

Plain common sense argues that we give greater priority to acquiring now the lands that will be so greatly needed in a few years. Good sense also argues that the Federal government itself, as the nation's largest landholder, should address itself more imaginatively to the question of making optimum use of its own holdings in a recreation-hungry era.

—*I propose full funding in fiscal 1971 of the $327 million available through the Land and Water Conservation Fund for additional park and recreational facilities, with increased emphasis on locations that can be easily reached by the people in crowded urban areas.*

—*I propose that we adopt a new philosophy for the use of Federally owned lands, treating them as a precious resource—like money itself— which should be made to serve the highest possible public good.*

Acquiring needed recreation areas is a real estate transaction. One third of all the land in the United States—more than 750 million acres— is owned by by the Federal government. Thousands of acres in the heart of metropolitan areas are reserved for only minimal use by Federal installations. To supplement the regularly appropriated funds available, nothing could be more appropriate than to meet new real estate needs through use of presently owned real estate, whether by transfer, sale, or conversion to a better use.

Until now the uses to which Federally owned properties were put has largely been determined by who got them first. As a result countless properties with enormous potential as recreation areas linger on in the hands of agencies that could just as well—or better—locate elsewhere. Bureaucratic inertia is compounded by a quirk of present accounting procedures, which has the effect of imposing a budgetary penalty on an agency that gives up one piece of property and moves to another, even if the vacated property is sold for ten times the cost of the new.

The time has come to make more rational use of our enormous wealth of real property, giving a new priority to our newly urgent concern with public recreation—and to make more imaginative use of properties now surplus to finance acquisition of properties now needed.

—*By Executive Order, I am directing the heads of all Federal agencies and the Administrator of General Services to institute a review of all Federally owned real properties that should be considered for other uses. The test will be whether a particular property's continued present use or another would better serve the public interest, considering both the agency's needs and the property's location. Special emphasis will be placed on identifying properties that could appropriately be converted to parks and recreation areas, or sold, so that proceeds can be made available to provide additional park and recreation lands.*

—*I am establishing a Property Review Board to review the GSA reports and recommend to me what properties should be converted or sold. This Board will consist of the Director of the Bureau of the Budget, the Chairman of the Council of Economic Advisers, the Chairman of the Council on Environmental Quality, and the Administrator of General Services, plus others that I may designate.*

—*I propose legislation to establish, for the first time, a program for relocating Federal installations that occupy locations that could better be used for other purposes.*

This would allow a part of the proceeds from the sales of surplus properties to be used for relocating such installations, thus making more land available.

—*I propose accompanying legislation to protect the Land and Water Conservation Fund, ensuring that its sources of income would be maintained and possibly increased for purchasing additional parkland.*

The net effect would be to increase our capacity to add new park and recreational facilities, by enabling us for the first time to use surplus property sales in a coordinated three-way program: a. by direct conversion from other uses; b. through sale of presently owned properties and purchase of others with the proceeds; and c. by sale of one Federal property, and use of the proceeds to finance the relocation and conversion costs of making another property available for recreational use.

—*I propose that the Department of the Interior be given authority to convey surplus real property to state and local governments for park and recreation purposes at a public benefit discount ranging up to 100 percent*

—*I propose that Federal procedures be revised to encourage Federal agencies to make efficient use of real property. This revision should remove the budgetary penalty now imposed on agencies relinquishing one site and moving to another.*

As one example of what such a property review can make possible, a sizeable stretch of one of California's finest beaches has long been closed to the public because it was part of Camp Pendleton. Last month the Defense Department arranged to make more than a mile of that beach available to the State of California for use as a state park. The remaining beach is sufficient for Camp Pendleton's needs; thus the released stretch represents a shift from low-priority to high-priority use. By carefully weighing alternative uses, a priceless recreational resource was returned to the people for recreational purposes.

Another vast source of potential parklands also lies untapped. We have come to realize that we have too much land available for growing crops and not enough land for parks, open space, and recreation.

—*I propose that instead of simply paying each year to keep this land idle, we help local governments buy selected parcels of it to provide recreational facilities for use by the people of towns in rural areas. This program has been tried, but allowed to lapse; I propose that we revive and expand it.*

—*I propose that we also adopt a program of long-term contracts with private owners of idled farmland, providing for its reforestation and public use for such pursuits as hunting, fishing, hiking, and picnicking.*

Organizing for Action

The environmental problems we face are deep-rooted and widespread. They can be solved only by a full national effort embracing not only sound, coordinated planning, but also an effective follow-through that reaches into every community in the land. Improving our surroundings is necessarily the business of us all.

At the Federal level we have begun the process of organizing for this effort.

The Council on Environmental Quality has been established. This Council will be the keeper of our environmental conscience, and a goad to our ingenuity; beyond this, it will have responsibility for ensuring that all our programs and actions are undertaken with a careful respect for the needs of environmental quality. I have already assigned it major responsibilities for new program development, and I shall look to it increasingly for new initiatives.

The Cabinet Committee on the Environment, which I created last year, acts as a coordinating agency for various departmental activities affecting the environment.

To meet future needs, many organizational changes will still be needed. Federal institutions for dealing with the environment and natural resources have developed piecemeal over the years in response to specific needs, not all of which were originally perceived in the light of the concerns we recognize today. Many of their missions appear to overlap, and even to conflict. Last year I asked the President's Advisory Council on Executive Organization, headed by Mr. Roy Ash, to make an especially thorough study of the organization of Federal environmental, natural resource, and oceanographic programs, and to report its recommendations to me by April 15. After receiving their report, I shall recommend needed reforms, which will involve major reassignments of responsibilities among Departments.

For many of the same reasons, overlaps in environmental programs extend to the Legislative as well as the Executive Branch, so that close consultation will be necessary before major steps are taken.

No matter how well organized government itself might be, however, in the final analysis the key to success lies with the people of America.

Private industry has an especially crucial role. Its resources, its technology, its demonstrated ingenuity in solving problems others only talk about—all these are needed, not only in helping curb the pollution industry itself creates but also in helping devise new and better ways of enhancing all aspects of our environment.

—I have ordered that the United States Patent Office give special priority to the processing of applications for patents which could aid in curbing environmental abuses.

Industry already has begun moving swiftly toward a fuller recognition of its own environmental responsibilities, and has made substantial progress in many areas. However, more must be done.

Mobilizing industry's resources requires organization. With a remarkable degree of unanimity, its leaders have indicated their readiness to help.

—*I will shortly ask a group of the nation's principal industrial leaders to join me in establishing a National Industrial Pollution Control Council.*

The Council will work closely with the Council on Environmental Quality, the Citizens' Advisory Committee on Environmental Quality, the Secretary of Commerce, and others as appropriate in the development of effective policies for the curbing of air, water, noise, and waste pollution from industrial sources. It will work to enlist increased support from business and industry in the drive to reduce pollution, in all its forms, to the minimum level possible. It will provide a mechanism through which, in many cases, government can work with key leaders in various industries to establish voluntary programs for accomplishing desired pollution-control goals.

Patterns of organization often turn out to be only as good as the example set by the organizer. For years, many Federal facilities have themselves been among the worst polluters. The Executive Order I issued last week not only accepts responsibility for putting a swift end to Federal pollution, but puts teeth into the commitment.

I hope this will be an example for others.

At the turn of the century our chief environmental concern was to conserve what we had—and out of this concern grew the often embattled but always determined "conservation" movement. Today, "conservation" is as important as ever—but no longer is it enough to conserve what we have; we must also restore what we have lost. We have to go beyond conservation to embrace restoration.

The task of cleaning up our environment calls for a total mobilization by all of us. It involves governments at every level; it requires the help of every citizen. It cannot be a matter of simply sitting back and blaming someone else. Neither is it one to be left to a few hundred leaders. Rather, it presents us with one of those rare situations in which each individual everywhere has an opportunity to make a special contribution to his country as well as his community.

Through the Council on Environmental Quality, through the Citizens' Advisory Committee on Environmental Quality, and working with governors and mayors and county officials and with concerned private groups, we shall be reaching out in an effort to enlist millions of helping hands, millions of willing spirits—millions of volunteer citizens who will put to themselves the simple question: "What can *I* do?"

It is in this way—with vigorous Federal leadership, with active enlistment of governments at every level, with the aid of industry and private groups, and above all with the determined participation by individual citizens in every state and every community—that we at last will succeed in restoring the kind of environment we want for ourselves, and the kind the generations that come after deserve to inherit.

This task is ours together. It summons our energy, our ingenuity, and our conscience in a cause as fundamental as life itself.

16

Desegregation

of

Our

Schools

President Nixon gave deep thought to new definitions of racial policy he felt were required by conflicting court decisions and varying practices in various sections of the country on desegregation of the public schools.

The election of 1968 brought into sharper focus regional and national attitudes on racial relationships, which had deteriorated after the murder of Dr. Martin Luther King, Jr., and the ensuing riots that year. These harder attitudes were described by commissions on civil rights and domestic violence.

The newest element was a more general understanding that racial integration in the North, particularly in the public schools, was in some leading cities less complete than in the South.

The "hypocrisy" of the North became the center of Congressional debate. Much controversy centered on the effectiveness or ineffectiveness of the Nixon Administration in establishing Federal requirements for school desegregation.

This controversy broadened into a wider re-examination of what was desirable, practicable, and morally supportable in improving racial relationships and reducing tension.

What began as a limited attempt to clarify the Nixon policy on school desegregation ended with the preparation and publication of an exhaustive document defining a workable philosophy of racial relations as Nixon saw it.

This document immediately became controversial in the sense that it was widely criticized and deplored by civil rights leaders and groups as a backward step.

The South, although now having no escape from school desegregation under Nixon's new definitions, appeared to respond favorably to his philosophy. There was no measure of the response elsewhere except to the extent that the idea of neighborhood schools as expressed by Nixon appeared to have wide acceptance, which was reflected in opinion polls.

The document itself was unique as the expression by an incumbent President of his basic doctrines on racial relationships. Its main purpose was equally novel. The President prepared the statement as if it were a legal brief for perusal by members of the Supreme Court in their consideration of unresolved issues on busing and neighborhood schools. The general questions to be considered had previously been outlined in an opinion by Chief Justice Warren Burger. Nixon gave, in effect, his own Presidential opinion on how these questions ought to be resolved.

He considered making a television broadcast summarizing

his views. A speech was prepared, but he decided that the issues were so complex that he could effectively discuss them only in a general statement of policy that could be studied by the Supreme Court, the affected interests and, finally, the general public.

DESEGREGATION OF OUR SCHOOLS
A White House Policy Statement
MARCH 24, 1970

My purpose in this statement is to set forth in detail this Administration's policies on the subject of desegregation of America's elementary and secondary schools.

Few public issues are so emotionally charged as that of school desegregation, few so wrapped in confusion and clouded with misunderstanding. None is more important to our national unity and progress.

This issue is not partisan. It is not sectional. It is an American issue, of direct and immediate concern to every citizen.

I hope that this statement will reduce the prevailing confusion and will help place public discussion of the issue on a more rational and realistic level in all parts of the nation. It is time to strip away the hypocrisy, the prejudice, and the ignorance that too long have characterized discussion of this issue.

My specific objectives in this statement are:

—To reaffirm my personal belief that the 1954 decision of the Supreme Court in *Brown v. Board of Education* was right in both constitutional and human terms.

—To assess our progress in the sixteen years since *Brown* and to point the way to continuing progress.

—To clarify the present state of the law, as developed by the courts and the Congress, and the Administration policies guided by it.

—To discuss some of the difficulties encountered by courts and communities as desegregation has accelerated in recent years, and to suggest approaches that can mitigate such problems as we complete the process of compliance with *Brown*.

—To place the question of school desegregation in its larger context as part of America's historic commitment to the achievement of a free and open society.

Anxiety over this issue has been fed by many sources:

On the one hand, some have interpreted various Administration statements and actions as a backing away from the principle of *Brown* —and have therefore feared that the painstaking work of a decade and a half might be undermined. We are not backing away. The constitutional mandate will be enforced.

On the other hand, several recent decisions by lower courts have raised widespread fears that the nation might face a massive disruption of public education—that wholesale compulsory busing may be ordered and the neighborhood school virtually doomed. A comprehensive review of school desegregation cases indicates that these latter are untypical decisions and that the prevailing trend of judicial opinion is by no means so extreme.

Certain changes are needed in the nation's approach to school desegregation. It would be remarkable if sixteen years of hard, often tempestuous experience had not taught us something about how better to manage the task with a decent regard for the legitimate interests of all concerned—and especially the children. Drawing on this experience, I am confident the remaining problems can be overcome.

What the Law Requires

In order to determine what ought to be done, it is important first to be as clear as possible about what *must* be done.

We are dealing fundamentally with inalienable human rights— some of them constitutionally protected. The final arbiter of constitutional questions is the United States Supreme Court.

THE PRESIDENT'S RESPONSIBILITY

There are a number of questions involved in the school controversy on which the Supreme Court has not yet spoken definitively. Where it has spoken, its decrees are the law. Where it has not spoken, where Congress has not acted, and where differing lower courts have left the issue in doubt, my responsibilities as Chief Executive make it necessary that I determine, on the basis of my best judgment, what must be done.

In reaching that determination, I have sought to ascertain the prevailing judicial view as developed in decisions by the Supreme Court and the various circuit courts of appeals. In this statement I list a number of principles derived from that prevailing judicial view.

I accept those principles and shall be guided by them. The departments and agencies of the government will adhere to them.

A few recent cases in the lower courts have gone beyond those generally accepted principles. Unless affirmed by the Supreme Court, I will not consider them as precedents to guide Administration policy elsewhere.

WHAT THE SUPREME COURT HAS SAID

To determine the present state of the law, we must first remind ourselves of the recent history of Supreme Court rulings in this area.

This begins with the *Brown* case in 1954, when the Court laid down the principle that deliberate segregation of students by race in the public schools was unconstitutional. In that historic ruling the Court gave legal sanction to two fundamental truths: that separation by law establishes schools that are inherently unequal, and that a promise of equality before the law cannot be squared with use of the law to establish two classes of people, one black and one white. The Court requested further argument, however, and propounded the following questions, among others:

"Assuming it is decided that segregation in public school violates the Fourteenth Amendment—

"a. Would a decree necessarily follow providing that, within the limit set by normal geographic school districting, Negro children should forthwith be admitted to schools of their choice, or

"b. May this Court, in the exercise of its equity powers, permit an effective gradual adjustment to be brought about from existing segregated systems to a system not based on color distinctions?"

In its second *Brown* decision, the following year, the Court addressed itself to these questions of manner and timing of compliance. Its ruling included these principles:

Local school problems vary. School authorities have the primary responsibility for solving these problems. Courts must consider whether these authorities are acting in good faith.

The courts should be guided by principles of equity, which traditionally are "characterized by a practical flexibility in shaping its remedies and by a facility for adjusting and reconciling public and private needs."

Compliance must be achieved "with all deliberate speed," including "a prompt and reasonable start" toward achieving full compliance "at the earliest practicable date."

In 1964 the Supreme Court spoke again: "The time for mere 'deliberate speed' has run out, and that phrase can no longer justify denying these . . . children their constitutional rights."

At the same time Congress also added to the impetus of desegregation by passing the Civil Rights Act of 1964—an Act that as a private citizen I endorsed and supported.

Although the Supreme Court in the *Brown* cases concerned itself primarily, if not exclusively, with pupil assignments, its decree applied also to teacher assignments and school facilities as a whole.

In 1968 the Supreme Court reiterated the principle enunciated in prior decisions—that teacher assignments are an important aspect of the basic task of achieving a public school system wholly freed from racial discrimination. During that same year, in another group of Supreme Court decisions, a significant and new set of principles also emerged:

That a school board must establish "that its proposed plan promises meaningful and immediate progress toward disestablishing state-imposed segregation," and that the plan must "have real prospects for dismantling the state-imposed dual system 'at the earliest practicable date.' "

That one test of whether a school board has met its "affirmative duty to take whatever steps might be necessary to convert to a unitary system in which racial discrimination would be eliminated root and branch" is the extent to which racial separation persists under its plan.

That the argument that effective desegregation might cause white families to flee the neighborhood cannot be used to sustain devices designed to perpetuate segregation.

That when geographic zoning is combined with "free transfers" and the effect of the transfer privilege is to perpetuate segregation despite the zoning, the plan is unacceptable.

The most recent decisions by the Supreme Court have now rejected any further delay, adding to the Court's mandate:

"The obligation of every school district is to terminate dual systems at once and to operate now and hereafter only unitary schools."

That the obligation of such districts is an affirmative one and not a passive one.

That freedom-of-choice plans could no longer be considered as an appropriate substitute for the affirmative obligation imposed by the Court unless they, in fact, discharge that obligation immediately.

The Court has dealt only in very general terms with the question of what constitutes a "unitary" system, referring to it as one "within which no person is to be effectively excluded from any school because of race or color." It has not spoken definitely on whether or not—or the extent to which—"desegregation" may mean "integration."

In an opinion earlier this month Chief Justice Burger pointed out a number of "basic practical problems" which the Court had not yet resolved, "including whether, as a constitutional matter, any particular racial balance must be achieved in the schools; to what extent school districts and zones may or must be altered as a constitutional matter; to what extent transportation may or must be provided to achieve the ends sought by prior holdings of this Court."

One of these areas of legal uncertainty cited by Chief Justice Burger —school transportation—involves Congressional pronouncements.

In the 1964 Civil Rights Act the Congress stated: "Nothing herein shall empower any official or court of the United States to issue any order seeking to achieve a racial balance in any school by requiring the transportation of pupils or students from one school to another or one school district to another in order to achieve such racial balance, or otherwise enlarge the existing power of the court to insure compliance with constitutional standards."

In the 1966 amendments to the Elementary and Secondary Education Act, the Congress further stated: "Nothing contained in this Act shall . . . require the assignment or transportation of students or teachers in order to overcome racial imbalance."

I am advised that these provisions cannot constitutionally be applied to *de jure* segregation. However, not all segregation as it exists today is *de jure*.

I have consistently expressed my opposition to any compulsory busing of pupils beyond normal geographic school zones for the purpose of achieving racial balance.

WHAT THE LOWER COURTS HAVE SAID

In the absence of definitive Supreme Court rulings, these and other "basic practical problems" have been left for case-by-case determination in the lower courts—and both real and apparent contradictions among some of these lower-court ruling have generated considerable public confusion about what the law really requires.

In an often-cited case in 1955 (*Briggs v. Elliott*), a district court held that "the Constitution . . . does not require integration. . . . It merely forbids the use of governmental power to enforce segregation."

But in 1966 another court took issue with this doctrine, pointing out that it had been used as justifying "techniques for perpetuating school segregation," and declaring that "the only adequate redress for a previously overt systemwide policy of segregation directed against Negroes as a collective entity is a systemwide policy of integration."

In 1969 the Fourth Circuit Court of Appeals declared: "The famous *Briggs v. Elliott* dictum—adhered to by this court for many years—that the Constitution forbids segregation but does not require integration . . . is now dead."

Cases in two circuit courts have held that the continued existence of some all-black schools in a formerly segregated district did *not* demonstrate unconstitutionality—with one noting that there is "no duty to balance the races in the school system in conformity with some mathematical formula."

Another circuit court decision declared that even though a district's geographic zones were based on objective, non-racial criteria, the fact that they failed to produce any significant degree of integration meant that they *were* unconstitutional.

Two very recent Federal court decisions continue to illustrate the range of opinion: A plan of a Southern school district has been upheld even though three schools would remain all-black, but a Northern school system has been ordered by another Federal court to integrate all of its schools completely "by the revising of boundary lines for attendance purposes as well as busing so as to achieve maximum racial integration."

This range of differences demonstrates that lawyers and judges have honest disagreements about what the law requires. There have been some rulings that would divert such huge sums of money to non-educational purposes and would create such severe dislocations of public school systems as to impair the primary function of providing a good education.

In one, for example—probably the most extreme judicial decree so far—a California state court recently ordered the Los Angeles School Board to establish a virtually uniform racial balance throughout its 711-square-mile district, with its 775,000 children in 561 schools. Local leaders anticipate that this decree would impose an expenditure of $40 million over the next school year to lease 1,600 buses, to acquire site locations to house them, to hire drivers and to defray operating costs. Subsequent costs would approximate $20 million annually.

Some recent rulings by Federal district courts applicable to other school districts appear to be no less severe.

I am dedicated to continued progress toward a truly desegregated public school system. But considering the always heavy demands for more school-operating funds, I believe it is preferable, when we have to make the choice, to use limited financial resources for the improvement of education—for better teaching facilities, better methods, and advanced educational materials—and for the upgrading of the disadvantaged areas in the community rather than buying buses, tires, and gasoline to transport young children miles away from their neighborhood schools.

WHAT MOST OF THE COURTS AGREE ON

Despite the obvious confusion, a careful survey of rulings both by the Supreme Court and by the circuit courts of appeals suggests that the basic judicial approach may be more reasonable than some have feared. Whatever a few lower courts might have held to the contrary, the prevailing trend of judicial opinion appears to be summed up in these principles:

There is a fundamental distinction between so-called *de jure* and *de facto* segregation: *de jure* segregation arises by law or by the deliberate act of school officials and is unconstitutional; *de facto* segregation results from residential housing patterns and does not violate the Constitution. The clearest example of *de jure* segregation is the dual school system as it existed in the South prior to the decision in *Brown*—two schools, one Negro and one white, comprised of the same grades and serving the same geographical area. This is the system with which most of the decisions and the Supreme Court cases up until now have been concerned.

Where school boards have demonstrated a good-faith effort to comply with court rulings, the courts have generally allowed substantial latitude as to method—often making the explicit point that administrative choices should, wherever possible, be made by the local school authorities themselves.

In devising particular plans, questions of cost, capacity, and convenience for pupils and parents are relevant considerations.

Whatever the racial composition of student bodies, faculties and staff must be assigned in a way that does not contribute to identifying a given school as "Negro" or "white."

In school districts that previously operated dual systems, affirmative steps toward integration are a key element in disestablishing the dual result in "racial balance" throughout the system. When there is a racial separation in housing, the constitutional requirement has been held satisfied even though some schools remained all-black.

While the dual school system is the most obvious example, *de jure* segregation is also found in more subtle forms. Where authorities have deliberately drawn attendance zones or chosen school locations for the express purpose of creating and maintaining racially separate schools, *de jure* segregation is held to exist. In such a case the school board has a positive duty to remedy it. This is so even though the board ostensibly operates a unitary system.

In determining whether school authorities are responsible for existing racial separation—and thus whether they are constitutionally required to remedy it—the *intent* of their action in locating schools, drawing zones, etc., is a crucial factor.

In the case of genuine *de facto* segregation (*i.e.*, where housing patterns produce substantially all-Negro or all-white schools, and where this racial separation has not been caused by deliberate official action) school authorities are not constitutionally required to take any positive steps to correct the imbalance.

To summarize: There is a constitutional mandate that dual school systems and other forms of *de jure* segregation be eliminated totally. But within the framework of that requirement an area of flexibility—a "rule of reason"—exists in which school boards, acting in good faith, can formulate plans of desegregation which best suit the needs of their own localities.

De facto segregation, which exists in many areas both North and South, is undesirable but is not generally held to violate the Constitution. Thus, residential housing patterns may result in the continued existence of some all-Negro schools even in a system which fully meets constitutional standards. But in any event, local school officials may, if they so choose, take steps beyond the constitutional minimums to diminish racial separation.

School Desegregation Today

THE PROGRESS

Though it began slowly, the momentum of school desegregation has become dramatic.

Thousands of school districts throughout the South have met the requirements of law.

In the past year alone the number of black children attending Southern schools held to be in compliance has doubled, from less than 600,000 to nearly 1.2 milion—representing 40 percent of the Negro student population.

In most cases, this has been peacefully achieved.

However, serious problems are being encountered both by communities and by courts—in part as a consequence of this accelerating pace.

THE PROBLEMS

In some communities, racially mixed schools have brought the community greater interracial harmony; in others they have heightened racial tension and exacerbated racial frictions. Integration is no longer seen automatically and necessarily as an unmixed blessing for the Negro, Puerto Rican, or Mexican-American child. "Racial balance" has been discovered to be neither a static nor a finite condition; in many cases it has turned out to be only a way-station on the road to resegregation.

Whites have deserted the public schools, often for grossly inadequate private schools. They have left the now resegregated public schools foundering for lack of support. And when whites flee the central city in pursuit of all- or predominantly white schools in the suburbs, it is not only the central-city schools that become racially isolated, but the central city itself.

These are not theoretical problems, but actual problems. They exist not just in the realm of law, but in the realm of human attitudes and human behavior. They are part of the real world, and we have to take account of them.

THE COMPLEXITIES

Courts are confronted wih problems of equity and administrators with problems of policy. For example: To what extent does desegregation of dual systems require positive steps to achieve integration? How are the rights of individual children and their parents to be guarded in the process of enforcement? What are the educational impacts of the various means of desegregation—and where they appear to conflict, how should the claims of education be balanced against those of integration? To what extent should desegregation plans attempt to anticipate the problem of resegregation?

These questions suggest the complexity of the problems. These problems confront us in the North as well as the South, and in rural communities, suburbs, and central cities.

The troubles in our schools have many sources. They stem in part from deeply rooted racial attitudes; in part from differences in social, economic, and behavioral patterns; in part from weaknesses and inequities in the educational system itself; in part from the fact that by making schools the primary focus of efforts to remedy longstanding social ills, in some cases greater pressure has been brought to bear on the schools than they could withstand.

THE CONTEXT

Progress toward school desegregation is part of two larger processes, each equally essential:

—The improvement of educational opportunities for all of America's children.

—The lowering of artificial racial barriers in all aspects of American life.

Only if we keep each of these considerations clearly in mind—and only if we recognize their separate natures—can we approach the question of school desegregation realistically.

It may be helpful to step back for a moment, and to consider the problem of school desegregation in its larger context.

The school stands in a unique relationship to the community, to the family, and to the individual student. It is a focal point of community life. It has a powerful impact on the future of all who attend. It is a place not only of learning, but also of living—where a child's friendships center, where he learns to measure himself against others, to share, to compete, to cooperate—and it is the one institution above all others with which the parent shares his child.

Thus it is natural that whatever affects the schools stirs deep feelings among parents, and in the community at large.

Whatever threatens the schools, parents perceive—rightly—as a threat to their children.

Whatever makes the schools more distant from the family undermines one of the important supports of learning.

Quite understandably, the prospect of any abrupt change in the schools is seen as a threat.

As we look back over these sixteen years we find that many changes that stirred fears when they first were ordered have turned out well. In many Southern communities black and white children now learn together—and both the schools and the communities are better where the essential changes have been accomplished in a peaceful way.

But we also have seen situations in which the changes have not worked well. These have tended to command the headlines, thus increasing the anxieties of those still facing change.

OVERBURDENING THE SCHOOLS

One of the mistakes of past policy has been to demand too much of our schools: They have been expected not only to educate, but also to accomplish a social transformation. Children in many instances have not been served but used—in what all too often has proved a tragically futile effort to achieve in the schools the kind of a multiracial society which the adult community has failed to achieve for itself.

If we are to be realists, we must recognize that in a free society there are limits to the amount of government coercion that can reasonably be used; that in achieving desegregation, we must proceed with the least possible disruption of the education of the nation's children; and that our children are highly sensitive to conflict, and highly vulnerable to lasting psychic injury.

Failing to recognize these factors, past policies have placed on the schools and the children too great a share of the burden af eliminating racial disparities throughout our society. A major part of this task falls to the schools. But they cannot do all or even most of it by themselves. Other institutions can share the burden of breaking down racial barriers but only the schools can perform the task of education itself. If our schools fail to educate, then whatever they may achieve in integrating the races will turn out to be only a pyrrhic victory.

With housing patterns what they are in many places in the nation, the sheer numbers of pupils and the distances between schools make full and prompt school integration in every such community impractical— even if there were a sufficient desire on the part of the community to achieve it. In Los Angeles 78 percent of all Negro pupils attend schools that are 95-percent or more black. In Chicago the figure is 85 percent— the same as in Mobile, Alabama. Many smaller cities have the same patterns. Nationwide, 61 percent of all Negro students attend schools which are 95-percent or more black.

Demands that an arbitrary "racial balance" be established as a matter of right misinterpret the law and misstate the priorities.

As a matter of educational policy some school boards have chosen to arrange their school systems in such a way as to provide a greater measure of racial integration. The important point to bear in mind is that where the existing racial separation has not been caused by official action, this increased integration is and should remain a matter for local determination.

Pupil assignments involve problems which do not arise in the case of the assignment of teachers. If school administrators were truly color-blind and teacher assignments did not reflect the color of the teacher's skin, the law of averages would eventually dictate an approximate racial balance of teachers in each school within a system.

NOT JUST A MATTER OF RACE

Available data on the educational effects of integration are neither definitive nor comprehensive. But such data as we have suggest strongly that, under the appropriate conditions, racial integration in the class-room can be a significant factor in improving the quality of education · for the disadvantaged. At the same time, the data lead us into several more of the complexities that surround the desegregation issue.

For one thing, they serve as a reminder that, from an educational standpoint, to approach school questions solely in terms of race is to go astray. The data tell us that in educational terms the significant factor is not race but rather the educational environment in the home—and indeed, that the single most important educational factor in a school is the kind of home environment its pupils come from. As a general rule, children from families whose home environment encourages learning—

whatever their race—are higher achievers; those from homes offering little encouragement are lower achievers.

Which effect the home environment has depends on such things as whether books and magazines are available, whether the family subscribes to a newspaper, the educational level of the parents, and their attitude toward the child's education.

The data strongly suggest, also, that in order for the positive benefits of integration to be achieved, the school must have a majority of children from environments that encourage learning—recognizing, again, that the key factor is not race but the kind of home the child comes from. The greater concentration of pupils whose homes encourage learning—of whatever race—the higher the achievement levels not only of those pupils, but also of others in the same school. Students learn from students. The reverse is also true: The greater concentration of pupils from homes that discourage learning, the lower the achievement levels of all.

We should bear very carefully in mind, therefore, the distinction between educational difficulty as a result of race and educational difficulty as a result of social or economic levels, of family background, of cultural patterns, or simply of bad schools. Providing bettter education for the disadvantaged requires a more sophisticated approach than mere racial mathematics.

In this same connection we should recognize that a smug paternalism has characterized the attitudes of many white Americans toward school questions. There has been an implicit assumption that blacks or others of minority races would be improved by association with whites. The notion that an all-black or predominantly black school is automatically inferior to one which is all- or predominantly white—even though not a product of a dual system—inescapably carries racist overtones. And, of course, we know of hypocrisy: not a few of those in the North most stridently demanding racial integration of public schools in the South at the same time send their children to private schools to avoid the assumed inferiority of mixed public schools.

It is unquestionably true that most black schools—though by no means all—are in fact inferior to most white schools. This is due in part to past neglect or shortchanging of the black schools; and in part to long-term patterns of racial discrimination which caused a greater proportion of Negroes to be left behind educationally, left out culturally, and trapped in low-paying jobs. It is not really because they serve black children that most of these schools are inferior, but rather because they serve poor children who often lack the home environment that encourages learning.

INNOVATIVE APPROACHES

Most public discussion of overcoming racial isolation centers on such concepts as compulsory "busing"—taking children out of the schools they would normally attend, and forcing them instead to attend others more distant, often in strange or even hostile neighborhoods. Massive "busing" is seen by some as the only alternative to massive racial isolation.

However, a number of new educational ideas are being developed, designed to provide the educational benefits of integration without depriving the student of his own neighborhood school.

For example, rather than attempting dislocation of whole schools, a portion of a child's educational activities may be shared with children from other schools. Some of his education is in a "home-base" school, but some outside it. This "outside learning" is in settings that are defined neither as black nor white, and sometimes in settings that are not even in traditional school buildings. It may range all the way from intensive work in reading to training in technical skills, and to joint efforts such as drama and athletics.

By bringing the children together on "neutral" territory, friction may be dispelled; by limiting it to part-time activities no one would be deprived of his own neighborhood school; and the activities themselves provide the children with better education.

This sort of innovative approach demonstrates that the alternatives are not limited to perpetuating racial isolation on the one hand, and massively disrupting existing school patterns on the other. Without uprooting students, devices of this kind can provide an additional educational experience within an integrated setting. The child gains both ways.

GOOD FAITH AND THE COURTS

Where desegregation proceeds under the mandate of law, the best results require that the plans be carefully adapted to local circumstances.

A sense of compassionate balance is indispensable. The concept of balance is no stranger to our Constitution. Even First Amendment freedoms are not absolute and unlimited; rather the scales of that "balance" have been adjusted with minute care, case by case, and the process continues.

In my discussion of the status of school desegregation law I indicated that the Supreme Court has left a substantial degree of latitude within which specific desegregation plans can be designed. Many lower courts have left a comparable degree of latitude. This does not mean that the courts will tolerate or the Administration condone evasions or subterfuges; it does mean that if the essential element of good faith is present, it should ordinarily be possible to achieve legal compliance with a minimum of educational disruption and through a plan designed to be responsive to the community's own local circumstances.

This matter of good faith is critical.

Thus the farsighted local leaders who have demonstrated good faith by smoothing the path of compliance in their communities have helped lay the basis for judicial attitudes which take more fully into account the practical problems of compliance.

How the Supreme Court finally rules on the major issues it has not yet determined can have a crucial impact on the future of public education in the United States.

Traditionally, the Court has refrained from deciding constitutional questions until it became necessary. This period of legal uncertainty has occasioned vigorous controversy over what the thrust of the law should be.

As a nation, we should create a climate in which these questions, when they finally are decided by the Court, can be decided in a framework most conducive to reasonable and realistic interpretation.

We should not provoke any court to push a constitutional principle beyond its ultimate limit in order to compel compliance with the Court's essential but more modest mandate. The best way to avoid this is for the nation to demonstrate that it does intend to carry out the full spirit of the constitutional mandate.

Policies of this Administration

It will be the purpose of this Administration to carry out the law fully and fairly. And where problems exist that are beyond the mandate of legal requirements, it will be our purpose to seek solutions that are both realistic and appropriate.

I have instructed the Attorney General, the Secretary of Health, Education and Welfare, and other appropriate officials of the government to be guided by these basic principles and policies:

PRINCIPLES OF ENFORCEMENT

Deliberate racial segregation of pupils by official action is unlawful, wherever it exists. In the words of the Supreme Court, it must be eliminated "root and branch"—and it must be eliminated at once.

Segregation of teachers must be eliminated. To this end each school system in this nation, North and South, East and West, must move immediately, as the Supreme Court has ruled, toward a goal under which "in each school the ratio of white to Negro faculty members is substantially the same as it is throughout the system."

With respect to school facilities, school administrators throughout the nation, North and South, East and West, must move immediately, also in conformance wih the Court's ruling, to assure that schools within individual school districts do not discriminate with respect to the quality of facilities or the quality of education delivered to the children within the district.

In devising local compliance plans, primary weight should be given to the considered judgment of local school boards—provided they act in good faith and within constitutional limits.

The neighborhood school will be deemed the most appropriate base for such a system.

Transportation of pupils beyond normal geographic school zones for the purpose of achieving racial balance will not be required.

Federal advice and assistance will be made available on request, but Federal officials should not go beyond the requirements of law in attempting to impose their own judgment on the local school district.

School boards will be encouraged to be flexible and creative in formulating plans that are educationally sound and that result in effective desegregation.

Racial imbalance in a school system may be partly *de jure* in origin and partly *de facto*. In such a case it is appropriate to insist on remedy for the *de jure* portion, which is unlawful, without insisting on a remedy for the lawful *de facto* portion.

De facto racial separation, resulting genuinely from housing patterns, exists in the South as well as the North; in neither area should this condition by itself be cause for Federal enforcement actions. *De jure* segregation brought about by deliberate school board gerrymandering exists in the North as the South; in both areas this must be remedied. In all respects the law should be applied equally, North and South, East and West.

This is one nation. We are one people. I feel strongly that as Americans we must be done, now and for all future time, with the divisive notion that these problems are sectional.

POLICIES FOR PROGRESS

In those communities facing desegregation orders, the leaders of the communities will be encouraged to lead—not in defiance, but in smoothing the way of compliance. One clear lesson of experience is that local leadership is a fundamental factor in determining success or failure. Where leadership has been present, where it has been mobilized, where it has been effective, many districts have found that they could, after all, desegregate their schools successfully. Where local leadership has failed, the community has failed—and the schools and the children have borne the brunt of that failure.

We shall launch a concerted, sustained, and honest effort to assemble and evaluate the lessons of experience: to determine what methods of school desegregation have worked, in what situations, and why—and also what has not worked. The Cabinet-level working group I recently appointed will have as one of its principal functions amassing just this sort of information and helping make it available to the communities in need of assistance.

We shall attempt to develop a far greater body of reliable data than now exists on the effects of various integration patterns on the learning process. Our effort must always be to preserve the education benefit for the children.

We shall explore ways of sharing more broadly the burdens of social transition that have been laid disproportionately on the schools—ways, that is, of shifting to other public institutions a greater share of the task of undoing the effects of racial isolation.

We shall seek to develop and test a varied set of approaches to the problems associated with "*de facto*" segregation, North as well as South.

We shall intensify our efforts to ensure that the gifted child—the potential leader—is not stifled intellectually merely because he is black or brown or lives in a slum.

While raising the quality of education in all schools, we shall concentrate especially on racially impacted schools, and particularly on equalizing those schools that are furthest behind.

Words often ring empty without deeds. In government words can ring even emptier without dollars.

In order to give substance to these commitments, I shall ask Congress to divert $500 million from my previous budget requests for other domestic programs for fiscal 1971, to be put instead into programs for improving education in racially impacted areas, North and South, and for assisting school districts in meeting special problems incident to court-ordered desegregation. For fiscal 1972 I have ordered that $1 billion be budgeted for the same purposes.

I am not content simply to see this money spent, and then to count the spending as the measure of accomplishment. For much too long national "commitments" have been measured by the number of Federal dollars spent rather than by more valid measures such as the quality of imagination displayed, the amount of private energy enlisted, or, even more to the point, the results achieved.

If this $1.5 billion accomplishes nothing, then the commitment will mean nothing.

If it enables us to break significant new ground, then the commitment will mean everything.

This I deeply believe: Communities desegregating their schools face special needs—for classrooms, facilities, teachers, teacher training—and the nation should help meet those needs.

The nation also has a vital and special stake in upgrading education where *de facto* segregation persists—and where extra efforts are needed if the schools are to do their job. These schools, too, need extra money for teachers and facilities.

Beyond this, we need to press forward with innovative new ways of overcoming the effects of racial isolation and of making up for environmental deficiencies among the poor.

I have asked the Vice President's Cabinet Committee on School Desegregation, together with the Secretary of Health, Education and Welfare, to consult with experts in and out of government and prepare a set of recommended criteria for the allocation of these funds.

I have specified that these criteria should give special weight to four categories of need:

—The special needs of desegregating (or recently desegregated) districts for additional facilities, personnel, and training required to get the new unitary system successfully started.

—The special needs of racially impacted schools where *de facto* segregation persists—and where immediate infusions of money can make a real difference in terms of educational effectiveness.

—The special needs of those districts that have the furthest to go to catch up educationally with the rest of the nation.

—The financing of innovative techniques for providing educationally sound interracial experiences for children in racially isolated schools.

This money—the $500 million next year and the $1 billion in fiscal 1972—must come from other programs. Inevitably, it represents a further reordering of priorities on the domestic scene. It represents a heightened priority for making school desegregation work, and for helping the victims of racial isolation learn.

Nothing is more vital to the future of our nation than the education of its children; and at the heart of equal opportunity is equal educational opportunity. These funds wil be an investment in both the quality and the equality of that opportunity.

This money is meant to provide help *now*, where help is needed now.

As we look to the longer-term future, it is vital that we concentrate more effort on understanding the process of learning—and improving the process of teaching. The educational needs we face cannot be met simply with more books, more classrooms, and more teachers—however urgently these are needed now in schools that face shortages. We need more effective methods of teaching, and especially of teaching those children who are hardest to reach and most lacking in a home environment that encourages learning.

In my message on education reform earlier this month I proposed creation of a National Institute of Education to conduct and to sponsor basic and applied educational research—with special emphasis on compensatory education for the disadvantaged, on the Right to Read, on experimental schools, and on the use of television for educational purposes.

I repeat that proposal—and I ask that the Congress consider it a matter of high priority.

A Free and Open Society

The goal of this Administration is a free and open society. In saying this, I use the words "free" and "open" quite precisely.

Freedom has two essential elements: the *right* to choose, and the *ability* to choose. The right to move out of a mid-city slum, for example, means little without the means of doing so. The right to apply for a good job means little without access to the skills that make it attainable. By the same token, those skills are of little use if arbitrary policies exclude the person who has them because of race or other distinction.

Similarly, an "open" society is one of open choices—and one in which the individual has the mobility to take advantage of those choices.

In speaking of "desegregation" or "integration," we often lose sight of what these mean within the context of a free, open, pluralistic society. We cannot be free, and at the same time be required to fit our lives into prescribed places on a racial grid—whether segregated or integrated, and whether by some mathematical formula or by automatic assignment. Neither can we be free, and at the same time be denied—because of race; the right to associate with our fellow citizens on a basis of human equality.

An open society does not have to be homogeneous, or even fully integrated. There is room within it for many communities. Especially in a nation like America, it is natural that people with a common heritage retain special ties; it is natural and right that we have Italian or Irish or Negro or Norwegian neighborhoods; it is natural and right that members of those communities feel a sense of group identity and group pride. In terms of an open society, what matters is mobility: the right and the ability of each person to decide for himself where and how he wants to live, whether as part of the ethnic enclave or as part of the larger society—or, as many do, share the life of both.

We are richer for our cultural diversity; mobility is what allows us to enjoy it.

Economic, educational, social mobility—all these, too, are essential elements of the open society. When we speak of equal opportunity we mean just that: that each person should have an equal chance at the starting line, and an equal chance to go just as high and as far as his talents and energies will take him.

This Administration's programs for helping the poor, for equal opportunity, for expanded opportunity, all have taken a significantly changed direction from those of previous years—and those principles of a free and open society are the keys to the new direction.

Instead of making a man's decisions for him, we aim to give him both the *right* and *ability* to choose for himself—and the mobility to move upward. Instead of creating a permanent welfare class catered to by a permanent welfare bureaucracy, for example, my welfare reform proposal provides job training and a job requirement for all those able to work—and also a regularly Family Assistance payment instead of the demeaning welfare handout.

By pressing hard for the "Philadelphia Plan," we have sought to crack the color bar in the construction unions—and thus to give black and other minority Americans both the right and the ability to choose jobs in the construction trades, among the highest paid in the nation.

We have inaugurated new Minority Business Enterprise programs— not only to help minority members get started in business themselves, but also, by developing more black and brown entrepreneurs, to demonstrate to young blacks, Mexican-Americans, and others that they, too, can aspire to this same sort of upward economic mobility.

In our education programs we have stressed the need for far greater diversity of individual needs—including more and better vocational and technical training, and a greater development of two-year community colleges.

Such approaches have been based essentially on faith in the individual—knowing that he sometimes needs help, but believing that in the long run he usually knows what is best for himself. Through them also runs a belief that education is the key that opens the door to personal progress.

As we strive to make our schools places of equal educational opportunity, we should keep our eye fixed on this goal: to achieve a set of conditions in which neither the laws nor the institutions supported by law any longer draw an invidious distinction based on race; and going one step further, we must seek to repair the human damage wrought by past segregation. We must give the minority child that equal place at the starting line that his parents were denied—and the pride, the dignity, the self-respect, that are the birthright of a free American.

We can do no less and still be true to our conscience and our Constitution. I believe that most Americans today, whether North or South, accept this as their duty.

The issues involved in desegregating schools, reducing racial isolation, and providing equal educational opportunity are not simple. Many of the questions are profound, the factors complex, the legitimate considerations in conflict, and the answers elusive. Our continuing search, therefore, must be not for the perfect set of answers, but for the most nearly perfect and the most constructive.

I am aware that there are many sincere Americans who believe deeply in instant solutions and who will say that my approach does not go far enough fast enough. They feel that the only way to bring about social justice is to integrate all schools now, everywhere, no matter what the cost in the disruption of education.

I am aware, too, that there are many equally sincere citizens—North and South, black and white—who believe that racial separation is right, and wish the clock of progress would stop or be turned back to 1953. They will be disappointed, too.

But the call for equal educational opportunity today is in the American tradition. From the outset of the nation, one of the great struggles in America has been to transform the system of education into one that truly provided equal opportunity for all. At first, the focus was on economic discrimination. The system of "fee schools" and "pauper schools" persisted well into the nineteenth century.

Heated debates preceded the establishment of universal free public education—and even in such states as New York, New Jersey, and Connecticut the system is barely a century old.

Even today inequities persist. Children in poor areas often are served by poor schools—and unlike the children of the wealthy, they cannot escape to private schools. But we have been narrowing the gap— providing more and better education in more of the public schools, and making higher education more widely available through free tuition, scholarships, and loans.

In other areas, too, there were long struggles to eliminate discrimination that had nothing to do with race. Property and even religious qualifications for voting persisted well into the nineteenth century—and not until 1920 were women finally guaranteed the right to vote.

Now the focus is on race—and on the dismantling of all racial bars to equality of opportunity in the schools. As with the lowering of economic barriers, the pull of conscience and the pull of national self-interest both are in the same direction. A system that leaves any segment of its people poorly educated serves the nation badly; a system that educates all of its people well serves the nation well.

We have overcome many problems in our hundred and ninety years as a nation. We can overcome this problem. We have managed to extend opportunity in other areas. We can extend it in this area. Just as other rights have been secured, so too can these rights be secured—and once again the nation will be better for having done so.

I am confident that we can preserve and improve our schools, carry out the mandate of our Constitution, and be true to our national conscience.

17

State
of
the
Union

On January 22, 1970, a year and two days after he took office, President Nixon went to the House of Representatives to deliver his first formal State-of-the-Union address to a joint session of Congress. The Constitution prescribes as a President's duty that "he shall from time to time give to the Congress information of the state of the union and recommend to their consideration such measures as he shall judge necessary and expedient."

It was known in advance of the President's speech that he would launch a long-range program for environmental improvement as a major new initiative of his Administration. The extent and scope of his program was treated as the major news focus of his address.

On further consideration, however, more weight was attached to his extension of the Nixon doctrine of lowered profile in the Far East to the entire world. The Guam Doctrine made worldwide became the Nixon Doctrine in which the nations of each part of the world should assume the primary responsibility for their own well-being.

The address was well received in Congress, both for its foreign policy and domestic content. Following as it did numerous specific reform proposals of the previous year, the State-of-the-Union address gave general form and direction to the purposes of his Administration.

Thus ended a year in which the President, after a slow beginning, had erected and articulated a general program of large proportions. It was, in effect, a two-year program and much more than Congress could act upon in one year.

The January 22 address is one to which historians are more likely to turn for general definitions of President Nixon's policies than to any other speech or statement.

STATE OF THE UNION
Address to a Joint Session of the Congress of the United States
JANUARY 22, 1970

Mr. Speaker, Mr. President, my colleagues in the Congress, our distinguished guests, and my fellow Americans:

373

To address a joint session of the Congress in this great chamber in which I was privileged to serve is an honor for which I am deeply grateful.

The State of the Union Address is traditionally an occasion for lengthy and detailed account by the President of what he has accomplished in the past, what he wants the Congress to do in the future, and, in an election year, to lay the basis for the political issues which might be decisive in the fall.

Occasionally there comes a time when profound and far-reaching events command a break with tradition.

This is such a time.

I say this not only because 1970 marks the beginning of a new decade in which America will celebrate its two-hundredth birthday. I say it because new knowledge and hard experience argue persuasively that both our programs and our institutions in America need to be reformed.

The moment has arrived to harness the vast energies and abundance of this land to the creation of a new American experience, an experience richer and deeper and more truly a reflection of the goodness and grace of the human spirit.

The '70s will be a time of new beginnings, a time of exploring both on the earth and in the heavens, a time of discovery. But the time has also come for emphasis on developing better ways of managing what we have and of completing what man's genius has begun but left unfinished.

Our land, this land that is ours together, is a great and a good land. It is also an unfinished land. The challenge of perfecting it is the summons of the '70s.

It is in that spirit that I address myself to those great issues facing our nation which are above partisanship.

When we speak of America's priorities the first priority must always be peace for America and the world.

The major immediate goal of our foreign policy is to bring an end to the war in Vietnam in a way that our generation will be remembered, not so much as the generation that suffered in war, but more for the fact that we had the courage and character to win the kind of a just peace that the next generation was able to keep.

We are making progress toward that goal.

The prospects for peace are far greater today than they were a year ago.

A major part of the credit for this development goes to the members of this Congress who, despite their differences on the conduct of the war, have overwhelmingly indicated their support of a just peace. By this action you have completely demolished the enemy's hopes that they can gain in Washington the victory our fighting men have denied them in Vietnam.

No goal could be greater than to make the next generation the first in this century in which America was at peace with every nation in the world.

I shall discuss in detail the new concepts and programs designed to achieve this goal in a separate report on foreign policy, which I shall submit to the Congress at a later date.

Today, let me describe the directions of our new policies.

We have based our policies on an evaluation of the world as it is, not as it was twenty-five years ago at the conclusion of World War II. Many of the policies which were necessary and right then are obsolete today.

Then, because of America's overwhelming military and economic strength, because of the weakness of other major free world powers and the inability of scores of newly independent nations to defend or even govern themselves, America had to assume the major burden for the defense of freedom in the world.

In two wars, first in Korea and now in Vietnam, we furnished most of the money, most of the arms, most of the men to help other nations defend their freedom.

Today the great industrial nations of Europe, as well as Japan, have regained their economic strength, and the nations of Latin America—and many of the nations that acquired their freedom from colonialism after World War II in Asia and Africa—have a new sense of pride and dignity, and a determination to assume the responsibility for their own defense.

That is the basis of the doctrine I announced at Guam.

Neither the defense nor the development of other nations can be exclusively or primarily an American undertaking.

The nations of each part of the world should assume the primary responsibility for their own well-being; and they themselves should determine the terms of that well-being.

We shall be faithful to our treaty commitments, but we shall reduce our involvement and our presence in other nations' affairs.

To insist that other nations play a role is not a retreat from responsibility; it is a sharing of responsibility.

The result of this new policy has been not to weaken our alliances, but to give them new life, new strength, a new sense of common purpose.

Relations with our European allies are once again strong and healthy, based on mutual consultation and mutual responsibility.

We have initiated a new approach to Latin America, in which we deal with those nations as partners rather than patrons.

The new partnership concept has been welcomed in Asia. We have developed an historic new basis for Japanese-American friendship and cooperation which is the linchpin for peace in the Pacific.

If we are to have peace in the last third of the twentieth century, a major factor will be the development of a new relationship between the United States and the Soviet Union.

I would not underestimate our differences, but we are moving with precision and purpose from an era of confrontation to an era of negotiation. Our negotiations on strategic arms limitations and in other areas will have far greater chance for success if both sides enter them motivated by mutual self-interest rather than naïve sentimentality.

It is this same spirit with which we have resumed discussions with Communist China in our talks at Warsaw.

Our concern in our relations with both these nations is to avoid a catastrophic collision and to build a solid basis for peaceful settlement of our differences.

I would be the last to suggest that the road to peace is not difficult and dangerous, but I believe our new policies have contributed to the prospect that America may have the best chance since World War II to enjoy a generation of uninterrupted peace. And that chance will be enormously increased if we continue to have a relationship between Congress and the Executive in which, despite differences in detail, where the security of America and the peace of mankind are concerned, we act not as Republicans, not as Democrats—but as Americans.

As we move into the decade of the '70s we have the greatest opportunity for progress at home of any people in world history.

Our gross national product will increase by $500 billion in the next ten years. This increase alone is greater than the entire growth of the American economy from 1790 to 1950.

The critical question is not whether we will grow, but how we will use that growth.

The decade of the '60s was also a period of great growth economically. But in that same ten-year period we witnessed the greatest growth of crime, the greatest increase in inflation, the greatest social unrest in America in a hundred years. Never has a nation seemed to have had more and enjoyed it less.

At heart the issue is the effectiveness of government.

Ours had become, as it continues to be—and should remain—a society of large expectations. Government helped to generate these expectations. It undertook to meet them. Yet, increasingly, it proved unable to do so.

As a people we had too many visions—and too little vision.

Now, as we enter the '70s, we should enter a great age of reform of the institutions of American government.

Our purpose in this period should not be simply better management of the programs of the past. The time has come for a new quest —a quest not for a greater quantity of what we have—but for a new quality of life in America.

A major part of the substance for an unprecedented advance in this nation's approach to its problems and opportunities is contained in more than two score legislative proposals which I sent to the Congress last year and which still await enactment.

I will offer at least a dozen more major programs in the course of this session.

At this point I do not intend to go through a detailed listing of what I have proposed or will propose, but I would like to mention three areas in which urgent priorities demand that we move and move now.

First, we cannot delay longer in accomplishing a total reform of our welfare system. When a system penalizes work, breaks up homes, and robs recipients of dignity, there is no alternative to abolishing that system and adopting in its place the program of income support, job training, and work incentives which I recommended to the Congress last year.

Second, the time has come to assess and reform all of our institutions of government at the Federal, state, and local level. It is time for a New Federalism, in which, after a hundred and ninety years of power flowing from the people and local and state governments to Washington, D.C., it will begin to flow from Washington back to the states and to the people of the United States.

Third, we must adopt reforms which will expand the range of opportunities for all Americans. We can fulfill the American Dream only when each person has a fair chance to fulfill his own dreams. This means equal voting rights, equal employment opportunity, and new opportunities for expanded ownership. Because in order to be secure in their human rights, people need access to property rights.

I could give similar examples of the need for reform in our programs for health, education, housing, transportation, as well as in other critical areas which directly affect the well-being of millions of Americans.

The people of the United States should wait no longer for these reforms that would so deeply enhance the quality of their life.

When I speak of actions which would be beneficial to the American people, I can think of none more important than for the Congress to join this Administration in the battle to stop the rise in the cost of living.

Now I realize it is tempting to blame someone else for inflation.

Some blame business for raising prices.

Some blame unions for asking for more wages.

But a review of the stark fiscal facts of the 1960s clearly demonstrates where the primary blame for rising prices must be placed.

In the decade of the '60s the Federal government spent $57 billion more than it took in in taxes.

In that same decade the American people paid the bill for that deficit in price increases which raised the cost of living for the average American family of four by $200 per month.

Now millions of Americans are forced to go into debt today because the Federal government decided to go into debt yesterday. We must balance our Federal budget so that American families will have a better chance to balance their family budgets.

Only with the cooperation of the Congress can we meet this highest priority objective of responsible government.

We are on the right track.

We had a balanced budget in 1969.

This Administration cut more than $7 billion out of spending plans in order to produce a surplus in 1970.

In spite of the fact that Congress reduced revenues by $3 billion, I can recommend a balanced budget for 1971.

But I can assure you that not only to present, but to stay within a balanced budget requires some very hard decisions. It means rejecting spending programs which would benefit some of the people when their net effect would result in price increases for all the people.

It is time to quit putting good money into bad programs. Otherwise, we will end up with bad money and bad programs.

I recognize the political popularity of spending programs, particularly in an election year. But unless we stop the rise in prices, the cost of living for millions of American families will become unbearable and government's ability to plan programs for progress for the future will become impossible.

In referring to budget cuts, there is one area where I have ordered an increase rather than a cut—that is the request of those agencies with the responsibility for law enforcement.

We have heard a great deal of overblown rhetoric during the '60s in which the word "war" has perhaps too often been used—the war on poverty, the war on misery, the war on disease, the war on hunger. But if there is one area where the word "war" is appropriate it is in the fight against crime. We must declare and win the war against the criminal elements which increasingly threaten our cities, our homes, and our lives.

We have a tragic example of this problem in the nation's Capital, for whose safety the Congress and the Executive have the primary responsibility. I doubt if there are many members of this Congress who live more than a few blocks from here who would dare leave their cars in the Capitol Garage and walk home alone tonight.

This year this Administration sent to the Congress thirteen separate pieces of legislation dealing with organized crime, pornography, street crime, narcotics, and crime in the District of Columbia.

None of these bills has reached my desk for signature.

I am confident that the Congress will act now to adopt the legislation I placed before you last year. We in the Executive have done everything we can under existing law, but new and stronger weapons are needed in that fight.

While it is true that state and local law enforcement agencies are the cutting edge in the effort to eliminate street crime, burglaries, and murder, my proposals to you have embodied my belief that the Federal government should play a greater role in working in partnership with these agencies.

That is why 1971 Federal spending for aiding local law enforcement will double that budgeted for 1970.

The primary responsibility for crimes that affect individuals is with local and state rather than with Federal government. But in the field of organized crime, narcotics, and pornography, the Federal government has a special responsibility it should fulfill. And we should make Washington, D.C., where we have the primary responsibility, an example to the nation and the world of respect for law rather than lawlessness.

I now turn to a subject which, next to our desire for peace, may well become the major concern of the American people in the decade of the '70s.

In the next ten years we shall increase our wealth by 50 percent. The profound question is, Does this mean we will be 50-percent richer in a real sense, 50-percent better off, 50-percent happier?

Or does it mean that in the year 1980 the President standing in this place will look back on a decade in which 70 percent of our people lived in metropolitan areas choked by traffic, suffocated by smog, poisoned by water, deafened by noise, and terrorized by crime?

These are not the great questions that concern world leaders at Summit Conferences. But people do not live at the summit. They live in the foothills of everyday experience. It is time for us all to concern ourselves with the way real people live in real life.

The great question of the '70s is, Shall we surrender to our surroundings, or shall we make our peace with nature and begin to make reparations for the damage we have done to our air, to our land, and to our water?

Restoring nature to its natural state is a cause beyond party and beyond factions. It has become a common cause of all the people of this country. It is a cause of particular concern to young Americans —because they more than we will reap the grim consequences of our failure to act on programs which are needed now if we are to prevent disaster later.

Clean air, clean water, open spaces—these should once again be the birthright of every American. If we act now—they can be.

We still think of air as free. But clean air is not free, and neither is clean water. The price tag on pollution control is high. Through our years of past carelessness we incurred a debt to nature, and now that debt is being called.

The program I shall propose to Congress will be the most comprehensive and costly program in this field in America's history.

It is not a program for just a year. A year's plan in this field is no plan at all. This is a time to look ahead not a year, but five or ten years—whatever time is required to do the job.

I shall propose to this Congress a $10-billion nationwide clean waters program to put modern municipal waste treatment plants in every place in America where they are needed to make our waters clean again, and to do it now.

We have the industrial capacity, if we begin now, to build them all within five years. This program will get them built within five years.

As our cities and suburbs relentlessly expand, those priceless open spaces needed for recreation areas accessible to their people are swallowed up—often forever. Unless we preserve these spaces while they are still available, we will have none to preserve. Therefore, I shall propose new financing methods for purchasing open space and parklands, now, before they are lost to us.

The automobile is our worst polluter of the air. Adequate control requires further advances in engine design and fuel composition. We shall intensify our research, set increasingly strict standards, and strengthen enforcement procedures—and we shall do it now.

We no longer can afford to consider air and water common property, free to be abused by anyone without regard to the consequences. Instead, we should begin now to treat them as scarce resources, which we are no more free to contaminate than we are free to throw garbage in our neighbor's yard.

This requires comprehensive new regulations. It also requires that, to the extent possible, the price of goods should be made to include the costs of producing and disposing of them without damage to the environment.

Now I realize that the argument is often made that there is a fundamental contradiction between economic growth and the quality of life, so that to have one we must forsake the other.

The answer is not to abandon growth, but to redirect it. For example, we should turn toward the ending of congestion and eliminating smog the same reservoir of inventive genius that created them in the first place.

Continued vigorous economic growth provides us with the means to enrich life itself and to enhance our planet as a place hospitable to man.

Each individual must enlist in this fight if it is to be won.

It has been said that no matter how many national parks and historical monuments we buy and develop, the truly significant environment for each of us is that in which we spend 80 percent of our time —in our homes, in our places of work, and the streets over which we pass.

Street litter, rundown parking strips and yards, dilapidated fences, broken windows, smoking automobiles, dingy working places, all should be the object of our fresh view.

We have been too tolerant of our surroundings and too willing to leave it to others to clean up our environment. It is time for those who make massive demands on society to make some minimal demands on themselves. Each of us must resolve that each day he will leave his home, his property, the public places of his city or town a little cleaner, a little better, a little more pleasant for himself and those around him.

With the help of people we can do anything. Without their help we can do nothing. In this spirit, together, we can reclaim our land for ours and generations to come.

Between now and the year 2000 over 100 million children will be born in the United States. Where they grow up—and how—will, more than any one thing, measure the quality of American life in these years ahead.

This should be a warning to us.

For the past thirty years our population has also been growing and shifting. The result is exemplified in the vast areas of rural America emptying out of people and of promise—a third of our counties lost population in the 1960s.

The violent and decayed central cities of our great metropolitan complexes are the most conspicuous area of failure in American life today.

I propose that before these problems become insoluble, the nation develop a national growth policy.

In the future decisions as to where to build highways, locate airports, acquire land, or sell land should be made with a clear objective of aiding a balanced growth.

In particular, the Federal government must be in a position to assist in the building of new cities and rebuilding of old ones.

At the same time, we will carry our concern with the quality of life in America to the farm as well as the suburb, to the village as well as the city. What rural America needs most is a new kind of assistance. It needs to be dealt with, not as a separate nation, but as part of an overall growth policy for America. We must create a new rural environment that will not only stem the migration to urban centers, but reverse it. If we seize our growth as a challenge, we can make the 1970s an historic period when by conscious choice we transformed our land into what we want it to become.

America, which has pioneered in the new abundance and in the new technology, is called upon today to pioneer in meeting the concerns which have followed in their wake—in turning the wonders of science to the service of man.

In the majesty of this great chamber we hear the echoes of America's history, of debates that rocked the Union and those that repaired it, of the summons to war and the search for peace, of the uniting of the people and the building of a nation.

Those echoes of history remind us of our roots and strengths.

They remind us also of that special genius of American democracy, which at one critical turning-point after another has led us to spot the new road to the future and given us the wisdom and courage to take it.

As I look down that new road which I have tried to map out today, I see a new America as we celebrate our two-hundredth birthday six years from now.

I see an America in which we have abolished hunger, provided the means for every family in the nation to obtain a minimum income, made enormous progress in providing better housing, faster transportation, improved health, and superior education.

I see an America in which we have checked inflation and waged a winning war against crime.

I see an America in which we have made great strides in stopping the pollution of our air, cleaning up our water, opening up new parks, and continuing to explore in space.

Most important, I see an America at peace with all the nations of the world.

This is not an impossible dream. These goals are all within our reach.

In times past our forefathers had the vision but not the means to achieve such goals.

Let it not be recorded that we were the first American generation that had the means but not the vision to make this dream come true.

But let us, above all, recognize a fundamental truth. We can be the best-clothed, best-fed, best-housed people in the world, enjoying clear air, clean water, and beautiful parks, but we could still be the unhappiest people in the world without an indefinable spirit—the lift of a driving dream which has made America from its beginning the hope of the world.

Two hundred years ago this was a new nation of 3 million people, weak militarily, poor economically. But America meant something to the world then which could not be measured in dollars, something far more important than military might.

Listen to President Thomas Jefferson in 1802: "We act not for ourselves alone, but for the whole human race."

We had a spiritual quality which caught the imagination of millions of people in the world.

Today, when we are the richest and strongest nation in the world, let it not be recorded that we lack the moral and spiritual idealism which made us the hope of the world at the time of our birth.

The demands on us in 1976 are even greater than in 1776.

It is no longer enough to live and let live. Now we must live and help live.

We need a fresh climate in America, one in which a person can breathe freely and breathe in freedom.

Our recognition of the truth that wealth and happiness are not the same thing requires us to measure success or failure by new criteria.

Even more than the programs I have described today, what this nation needs is an example from its elected leaders in providing spiritual and moral leadership.

Above all, let us inspire young Americans with a sense of excitement, a sense of destiny, a sense of involvement in meeting the challenges we face in this great period of our history. Only then are they going to have any sense of satisfaction in their lives.

The greatest privilege an individual can have is to serve in a cause bigger than himself. We have such a cause.

How we seize the opportunities I have described today will determine not only our future, but the future of peace and freedom in this world in the last third of this century.

May God give us the wisdom, the strength, and above all the idealism to be worthy of that challenge, so that America can fulfill its destiny of being the world's best hope for liberty, for opportunity, for progress and peace for all peoples.

18

Farewell
to
an
Old
Friend

FAREWELL TO AN OLD FRIEND

The President's Eulogy of Dwight D. Eisenhower
in the Rotunda of the Capitol, Washington, D.C.
MARCH 30, 1969

Mrs. Eisenhower, Your Excellencies, friends of Dwight David Eisenhower in America and throughout the world:

We gather today in mourning, but also in gratitude.

We mourn Dwight Eisenhower's death, but we are grateful for his life.

We gather, also conscious of the fact that in paying tribute to Dwight Eisenhower, we celebrate greatness. When we think of his place in history, we think, inevitably, of the other giants of those days of World War II and we think of the qualities of greatness and what his were that made him unique among all.

Once, perhaps without intending to do so, he himself put his finger on it. It was 1945, shortly after V-E Day, at a ceremony in London's historic Guild Hall. The triumphant Supreme Commander of the Allied Forces in Europe was officially given the Freedom of the City of London.

In an eloquent address that day Dwight Eisenhower said, "I come from the heart of America."

Perhaps no one sentence could better sum up what Dwight Eisenhower meant to a whole generation of Americans. He did come from the heart of America, not only from its geographical heart, but from its spiritual heart.

He exemplified what millions of parents hoped that their sons would be—strong, courageous, honest, and compassionate.

And with his own great qualities of heart, he personified the best in America.

It is, I think, a special tribute to Dwight Eisenhower that despite all of his honors, despite all of his great deeds and his triumphs, we find ourselves today thinking, first, not of his deeds but of his character. It was the character of the man, not what he did but what he was, that so captured the trust and faith and affection of his own people and of the people of the world.

Dwight Eisenhower touched something fundamental in America which only a man of immense force of mind and spirit could have brought so vibrantly alive. He was a product of America's soil and of its ideals, driven by a compulsion to do right and to do well; a man of deep faith who believed in God and trusted in His will; a man who truly loved his country and for whom words like "freedom" and "democracy" were not clichés, but they were living truths.

I know Mrs. Eisenhower would permit me to share with you the last words he spoke to her on the day he died. He said, "I have always loved my wife. I have always loved my children. I have always loved my grandchildren. And I have always loved my country." That was Dwight Eisenhower.

He was a man who gave enormously of himself. His way of relaxing from the intense pressures of office or command was to do something else intensely, whether as a fierce competitor on the golf course or executing one of those hauntingly beautiful paintings that he did with such meticulous care. But even more than this, he gave enormously of himself to people. People loved Dwight Eisenhower. But the other side of this coin was that he loved people.

He had the great leader's capacity to bring out the best in people. He had the great humanist's capacity to inspire people, to cheer them, to give them lift.

I remember, for example, just a few months ago when I asked all of the members of the Cabinet to go out and call on him. Each of them returned with wonder and admiration and said, "You know, I went out there to cheer him up and instead I found he cheered me up."

His great love of people was rooted in his faith. He had a deep faith in the goodness of God and in the essential goodness of man as a creature of God.

This feeling toward people had another side. In the political world strong passions are the norm and all too often these turn toward personal vindictiveness. People often disagreed with Dwight Eisenhower, but almost nobody ever hated him.

And this, I think, was because he himself was a man who did not know how to hate.

Oh, he could be aroused by a cause, but he could not hate a person. He could disagree strongly, even passionately, but never personally.

When people disagreed with him, he never thought of them as enemies. He simply thought, "Well, they don't agree with me."

I remember time after time, when critics of one sort or another were misrepresenting him or reviling him, he would sit back in his chair and with that wonderful half-smile and half-frown, he would say, "I am puzzled by those fellows." And he was genuinely puzzled by frenzy and by hate. Because he was incapable of it himself, he could never quite understand it in others.

The last time I saw him that was what he talked about. He was puzzled by the hatreds he had seen in our times. And he said the thing the world needs most today is understanding, an ability to see the other person's point of view and not to hate him because he disagrees.

That was Dwight Eisenhower.

And yet, of course, he was more than all that. He had a side more evident to those of us who worked with him than to the rest of the world. He was a strong man. He was shrewd. He was decisive.

Time and again I have seen him make decisions that probably made the difference between war and peace for America and the world.

That was always when he was at his best. No matter how heated the arguments were, he was always then the coolest man in the room.

Dwight Eisenhower was that rarest of men—an authentic hero.

Wars bring the names of many men into the headlines and of those some few become national or even international heroes. But as the years then pass, their fame goes down.

But not so with Dwight Eisenhower. As the years passed, his stature grew: commander of the mightiest expeditionary force ever assembled; receiver of the surrender of the German Armies in World War II; President of Columbia University; Supreme Commander of NATO; thirty-fourth President of the United States. The honors, the offices were there in abundance. Every trust that the American people had it in their power to bestow he was given.

And yet he always retained a saving humility. His was the humility not of fear but of confidence. He walked with the great of the world, and he knew that the great are human.

His was the humility of man before God and before the truth. His was the humility of a man too proud to be arrogant.

The pursuit of peace was uppermost in his mind when he ran for the Presidency. And it was uppermost in his conduct of that office. And it is a tribute to his skill and determination that not since the 1930s has the nation enjoyed so long a period of peace, both at home and abroad, as the one that began in 1953 and continued through his Presidency.

As commander of the mightiest allied force ever assembled he was the right man at the right place at the right time.

And as President once again, he was the right man at the right place at the right time.

He restored calm to a divided nation. He gave Americans a new measure of self-respect. He invested his office with dignity and respect and trust. He made Americans proud of their President, proud of their country, proud of themselves.

And if we in America were proud of Dwight Eisenhower, it was partly because he made us proud of America.

He came from the heart of America. And he gave expression to the heart of America and he touched the hearts of the world.

Many leaders are known and respected outside their own countries. Very few are loved outside their own countries. Dwight Eisenhower was one of those few. He was probably loved by more people in more parts of the world than any President America has ever had.

He captured the deepest feelings of free men everywhere. The principles he believed in, the ideals he stood for, these were bigger than his own country.

Perhaps he himself put it best again in that Guild Hall speech in 1945. He said then, "Kinship among nations is not determined in such measurements as proximity, size, and age. Rather, we should turn to those inner things—call them what you will—I mean those intangibles that are the real treasures free men possess.

"To preserve his freedom of worship, his equality before law, his liberty to speak and act as he sees fit, subject only to provisions that he trespass not upon similar rights of others—a Londoner will fight. So will a citizen of Abilene.

"When we consider these things, then the Valley of the Thames draws closer to the farms of Kansas and the plains of Texas."

Some men are considered great because they lead great armies or they lead powerful nations. For eight years now Dwight Eisenhower has neither commanded an army nor led a nation. And yet he remained through his final days the world's most admired and respected man— truly the first citizen of the world.

As we marvel at this, it leads us once again to ponder the mysteries of greatness. Dwight Eisenhower's greatness derived not from his office, but from his character, from a unique moral force that transcended national boundaries, even as his own deep concern for humanity transcended national boundaries.

His life reminds us that there is a moral force in this world more powerful than the might of arms or the wealth of nations. This man who led the most powerful armies that the world has ever seen, this man who led the most powerful nation in the world, this essentially good and gentle and kind man—that moral force was his greatness.

For a quarter of a century to the very end of his life Dwight Eisenhower exercised a moral authority without parallel in America and in the world. And America and the world are better because of it.

And so today we render our final salute. It is a fond salute to a man we loved and cherished. It is a grateful salute to a man whose whole extraordinary life was consecrated to service. It is a profoundly respectful salute to a man larger than life who by any standard was one of the giants of our time.

Each of us here will have a special memory of Dwight Eisenhower.

I can see him now standing erect, straight, proud, and tall sixteen years ago as he took the oath of office as the thirty-fourth President of the United States of America.

We salute Dwight David Eisenhower standing there in our memories, first in war, first in peace, and, wherever freedom is cherished, first in the hearts of his fellow men.

Appendix

United States

Foreign

Policy

for the

1970s

A NEW STRATEGY FOR PEACE
A Report to the Congress

INTRODUCTION
BY RICHARD WILSON

In simple and direct language President Nixon said in the Presidential campaign of 1968 that he intended to change American foreign policy.

"I say that it's time that we look at the balance in the world," he said. "When there are 200 million Americans and when there are 2 billion people that live in the free world, I think we need a foreign policy where other nations in the free world bear their fair share of the defense of freedom, and that's what I will work for.

". . . one of the major objectives of our new foreign policy," Candidate Nixon continued, "will be to develop in consultation with our friends and our allies new policies so that in the future if something comes up like Vietnam, the United States will not do as we did in Korea and in Vietnam—shoulder the burden not only of furnishing the arms and the money but most of the men."

Soon after assuming office in 1969, Nixon ordered a thorough foreign policy review in many agencies of the government, enlisting hundreds of policy-makers in the search for new directions and definitions under the general guidance of Dr. Henry A. Kissinger, Adviser on National Security.

This intent alone was unprecedented over such a wide range of commitments as the United States had assumed in the post-World War II period. In world relationships evasion and ambiguity are familiar even in treaty obligations. Definitions are frequently avoided or merely implied and usually limited. The absolute commitment is foreign to the art of diplomacy; it is usually contingent and not automatic.

Ambiguity notwithstanding, the whole structure of postwar treaty obligations created a presumption that America bore the major responsibility—in some cases the sole responsibility— for keeping the free world at peace and secure. How to preserve that structure and the confidence it gave to the free world while reducing America's share of the commitment became of crucial importance in Nixon's search for new definitions.

The President's forty-three-thousand-word statement finally emerged, after a year of study and consideration, in the form of a special message to Congress on foreign affairs, the

395

first of its kind. Dr. Kissinger, it was understood, was the chief draftsman.

Nixon appeared before newsmen gathered in the East Room of the White House at 5 P.M., Monday, February 16, 1970, for a background briefing on the contents of the message in advance of its submission to Congress on February 18.

Nixon described this document as "a watershed in American foreign policy. . . . This report . . . shows a very significant shift from those policies of the past to the new policies dealing with the world as it is today," he said.

The essence of the change was contained in a single sentence of the exhaustive report: "We are not involved in the world because we have commitments; we have commitments because we are involved. Our interests must shape our commitments, rather than the other way around."

For the future: "We will view new commitments in the light of a careful assessment of our own national interests and those of other countries, of the specific threats to those interests and of our capacity to counter those threats at an acceptable risk and cost."

In his briefing of newsmen on the significance of the foregoing passages the President cautioned that the report does not indicate any abandonment on the part of the United States of its alliances around the world. "On the contrary, peace cannot be built by abandoning allies."

The message does mean, the President said, "that we have re-examined our commitments around the world to see that they are consistent with our interests. We have re-examined our defense policy and we are trying to present here a policy not just for a year, but a policy for a decade, and even beyond that."

The message, he observed, represents not only the studies made by the National Security Council, the Defense and State Departments, but his own experience in twenty-two years at high levels in the government and in extensive travels over the world.

Nixon pointedly referred to the fact that he and Defense Secretary Melvin R. Laird, who was at his side during his brief statement, were identified with the policies of the Eisenhower Administration from 1953 to early 1961. Before this, in Congress, the President said, both he and Laird supported the institutions for peace and security that were created in the period immediately after World War II and fashioned for the world as it then existed.

His new definitions were for the world that now exists, with the renaissance of Western Europe, the emergence of Japan as the world's third industrial power, and the hope that new avenues of cooperation may ultimately be opened with both Russia and China. After his brief statement the President called on Dr. Kissinger to continue the briefing of newsmen and left the East Room.

This document was too long, too complex, and too novel to be immediately absorbed by its chief audience in Congress, the public, foreign governments, and students of international affairs. Not the least of the audience Nixon addressed was the American foreign affairs establishment, the immense bureaucracy, largely undisciplined, that carries on the affairs of the United States throughout the world.

This establishment is not confined to the State Department and the Foreign Service, but ranges loosely coordinated through a score of different agencies from the Central Intelligence Agency to the Peace Corps. An uncertain diplomat in a far-off post might not find the answer to his immediate problems in the new declaration of policy but he could at least sense in what direction he was supposed to go. The message was intended as a general guide or manual of the Nixon foreign policy.

A President can define a policy, but implementing it is more difficult if only because the policy must be executed by an entrenched bureaucracy that came into being largely under his predecessors. Fixed views and vested interests in Congress may also circumscribe the execution of policy.

In general, it was noted at the time the foreign affairs message was submitted that it appeared to conform to the public and Congressional mood. The foreign reaction in the free world was less fathomable but seemed to accept as inevitable a drawing-back by the United States from the extent if not the spirit of its previous commitments. The concern that might have been felt in foreign capitals that the United States was slowly withdrawing into some new form of isolationism was not pronounced. At the worst, this was merely a speculative matter in diplomatic conversation and not apprehension of an immediate event.

Certain other limiting factors entered into reaction to the President's message. These had to do with the actual determination or capability of American allies in assuming their share of the responsibilities that the United States might wish to lay down. What, it was asked, would the United States do if this proved to be the case in some future emergency in which it considered its vital interests to be affected?

Many other questions were propounded. Was the Nixon Doctrine realistically compatible with such action as the President would later take in Cambodia? Would the policy stand the test of a hard freeze in Soviet-American relations? Could it be made applicable in the circumstances existing in the Middle East?

Whatever the immediate consistencies or contradictions, the President's emphasis was on the farther future and the general direction he felt American policy must take in a changed world.

The statement confirmed and expanded upon the President's extemporaneous press conference on the island of Guam the previous summer and his State of the Union message in January, 1970. It replaced military and diplomatic posture statements made by Secretaries of Defense and State in other Administrations. The President hinted that he might make such statements annually.

CONTENTS

TO THE CONGRESS OF THE UNITED STATES

In my State of the Union Message to the Congress and on other occasions I report to the Congress and the American people on specific aspects of foreign affairs. The Secretary of State also frequently makes reports to the appropriate committees of the Congress on foreign affairs, and the Secretary of Defense must deal with such matters as they relate to military programs.

Up to now, however, there has been no comprehensive report on foreign affairs submitted to the Congress on behalf of the Administration as a whole. I am, therefore, transmitting to the Congress this report on my Administration's stewardship of foreign relations. I hope the report will lead to a better understanding by the Congress and the American people of the spirit in which this Administration has sought to guide our foreign affairs, of what has been accomplished so far, and of our new approach to the challenges and opportunities of the world of the 1970s.

Richard Nixon

The White House

February 18, 1970

INTRODUCTION

A nation needs many qualities, but it needs faith and confidence above all. Skeptics do not build societies; the idealists are the builders. Only societies that believe in themselves can rise to their challenges. Let us not, then, pose a false choice between meeting our responsibilities abroad and meeting the needs of our people at home. We shall meet both or we shall meet neither.

—*The President's Remarks at the Air Force Academy Commencment, June 4, 1969.*

When I took office, the most immediate problem facing our nation was the war in Vietnam. No question has more occupied our thoughts and energies during this past year.

Yet the fundamental task confronting us was more profound. We could see that the whole pattern of international politics was changing. Our challenge was to understand that change, to define America's goals for the next period, and to set in motion policies to achieve them. For all Americans must understand that because of its strength, its history, and its concern for human dignity, this nation occupies a special place in the world. Peace and progress are impossible without a major American role.

This first annual report on U.S. foreign policy is more than a record of one year. It is this Administration's statement of a new approach to foreign policy, to match a new era of international relations.

A New Era

The postwar period in international relations has ended.

Then we were the only great power whose society and economy had escaped World War II's massive destruction. Today the ravages of that war have been overcome. Western Europe and Japan have recovered their economic strength, their political vitality, and their national self-confidence. Once the recipients of American aid, they have now begun to share their growing resources with the developing world. Once almost totally dependent on American military power, our European allies now play a greater role in our common policies, commensurate with their growing strength.

Then new nations were being born, often in turmoil and uncertainty. Today these nations have a new spirit and a growing strength of independence. Once, many feared that they would become simply a battleground of Cold War rivalry and fertile ground for communist penetration. But this fear misjudged their pride in their national identities and their determination to preserve their newly won sovereignty.

Then we were confronted by a monolithic communist world. Today the nature of that world has changed—the power of individual communist nations has grown, but international communist unity has been shattered. Once a unified bloc, its solidarity has been broken by the powerful forces of nationalism. The Soviet Union and Communist China, once bound by an alliance of friendship, had become bitter adversaries by the mid-1960s. The only times the Soviet Union has used the Red Army since World War II have been against its own allies—in East Germany in 1953, in Hungary in 1956, and in

Czechoslovakia in 1968. The Marxist dream of international communist unity has disintegrated.

Then the United States had a monopoly or overwhelming superiority of nuclear weapons. Today a revolution in the technology of war has altered the nature of the military balance of power. New types of weapons present new dangers. Communist China has acquired thermonuclear weapons. Both the Soviet Union and the United States have acquired the ability to inflict unacceptable damage on the other, no matter which strikes first. There can be no gain and certainly no victory for the power that provokes a thermonuclear exchange. Thus, both sides have recognized a vital mutual interest in halting the dangerous momentum of the nuclear arms race.

Then the slogans formed in the past century were the ideological accessories of the intellectual debate. Today the "isms" have lost their vitality—indeed the restlessness of youth on both sides of the dividing line testifies to the need for a new idealism and deeper purposes.

This is the challenge and the opportunity before America as it enters the 1970s.

The Framework for a Durable Peace

In the first postwar decades American energies were absorbed in coping with a cycle of recurrent crises, whose fundamental origins lay in the destruction of World War II and the tensions attending the emergence of scores of new nations. Our opportunity today—and challenge—is to get at the causes of crises, to take a longer view, and to help build the international relationships that will provide the framework of a durable peace.

I have often reflected on the meaning of "peace," and have reached one certain conclusion: Peace must be far more than the absence of war. Peace must provide a durable structure of international relationships which inhibits or removes the causes of war. Building a lasting peace requires a foreign policy guided by three basic principles:

—Peace requires *partnership*. Its obligations, like its benefits, must be shared. This concept of partnership guides our relations with all friendly nations.

—Peace requires *strength*. So long as there are those who would threaten our vital interests and those of our allies with military force, we must be strong. American weakness could tempt would-be aggressors to make dangerous miscalculations. At the same time, our own strength is important only in relation to the strength of others. We—like others—must place high priority on enhancing our security through cooperative arms control.

—Peace requires a *willingness to negotiate*. All nations—and we are no exception—have important national interests to protect. But the most fundamental interest of all nations lies in building the structure of peace. In partnership with our allies, secure in our own strength, we will seek those areas in which we can agree among ourselves and with others to accommodate conflicts and overcome rivalries. We are working toward the day when *all* nations will have a stake in peace, and will therefore be partners in its maintenance.

Within such a structure international disputes can be settled and clashes contained. The insecurity of nations, out of which so much conflict arises, will be eased, and the habits of moderation and compromise will be nurtured. Most important, a durable peace will give full opportunity to the powerful forces driving toward economic change and social justice.

This vision of a peace built on partnership, strength, and willingness to negotiate is the unifying theme of this report. In the sections that follow, the first steps we have taken during this past year—the policies we have devised and the programs we have initiated to realize this vision—are placed in the context of these three principles.

1. Peace Through Partnership—The Nixon Doctrine

As I said in my address of November 3, "We Americans are a do-it-yourself people—an impatient people. Instead of teaching someone else to do a job, we like to do it ourselves. This trait has been carried over into our foreign policy."

The postwar era of American foreign policy began in this vein in 1947 with the proclamation of the Truman Doctrine and the Marshall Plan, offering American economic and military assistance to countries threatened by aggression. Our policy held that democracy and prosperity, buttressed by American military strength and organized in a worldwide network of American-led alliances, would ensure stability and peace. In the formative years of the postwar period this great effort of international political and economic reconstruction was a triumph of American leadership and imagination, especially in Europe.

For two decades after the end of the Second World War, our foreign policy was guided by such a vision and inspired by its success. The vision was based on the fact that the United States was the richest and most stable country, without whose initiative and resources little security or progress was possible.

This impulse carried us through into the 1960s. The United States conceived programs and ran them. We devised strategies, and proposed them to our allies. We discerned dangers, and acted directly to combat them.

The world has dramatically changed since the days of the Marshall Plan. We deal now with a world of stronger allies, a community of independent developing nations, and a communist world still hostile but now divided.

Others now have the ability and responsibility to deal with local disputes which once might have required our intervention. Our contribution and success will depend not on the frequency of our involvement in the affairs of others, but on the stamina of our policies. This is the approach which will best encourage other nations to do their part, and will most genuinely enlist the support of the American people.

This is the message of the doctrine I announced at Guam—the "Nixon Doctrine." Its central thesis is that the United States will participate in the defense and development of allies and friends, but that America cannot—and will not—conceive all the plans, design all the programs, execute all the decisions, and undertake all the defense of the free nations of the world. We will help where it makes a real difference and is considered in our interest.

America cannot live in isolation if it expects to live in peace. We have no intention of withdrawing from the world. The only issue before us is how we can be most effective in meeting our responsibilities, protecting our interests, and thereby building peace.

A more responsible participation by our foreign friends in their own defense and progress means a more effective common effort toward the goals we all seek. Peace in the world will continue to require us to maintain our commitments—and we will. As I said at the United Nations, "It is not my belief that the way to peace is by giving up our friends or letting down our allies." But a more balanced and realistic American role in the world is essential if American commitments are to be sustained over the long pull. In my State of the Union Address I affirmed that "to insist that other nations play a role is not a retreat from responsibility; it is a sharing of responsibility." This is not a way for America to withdraw from its indispensable role in the world. It is a way—the only way—we can carry out our responsibilities.

It is misleading, moreover, to pose the fundamental question so largely in terms of commitments. Our objective, in the first instance, is to support our *interests* over the long run with a sound foreign policy. The more that policy is based on a realistic assessment of our and others' interests, the more effective our role in the world can be. We are not involved in the world because we have commitments; we have commitments because we are involved. Our interests must shape our commitments, rather than the other way around.

We will view new commitments in the light of a careful assessment of our own national interests and those of other countries, of the specific threats to those interests, and of our capacity to counter those threats at an acceptable risk and cost.

We have been guided by these concepts during the past year in our dealings with free nations throughout the world.

—In Europe our policies embody precisely the three principles of a durable peace: partnership, continued strength to defend our common interests when challenged, and willingness to negotiate differences with adversaries.

—Here in the Western Hemisphere we seek to strengthen our special relationship with our sister republics through a new program of action for progress in which all voices are heard and none predominates.

—In Asia, where the Nixon Doctrine was enunciated, partnership will have special meaning for our policies—as evidenced by our strengthened ties with Japan. Our cooperation with Asian nations will be enhanced as they cooperate with one another and develop regional institutions.

—In Vietnam we seek a just settlement which all parties to the conflict, and all Americans, can support. We are working closely with the South Vietnamese to strengthen their ability to defend themselves. As South Vietnam grows stronger, the other side will, we hope, soon realize that it becomes ever more in their interest to negotiate a just peace.

—In the Middle East we shall continue to work with others to establish a possible framework within which the parties to the Arab-Israeli conflict can negotiate the complicated and difficult questions at issue. Others must join us in recognizing that a settlement will require sacrifices and restraints by all concerned.

—Africa, with its historic ties to so many of our own citizens, must always retain a significant place in our partnership with the new nations. Africans will play the major role in fulfilling their just aspirations—an end to racialism, the building of new nations, freedom from outside interference, and cooperative economic development. But we will add our efforts to theirs to help realize Africa's great potential.

—In an ever more interdependent world economy American foreign policy will emphasize the freer flow of capital and goods between nations. We are proud to have participated in the successful cooperative effort which created Special Drawing Rights, a form of international money which will help ensure the stability of the monetary structure on which the continued expansion of trade depends.

—The great effort of economic development must engage the cooperation of all nations. We are carefully studying the specific goals of our economic assistance programs and how most effectively to reach them.

—Unprecedented scientific and technological advances as well as explosions in population, communications, and knowledge require new forms of international cooperation. The United Nations, the symbol of international partnership, will receive our continued strong support as it marks its twenty-fifth anniversary.

2. *America's Strength*

The second element of a durable peace must be America's strength. Peace, we have learned, cannot be gained by good will alone.

In determining the strength of our defenses, we must make precise and crucial judgments. We should spend no more than is necessary. But there is an irreducible minimum of essential military security: for if we are less strong than necessary, and if the worst happens, there will be no domestic society to look after. The magnitude of such a catastrophe, and the reality of the opposing military power that could threaten it, present a risk which requires of any President the most searching and careful attention to the state of our defenses.

The changes in the world since 1945 have altered the context and requirements of our defense policy. In this area, perhaps more than in any other, the need to re-examine our approaches is urgent and constant.

The last twenty-five years have seen a revolution in the nature of military power. In fact, there has been a series of transformations—from the atomic to the thermonuclear weapon, from the strategic bomber to the intercontinental ballistic missile, from the surface missile to the hardened silo and the missile-carrying submarine, from the single to the multiple warhead, and from air defense to missile defense. We are now entering an era in which the sophistication and destructiveness of weapons present more formidable and complex issues affecting our strategic posture.

The last twenty-five years have also seen an important change in the relative balance of strategic power. From 1945 to 1949 we were the only nation in the world possessing an arsenal of atomic weapons. From 1950 to 1966 we possessed an overwhelming superiority in strategic weapons. From 1967 to 1969 we retained a significant superiority. Today the Soviet Union possesses a powerful and sophisticated strategic force approaching our own. We must consider, too, that Communist China will deploy its own intercontinental missiles during the coming decade, introducing new and complicating factors for our strategic planning and diplomacy.

In the light of these fateful changes, the Administration undertook a comprehensive and far-reaching reconsideration of the premises and procedures for designing our forces. We sought—and I believe we have achieved—a rational and coherent formulation of our defense strategy and requirements for the 1970s.

The importance of comprehensive planning of policy and objective scrutiny of programs is clear:

—Because of the lead time in building new strategic systems, the decisions we make today substantially determine our military posture—and thus our security—five years from now. This places a premium on foresight and planning.

—Because the allocation of national resources between defense programs and other national programs is itself an issue of policy, it must be considered on a systematic basis at the early stages of the national security planning process.

—Because we are a leader of the Atlantic Alliance, our doctrine and forces are crucial to the policy and planning of NATO. The mutual confidence that holds the allies together depends on understanding, agreement, and coordination among the fifteen sovereign nations of the Treaty.

—Because our security depends not only on our own strategic strength, but also on cooperative efforts to provide greater security for everyone through arms control, planning weapons systems and planning for arms control negotiations must be closely integrated.

For these reasons, this Administration has established procedures for the intensive scrutiny of defense issues in the light of overall national priorities. We have re-examined our strategic forces; we have reassessed our general purpose forces; and we have engaged in the most painstaking preparation ever undertaken by the United States government for arms control negotiations.

3. Willingness to Negotiate—An Era of Negotiation

Partnership and strength are two of the pillars of the structure of a durable peace. Negotiation is the third. For our commitment to peace is most convincingly demonstrated in our willingness to negotiate our points of difference in a fair and businesslike manner with the communist countries.

We are under no illusions. We know that there are enduring ideological differences. We are aware of the difficulty in moderating tensions that arise from the clash of national interests. These differences will not be dissipated by changes of atmosphere or dissolved in cordial personal relations between statesmen. They involve strong convictions and contrary philosophies, necessities of national security, and the deep-seated differences of perspectives formed by geography and history.

The United States, like any other nation, has interests of its own, and will defend those interests. But any nation today must define its interests with special concern for the interests of others. If some nations define their security in a manner that means insecurity for other nations, then peace is threatened and the security of all is diminished. This obligation is particularly great for the nuclear superpowers on whose decisions the survival of mankind may well depend.

The United States is confident that tensions can be eased and the danger of war reduced by patient and precise efforts to reconcile conflicting interests on concrete issues. Coexistence demands more than a spirit of good will. It requires the definition of positive goals which can be sought and achieved co-operatively. It requires real progress toward resolution of specific differences. This is our objective.

As the Secretary of State said on December 6: "We will continue to probe every available opening that offers a prospect for better East-West relations, for the resolution of problems large or small, for greater security for all.

"In this the United States will continue to play an active role in concert with our allies."

This is the spirit in which the United States ratified the Non-Proliferation Treaty and entered into negotiation with the Soviet Union on control of the military use of the seabeds, on the framework of a settlement in the Middle East, and on limitation of strategic arms. This is the basis on which we and our Atlantic allies have offered to negotiate on concrete issues affecting the security and future of Europe, and on which the United States took steps last year to improve our relations with nations of Eastern Europe. This is also the spirit in which we have resumed formal talks in Warsaw with Communist China. No nation need be our permanent enemy.

America's Purpose

These policies were conceived as a result of change, and we know they will be tested by the change that lies ahead. The world of 1970 was not predicted a decade ago, and we can be certain that the world of 1980 will render many current views obsolete.

The source of America's historic greatness has been our ability to see what had to be done, and then to do it. I believe America now has the chance to move the world closer to a durable peace. And I know that Americans working with each other and with other nations can make our vision real.

PART I: THE NATIONAL SECURITY COUNCIL SYSTEM

If we were to establish a new foreign policy for the era to come, we had to begin with a basic restructuring of the process by which policy is made.

Our fresh purposes demanded new methods of planning and a more rigorous and systematic process of policymaking. We required a system which would summon and gather the best ideas, the best analyses, and the best information available to the government and the nation.

Efficient procedure does not ensure wisdom in the substance of policy. But given the complexity of contemporary choices, adequate procedures are an indispensable component of the act of judgment. I have long believed that the most pressing issues are not necessarily the most fundamental ones; we know that an effective American policy requires clarity of purpose for the future as well as a procedure for dealing with the present. We do not want to exhaust ourselves managing crises; our basic goal is to shape the future.

At the outset, therefore, I directed that the National Security Council be re-established as the principal forum for Presidential consideration of foreign-policy issues. The revitalized Council—composed by statute of the President, the Vice President, the Secretaries of State and Defense, and the Director of the Office of Emergency Preparedness—and its new system of supporting groups are designed to respond to the requirements of leadership in the 1970s:

—Our policy must be *creative:* foreign policy must mean more than reacting to emergencies; we must fashion a new and positive vision of a peaceful world, and design new policies to achieve it.

—Our policymaking must be *systematic:* our actions must be the products of thorough analysis, forward planning, and deliberate decision. We must master problems before they master us.

—We must know the *facts:* intelligent discussions in the National Security Council and wise decisions require the most reliable information available. Disputes in the government have been caused too often by an incomplete awareness or understanding of the facts.

—We must know the *alternatives:* we must know what our real options are and not simply what compromise has found bureaucratic acceptance. Every view and every alternative must have a fair hearing. Presidential leadership is not the same as ratifying bureaucratic consensus.

—We must be prepared if *crises* occur: we must anticipate crises where possible. If they cannot be prevented, we must plan for dealing with them. All the elements of emergency action, political as well as military, must be related to each other.

—Finally, we must have effective *implementation:* it does little good to plan intelligently and imaginatively if our decisions are not well carried out.

Creativity. Above all, a foreign policy for the 1970s demands imaginative thought. In a world of onrushing change we can no longer rest content with familiar ideas or assume that the future will be a projection of the present. If we are to meet both the peril and the opportunity of change, we require a clear and positive vision of the world we seek—and of America's contribution to bringing it about.

As modern bureaucracy has grown, the understanding of change and the formulation of new purposes have become more difficult. Like men, governments find old ways hard to change and new paths difficult to discover.

The mandate I have given to the National Security Council system, and the overriding objective of every policy review undertaken, is to clarify our

410

view of where we want to be in the next three to five years. Only then can we ask, and answer, the question of how to proceed.

In central areas of policy we have arranged our procedure of policy-making so as to address the broader questions of long-term objectives first; we define our purposes and then address the specific operational issues. In this manner, for example, the NSC first addressed the basic questions of the rationale and doctrine of our strategic posture, and then considered—in the light of new criteria of strategic sufficiency—our specific weapons programs and our specific policy for the negotiations on strategic arms limitation. We determined that our relationship with Japan for the 1970s and beyond had to be founded on our mutual and increasingly collaborative concern for peace and security in the Far East; we then addressed the issue of Okinawa's status in the light of this fundamental objective.

Systematic Planning. American foreign policy must not be merely the result of a series of piecemeal tactical decisions forced by the pressures of events. If our policy is to embody a coherent vision of the world and a rational conception of America's interests, our specific actions must be the products of rational and deliberate choice. We need a system which forces consideration of problems before they become emergencies, which enables us to make our basic determinations of purpose before being pressed by events, and to mesh policies.

The National Security Council itself met thirty-seven times in 1969, and considered over a score of different major problems of national security. Each Council meeting was the culmination of an interagency process of systematic and comprehensive review.

This is how the process works: I assign an issue to an Interdepartmental Group—chaired by an Assistant Secretary of State—for intensive study, asking it to formulate the policy choices and to analyze the pros and cons of the different courses of action. This group's report is examined by an interagency review group of senior officials—chaired by the Assistant to the President for National Security Affairs—to ensure that the issues, options, and views are presented fully and fairly. The paper is then presented to me and the full National Security Council.

Some topics requiring specialized knowledge are handled through different channels before reaching the National Security Council. But the purpose is the same—systematic review and analysis, bringing together all the agencies concerned:

—The major issues of defense policy are treated in systematic and integrated fashion by the NSC Defense Program Review Committee. This group reviews at the Under Secretary level the major defense policy and program issues which have strategic, political, diplomatic, and economic implications in relation to overall national priorities.

—Through other NSC interagency groups the United States government has undertaken its first substantial effort to review all its resource programs within certain countries on a systematic and integrated basis, instead of haphazardly and piecemeal.

Determination of the Facts. Intelligent discussions and decisions at the highest level demand the fullest possible information. Too often in the past the process of policymaking has been impaired or distorted by incomplete information and by disputes in the government which resulted from the lack of a common appreciation of the facts. It is an essential function of the NSC system, therefore, to bring together all the agencies of the government concerned with foreign affairs to elicit, assess, and present to me and the Council all the pertinent knowledge available.

Normally, NSC Interdepartmental Groups are assigned this task. But other interagency groups perform this function for certain special topics. For example:

—The Verification Panel was formed to gather the essential facts relating to a number of important issues of strategic arms limitation, such as Soviet strategic capabilities, and our potential means of verifying compliance with various possible agreements. This Panel was designed not to induce agreement on policy views, but to establish as firmly as possible the *data* on which to base policy discussions. It helped to resolve many major policy differences which might otherwise have been intractable. As the section on Arms Control in this report explains in detail, the Panel played a central part in making our preparation for the Strategic Arms Limitation Talks with the Soviet Union the most thorough in which the U.S. government has ever engaged.

—The Vietnam Special Studies Group (VSSG) gathers and presents to the highest levels of the United States government the fullest and most up-to-date information on trends and conditions in the countryside in Vietnam. This group is of key assistance in our major and sustained effort to understand the factors which will determine the course of Vietnamization.

Full Range of Options. I do not believe that Presidential leadership consists merely in ratifying a consensus reached among departments and agencies. The President bears the Constitutional responsibility of making the judgments and decisions that form our policy.

The new NSC system is designed to make certain that clear policy choices reach the top, so that the various positions can be fully debated in the meeting of the Council. Differences of view are identified and defended, rather than muted or buried. I refuse to be confronted with a bureaucratic consensus that leaves me no options but acceptance or rejection, and that gives me no way of knowing what alternatives exist.

The NSC system also ensures that all agencies and departments receive a fair hearing before I make my decisions. All departments concerned with a problem participate on the groups that draft and review the policy papers. They know that their positions and arguments will reach the Council without dilution, along with the other alternatives. Council meetings are not rubber-stamp sessions. And as my decisions are reached, they are circulated in writing, so that all departments concerned are fully informed of our policy and so that implementation can be monitored.

Crisis Planning. Some events in the world over which we have little control may produce crises that we cannot prevent, even though our systematized study forewarns us of their possibility. But we can be the masters of events when crises occur, to the extent that we are able to prepare ourselves in advance.

For this purpose we created within the NSC system a special senior panel known as the Washington Special Actions Group (WSAG). This group drafts contingency plans for possible crises, integrating the political and military requirements of crisis action. The action responsibilities of the departments of the government are planned in detail, and specific responsibilities assigned in an agreed time sequence in advance. While no one can anticipate exactly the timing and course of a possible crisis, the WSAG's planning helps ensure that we have asked the right questions in advance, and thought through the implications of various responses.

Policy Implementation. The variety and complexity of foreign-policy issues in today's world places an enormous premium on the effective implementation of policy. Just as our policies are shaped and our programs formed through a constant process of interagency discussion and debate within the NSC framework, so the implementation of our major policies needs review and coordination on a continuing basis. This is done by an interdepartmental committee at the Under Secretary level chaired by the Under Secretary of State.

Conclusions

There is no textbook prescription for organizing the machinery of policy-making, and no procedural formula for making wise decisions. The policies of this Administration will be judged on their results, not on how methodically they were made.

The NSC system is meant to help us address the fundamental issues, clarify our basic purposes, examine all alternatives, and plan intelligent actions. It is meant to promote the thoroughness and deliberation which are essential for an effective American foreign policy. It gives us the means to bring to bear the best foresight and insight of which the nation is capable.

PART II: PARTNERSHIP AND THE NIXON
DOCTRINE

EUROPE

> I believe we must build an alliance strong enough to deter those who might threaten war; close enough to provide for continuous and far-reaching consultation; trusting enough to accept a diversity of views; realistic enough to deal with the world as it is; flexible enough to explore new channels of constructive cooperation.
>
> —*Address by the President to the North Atlantic Council, April 10, 1969.*

The peace of Europe is crucial to the peace of the world. This truth, a lesson learned at a terrible cost twice in the twentieth century, is a central principle of United States foreign policy. For the foreseeable future Europe must be the cornerstone of the structure of a durable peace.

Since 1945, the nations of Western Europe and North America have built together an alliance and a mutual respect worthy of the values and heritage we share. Our partnership is founded not merely on a common perception of common dangers but on a shared vision of a better world.

It was essential, therefore, that my first trip abroad as President should be to the capitals of our Western European allies. It was time to reaffirm the importance of those ties, and to strengthen the collaboration with which we shall develop, together, new policies for the new issues of the 1970s.

We must adapt to the conditions created by the past successes of our alliance. European politics are more fluid, and the issues facing the alliance are more subtle and profound, than ever in the past twenty years. These issues challenge our mastery of each of the three elements of a durable peace:

—Genuine *partnership* must increasingly characterize our alliance. For if we cannot maintain and develop further such a relationship with our North Atlantic allies, the prospects for achieving it with our other friends and allies around the world are slim indeed. But the evolution—past and future—of Europe and of European-American relations presents new issues. We must change the pattern of American predominance, appropriate to the postwar era, to match the new circumstances of today. We must extend our joint endeavor into another dimension of common challenges—bringing twentieth-century man and his environment to terms with one another in modern industrial societies.

—Jointly with our allies we must maintain the *strength* required to defend our common interests against external dangers, so long as those dangers exist. We have learned to integrate our forces; we now need better means of harmonizing our policies. We need a rational alliance defense posture for the longer term. This requires a common understanding of the nature of the dangers today and tomorrow, and on nuclear and non-nuclear strategy and forces. We must fashion common policies for the pursuit of security through arms control, as well as through military strength.

—Together with our allies, we must be prepared to *negotiate*. The problems and dangers of the division of Europe persist. Our association with our friends and allies in Europe is the starting point from which we seek to resolve those problems and cope with those dangers. Our efforts to pursue genuine relaxation of tensions between East and West will be a test of the new transatlantic partnership.

416

A New and Mature Partnership

I went to Western Europe in February, 1969, to reaffirm America's commitment to partnership with Europe.

A reaffirmation was sorely needed. We had to re-establish the principle and practice of consultation. For too long in the past, the United States had led without listening, talked *to* our allies instead of *with* them, and informed them of new departures instead of deciding with them. Inspired by the success of the Marshall Plan, we had taken such pride in our leadership of the alliance that we forgot how much even the origin and success of the Marshall Plan grew from European ideas and European efforts as well as our own.

After twenty years the economic prostration, military weakness, and political instability in postwar Europe that had required a predominant American effort were things of the past. Our *common* success in rebuilding Western Europe had restored our allies to their proper strength and status. It was time that our own leadership, in its substance and its manner, took account of this fact. As I stated to the NATO Council in Brussels on my trip in February, 1969: "The nations of NATO are rich in physical resources— but they are even richer in their accumulated wisdom and their experience of the world today. In fashioning America's policies, we need the benefit of that wisdom and that experience."

But the issue we face is not simply improved communication. It is the fundamental question of what shall be the content and purpose of the European-American relationship in the 1970s. In today's world what kind of an alliance shall we strive to build?

Last April the North Atlantic Treaty completed its second decade and began its third. I stated on that occasion: "When NATO was founded, the mere fact of cooperation among the Western nations was of tremendous significance, both symbolically and substantively. Now the symbol is not enough; we need substance. The alliance today will be judged by the content of its cooperation, not merely by its form."

The durability of the alliance is itself a triumph, but also a challenge: It would be unreasonable to imagine that a structure and relationship developed in the late 1940s can remain the same in content and purpose in the 1970s.

The fundamentals of the relationship are not in question. The original aims of the Western Alliance are still our basic purposes: the defense of Western Europe against common challenges, and ultimately the creation of a viable and secure European order.

But what pattern of relations will serve these objectives best today? There is a natural tendency to prefer the status quo and to support established forms and relationships that have served well in the past. But we can see in 1970 that there is no "status quo"—the only constant is the inevitability of change. Evolution within Western Europe has changed the region's position in the world, and therefore its role in the Western Alliance.

Since 1945, West Germany has achieved a position of mutual respect and partnership with its Western neighbors. From this reconciliation a larger European entity has developed, with prospects of further growth. Americans have welcomed this transformation and see it as a vindication of the historic choices made twenty years ago. We contributed, not only by ensuring the physical safety of Western Europe from outside attack or pressure, and in the early years by providing economic support, but also by giving a powerful impetus to the building of European institutions.

But today, European vitality is more self-sustaining. The preponderant American influence that was a natural consequence of postwar conditions would be self-defeating today. For nations which did not share in the responsibility to make the vital decisions for their own defense and diplomacy could retain neither their self-respect nor their self-assurance.

A more balanced association and a more genuine partnership are in America's interest. As this process advances, the balance of burdens and responsibilities must gradually be adjusted to reflect the economic and political realities of European progress. Our allies will deserve a voice in the alliance and its decisions commensurate with their growing power and contributions.

As we move from dominance to partnership, there is the possibility that some will see this as a step toward disengagement. But in the third decade of our commitment to Europe the depth of our relationship is a fact of life. We can no more disengage from Europe than from Alaska.

We recognize that America's contribution will continue to be unique in certain areas, such as in maintaining a nuclear deterrent and a level of involvement sufficient to balance the powerful military position of the U.S.S.R. in Eastern Europe. But we have no desire to occupy such a position in Europe that European affairs are not the province of the sovereign states that conduct them.

Intra-European institutions are in flux. We favor a definition by Western Europe of a distinct identity, for the sake of its own continued vitality and independence of spirit. Our support for the strengthening and broadening of the European Community has not diminished. We recognize that our interests will necessarily be affected by Europe's evolution, and we may have to make sacrifices in the common interest. We consider that the possible economic price of a truly unified Europe is outweighed by the gain in the political vitality of the West as a whole.

The structure of Western Europe itself—the organization of its unity— is fundamentally the concern of the Europeans. We cannot unify Europe and we do not believe that there is only one road to that goal. When the United States in previous Administrations turned into an ardent advocate, it harmed rather than helped progress.

We believe that we can render support to the process of European coalescence not only by our role in the North Atlantic Alliance and by our relationships with European institutions, but also by our bilateral relations with the several European countries. For many years to come these relations will provide essential trans-Atlantic bonds; and we will therefore continue to broaden and deepen them.

European Defense and Security

In choosing a strategy for our general purpose forces for the 1970s, we decided to continue our support for the present NATO strategy. And the Secretary of State and the Secretary of Defense announced at the NATO

Council meeting in December that we would maintain current U.S. troop levels in Europe at least through mid-1971.

At the same time, we recognized that we must use this time to conduct a thorough study of our strategy for the defense of Western Europe, including a full and candid exchange of views with our allies.

The need for this study is based on several considerations:

First, at the beginning of the last decade the United States possessed overwhelming nuclear superiority over the Soviet Union. However, that superiority has been reduced by the growth in Soviet strategic forces during the 1960s. As I point out elsewhere, the prospect for the 1970s is that the Soviets will possess strategic forces approaching and in some categories exceeding our own.

This fundamental change in the strategic balance raises important questions about the relative role of strategic nuclear forces, conventional forces, and tactical nuclear weapons.

Second, there are several views among Western strategists concerning the answers to several key questions:

—What is a realistic assessment of the military threats to Western Europe that should be used as the basis for Allied strategic and force structure planning?

—For how long could NATO sustain a conventional forward defense against a determined Warsaw Pact attack?

—Beyond their value as a deterrent to war, how should our tactical nuclear weapons in Europe be used to counter specific Warsaw Pact military threats?

—How does the contemplated use of tactical nuclear weapons affect the size, equipment, and deployment of Allied conventional forces?

Third, even though the NATO Allies have reached agreement on the strategy of flexible response, there are disagreements about the burdens that should be borne by the several partners in providing the forces and other resources required by that strategy. Further, questions have been raised concerning whether, for example, our logistics support, the disposition of our forces in Europe, and our airlift and sealift capabilities are sufficient to meet the needs of the existing strategy.

These questions must be addressed in full consultation with our allies. This is the process we have followed in the preparations for and conduct of the strategic arms limitation talks with the Soviet Union. We are consulting our allies closely at every stage, not on a take-it-or-leave-it basis but by seeking their advice on the whole range of options we have under consideration.

In assessing our common security, we must not be satisfied with formal agreements which paper over dissimilar views on fundamental issues or with language that is acceptable precisely because it permits widely divergent interpretations. Disagreements must be faced openly and their bases carefully explored. Because our security is inseparable, we can afford the most candid exchange of views.

In the past year, in the NATO Nuclear Planning Group, where the Secretary of Defense represents this government, the allies have taken significant steps to explore the principal problems of defining a common political rationale for the resort to tactical nuclear weapons. The completion of this process in close collaboration with all of our allies, including those possessing national nuclear capabilities, will be a major contribution to the credible defense of Europe.

The forging of a common understanding on basic security issues will materially improve our ability to deal sensibly and realistically with the opportunities and pressures for change that we face, including suggestions in this country for substantial reductions of U.S. troop levels in Europe and the possibility that balanced force reductions could become a subject of East-West discussions.

An Era of Negotiation in Europe

Our association with Western Europe is fundamental to the resolution of the problems caused by the unnatural division of the continent. We recognize that the reunion of Europe will come about not from one spectacular negotiation, but from an extended historical process.

We must be under no illusion about the difficulties. As I remarked last April, addressing the NATO Council in Washington: "It is not enough to talk of relaxing tension, unless we keep in mind the fact that twenty years of tension were not caused by superficial misunderstandings. A change of mood is useful only if it reflects some change of mind about political purpose.

"It is not enough to talk of European security in the abstract. We must know the elements of insecurity and how to remove them. Conferences are useful if they deal with concrete issues, which means they must, of course, be carefully prepared."

The division of Europe gives rise to a number of interrelated issues—the division of Germany, access to Berlin, the level of military forces on both sides of the line, the barriers to economic and cultural relations, and other issues. We are prepared to negotiate on these issues, in any suitable forum.

We have already joined with the three allies involved—the United Kingdom, France, and the Federal Republic of Germany—in suggesting to the Soviet Union that an attempt should be made to improve the situation regarding Berlin. Even if progress on broader issues cannot soon be made, the elimination of recurrent crises around Berlin would be desirable.

Our German ally has also undertaken steps to seek a normalization of its relations with its Eastern neighbors. Since the problem of Germany remains the key to East-West problems in Europe, we would welcome such a normalization. Just as the postwar era has ended in Western Europe, it is our hope that a more satisfactory and enduring order will come into being in the center of the continent.

Within NATO, meanwhile, we have joined wtih our allies in canvassing other issues that might offer prospects for fruitful negotiation, including the possibility of reciprocal adjustments in the military forces on both sides of the present demarcation line in Europe.

There is no dearth of subjects to negotiate. But there is no one way to go about it or any preferable forum. Relations between East and West must be dealt with on several levels and it would be wrong to believe that one single grand conference can encompass all existing relationships.

High on the agenda of the Western Alliance is the complex responsibility of integrating our individual and collective efforts. Together with our allies we seek to answer these questions: Should we consider the relaxation of tensions in terms of an overall settlement between NATO and the Warsaw Pact? Or is there scope for a series of bilateral efforts? What are the limits of bilateral efforts and how can they be related to the NATO system of consultations? What would be the contribution of a unified Western Europe?

Last April 10, in my talk at the twentieth anniversary celebration of NATO, I stated this problem as follows: "Up to now, our discussions [within NATO] have mainly had to do with tactics—ways and means of carrying out the provisions of a treaty drawn a generation ago. We have discussed clauses in proposed treaties; in the negotiations to come, we must go beyond these to the processes which these future treaties will set in motion. We must shake off our preoccupation with formal structure to bring into focus a common world view."

Without such a general understanding on the issues and our respective roles, we run a risk of failures and frustrations which have nothing to do with the intentions of the principals, but which could result from starting a sequence of events that gets out of control.

In the last analysis, progress does not depend on us and our allies alone. The prospects for durable agreement also involve the attitudes, interests, and policies of the Soviet Union and its allies in Eastern Europe. Ultimately, a workable system of security embracing all of Europe will require a willingness on the part of the Soviet Union to normalize its own relations with Eastern Europe—to recover from its anachronistic fear of Germany, and to recognize that its own security and the stability of Central Europe can best be served by a structure of reconciliation. Only then will an era of negotiation in Europe culminate in an era of peace.

A New Dimension

The common concerns and purposes of the Western allies reach beyond the military and political dimensions of traditional alliances.

Article 2 of the North Atlantic Treaty anticipated these further dimensions of partnership by pledging the allies to "strengthening their free institutions, . . . promoting conditions of stability and well-being," and "encourag[ing] economic collaboration." These are not goals limited to the Treaty area. They go beyond partnership among allies, military security, and negotiations with adversaries. As I said last April on NATO's twentieth anniversary, the relationship of Europe and the United States "also needs a social dimension to deal with our concern for the quality of life in this last third of the twentieth century."

At America's initiative the alliance created in 1969 a Committee on the Challenges of Modern Society—to pool our skills, our intellects, and our inventiveness in finding new ways to use technology to enhance our environments, and not to destroy them. For as I said last April: "The Western nations share common ideals and a common heritage. We are all advanced societies, sharing the benefits and the gathering torments of a rapidly advancing industrial technology. The industrial nations share no challenge more urgent than that of bringing twentieth-century man and his environment to terms with one another—of making the world fit for man and helping man to learn how to remain in harmony with the rapidly changing world."

If this view was not at first uniformly held among the allied nations, it emerged with increasing strength as the matter was considered—evidence both of the validity of the proposition and of the lessons learned and skills acquired in the course of two decades of intensive and detailed consultation and cooperation.

Environmental problems are secondary effects of technological change; international environmental cooperation is therefore an essential requirement of our age. This has now begun in the Committee on the Challenges of Modern Society. We have established a procedure whereby individual nations offer to "pilot" studies in a specific area and are responsible for making recommendations for action. Eight projects have been agreed upon. These are road safety, disaster relief, air pollution, sea pollution, inland water pollution, scientific knowledge and governmental decision-making, group and individual motivation, and regional planning. The United States is pilot nation for the first three of these.

A provision of the charter of the Committee on the Challenges of Modern Society looks to expanding the number of nations involved in these efforts, and to the support of similar undertakings in other international organizations such as the Organization for Economic Cooperation and Development, the Economic Commission for Europe, and the United Nations, which is holding a worldwide conference on environmental problems in 1972. We see this new dimension of international cooperation as an urgent and positive area of work. Cooperative research, technological exchange, education, institution building, and international regulatory agreements are all required to reverse the trend toward pollution of our planet's environment within this critical decade.

Agenda for the Future

The agenda for the future of American relations with Europe is implicit in the statement of the issues we face together:

—The evolution of a mature partnership reflecting the vitality and the independence of Western Eoropean nations.

—The continuation of genuine consultation with our allies on the nature of the threats to alliance security, on maintenance of a common and credible strategy, and on an appropriate and sustainable level of forces.

—The continuation of genuine consultations with our allies on the mutual interests affected by the U.S.-Soviet talks on strategic arms limitation.

—The development of a European-American understanding on our common purposes and respective roles in seeking a peaceful and stable order in all of Europe.

—The expansion of allied and worldwide cooperation in facing the common social and human challenges of modern societies.

In 1969 the United States and its allies discussed most of these issues—some in the context of new proposals, but most of them in the form of new questions. These questions will not be answered in a year. As I said last February in Brussels, "They deal with the vast sweep of history, they need the most thorough deliberations." The deliberations will continue; we have the chance today to build a tomorrow worthy of our common heritage.

WESTERN HEMISPHERE

Understandably, perhaps, a feeling has arisen in many Latin American countries that the United States "no longer cares."

My answer to that is simple.

We do care. I care. I have visited most of your countries. I have met most of your leaders. I have talked with your people. I have seen your great needs as well as your great achievements.

And I know this, in my heart as well as in my mind: If peace and freedom are to endure in the world, there is no task more urgent than lifting up the hungry and helpless, and putting flesh on the dreams of those who yearn for a better life.

—*The President's Remarks at the Annual Meeting of the Inter-American Press Association, Washington, October 31, 1969.*

The Setting

This concern which I expressed last year is central to our policies in the Western Hemisphere. Our relationship with our sister republics has special relevance for this Administration's general approach to foreign relations. We must be able to forge a constructive relationship with nations historically linked to us if we are to do so with nations more removed.

A new spirit and a new approach were needed to pursue this objective in the Americas. It meant recalling our special relationship but changing our attitude to accommodate the forces of change. And it meant translating our new attitude into an action program for progress that offers cooperative action rather than paternal promises and panaceas.

Throughout our history we have accorded the other American nations a special place in our foreign policy. This unique relationship is rooted in geography, in a common Western heritage, and in a shared historical experience of independence born through revolution.

This relationship has evolved over time. Our long and close political and economic association, and our articulation of the concept of hemispheric community, have been self-fulfilling: it is now a political and psychological fact that the relations between the United States and Latin America have a special meaning for us both. We share a concept of hemispheric community, as well as a web of treaties, commitments, and organizations that deserves the name of an Inter-American System.

But the character of that relationship has not been immune to the upheavals and transformations of past decades. Indeed, the continuing challenge throughout this hemisphere's history has been how to redefine and readjust this special relationship to meet changed circumstances, new settings, different problems.

That challenge is all the more compelling today.

Forces of Change

The powerful tides of change that have transformed the world since the Second World War have also swept through the Western Hemisphere, particularly in the 1960s. They have altered the nature of our relationship, and the expectations and obligations that flow from it.

When this Administration took office, it was evident that United States policies and programs had not kept pace with these fundamental changes. The state of the hemisphere and of our relationship was satisfying neither to North nor to South Americans:

—Our power overshadowed the formal relationship of equality, and even our restrained use of this power was not wholly reassuring. As a result, tension between us grew.

—Too many of our development programs were made *for* our neighbors instead of *with* them. This directive and tutorial style clashed with the growing self-assertiveness and nationalism of the other Western Hemisphere nations.

—Development problems had become more intense and complex; exploding population growth and accelerating urbanization added to social stress; frustrations were rising as expectations outstripped accomplishments.

—Political and social instability were therefore on the rise. Political radicalism increased, as well as the resort to violence and the temptation to turn to authoritarian methods to handle internal problems.

—Nationalism was taking on anti-U.S. overtones.

—Other Western Hemisphere nations seriously questioned whether our assistance, trade, and investment policies would match the realities of the 1970s.

Toward a Policy for the 1970s

From the outset, the Administration recognized the need to redefine the special concern of the United States for the nations of the hemisphere. We were determined to reflect the forces of change in our approach and in our actions.

We approached this task in two phases: first, we sought to appraise the state of the hemisphere, to analyze the problems that existed, and to determine fundamental policy objectives; then we expressed our conclusions in specific policies and programs.

To get a fresh perspective, early in my Administration I asked Governor Nelson A. Rockefeller to undertake a fact-finding mission throughout the region. His conclusions and recommendations, together with other government studies, were intensively reviewed by the NSC during the summer and early fall. This review addressed some of the basic questions: whether we should continue to have a "special relationship"; if so, what its essential purpose and substance ought to be and how best to achieve it.

We concluded that:

—A "special relationship" with Latin America has existed historically, and there are compelling reasons to maintain and strengthen our ties.

—The goal of such a relationship today should be to create a community of independent, self-reliant states linked together in a vital and useful association.

—United States assistance to its neighbors is an essential part of that relationship.

—The United States should contribute, not dominate. We alone cannot assume the responsibility for the economic and social development of other nations. This is a process deeply rooted in each nation's history and evolution. Responsibility has to be shared for progress to be real.

—For the '70s we therefore had to shape a relationship that would encourage other nations to help themselves. As elsewhere in the world, our basic role is to persuade and supplement, not to prescribe. Each nation must be true to its own character.

On October 31 I proposed a new partnership in the Americas to reflect these concepts, a partnership in which all voices are heard and none is predominant. I outlined the five basic principles governing this new approach:

"First, a firm commitment to the inter-American system, to the compacts which bind us in that system—as exemplified by the Organization of American States and by the principles so nobly set forth in its charter.

"Second, respect for national identity and national dignity, in a partnership in which rights and responsibilities are shared by a community of independent states.

"Third, a firm commitment to continued United States assistance for hemispheric development.

"Fourth, a belief that the principal future pattern of this assistance must be U.S. support for Latin American initiatives, and that this can best be achieved on a multilateral basis within the inter-American system.

"Finally, a dedication to improving the quality of life in this new world of ours—to making people the center of our concerns, and to helping meet their economic, social, and human needs."

In this speech we also began laying the foundations of an action program for progress. These are actions that reflect our new approach of enabling other Western Hemisphere nations to help themselves. And they are actions that can realistically be implemented. I refused to propose grandiose spending programs that had no prospect of Congressional approval, or to make promises that could not be fulfilled.

A less than realistic approach would have blunted our partners' sense of participation and generated false hopes. The time for dependency and slogans was over. The time for partnership and action was at hand.

Action

We are shaping programs together with the other nations of the Western Hemisphere, not devising them on our own. And where we once relied on bilateral exchanges, we are turning more to multilateral groups.

One of the principal cooperative forums is the Inter-American Economic and Social Council, the economic and development channel of the Organization of American States. Shortly after my speech, and again early this year, this body met to consider our proposals and those of our friends. In these continuing meetings and in other multilateral exchanges we are putting forward our suggestions for give-and-take discussions.

We have made realistic action proposals to meet specific objectives:

—*Share Responsibility.* To ensure that the shaping of the Western Hemisphere's future reflects the will of the other nations of this hemisphere, I affirmed the need for a fundamental change in the way we manage development assistance. I proposed that the nations of the hemisphere evolve an effective multilateral mechanism for bilateral assistance. The precise form this takes will be worked out with our partners. IA–ECOSOC has directed the Inter-American Committee for the Alliance for Progress (CIAP) and the Inter-American Bank to explore ways to increase their participation in development decisions. The goal is to enable the other Western Hemisphere nations to assume a primary role in setting priorities within the hemisphere, developing realistic programs, and keeping their own performance under critical review. To demonstrate United States interest in improving and strengthening our multilateral institutions, I authorized financial support— totaling $23 million in grant funds—to strengthen the activities of CIAP and the Inter-American Bank. I also authorized our representatives to agree to submit to CIAP, for its review, United States economic and financial programs as they affect the other nations of the hemisphere. Similar reviews are made of the other hemisphere countries' policies, but the United States had not, prior to this decision, opened its policies to such a consultation.

—*Expand Trade.* To help other Western Hemisphere nations to increase their export earnings and thus contribute to balanced development and economic growth, I have committed the United States to a program which would help these countries improve their access to the expanding markets of the industrialized world:

• The U.S. will press for a liberal system of generalized tariff preferences for all developing countries. We are working toward a system that would eliminate discriminations against South American exports that exist in other countries. Through the Organization for Economic Cooperation and Development and the United Nations Conference on Trade and Development, we are pressing other developed nations to recognize the need for a genuinely progressive tariff preference system.

• I committed the U.S. to lead an effort to reduce non-tariff barriers to trade maintained by nearly all industrialized countries. We seek to lead a concerted multilateral reduction in non-tariff barriers on products of major interest to South America, taking advantage of the work going on in the General Agreement on Tariffs and Trade.

• I pledged to support increased technical and financial assistance to promote Latin American trade expansion.

• I promised to support the establishment within the inter-American system of regular procedures for advance consultations on all trade matters, and we proposed specific mechanisms for this purpose. In early February, IA–ECOSOC agreed to establish a standing special committee which will meet regularly for consultation on mutual economic problems, including trade and development.

—*Ease AID Restrictions.* To make development assistance more helpful and effective, we are taking several actions:

• I ordered that from November 1 all loan dollars sent to Latin America under AID be freed to allow purchases not only in the U.S. but anywhere in Latin America. This partial "untying" of our assistance loans removed restrictions that had burdened borrowers and promised to provide an incentive for industrial development in the region.

• We have removed a number of other procedural restrictions on the use of AID funds. We eliminated, for example, the requirement under which recipient countries were forced to import U.S. goods they would not have imported under normal trade conditions—the "additionality" provision.

• The Peterson Task Force (which is studying our overall assistance programs) is reviewing other procedural and administrative restrictions. We aim to streamline our lending and make it more effective.

—*Assure Special Representation.* To reflect our special concern for this region, I proposed establishing the position of Under Secretary of State for Western Hemisphere Affairs. The new Under Secretary will be given authority to coordinate all of our activities in this region. On December 20 the Secretary of State submitted implementing legislation to Congress.

—*Support Regionalism.* To encourage regional cooperation we have offered to support economic integration efforts. We have reiterated our offer of financial assistance to the Central American Common Market, the Caribbean Free Trade Area, the Andean Group, and to an eventual Latin American Common Market.

—*Ease Debt Burdens.* To help nations heavily burdened by large debts and their servicing we have urged the Inter-American Committee for the Alliance for Progress (CIAP) to join us in approaching other creditor nations and international lending agencies to study these problems. In February the IA–ECOSOC authorized CIAP to proceed along this line. As members of CIAP we have offered our full cooperation and expressed our willingness to join in an approach to other creditor nations.

—*Share Science and Technology.* To help turn science to the service of the hemisphere:

• We will contribute to the support and financing of initiatives in these fields, including research and development, regional training centers, and transfer of technology.

• We are developing a program for training and orientation of Latin American specialists in the field of scientific and technical information.

• The OAS will sponsor a conference next year on the application of science and technology to Latin America.

This is the beginning of action for progress. But it is only a beginning. There is a long way to go.

Agenda for the Future

During the 1970s the nations of this hemisphere will continue to experience profound change in their societies and institutions. Aspirations rise while the intensity and complexity of social and economic problems increase, and most American governments must straddle the widening gap between demands and resources. If these governments cannot find greater resources, their prospects for solving their problems through rational policies will fade. The results will be more instability, more political radicalism, more of the wrong kind of nationalism.

This is the dilemma which the hemisphere faces in the 1970s. It prompted the efforts made by the hemisphere nations to forge new development and trade policies in the series of meetings of the Inter-American Economic and Social Council during the latter half of 1969. Against this backdrop our friends will seek our cooperation, judge the credibility of our words, and measure the value of our actions.

In practical terms, we shall confront increased pressures:

—*For capital resources to finance development and reform.* We shall have to find ways to achieve adequate levels of resources, to use them more effectively, and to transfer them through improved institutions and channels. We believe we can meet these needs through partnership, with shared responsibility for development decisions and major efforts by the United States and other developed nations.

—*For growing markets to expand exports.* We shall have to face frankly the contradictions we will find between our broader foreign policy interests and our more particular domestic interests. Unless we can demonstrate to our sister nations evidence of our sincerity and of our help in this area while recognizing practical constraints, we cannot achieve the effective partnership we seek. A liberal trade policy that can support development is necessary to sustain a harmonious hemispheric system.

—*Against foreign investments.* Foreign investments are the most exposed targets of frustration, irrational politics, misguided nationalism. Their potential for mutual benefits will only be realized through mutual perception and tact. The nations of this hemisphere must work out arrangements which can attract the needed technical and financial resources of foreign investment. For their part, investors must recognize the national sensitivities and political needs of the 1970s. There is no more delicate task than finding new modes which permit the flow of needed investment capital without a challenge to national pride and prerogative.

There will be political and diplomatic pressures as well. The Inter-American community will have to consider:

—How to maintain peace in the face of border disputes and neighbors' quarrels.

—How to meet the problems of subversive threats to internal security and order.

—How to handle legitimate desires to modernize security forces without starting arms races.

—How to view internal political instabilities and extra-legal changes of government among us.

In both the development and security spheres we shall have to adapt the formalities of the inter-American system to rapidly changing realities. An amended OAS charter will very soon take effect. We shall need to work to enhance the effectiveness of its constituent organizations. Above all, our special partnership must accommodate the desire of the Latin Americans to consult among themselves and formulate positions which they can then discuss with us.

Within the broad commonality of our relationship there is great diversity. In a period of such profound social and cultural change emerging domestic structures will differ by country, reflecting various historical roots, particular contexts, and national priorities. We can anticipate different interpretations of reality, different conceptions of self-interest, and different conclusions on how to resolve problems.

The United States must comprehend these phenomena. We must recognize national interests may indeed diverge from ours rather than merge. Our joint task is to construct a community of institutions and interests broad and resilient enough to accommodate our national divergencies. It is in this context that we are giving intensive study to Governor Rockefeller's recommendations for additional actions.

Our concepts of future American relations must thus be grounded in differences as well as similarities. Our mandate is to produce creativity from diversity. Our challenge is the vision I painted in my October 31 speech: "Today, we share an historic opportunity.

"As we look together down the closing decades of this century, we see tasks that summon the very best that is in us. But those tasks are difficult precisely because they do mean the difference between despair and fulfillment for most of the 600 million people who will live in Latin America in the year 2000. Those lives are our challenge. Those lives are our hope. And we could ask no prouder reward than to have our efforts crowned by peace, prosperity, and dignity in the lives of those 600 million human beings, each so precious and each so unique—our children and our legacy."

ASIA AND THE PACIFIC

What we seek for Asia is a community of free nations able to go their own way and seek their own destiny with whatever cooperation we can provide—a community of independent Asian countries, each maintaining its own traditions and yet each developing through mutual cooperation. In such an arrangement, we stand ready to play a responsible role in accordance with our commitments and basic interests.

—*Statement by the President at Bangkok, Thailand, July 28, 1969.*

Three times in a single generation Americans have been called upon to cross the Pacific and fight in Asia. No region of the world has more engaged our energies in the postwar period. No continent has changed more rapidly or with greater complexity since World War II. Nowhere has the failure to create peace been more costly or led to greater sacrifice.

America's Asian policy for the 1970s must be based on the lessons of this sacrifice. Does it mean that the United States should withdraw from Asian affairs? If not, does it mean that we are condemned to a recurring cycle of crisis and war in a changing setting beyond the understanding or influence of outsiders?

Our answers to these questions provide the concepts behind this Administration's approach to Asia.

First, we remain involved in Asia. We are a Pacific power. We have learned that peace for us is much less likely if there is no peace in Asia.

Second, behind the headlines of strife and turmoil the fact remains that no region contains a greater diversity of vital and gifted peoples, and thus a greater potential for cooperative enterprises. Constructive nationalism and economic progress since World War II have strengthened the new nations of Asia internally. A growing sense of Asian identity and concrete action toward Asian cooperation are creating a new and healthy pattern of international relationships in the region. Our Asian friends, especially Japan, are in a position to shoulder larger responsibilities for the peaceful progress of the area. Thus, despite its troubled past, Asia's future is rich in promise. That promise has been nurtured in part by America's participation.

Third, while we will maintain our interests in Asia and the commitments that flow from them, the changes taking place in that region enable us to change the character of our involvement. The responsibilities once borne by the United States at such great cost can now be shared. America *can* be effective in helping the peoples of Asia harness the forces of change to peaceful progress, and in supporting them as they defend themselves from those who would subvert this process and fling Asia again into conflict.

Our friends in Asia have understood and welcomed our concept of our role in that continent. Those with whom the Vice President, the Secretary of State, and I spoke during our visits there agreed that this was the most effective way in which we can work together to meet the military challenges and economic opportunities of the new Asia.

Our new cooperative relationship concerns primarily two areas of challenge—military threats and the great task of development.

Defense

Our important interests and those of our friends are still threatened by those nations which would exploit change and which proclaim hostility to the United States as one of the fundamental tenets of their policies. We do not assume that these nations will always remain hostile, and will work toward improved relationships wherever possible. But we will not underestimate any threat to us or our allies, nor lightly base our present policies on untested assumptions about the future.

At the beginning of my trip last summer through Asia, I described at Guam the principles that underlie our cooperative approach to the defense of our common interests. In my speech on November 3 I summarized key elements of this approach:

—The United States will keep all its treaty commitments.

—We shall provide a shield if a nuclear power threatens the freedom of a nation allied with us, or of a nation whose survival we consider vital to our security and the security of the region as a whole.

—In cases involving other types of aggression we shall furnish military and economic assistance when requested and as appropriate. But we shall look to the nation directly threatened to assume the primary responsibility of providing the manpower for its defense.

This approach requires our commitment to helping our partners develop their own strength. In doing so, we must strike a careful balance. If we do too little to help them—and erode their belief in our commitments—they may lose the necessary will to conduct their own self-defense or become disheartened about prospects of development. Yet, if we do too much, and American forces do what local forces can and should be doing, we promote dependence rather than independence.

In providing for a more responsible role for Asian nations in their own defense, the Nixon Doctrine means not only a more effective use of common resources, but also an American policy which can best be sustained over the long run.

Economic and Political Partnership

The partnership we seek involves not only defense. Its ultimate goal must be equally close cooperation over a much broader range of concerns—economic as well as political and military. For in that close cooperation with our Asian friends lies our mutual commitment to peace in Asia and the world.

Our goal must be particularly close cooperation for economic development. Here, too, our most effective contribution will be to support Asian initiatives in an Asian framework.

Our partnership will rest on the solid basis of Asia's own wealth of human and material resources. Acting jointly, its peoples offer each other a wide range of energy and genius. Their benefits shared, its land and products can overcome the unmet needs which have often sparked conflict. Already, the Republics of Korea and China, Thailand, Singapore, and Malaysia can show a doubling of their Gross National Product[s] in the last decade. Korea's annual growth rate of 15 percent may be the highest in the world; the Republic of China, no longer an economic aid recipient, now conducts a technical assistance program of its own in twenty-seven other countries.

Thus, the potential for cooperation among Asian countries is strong, and progress is already apparent. New multinational organizations are sharing agricultural and technical skills. When the war in Vietnam is ended, reconstruction can be carried out in a regional context. And we look forward to continued cooperation with a regional effort to harness the power of the Mekong River.

The successful start of the Asian Development Bank, of which we are a member, illustrates the potential of Asian initiatives and regionalism. It is an *Asian* institution, with a requirement that the Bank's president, seven of its ten directors, and 60 percent of its capital come from Asia.

Our hopes for Asia are thus for a continent of strong nations drawing together for their mutual benefit on their own terms, and creating a new relationship with the rest of the international community.

Japan, as one of the great industrial nations of the world, has a unique and essential role to play in the development of the new Asia. Our policy toward Japan during the past year demonstrates our conception of the creative partnership we seek with all Asian nations.

Upon entering office, I faced a pivotal question concerning the future of our relations with Japan: the status of Okinawa. What did we consider more important—the maintenance of American administration of Okinawa with no adjustments in the conditions under which we operate our bases, or the strengthening of our relationship with Japan over the long term? We chose the second course because our cooperation with Japan will be crucial to our efforts to help other Asian nations develop in peace. Japan's partnership with us will be a key to the success of the Nixon Doctrine in Asia.

In November I therefore agreed with Prime Minister Sato during his visit to Washington that we would proceed with arrangements for the return of Okinawa in 1972, with our bases remaining after its reversion in the same status as our bases in Japan. This was among the most important decisions I have taken as President.

For his part, Prime Minister Sato expressed the intention of the Japanese government to expand and improve its aid programs in Asia in keeping with the economic growth of Japan. He agreed with me that attention to the economic needs of the developing countries was essential to the development of international peace and stability. He stated Japan's intention to accelerate the reduction and removal of its restrictions on trade and capital. He also stated that Japan was exploring what it could do to help bring about stability and reconstruction in postwar Southeast Asia. The Prime Minister affirmed that it is in Japan's interest that we carry out fully our defensive commitments in East Asia.

We have thereby laid the foundation for U.S.-Japanese cooperation in the 1970s.

Elsewhere, too, we have seen developments encouraging for the future of Asia. In Indonesia—which is virtually half of Southeast Asia—we have participated in multilateral efforts, aimed at achieving economic stability, which have already contributed much to the building of a prospering and peaceful nation.

The United States has a similar long-run interest in cooperation for progress in South Asia. The one-fifth of mankind who live in India and Pakistan can make the difference for the future of Asia. If their nation-building surmounts the centrifugal forces that have historically divided the subcontinent, if their economic growth keeps pace with popular demands, and if they can avert further costly rivalry between themselves, India and Pakistan can contribute their vast energies to the structure of a stable peace. But these are formidable "ifs." We stand ready to help the subcontinent overcome them. These nations' potential contribution to peace is too great for us to do otherwise.

Like the rest of Asia, India and Pakistan have changed significantly over the past decade. They have registered steady economic progress in many areas, and established a hopeful precedent for mutual cooperation in the Indus development scheme. Yet in the same period, each has felt the strains of continuing tension in their relations and their old bitter dispute flared again in brief warfare in 1965.

They have reordered their international relationships with East and West; each remains staunchly independent.

Over the next decade India, Pakistan, and their friends have an opportunity to build substantially on the constructive elements in this record, and above all, to work together to avert further wasteful and dangerous conflict in the area.

While I was in South Asia, I stated our view of the method and purpose of our economic assistance to Asia. These words were spoken in Pakistan, but they express our goals as well for India and all of Asia: "I wish to communicate my Government's conviction that Asian hands must shape the Asian future. This is true, for example, with respect to economic aid, for it must be related to the total pattern of a nation's life. It must support the unique aspirations of each people. Its purpose is to encourage self-reliance, not dependence."

Issues for the Future

The fostering of self-reliance is the new purpose and direction of American involvement in Asia. But we are only at the beginning of a new road. However clear our conception of where we wish to go, we must be under no illusion that any policy can provide easy answers to the hard, specific issues which will confront us in Asia in coming years.

—While we have established general guidelines on American responses to Asian conflicts, in practice the specific circumstances of each case require careful study. Even with careful planning, we will always have to consider a basic and delicate choice. If we limit our own involvement in the interest of encouraging local self-reliance, and the threat turns out to have been more serious than we had judged, we will only have created still more dangerous choices. On the other hand, if we become unwisely involved, we risk stifling the local contribution which is the key to our long-run commitment to Asia.

—The success of our Asian policy depends not only on the strength of our partnership with our Asian friends, but also on our relations with Mainland China and the Soviet Union. We have no desire to impose our own prescriptions for relationships in Asia. We have described in the Nixon Doctrine our conception of our relations with Asian nations. We hope that other great powers will act in a similar spirit and not seek hegemony.

—Just as we and our allies have an interest in averting Great Power dominance over Asia, we believe that peace in the world would be endangered by Great Power conflict there—whether it involves us or not. This characterizes our attitude toward the Sino-Soviet dispute.

—Asian regional cooperation is at its beginning. We will confront subtle decisions as we seek to help maintain its momentum without supplanting Asian direction of the effort.

—A sound relationship with Japan is crucial in our common effort to secure peace, security, and a rising living standard in the Pacific area. We look forward to extending the cooperative relationship we deepened in 1969. But we shall not ask Japan to assume responsibilities inconsistent with the deeply felt concerns of its people.

—In South Asia our good relations with India and Pakistan should not obscure the concrete dilemmas we will face. How can we bring home to both, for example, our serious concern over the waste of their limited resources in an arms race, yet recognize their legitimate interests in self-defense?

All these issues will confront this Administration with varying intensity over the coming years. We are planning now to meet challenges and anticipate crises. Our purpose in 1969 has been to make sure none was ignored or underestimated. The task ahead—for Asians and Americans—is to address all these issues with the imagination, realism, and boldness their solutions demand if lasting peace is to come to Asia.

VIETNAM

The people of Vietnam, North and South alike, have demonstrated heroism enough to last a century. And I speak from personal observation. I have been to North Vietnam, to Hanoi, in 1953, and all over South Vietnam. I have seen the people of the North and the people of the South. The people of Vietnam, North and South, have endured an unspeakable weight of suffering for a generation. And they deserve a better future.

—*The President's Address to the 24th Session of the UN General Assembly, September, 18, 1969.*

A just peace in Vietnam has been, and remains, our goal.

The real issues are the nature of that peace and how to achieve it. In addressing these issues at the beginning of my Administration, I had to consider the great consequences of our decisions.

I stated the consequences of a precipitate withdrawal in these terms in my speech of May 14: "When we assumed the burden of helping defend South Vietnam, millions of South Vietnamese men, women, and children placed their trust in us. To abandon them now would risk a massacre that would shock and dismay everyone in the world who values human life.

"Abandoning the South Vietnamese people, however, would jeopardize more than lives in South Vietnam. It would threaten our long-term hopes for peace in the world. A great nation cannot renege on its pledges. A great nation must be worthy of trust.

"When it comes to maintaining peace, 'prestige' is not an empty word. I am not speaking of false pride or bravado—they should have no place in our policies. I speak, rather, of the respect that one nation has for another's integrity in defending its principles and meeting its obligations.

"If we simply abandoned our effort in Vietnam, the cause of peace might not survive the damage that would be done to other nations' confidence in our reliability.

"Another reason for not withdrawing unilaterally stems from debates within the Communist world. . . . If Hanoi were to succeed in taking over South Vietnam by force—even after the power of the United States had been engaged—it would greatly strengthen those leaders who scorn negotiation, who advocate aggression, who minimize the risks of confrontation with the United States. It would bring peace now but it would enormously increase the danger of a bigger war later."

My trip through Asia last summer made this fact more vivid to me than ever. I did not meet a single Asian leader who urged a precipitate U.S. withdrawal. The closer their nations were to the battlefield, the greater was their concern that America meet its responsibilities in Vietnam.

Less attention had been given to another important consequence of our decisions—within the United States itself. When the Administration took office, Vietnam had already led to a profound national debate. In considering our objectives there, I could only conclude that the peace must not intensify the bitter recrimination and divisions which the war had already inflicted on American society. Were we to purchase peace in Vietnam at the expense of greater suffering later, the American people would inevitably lose confidence in their leaders—not just in the Presidency or in either political party, but in the whole structure of American leadership.

For all these reasons, I resolved to seek a peace which all Americans could support, a peace in which all parties to the conflict would have a stake. I resolved also to be completely candid with the American public and Congress in presenting our policies, except for some details on matters of great sensitivity. I was determined to report the setbacks as well as achievements, the uncertainties as well as the hopeful signs.

To seek a just peace, we pursued two distinct but mutually supporting courses of action: negotiations and Vietnamization. We want to achieve an early and fair settlement through negotiations. But if the other side refuses, we shall proceed to strengthen the South Vietnamese forces. This will allow us to replace our troops on an orderly timetable. We hope that as Vietnamization proceeds the government of North Vietnam will realize that it has more to gain in negotiations than in continued fighting.

We do not pretend that our goals in Vietnam have been accomplished, or that the way ahead will be easy.

—In South Vietnam we have helped the South Vietnamese make progress in increasing their defense capacity, and we have reduced the number of American men and casualties. Yet Vietnamization is still a developing process, and enemy intentions on the battlefield are unclear.

—At the conference table we have made generous and reasonable proposals for a settlement. Yet the other side still refuses to negotiate seriously.

Despite these uncertainties, I believe that we are on the right road, and that we are moving toward our goals.

Negotiations

In seeking a negotiated settlement of the war, we did not underestimate the difficulties ahead:

—We knew that the basic questions at issue in negotiations—particularly the resolution of political power in such a war—were enormously complex. There could be no rigid formula or strict agenda.

—We were aware that Hanoi's actions and doctrinal statements about "protracted conflict" caused it to view negotiations as a means of pressure, rather than as an avenue to a fair compromise.

—We realized that our opponent had sacrificed heavily; he had demonstrated a tenacious commitment to the war, and obviously harbored a deep mistrust of negotiations as a means of settling disputes. As I wrote to the late President Ho Chi Minh last July in an appeal to him to join us in finding a rapid solution: "It is difficult to communicate meaningfully across the gulf of four years of war."

These were formidable obstacles. But we were equally convinced that negotiations offered the best hope of a rapid settlement of the war. The specific issues were complex but could be resolved, once both sides made the fundamental decision to negotiate in a spirit of goodwill. Therefore we and the government of the Republic of Vietnam moved to demonstrate to a mistrustful adversary our willingness to negotiate seriously and flexibly.

On May 14 I made a number of far-reaching proposals for a settlement. They included a mutual withdrawal of all non-South Vietnamese forces from South Vietnam and internationally supervised free elections.

I also indicated that we seek no bases in Vietnam and no military ties, that we are willing to agree to neutrality or to unification of Vietnam if that is what the South Vietnamese people choose.

In order to encourage the other side to negotiate, I indicated that our proposals were flexible, and that we were prepared to consider other approaches consistent with our principles. We insist only on one general proposition for which the government of North Vietnam itself has claimed to be fighting—that the people of South Vietnam be able to decide their own future free of outside interference.

The proposals I made on May 14 still stand. They offer all parties an opportunity to end the war quickly and on an equitable basis.

In a similar spirit President Thieu of the Republic of Vietnam on July 11 offered a comprehensive set of proposals. They include free elections in which all the people and parties of South Vietnam can participate, including the National Liberation Front and its adherents, and a mixed Electoral Commission on which all parties can be represented. We have supported those proposals.

At Midway, in early June, President Thieu and I both publicly pledged to accept *any* outcome of free elections, regardless of what changes they might bring.

Throughout the year we explored every means of engaging the other side in serious negotiations—in the public talks in Paris, in private conversations, and through reliable third parties.

To demonstrate our willingness to wind down the war, I also ordered a reduction in the level of our military operations in Vietnam. Our tactical air and B-52 operations have been reduced by over 25 percent. Our combat deaths have dropped by two thirds.

Nor were our proposals put forward on a take-it-or-leave-it basis. We have repeatedly expressed our willingness to discuss the other side's Ten Point Program. But Hanoi has adamantly refused even to discuss our proposals. It has refused to negotiate with the government of the Republic of Vietnam, although it had agreed to do so as one of the "understandings" that led to the bombing halt. It has insisted that we must unconditionally and totally accept its demands for unilateral U.S. withdrawal and for the removal of the leaders of the government of South Vietnam. It has demanded these things as conditions for just *beginning* negotiations. If we were to accept these demands, we would have conceded the fundamental points at issue. There would be nothing left to negotiate.

If the other side is interested in genuine negotiations, there are many ways they can let us know and there are many channels open to them.

The key to peace lies in Hanoi—in its decision to end the bloodshed and to negotiate in the true sense of the word.

The United States has taken three major steps which we were told repeatedly would lead to serious negotiations. We stopped the bombing of North Vietnam; we began the withdrawal of U.S. forces from Vietnam; and we agreed to negotiate with the National Liberation Front as one of the parties to the negotiation. But none of those moves brought about the response or the reaction which their advocates had claimed. It is time for Hanoi to heed the concern of mankind and turn our negotiations into a serious give-and-take. Hanoi will find us forthcoming and flexible.

Vietnamization

The other course of action we are pursuing—Vietnamization—is a program to strengthen the ability of the South Vietnamese government and people to defend themselves. It emphasizes progress in providing physical security for the Vietnamese people and in extending the authority of the South Vietnamese government throughout the countryside.

Vietnamization is not a substitute for negotiations, but a spur to negotiations. In strengthening the capability of the government and people of South

Vietnam to defend themselves, we provide Hanoi with an authentic incentive to negotiate seriously now. Confronted by Vietnamization, Hanoi's alternative to a reasonable settlement is to continue its costly sacrifices while its bargaining power diminishes.

Vietnamization has two principal components. The first is the strengthening of the armed forces of the South Vietnamese in numbers, equipment, leadership and combat skills, and overall capability. The second component is the extension of the pacification program in South Vietnam.

Tangible progress has been made toward strengthening the South Vietnamese armed forces. Their number has grown, particularly the local and territorial forces. For example the numerical strength of the South Vietnamese Regional Forces and Popular Forces—important elements in resisting guerrilla attacks—has grown by more than 75,000 in the last year. The effectiveness of these forces is improving in most areas. In addition, about 400,000 weapons have been supplied to South Vietnamese villagers who have become part of the Peoples' Self-Defense force, a local militia.

Under the Vietnamization program, we have reversed the trend of American military engagement in Vietnam and the South Vietnamese have assumed a greater role in combat operations. We have cut the authorized strength of American forces by 115,000 as of April 15, 1970. American forces will continue to be withdrawn in accordance with an orderly schedule based on three criteria: the level of enemy activity, progress in the negotiations, and the increasing ability of the South Vietnamese people to assume for themselves the task of their own defense.

During this process we have kept in close consultations with the allied nations—Australia, Korea, New Zealand, and Thailand—which also contribute troops to assist the Vietnamese. Their forces continue to bear a significant burden in this common struggle.

As the Vietnamese government bears the growing cost of these augmented forces, and as U.S. military spending in Vietnam is reduced with the continuing reduction of the U.S. military presence there, there will be additional strains on the Vietnamese economy. The Vietnamese will require assistance in dealing with these economic problems. Although our spending for purely military purposes in Vietnam can be expected to decrease substantially during the process of Vietnamization, some increases in our spending for economic purposes will be required.

Vietnamization also involves expansion of the pacification program. Our understanding of the pacification program and of the criteria for measuring its success needed improvement. I therefore ordered a comprehensive study of conditions in the countryside by a committee charged with analyzing the statistics of Vietnam and keeping the situation under constant review.

The study has concluded that the most meaningful criteria for South Vietnamese government success in the countryside are the establishment in each hamlet of (1) an adequate defense, and (2) a fully functioning government resident in the hamlet twenty-four hours a day. If the government can achieve these two objectives, it can prevent the enemy from subverting and terrorizing the population or mobilizing it for its own purposes. The enemy will be denied any but the most limited and furtive access to the people, and will encounter increasing hostility or indifference as they seek the assistance they formerly enjoyed. The enemy forces will be isolated and forced to fight as a conventional expeditionary force, being dependent on external sources of supply and reinforcement.

This is very important: Enemy main force activities have in the past relied on active assistance from the population in the countryside for intelligence, food, money, and manpower. This has enabled the enemy to use the countryside as a springboard from which to strike at key Vietnamese cities and installations. If they are forced to fight as a conventional army, with their support provided from their own resources rather than from the population, the enemy will lose momentum as they move forward because their supply lines will lengthen and they will encounter increasing opposition.

To date, the pacification program is succeeding.

Enemy forces have suffered heavy casualties, many in the course of their own offensives of 1968 and early 1969. The operations of U.S. and South Vietnamese troops against enemy main force units have prevented those units from moving freely through the populated areas and have more and more forced them back into bases in remote areas and along the borders of South Vietnam.

Since 1967, the percentage of the rural population living in areas with adequate defense and a fully functioning local government—the two criteria for government success mentioned above—has more than doubled. By a similar standard, Viet Cong control over the rural population has dropped sharply to less than 10 percent.

The enemy is facing greater difficulty in recruitment and supply. North Vietnamese fillers are being used to bolster Viet Cong main force and local force units, whose strength appears to be declining in most areas. More of the enemy's time is taken up in gaining strength for new offensives which appear to be progressively less efficient.

Claims of progress in Vietnam have been frequent during the course of our involvement there—and have often proved too optimistic. However careful our planning, and however hopeful we are for the progress of these plans, we are conscious of two basic facts:

—We cannot try to fool the enemy, who knows what is actually happening.

—Nor must we fool ourselves. The American people must have the full truth. We cannot afford a loss of confidence in our judgment and in our leadership.

Because the prospects and the progress of Vietnamization demand the most careful study and thoughtful analysis—by ourselves and our critics alike —we have made major efforts to determine the facts.

At my request Secretary Laird and the Chairman of the Joint Chiefs of Staff, General Wheeler, have just traveled to Vietnam to look into the situation. Last fall I asked Sir Robert Thompson, an objective British expert with long experience in the area, to make his own candid and independent appraisal for me.

We have established a Vietnam Special Studies Group whose membership includes my Assistant for National Security Affairs as Chairman, the Under Secretary of State, the Deputy Secretary of Defense, the Director of Central Intelligence, and the Chairman of the Joint Chiefs of Staff. I have directed this group to:

—Sponsor and direct on a continuous basis systematic analyses of U.S. programs and activities in Vietnam;

—Undertake special analytical studies on a priority basis as required to support broad policy and related program decisions; and

—Provide a forum for and encourage systematic interagency analysis of U.S. activities in Vietnam.

Essentially the purpose of this group is to direct studies of the factual situation in Vietnam. These studies are undertaken by analysts and individuals with experience in Vietnam drawn from throughout the government. Their findings are presented to the Vietnam Special Studies Group and the National Security Council.

As described below, the group has helped us identify problems for the future. It has provoked the most searching questions, as well as measured the progress we have achieved.

Prisoners of War

In human terms no other aspect of conflict in Vietnam more deeply troubles thousands of American families than the refusal of North Vietnam to agree to humane treatment of prisoners of war or to provide information about men missing in action. Over fourteen hundred Americans are now listed as missing or captured, some as long as five years, most with no word ever to their families. In the Paris meetings we have sought repeatedly to raise this subject—to no avail. Far from agreeing to arrangements for the release of prisoners, the other side has failed even to live up to the humane standards of the 1949 Geneva Convention on prisoners of war: the provision of information about all prisoners, the right of all prisoners to correspond with their families and to receive packages, inspection of POW camps by an impartial organization such as the International Red Cross, and the early release of seriously sick and wounded prisoners.

This is not a political or military issue, but a matter of basic humanity. There may be disagreement about other aspects of this conflict, but there can be no disagreement on humane treatment for prisoners of war. I state again our readiness to proceed at once to arrangements for the release of prisoners of war on both sides.

Tasks for the Future

This Administration is carrying out a concerted and coordinated plan for peace in Vietnam. But the following tasks still remain:

—*Negotiations.* One task is to persuade the North Vietnamese government to join us in genuine negotiations leading toward a compromise settlement which would assure the self-determination of the South Vietnamese people and would also ensure the continued neutrality of Laos. The fact that it has not yet given any indication of doing so does not necessarily mean that such a decision cannot come at any point. While we harbor no undue optimism, the history of negotiations on Vietnam shows that breakthroughs have always come with little warning after long deadlocks.

Hanoi faces serious complicated issues in making the fundamental decision to seek a genuine settlement. Allied military pressures, uncertainties in its international support, strains within North Vietnam, the recent display of American public support for a just peace, and the strengthening of the South Vietnamese government under Vietnamization all argue for seeking a settlement now. On the other hand, Hanoi's mistrust of our intentions before and after a settlement, its hope that American domestic pressures will force us to withdraw rapidly or make major concessions, its hope for political instability and collapse in South Vietnam, its emotional commitment to the struggle, and its own political weakness in the South must weigh heavily against its willingness to negotiate.

We do not know what choice the North Vietnamese government will make. For our part, we shall continue to try to make clear to that government that its true long-range interests lie in the direction of negotiations. As we have often said, we shall be flexible and generous when serious negotiations start at last.

—*Enemy Intentions.* Another crucial task is to evaluate Hanoi's intentions on the battlefield. We hope that the level of combat can be further reduced, but we must be prepared for new enemy offensives. The government of North Vietnam could make no greater mistake than to assume that an increase in violence would be to its advantage. As I said on November 3, and have repeated since, if I conclude that increased enemy action jeopardizes our remaining forces in Vietnam, I will not hesitate to take strong and effective measures to deal with that situation.

—*Vietnamization.* A major problem we must face is whether the Vietnamization program will succeed. The enemy is determined and able, and will continue to fight unless he can be persuaded that negotiation is the best solution. The success of Vietnamization is a basic element in Hanoi's assessment of its policies, just as it is in our own.

—We are now attempting to determine the depth and durability of the progress which has been made in Vietnam. We are studying the extent to which it has been dependent on the presence of American combat and support forces as well as on expanded and improved South Vietnamese army and territorial forces. We are asking searching questions:

• What is the enemy's capability to mount sustained operations? Could they succeed in undoing our gains?

• What is the actual extent of improvement in allied capabilities? In particular, are the Vietnamese developing the leadership, logistics capabilities, tactical know-how, and sensitivity to the needs of their own people which are indispensable to continued success?

• What alternative strategies are open to the enemy in the face of continued allied success? If they choose to conduct a protracted, low-intensity war, could they simply wait out U.S. withdrawals and then, through reinvigorated efforts, seize the initiative again and defeat the South Vietnamese forces?

• Most important, what are the attitudes of the Vietnamese people, whose free choice we are fighting to preserve? Are they truly being disaffected from the Viet Cong, or are they indifferent to both sides? What do their attitudes imply about the likelihood that the pacification gains will stick?

These studies are continuing, as are our studies of the enemy situation and options. I have made it clear that I want the Vietnam Special Studies Group and the other agencies of the U.S. government to provide the fullest possible presentation of the facts, whatever their policy implications might be.

Our task is to continue to proceed carefully in the policy of Vietnamization, and to find the means which will best support our purposes of helping the South Vietnamese to strengthen themselves.

Even as the fighting continues in Vietnam, we must plan for the transition from war to peace. Much has already been done to bring relief to suffering people, to reconstruct war-torn areas, and to promote economic rehabilitation. We have been supporting those efforts. We shall continue to support them and we shall count on other nations to help.

I look forward to the day when I shall not have to report on the problems of ending a complex war but rather on the opportunities offered by a stable peace, when the men and nations who have fought so long and so hard will be reconciled.

I expressed my hope for the future of Vietnam when I spoke to the United Nations on September 18: "When the war ends, the United States will stand ready to help the people of Vietnam—all of them—in their tasks of renewal and reconstruction. And when peace comes at last to Vietnam, it can truly come with healing in its wings."

THE MIDDLE EAST

. . . a peace which speaks not only about the integrity of nations, but also for the integrity of individuals.
—*Letter to the President of American Near East Refugee Aid, October 21, 1969.*

. . . the peace that is not simply one of words but one which both parties will have a vested interest in maintaining.
—*Welcoming Remarks to [Golda Meir,] Prime Minister of Israel, September 25, 1969.*

These statements reflect some of my thoughts on the nature of the peace which must come to the Middle East. At the same time, this is an area with great resources and prospects for economic progress. It is the first region of developing nations that is near to meeting its capital needs from its own resources.

Yet this area presents one of the sternest tests of our quest for peace through partnership and accommodation of interests. It combines intense local conflict with great power involvement. This combination is all the more dangerous because the outside powers' interests are greater than their control.

Beyond the area of conflict and beyond this era of conflict, the United States is challenged to find new relationships in helping all the people of the area marshal their resources to share in progress.

The most important of the area's conflicts, between Arabs and Israel, is still far from settlement. It has serious elements of intractability, but its importance requires all concerned to devote their energies to helping to resolve it or make it less dangerous.

Local passions in the Middle East run so deep that the parties in conflict are seldom amenable to outside advice or influence. Each side is convinced that vital interests are at stake which cannot be compromised:

—Israel, having lived so long before on a thin margin of security, sees territories occupied in 1967 as providing physical security more tangible than Arab commitments to live at peace—commitments whose nature would be tested only after Israel had relinquished the buffer of the territories.

—For the Arabs a settlement negotiated directly with the Israelis would require recognition of Israel as a sovereign state even while Israeli troops still occupy territory taken in 1967 and while Arab refugees remain homeless.

—For both sides and for the international community Jerusalem is a special problem involving not only the civil and political concerns of two states but the interests of three great world religions.

A powerful legacy of fear and mistrust must be overcome if the parties are to be willing to subject their interests and grievances to the procedure of compromise. Until then, no formula acceptable to both sides, and no neutral definition of "a fair and reasonable settlement," can get very far.

However, a settlement should still be sought.

This Administration continues to believe that the United Nations cease-fire resolutions define the minimal conditions that must prevail on the ground if a settlement is to be achieved. We have persistently urged the parties in the area as well as the other major powers to do all possible to restore observance of the cease-fire.

Once those minimal conditions exist, we believe a settlement can only be achieved through the give and take of negotiation by those involved, in an atmosphere of mutual willingness to compromise. That is why this Administration has pressed this view in a series of consultations with leaders from the Middle East both in Washington and in their capitals, in bilateral discussions with the outside powers most concerned, and in formal talks with the Soviet Union and in the Four Power forum at the United Nations. In the course of these discussions we have advanced specific proposals—outlined by Secretary Rogers in his speech of December 9—for creating a framework for negotiation in accordance with the United Nations resolution of November 22, 1967. These have been written with the legitimate concerns of all parties firmly in mind. They were made in an effort to try to help begin the process of negotiation under UN Ambassador Jarring's auspices. Observing that the United States maintained friendly ties with both Arabs and Israelis, the Secretary of State said that to call for Israeli withdrawal as envisaged in the UN resolution without achieving agreement on peace would be partisan toward the Arabs, while calling on the Arabs to accept peace without Israeli withdrawal would be partisan toward Israel.

But the United States cannot be expected to assume responsibility alone for developing the terms of peace or for guaranteeing them. Others—in the Middle East and among the great powers—must participate in the search for compromise. Each nation concerned must be prepared to subordinate its special interests to the general interest in peace. In the Middle East, especially, everyone must participate in making the peace so all will have an interest in maintaining it.

We have not achieved as much as we had hoped twelve months ago through the discussions with the Soviet Union or the Four Power talks. We have gone as far as we believe useful in making new proposals until there is a response from other parties. But we shall continue to participate in the dialogue so long as we can make a contribution.

If the Arab-Israeli conflict cannot be finally resolved, at least its scope must be contained and the direct engagement of the major powers limited. For this is a second dimension of the conflict in the Middle East—the rivalries and interests of the major powers themselves.

The interests of the great powers are involved in the contests between local forces, but we also have a common interest in avoiding a direct confrontation. One of the lessons of 1967 was that the local events and forces have a momentum of their own, and that conscious and serious effort is required for the major powers to resist being caught up in them.

In its communications to the Soviet Union and others, this Administration has made clear its opposition to steps which could have the effect of drawing the major powers more deeply into the Arab-Israeli conflict—steps that could only increase the dangers without advancing the prospects for peace.

The activity of the Soviet Union in the Middle East and the Mediterranean has increased in recent years. This has consequences that reach far beyond the Arab-Israeli question. The United States has long-standing obligations and relationships with a number of nations in the Middle East and its policy is to help them enhance their own integrity and freedom. This Administration has shown its readiness to work with the Soviet Union for peace and to work alongside the Soviet Union in cooperation with nations in the area in the pursuit of peace. But the United States would view any effort by the Soviet Union to seek predominance in the Middle East as a matter of grave concern.

I believe that the time has passed in which powerful nations can or should dictate the future to less powerful nations. The policy of this Administration is to help strengthen the freedom of others nations to determine their own futures. Any effort by an outside power to exploit local conflict for its own advantage or to seek a special position of its own would be contrary to that goal.

For these reasons, this Administration has not only pressed efforts to restore observance of the cease-fire and to help begin the process of negotiating a genuine peace. It has also urged an agreement to limit the shipment of arms to the Middle East as a step which could help stabilize the situation in the absence of a settlement. In the meantime, however, I now reaffirm our stated intention to maintain careful watch on the balance of military forces and to provide arms to friendly states as the need arises.

This Administration clearly recognizes that the problem of the Middle East, rooted in a long history of local developments, will be solved only when the parties to the conflict—by reason or resignation—come to accommodate each other's basic, long-run interests. They must recognize that to do less will increasingly endanger everyone's basic goals.

Issues for the Future

We shall continue to seek to work together with all the region's nations, respecting their legitimate national interests and expecting that they will have the same regard for ours. But the emphasis must be on the word "together." The day is past when the large powers can or should be expected either to determine their course or to solve their problems for them. As the Secretary of State said on December 9: "[Peace] is . . . a matter of the attitudes and intentions of the parties. Are they ready to coexist with one another? Can a live-and-let-live attitude replace suspicion, mistrust, and hate? A peace agreement between the parties must be based on clear and stated intentions and a willingness to bring about basic changes in the attitudes and conditions which are characteristic of the Middle East today."

The Middle East poses many challenges for the United States. First, of course, is the problem of resolving or containing major causes of conflict. No one should believe that a settlement even of the Arab-Israeli conflict would lead to the complete relaxation of tensions in the area. Other local rivalries and the turmoil accompanying social and economic change will continue to produce possibilities for conflict.

Yet, beyond that, a new problem faces us—the character of a constructive American relationship with an area with large capital resources of its own.

A number of nations in the area are well-launched toward economic modernization. Some of them have substantial revenues to finance this effort, and those that do not will increasingly rely on the efforts of nearby nations to help through regional funds. Large numbers of skilled technicians have been trained, and many of them have crossed borders to help neighbors.

This means that—while the United States will continue to help where it can—the need will decline for capital assistance and for the type of economic assistance which AID and its forerunners have provided. Of course, American technology, investment, education, managerial skills are still much in demand and can offer much in helping break bottlenecks that remain.

The challenge to the United States, therefore, is to find new tools—new programs, new legislation, new policies—that will permit our government and our citizens to relate productively to the first major area of the developing world to be close to meeting most of its capital needs from its own resources. We want to continue to work together. We must therefore—while persisting in the quest for peace—develop new relationships to meet the circumstances and demands of the 1970s.

Beyond the dangerous conflict of today, our vision of the Middle East is of a common effort by all those—the people of the area and friends outside—whose high purpose is to erase the scars of the past and to build a future consistent with their great heritage and abundant resources.

AFRICA

We know you have no easy task in seeking to assure a fair share of Africa's wealth to all her peoples. We know that the realization of equality and human dignity throughout the continent will be long and arduous in coming. But you can be sure as you pursue these difficult goals that the United States shares your hopes and your confidence in the future.

—*The President's Message to the Sixth Annual Assembly of the Organization of African Unity, September 6, 1969.*

In this greeting last September to the summit meeting of the Organization of Africa Unity, I expressed America's determination to support our African friends as they work to fulfill their continent's high promise. The unprecedented visit of the Secretary of State to Africa this month is a confirmation of this support.

One of the most dramatic and far-reaching changes of the last decade was the emergence of an independent Africa.

Only ten years ago thirty-two countries covering nearly five sixths of the continent were still colonies, their voices silent in world affairs. Today, these are all sovereign nations, proudly determined to shape their own future. And contrary to fears so often voiced at their birth, these nations did not succumb to communist subversion. Africa is one of the world's most striking examples, in fact, of the failure of the appeal of communism in the new nations. African states now comprise one third of the membership of the United Nations. African issues have become important moral and political questions. African views justly merit and receive the attention of the world.

But this rebirth of a continent has been hazardous as well as hopeful. Africa was the scene of many of the recurrent crises of the 1960s. There was the factional strife and international rivalry in the Congo, an arms race between Ethiopia and Somalia, the establishment of white minority rule in Southern Rhodesia, and the agonizing human loss in the Nigerian civil war.

The continent still faces grave problems. The imbalances of economies and institutions once under full external control are only too evident today. Arbitrary boundaries drawn in European chancelleries left many African countries vulnerable to tribal strife; and nowhere is the task of nation-building more taxing. Not least, Africans face the formidable task of strengthening their sense of identity and preserving traditional culture as their societies make the transition to modernity.

Over the last decade America has not had a clear conception of its relationship with post-colonial Africa and its particular problems. Because of our traditional support of self-determination, and Africa's historic ties with so many of our own citizens, our sympathy and friendship for the new Africa were spontaneous. But without a coherent concept to structure our policies, we allowed ourselves to concentrate more on temporary crises than on their underlying causes. We expressed our support for Africa more by lofty phrases than by candid and constructive dialogue.

Just as we focus our policies elsewhere to meet a new era, we will be clear with ourselves and with our African friends on America's interests and role in the continent. We have two major concerns regarding the future of Africa:

—That the continent be free of great power rivalry or conflict in any form. This is even more in Africa's interest than in ours.

—That Africa realize its potential to become a healthy and prosperous region in the international community. Such an Africa would not only be a valuable economic partner for all regions, but would also have a greater stake in the maintenance of a durable world peace.

These interests will guide our policies toward the most demanding challenges facing Africa in the 1970s.

Development

The primary challenge facing the African continent is economic development.

If the 1960s were years of high hopes and high rhetoric, the 1970s will have to be years of hard work and hard choices. The African nations and those who assist them must decide together on strict priorities in employing the relatively limited development capital available to the continent. In doing this, Africa and its friends can benefit from several lessons of the past decade.

Certainly development will not always proceed as rapidly as the Africans and their friends hope. In many countries, needs will outrun local and international resources for some time. But solid and steady progress will be made if our common development investment concentrates on those basic if undramatic building blocks of economic growth—health, education, agriculture, transportation, and local development. In particular Africa will realize the full advantage of its own rich material resources only as it nurtures the wealth of its human resources. In close coordination with the Africans' own efforts the United States will direct our aid at these fundamental building blocks.

Another lesson we have learned from the 1960s is the need for close regional cooperation, in order for Africa to get the most from development resources. The United States will work with other donors and the Africans to help realize the potential for cooperative efforts—by the support which we are giving, for example, to the East African Economic Community and the promising regional groupings in West Africa. We will recognize, however, that regional action is not the only road for African development. In some cases, for geographic or political reasons, it will not work.

Our assistance throughout the continent will be flexible and imaginative. We will make a particular effort—including programs of technical assistance and new encouragement of private investment—to help those countries not in a position to participate in regional projects.

We have learned that there are no panaceas for African development. Each country faces its own problems, and the solutions to them must spring from the national experience of each country. Foreign ideologies have often proven notoriously irrelevant, and even tragically wasteful, as designs for African progress. The most creative conceptual approaches to African development should come, of course, from the Africans themselves. Outsiders cannot prescribe the political framework most conducive to Africa's economic growth. In some countries, progress has depended upon stability. Yet elsewhere, solutions to local problems have been found amid periods of uncertainty or even turmoil.

The United States will measure African progress in terms of long-run social and economic accomplishment, and not in the political flux which is likely to accompany growth.

In Africa, as throughout the developing world, our goal in providing development aid is clear. We want the Africans to build a better life for themselves and their children. We want to see an Africa free of poverty and disease, and free too of economic or political dependence on any outside power. And we want Africans to build this future as *they* think best, because in that way both our help and their efforts will be most relevant to their needs.

As Secretary Rogers said in Ethiopia on February 12: "As a developed nation, we recognize a special obligation to assist in the economic development of Africa. Our resources and our capacity are not unlimited. We have many demands at home. We will, however, continue to seek the means, both directly and in cooperation with others, to contribute more effectively to economic development in Africa."

Nationhood

Africa's second challenge in the 1970s will be to weather the inevitable strains which will come with the further development of nations which house a great diversity of peoples and cultures.

We have witnessed tragic manifestations of this problem in the civil strife in the Congo and Nigeria. The process of national integration may be stormy elsewhere.

Such turmoil presents a tempting target to forces outside Africa ready to exploit the problems of change to their own advantage. But foreign intervention, whatever its form or source, will not serve the long-run interests of the Africans themselves.

The United States approaches these problems of national integration with a policy which clearly recognizes the limits as well as the obligations of our partnership with Africa:

—We will not intervene in the internal affairs of African nations. We strongly support their right to be independent, and we will observe their right to deal with their own problems independently. We believe that the national integrity of African states must be respected.

—However, we will distinguish between non-interference politically and the humanitarian obligation to help lessen human suffering.

—Finally, consulting our own interests, we will help our friends in Africa to help themselves when they are threatened by outside forces attempting to subvert their independent development. It is another lesson of the 1960s, however, that African defense against subversion, like African development, must be borne most directly by Africans rather than by outsiders.

Southern Africa

The third challenge facing Africa is the deep-seated tension in the southern sixth of the continent.

Clearly there is no question of the United States condoning, or acquiescing in, the racial policies of the white-ruled regimes. For moral as well as historical reasons, the United States stands firmly for the principles of racial equality and self-determination.

At the same time the 1960s have shown all of us—Africa and her friends alike—that the racial problems in the southern region of the continent will not be solved quickly. These tensions are deeply rooted in the history of the region, and thus in the psychology of both black and white.

These problems must be solved. But there remains a real issue in how best to achieve their resolution. Though we abhor the racial policies of the white regimes, we cannot agree that progressive change in southern Africa is furthered by force. The history of the area shows all too starkly that violence and the counter-violence it inevitably provokes will only make more difficult the task of those on both sides working for progress on the racial question.

The United States warmly welcomes, therefore, the recent Lusaka

Manifesto, a declaration by African leaders calling for a peaceful settlement of the tensions in southern Africa. That statesmanlike document combines a commitment to human dignity with a perceptive understanding of the depth and complexity of the racial problem in the area—a combination which we hope will guide the policies of Africa and her friends as they seek practical policies to deal with this anguishing question.

Issues for the Future

American policy toward Africa, then, will illustrate our general approach to building an enduring peace. Our stake in the continent will not rest on today's crisis, on political maneuvering for passing advantage, or on the strategic priority we assign it. Our goal is to help sustain the process by which Africa will gradually realize economic progress to match its aspirations.

We must understand, however, that this process is only beginning. Its specific course is unclear. Its success depends in part on how we and the Africans move now in the climate as well as the substance of our relations.

—Africa's friends must find a new tone of candor in their essential dialogue with the continent. All too often over the past decade the United States and others have been guilty of telling proud young nations, in misguided condescension, only what we thought they wanted to hear. But I know from many talks with Africans, including two trips to the continent in 1957 and 1967, that Africa's new leaders are pragmatic and practical as well as proud, realistic as well as idealistic. It will be a test of diplomacy for all concerned to face squarely common problems and differences of view. The United States will do all it can to establish this new dialogue.

—Most important, there must be new and broader forms of mobilizing the external resources for African development. The pattern of the multilateral consortium which in the past few years has aided Ghana should be employed more widely elsewhere. This will require the closest cooperation between the Africans and those who assist them. There is much to be gained also if we and others can help devise ways in which the more developed African states can share their resources with their African neighbors.

—The United States is firmly committed to non-interference in the continent, but Africa's future depends also on the restraint of other great powers. No one should seek advantage from Africa's need for assistance, or from future instability. In his speech on February 12 Secretary Rogers affirmed that: "We have deep respect for the independence of the African nations. We are not involved in their internal affairs. We want our relations with them to be on a basis of mutual respect, mutual trust and equality. We have no desire for any domination of any country or any area and have no desire for any special influence in Africa, except the influences that naturally and mutually develop among friends."

The Africa of the 1970s will need schools rather than sympathy, roads rather than rhetoric, farms rather than formulas, local development rather than lengthy sermons. We will do what we can in a spirit of constructive cooperation rather than by vague declarations of good will. The hard facts must be faced by Africans and their friends; and the hard work in every corner of the continent must be done. A durable peace cannot be built if the nations of Africa are not true partners in the gathering prosperity and security which fortify that peace.

INTERNATIONAL ECONOMIC POLICY

Peace has an economic dimension. In a world of independent states and interdependent economies failure to collaborate is costly—in political as well as economic terms. Economic barriers block more than the free flow of goods and capital across national borders; they obstruct a more open world in which ideas and people, as well as goods and machinery, move among nations with maximum freedom.

Good U.S. economic policy is good U.S. foreign policy. The pre-eminent role that we play in the world economy gives us a special responsibility. In the economic sphere, more than in almost any other area, what we do has a tremendous impact on the rest of the world. Steady non-inflationary growth in our domestic economy will promote steady non-inflationary growth in the world as a whole. The stability of our dollar is essential to the stability of the world monetary system. Our continued support of a stronger world monetary system and freer trade is crucial to the expansion of world trade and investment on which the prosperity and development of most other countries depend.

As in other areas of foreign policy, our approach is a sharing of international responsibilities. Our foreign economic policy must be designed to serve our purpose of strengthening the ties that make partnership work.

We have an excellent foundation. In no other area of our foreign policy has the record of cooperation been so long and so successful. From the 1944 Bretton Woods Conference (which created the International Monetary Fund) and the 1947 General Agreement on Tariffs and Trade (which established a code for the orderly conduct of trade), to the Kennedy Round of tariff negotiations and the recent creation of Special Drawing Rights, free nations have worked together to build and strengthen a system of economic relationships. We derive strength from their strength; we collaborate for our common interest.

International Monetary Policy

International monetary matters pose most sharply the potential tug-of-war between interdependent economies and independent national policies. Each country's balance of payments encompasses the full range of its economic and political relations with other nations—trade, travel, investment, military spending, foreign aid. The international monetary system links these national payments positions, and hence the domestic economies of all countries. It thus lies at the heart of all international economic relations and it must function smoothly if world trade, international investment, and political relations among nations are to prosper—particularly since imbalances inevitably arise as some countries temporarily spend more abroad than they earn, while others correspondingly earn more than they spend.

The system must include two elements:

—Adequate supplies of internationally acceptable money and credit to finance payments imbalances among countries; and

—Effective means through which national economies can adjust to one another to avoid the development of excessive and prolonged imbalances.

The inadequacies of both elements caused the recurring monetary crises of the 1960s.

An *adequate money supply* is needed internationally just as it is domestically. Shortages of internationally acceptable money induce national authorities to take hasty and often restrictive measures to protect their own monetary reserves, or to pull back from liberalization of trade and investment. Such actions clash with the objective of the international economic system, which, precisely by freeing trade and capital, has helped promote the unparalleled prosperity of the postwar world. In short, an adequate world money supply can hinder the pursuit of world prosperity which, in turn, can generate serious political problems among nations.

At the other extreme, excessive levels of world reserves could contribute to world inflation. They could permit countries to finance imbalances indefinitely, delaying too long the actions needed to adjust their own economies to those of their trading partners. Since failure to adjust may permit a country to drain resources away from the rest of the world, excessive levels of reserves can also generate serious political problems.

In 1969 the world took a step of profound importance by creating international money to help provide for adequate—neither too small nor too large—levels of world reserves. Through the International Monetary Fund the United States joined with the other free nations to create, for an initial three-year period, almost $10 billion of Special Drawing Rights—a truly international money, backed by the entire community of free nations, created in amounts determined jointly by these nations, in recognition of the fact that a steadily growing world economy requires growing reserves.

There exist other types of internationally accepted money, particularly gold and dollars, which the world has previously relied upon and will continue to use. But it is clear that the relative role of gold must diminish. Our critical monetary arrangements must not rest on the vagaries of gold production. Nor should the world be forced to rely more heavily on dollars flowing from a U.S. payments deficit. This would appear to some as representing largely national determination of the international monetary supply, not wholly responsive to international needs. Moreover, prolonged deficits could jeopardize our own international financial position and cause concern about the stability of the dollar.

A truly international money was thus needed to meet a truly international problem. The nations of the world did not shrink from the bold innovation required to meet that need. As a result, the foundations of the world economy, and hence world stability, are far stronger today.

To be sure, the first creation of Special Drawing Rights does not by itself assure an adequate supply of internationally acceptable money. The international community will have to make periodic decisions on how many Special Drawing Rights to create. The relationship among the different types of international money—gold, dollars, and now Special Drawing Rights— could again cause problems. Most important, a steady economic performance by the United States will be necessary to maintain full international confidence in the dollar, whose stability remains crucial to the smooth functioning of the world economy. But we have gone a long way toward meeting the needs for an adequate supply of international money.

The second fundamental requirement of an international monetary system—*the mutual adjustment of national economies*—still calls for improvement. Imbalances among nations can only be financed temporarily.

Constructive means must exist by which they can be rectified in an orderly way. Such adjustment should not require countries to resort to prolonged restrictions on international transactions, for this runs counter to the fundamental objective of an open world. Neither should it force countries to adopt internal economic policies, such as excessive rates of inflation or unemployment, which conflict with their national economic and social objectives. Both approaches have been adopted all too frequently in the past.

Improved means of adjustment are thus high on the agenda for the further development of the international monetary system in the 1970s. As economic interdependence accelerates, better coordination among national economies will become even more necessary. Such coordination must rest on a solid base of effective internal policies. For example, we in the United States must squarely face the fact that our inflation of the past five years— left unchecked—would not only undermine our domestic prosperity but jeopardize the effort to achieve better international equilibrium. We look forward to the results of the international discussions, already under way, examining the means through which exchange rates between national currencies might be adjusted so that such changes, when they become necessary, can take place more promptly and less disruptively.

In this environment the remaining restrictions on international transactions can be steadily reduced. We will do our share. That intent was plain in the actions we took in 1969 to relax our restraints on capital outflows for U.S. corporations and banks and to eliminate the most onerous restrictions on our aid to developing countries.

Trade Policy

Freer trade among all nations provides greater economic benefits for each nation. It minimizes potential political frictions as well. These conclusions are truer today than ever before, as the growing interdependence of the world economy creates new opportunities for productive exchange.

But growing interdependence also means greater reliance by each nation on all other nations. Each is increasingly exposed to its trading partners. In today's world, all major countries must pursue freer trade if each country is to do so. The principle of true reciprocity must lie at the heart of trade policy —as it lies at the heart of all foreign policy.

In 1969 the United States took a series of steps toward dismantling trade barriers and assuring fair treatment for our own industry and agriculture in world commerce. I submitted new trade legislation which proposed:

—Elimination of the American Selling Price system of tariff valuation for certain chemicals and other products, which would bring us immediate trade concessions in Europe and elsewhere. Because it is seen by many abroad as our most important non-tariff barrier to trade, its elimination might also open the door to further reductions of barriers to U.S. exports.

—Improvement of the means to help U.S. industries, firms, and workers adjust to import competition.

—Restoration of Presidential authority to reduce tariffs by a modest amount, when necessary to promote U.S. trade interests.

—New Presidential authority to retaliate against other countries if their trading practices unfairly impede our own exports in world markets.

We called on our trading partners to begin serious discussions on the remaining non-tariff barriers to trade, which have become even more important as tariff levels have been reduced.

We took specific steps toward easing economic relations between the United States and Communist China.

Finally, we proposed a liberal system of tariff preferences for exports of the developing countries.

This proposal is designed to meet one of the world's major economic and political problems—the struggle of the developing countries to achieve a satisfactory rate of economic development. Development can be promoted by aid, but aid cannot and should not be relied on to do the whole job. The low-income countries need increased export earnings to finance the imports they need for development. They need improved access for their products to the massive markets of the industrialized nations. Such export increases must come largely in manufactured goods, since the demand for most primary commodities—their traditional exports—grows relatively slowly. And these countries are at early stages of industrialization, so they face major hurdles in competing with the industrialized countries for sales of manufactured goods.

Against this background, we proposed that all industrialized nations eliminate their tariffs on most manufactured products exported to them by all developing countries. Such preferential treatment would free an important and rapidly growing part of the trade between these two groups of nations. It would therefore provide an important new impetus to world economic development.

The main tasks for the immediate future are to complete the actions started in 1969:

—Passage of this Administration's trade bill,

—Progress in the international discussions on non-tariff barriers and impediments to trade in agricultural products.

—Successful resolution of the negotiations on tariff preferences.

Beyond these steps lie new challenges for U.S. trade policy. I am establishing a Commission on International Trade and Investment Policy to help develop our approaches to them:

—*Trade and Investment.* Foreign investment, symbolized by the multinational corporation, has become increasingly important in relation to the flows of goods which have been the focus of traditional trade policy. We must explore more fully the relationship between our trade and foreign investment policies.

—*Trade Adjustment.* We must learn how better to adjust our own economy to the dynamic forces of world trade, so that we can pursue our objective of freer trade without unacceptable domestic disruption.

—*East-West Trade.* We look forward to the time when our relations with the communist countries will have improved to the point where trade relations can increase between us.

—*The European Community.* We will watch with great interest the developing relations between the European Community and other nations, some of which have applied for membership. The Community's trade policies will be of increasing importance to our own trade policy in the years ahead.

International Assistance

The International economic successes of the past have been mainly among the industrial nations. The successes of the future must occur at least equally in the economic relations between the industrial nations and the developing world. These new achievements may not be as dramatic as the creation of the Common Market, or the completion of the Kennedy Round of trade negotiations, or the birth of Special Drawing Rights. But the needs are at least as compelling.

There will be a continued requirement for international assistance to developing countries. First, however, we must be clear about what aid can do and what it cannot do. If aid is to be effective, its function must be understood by both donor and recipient.

Economic assistance is not a panacea for international stability, for political development, or even for economic progress. It is, literally, "assistance." It is a means of helping and supplementing the efforts of nations which are able to mobilize the resources and energies of their own people. There are no shortcuts to economic and social progress.

This is a reality, but also a source of hope. For collaborative effort can achieve much. And it is increasingly understood among developed and developing nations that economic development is an international responsibility.

Many of the frustrations and disappointments of development have come not so much from the failure of programs as from the gap between results and expectations. A new understanding of the scope of the challenge and the capacity of programs will help us set feasible goals and then achieve them.

What will be America's part in this effort?

When I came into office, it was clear that our present assistance program did not meet the realities or needs of the 1970s. It was time for a searching reassessment of our objectives and the effectiveness of our institutions. I therefore named a Task Force on International Development, chaired by Mr. Rudolph Peterson, to explore the purposes and methods of our foreign assistance. Its report, due shortly, will provide the foundation for a new American policy.

One truth is already clear: A new American purpose and attitude are required, if our economic assistance is to contribute to development in the new environment of the 1970s. As I stated on October 31 in my address on Latin America: "For years, we in the United States have pursued the illusion that we alone could remake continents. Conscious of our wealth and technology, seized by the force of good intentions, driven by habitual impatience, remembering the dramatic success of the Marshall Plan in postwar Europe, we have sometimes imagined that we knew what was best for everyone else and that we could and should make it happen. Well, experience has taught us better.

"It has taught us that economic and social development is not an achievement of one nation's foreign policy, but something deeply rooted in each nation's own traditions.

"It has taught us that aid that infringes pride is no favor to any nation.

"It has taught us that each nation, and each region, must be true to its own character."

In our reappraisal of the purposes and techniques of foreign assistance, we have already reached several conclusions and we have adopted policies to begin to carry them out:

—*Multilateral institutions must play an increasing role in the provision of aid.* We must enlist the expertise of other countries and of international agencies, thereby minimizing the political and ideological complications which can distort the assistance relationship. We are already contributing to a number of international and regional institutions: the International Development Association, the Inter-American Development Bank, and the Asian Development Bank. I will shortly propose a new U.S. contribution to the Special Funds of the Asian Bank. And I am prepared to respond positively to proposals for replenishment of the resources of the Inter-American Bank and the International Development Association.

—*The developing countries themselves must play a larger part in formulating their own development strategies.* Their own knowledge of the needs must be applied, their own energies mobilized to the tasks. This is the approach I emphasized in my address on Latin America.

—*Our bilateral aid must carry fewer restrictions.* I have therefore eliminated some of the most onerous restrictions on the U.S. aid program and have directed that all remaining restrictions be reviewed with the objective of modifying or eliminating them.

—*Private investment must play a central role in the development process, to whatever extent desired by the developing nations themselves.* I proposed, and Congress has authorized, an Overseas Private Investment Corporation to improve our efforts to make effective use of private capital. And we have given special attention to the developing countries in our relaxation of restraints on foreign investment by U.S. corporations.

—*Trade policy must recognize the special needs of the developing countries.* Trade is a crucial source of new resources for them. Thus, as already described, I have proposed and am urging a worldwide and comprehensive system of tariff preferences for the products of developing nations.

But these are only first steps. We are already considering the proposals of the Pearson Commission on International Development, sponsored by the World Bank. When the report of the Task Force on International Development becomes available, I will propose a fresh American assistance program, more responsive to the conditions of the 1970s.

Our new foreign aid program must distinguish clearly among the various purposes our assistance is designed to serve. Economic development requires sustained effort by donor and recipient alike. Assistance for this purpose will be wasted if—prompted by political considerations—it is deflected by the recipient or the donor to other ends. Similarly, we shall not be putting our own resources to their most productive use if we are unable to ensure continuity in our support.

We must focus on the achievement of our real objective—effective development—rather than on some arbitrary level of financial transfer. We shall need to see that various policies affecting the development process—trade, aid, investment—are fully coordinated. And new institutions will be needed to meet the realities and the challenges of the 1970s.

Thus, our assistance program, like the rest of our foreign policy, will be changed to serve the future rather than simply continued to reflect the habits of the past. We have already begun that change. I expect a new approach to foreign assistance to be one of our major foreign policy initiatives in the coming years.

UNITED NATIONS

> . . . let us press toward an open world—a world of open doors, open hearts, open minds—a world open to the exchange of ideas and of people, and open to the reach of the human spirit—a world open in the search for truth, and unconcerned with the fate of old dogmas and old isms—a world open at last to the light of justice, and the light of reason, and to the achievement of that true peace which the people of every land carry in their hearts and celebrate in their hopes.

> —*The President's Address to the 24th session of the General Assembly, September 18, 1969.*

The United Nations is both a symbol of the worldwide hopes for peace and a reflection of the tensions and conflicts that have frustrated these hopes.

Its friends can now look back with pride on twenty-five years of accomplishment. They also have a responsibility to study and apply the lessons of those years, to see what the UN can and cannot do. The UN, and its supporters, must match idealism in purpose with realism in expectation.

Some of its accomplishments have been highly visible—particularly the various international peacekeeping efforts that have helped to damp down or control local conflicts. Other accomplishments have been quiet but no less important, and deserve greater recognition—such as its promotion of human rights and its extensive economic, social, and technical assistance programs.

The UN provides a forum for crisis diplomacy and a means for multilateral assistance. It has encouraged arms control and helped nations reach agreements extending the frontiers of international law. And it offers a framework for private discussions between world leaders, free of the inflated expectations of summit meetings.

These achievements are impressive. But we have had to recognize that the UN cannot by itself solve fundamental international disputes, especially among the superpowers. Thus, we can as easily undermine the UN by asking too much of it as too little. We cannot expect it to be a more telling force for peace than its members make it. Peace today still depends on the acts of nations.

Last September 18, in my address to the General Assembly, I said: "In this great assembly, the desirability of peace needs no affirmation. The methods of achieving it are what so greatly challenge our courage, our intelligence, our discernment.

"And surely if one lesson above all rings resoundingly among the many shattered hopes in this world, it is that good words are not a substitute for hard deeds and noble rhetoric is no guarantee of noble results."

I then suggested some specific tasks for the near future. These included:

—Securing the safety of international travelers from airplane hijackings, on which the General Assembly has already acted;

—Encouraging international voluntary service, which we stress both at home and in the Peace Corps overseas;

—Fostering the interrelated objectives of economic development and population control;

—Protecting the planet's threatened environment, a major challenge confronting us all, and to which our own nation and people are already addressing new programs and greater energies; and

—Exploring the frontiers of space, an adventure whose excitement and benefits we continue to share with other nations.

In addition, as man's uses of the oceans grow, international law must keep pace. The most pressing issue regarding the law of the sea is the need to achieve agreement on the breadth of the territorial sea, to head off the threat of escalating national claims over the ocean. We also believe it important to make parallel progress toward establishing an internationally agreed boundary between the Continental Shelf and the deep seabeds, and on a regime for exploitation of deep seabed resources..

These are issues that transcend national differences and ideology, and should respond to effective multilateral action.

In an era when man possesses the power both to explore the heavens and desolate the earth, science and technology must be marshaled and shared in the cause of peaceful progress, whatever the political differences among nations. In numerous and varied fields—the peaceful use of atomic energy, the exploration and uses of outer space, the development of the resources of the ocean and the seabeds, the protection of our environment, the uses of satellites, the development of revolutionary transportation systems—we are working with others to channel the products of technological progress to the benefit of mankind.

My speech at the General Asembly underlined this country's continuing support for the organization. My decisions to ask Congress for funds to assist the expansion of the UN's New York Headquarters and to submit to the Senate the UN Convention on Diplomatic Privileges and Immunities are examples of this support.

This year's twenty-fifth anniversary of the United Nations is an occasion for more than commemoration. It is a time to acknowledge its realistic possibilities and to devise ways to expand them. It is a time to set goals for the coming years, particularly in such areas as international peacekeeping, the economic and social programs symbolized by the Second Development Decade, and the new environmental challenges posed by man's technological advances.

As the United Nations begins its second quarter-century, America reaffirms its strong support for the principles and promise begun at San Francisco in 1945. Our task now—as for all UN members—is to help the organization in steady progress toward fulfillment of that promise.

PART III: AMERICA'S STRENGTH

SHAPING OUR MILITARY POSTURE

America's strength is the second pillar of the structure of a durable peace.

We aim for a world in which the importance of power is reduced; where peace is secure because the principal countries wish to maintain it. But this era is not yet here. We cannot entrust our future entirely to the self-restraint of countries that have not hesitated to use their power even against their allies. With respect to national defense, any President has two principal obligations: to be certain that our military preparations do not provide an incentive for aggression, but in such a way that they do not provoke an arms race which might threaten the very security we seek to protect.

A basic review of our defense policy was essential.

In January, 1969, the need for such a review was compelling. Profound changes in the world called for a fresh approach to defense policy just as they required a new approach to foreign policy. In the past technology was relatively stable; in the contemporary world a constantly changing technology produces a new element of insecurity. Formerly, any additional strength was strategically significant; today, available power threatens to outstrip rational objectives.

We had to examine the basic premises underlying our military planning and begin shaping a military posture appropriate to the environment of the 1970s.

We launched a thorough re-examination of past concepts and programs and the alternatives we should consider for the future. The review, which is continuing, produced a reform of both national security policies and decision-making processes which was the most far-reaching in almost two decades.

For the first time the National Security Council has had the opportunity to review a broad and complete range of national strategies for both conventional and strategic forces. This review was undertaken in terms of security and budgetary implications five years into the future. Also for the first time, the relationship of various levels of defense spending to domestic priorities was spelled out in detail for a five-year period.

As a result of this review, our interests, our foreign policy objectives, our strategies, and our defense budgets are being brought into balance—with each other and with our overall national priorities.

Four factors have a special relevance to our continuing reappraisal.

—*Military and Arms Control Issues.* First, we need to ask some fundamental questions to establish the premises for our military posture. For example:

• In shaping our strategic nuclear posture, to what extent should we seek to maintain our security through the development of our strength? To what extent should we adopt unilateral measures of restraint? The judgment is delicate: the former course runs the risk of an arms race, the latter involves the danger of an unfavorable shift in the balance of power.

• How would either course affect the prospects for a meaningful strategic arms limitation agreement with the Soviet Union in the years ahead?

• What spectrum of threats can the United States responsibly deal with? Is it reasonable to seek to protect against every contingency from nuclear conflict to guerrilla wars?

458

—*Forward Planning.* Second, we have to plan ahead. Today's national security decisions must flow from an analysis of their implications well into the future. Many decisions on defense policies and programs will not have operational consequences for several years, in some cases for as much as a decade. Because planning mistakes may not show up for several years, deferral of hard choices is often tempting. But the ultimate penalty may be disastrous. The only responsible course is to face up to our problems and to make decisions in a long-term framework.

—*National Priorities.* Third, we have to weigh our national priorities. We will almost certainly not have the funds to finance the full range of necessary domestic programs in the years ahead if we are to maintain our commitment to non-inflationary economic growth. Defense spending is of course in a special category. It must never fall short of the minimum needed for security. If it does, the problem of domestic programs may become moot. But neither must we let defense spending grow beyond that justified by the defense of our vital interests while domestic needs go unmet.

—*Integrated Planning.* Finally, planning our national security policies and programs in given countries and regions has often been fragmented among agencies. For example, our intelligence analysts, defense planners, economists, and political analysts dealing with a given country may have been using different assumptions about our policy objectives, our expectations about the future, and even the basic facts about our policy choices. There was a need for analyses which would provide a commonly understood set of facts, evaluations, and policy and program choices. These would serve as a basis for consideration by the National Security Council of what we should be doing in given countries and regions.

In summary, we asked the central doctrinal questions; we looked as much as a decade ahead; we weighed our national priorities; and we sought ways of integrating the diverse aspects of our planning. In this fashion, we have reviewed the premises of our military policies, discarded those that no longer serve our interests, and adopted new ones suited to the 1970s. The 1971 defense budget reflects the results of our re-examination, the transition from the old strategies and policies to the new.

THE PROCESS OF DEFENSE PLANNING

This Administration found a defense planning process which left vague the impact of foreign policy on our military posture and provided an inadequate role for other agencies with a major stake in military issues. And it did little to relate defense and domestic priorities.

We set out to correct these deficiencies.

Insuring Balanced Decisions

Virtually very major defense issue has complex diplomatic, political, strategic, and economic implications. To ensure balanced decisions, we see to it that every agency has a full opportunity to contribute. The Director of the Arms Control and Disarmament Agency participates in deliberations on defense policy decisions that affect arms control prospects. In turn, the Secretary of Defense and the Joint Chiefs of Staff participate directly in the evaluation of arms control proposals. The Departments of State and Defense review with the Bureau of the Budget and the Council of Economic Advisers economic conditions that influence the magnitude of defense spending. The Department of State examines with Defense officials issues that affect our relationships with allies.

These interagency exchanges ensure that I receive all views on key national security issues. Disagreements are identified and explored, not suppressed or papered over. The full range of choices is presented.

Setting Rational Priorities

Our great wealth and productive capacity still do not enable us to pursue every worthwhile national objective with unlimited means. Choices among defense strategies and budgets have a great impact on the extent to which we can pursue other national goals.

We have no precise way of measuring whether extra dollars spent for defense are more important than extra dollars spent for other needs. But we can and have described the domestic programs that are consistent with various levels of defense expenditures. The National Security Council thus has a basis for making intelligent choices concerning the allocation of available revenue among priority federal programs. I do not believe any previous President has had the benefit of such a comprehensive picture of the interrelationships among the goals he can pursue within the limits of the federal budget.

As a result, I have decided on defense strategy and budget guidelines for the next five years that are consistent not only with our national security and the maintenance of our commitments but with our national priorities as well. This Administration is now in a position to weigh the impact of future changes in defense policies and programs on the whole fabric of government objectives.

Controlling the Defense Posture—The Defense Program Review Committee

To meet the objective of balanced decisions and rational priorities, we made a basic addition to the National Security Council system. I directed the formation of the Defense Program Review Committee, consisting of the Assistant to the President for National Security Affairs (Chairman), the Under Secretary of State, the Deputy Secretary of Defense, the Chairman of the Joint Chiefs of Staff, the Director of the Bureau of the Budget, the Director of Central Intelligence, and the Chairman of the Council of Economic Advisers. The Director of the Arms Control and Disarmament Agency, the President's Science Adviser, and the Chairman of the Atomic Energy Commission participate as appropriate.

This permanent Committee reviews major defense, fiscal, policy, and program issues in terms of their strategic, diplomatic, political, and economic implications, and advises me and the National Security Council on its findings. For example, the Committee analyzed our options for proceeding with ballistic missile defenses on four separate occasions. This year it will analyze our major strategic and fiscal choices over the next five years, together with the doctrinal, diplomatic, and strategic implications of key weapons programs. It will do so while the defense budget for fiscal year 1972 is still in the earliest stages of formulation. The participation in this review by the Department of

State, the Arms Control and Disarmament Agency, the Council of Economic Advisers, and other agencies ensures that careful analysis and balanced evaluations will be available when the National Security Council next fall reviews our choices for 1972 and beyond.

Country and Regional Analysis and Program Budgeting

A major obstacle to the implementation of a consistent and coherent foreign policy is the multitude of the U.S. agencies and programs involved in activities in any one country or region. In the past it has been difficult for the President or the National Security Council to obtain a picture of the totality of our effort in any one country. Yet a rational foreign policy must start with such a comprehensive view.

To overcome this difficulty we have begun a series of country program analyses which will examine all U.S. programs in key countries and regions and their interrelationships.

The studies for the first time put every U.S. program into one budget framework. The basic tool for this analysis is the program budget, which allocates all of our expenditures in a country on the basis of the purposes served. It permits us to make decisions or set guidelines for all of our programs simultaneously; in the past, they were examined largely agency by agency in isolation from one another.

The results of the country analysis studies are presented to the NSC in the form of integrated policy and program options based on alternative statements of interest, threats, and U.S. foreign policy objectives. After the NSC has considered these options, a decision can be made about the course of action to follow over the next several years.

Of course, our efforts start from the clearly understood fundamental premise that U.S. policies and programs must relate in a logical and meaningful fashion to what our friends and allies wish to do for themselves. We are dealing with sovereign nations each of which has its own interests, its own priorities, and its own capabilities. All that our country programming is designed to do is to make our actions as effective as they can be, consistent with our mutual interests.

I am convinced that such a comprehensive approach to country programs will lead to decidedly improved foreign policy. We are conscious of the need not only to make sound policy decisions but also to execute them. The country analysis studies will result in both a decision document for all government agencies and firm five-year program guidelines, presented in the form of a program budget. The members of the NSC, as well as the country director in every agency and our ambassadors in the field, then have a means of making sure that our decisions are followed up.

STRATEGIC POLICY

The Changing Strategic Balance

Following World War II, the U.S. had a monopoly of strategic nuclear weapons. Throughout most of the 1950s our virtual monopoly of intercontinental nuclear delivery capability, in the form of a large force of Strategic Air Command bombers, gave us an overwhelming deterrent.

This assessment was unchallenged until it became apparent in the late 1950s that the Soviet Union possessed the potential for developing and deploying a force of intercontinental ballistic missiles that could destroy a large part of our strategic bomber force on the ground. The fear that our deterrent to nuclear war was in grave jeopardy, though it later proved exaggerated, focused our attention on maintaining our nuclear superiority.

In 1961 the new Administration accelerated our Polaris submarine and Minuteman ICBM programs and put more of our strategic bombers on alert. These measures provided a clear margin of U.S. nuclear superiority for several years. They restored our confidence in our deterrent; we now had two forces, our Polaris submarines and our Minuteman ICBMs deployed in hardened underground silos, that were virtually invulnerable to attack by the Soviet Union with the then existing technology.

However, after 1965, the Soviets stepped up their ICBM deployments and began to construct their own force of Polaris-type submarines. And they began to test multiple warheads for their SS-9 ICBM, a weapon which can carry roughly ten times as much as our Minuteman missile.

Once again U.S. strategic superiority was being challenged. However, this time the Johnson Administration decided not to step up deployments. This restraint was based on two judgments. First, it was believed that there was relatively little we could do to keep the Soviets from developing over a period of time a strategic posture comparable in capability to our own. Second, it was thought that nuclear superiority of the kind we had previously enjoyed would have little military or political significance because our retaliatory capability was not seriously jeopardized by larger Soviet forces and because their goal was in all likelihood a retaliatory capability similar to ours.

As a result of these developments an inescapable reality of the 1970s is the Soviet Union's possession of powerful and sophisticated strategic forces approaching and, in some categories, exceeding ours in numbers and capability.

Recent Soviet programs have emphasized both quantitative increases in offensive and defensive forces and qualitative improvements in the capabilities of these forces—such as a new, more accurate warhead and perhaps penetration aids for their Minuteman-type SS-11 missile, continued testing of the multiple warhead for the SS-9, and research and development on improved components for their ABM system, together with improved coverage by their ABM radars. The following table shows the growth in Soviet land- and submarine-based missile forces in the last five years.

OPERATIONAL UNITED STATES AND SOVIET MISSILES

	1965 (Midyear)	1970 (Projected) (For year end)
Intercontinental Ballistic Missiles:		
United States	934	1,054
Soviet	224	1,290
Submarine Launched Ballistic Missiles:		
United States	464	656
Soviet	107	300

The Soviet missile deployments are continuing, whereas ours have leveled off. In the 1970s we must also expect to see Communist China deploy intercontinental ballistic missiles, seriously complicating strategic planning and diplomacy.

The evolution of U.S. and Soviet strategic capabilities during the past two decades was accompanied by intense doctrinal debates over the political and military roles of strategic forces and the appropriate criteria for choosing them.

The strategic doctrine that had gained the greatest acceptance by the time my Administration took office was this: According to the theory of "assured destruction," deterrence was guaranteed if we were sure we could destroy a significant percentage of Soviet population and industry after the worst conceivable Soviet attack on our strategic forces. The previous Administration reasoned that since we had more than enough forces for this purpose, restraint in the build-up of strategic weapons was indicated, regardless of Soviet actions. Further, it hoped that U.S. restraint in strategic weapons developments and deployments would provide a strong incentive for similar restraint by the Soviet Union, thus enhancing the likelihood of a stable strategic relationship between the two nuclear superpowers.

A Policy for the 1970s

Once in office, I concluded that this strategic doctrine should be carefully reviewed in the light of the continued growth of Soviet strategic capabilities. Since the Soviets were continuing their ambitious strategic weapons program, we had to ask some basic questions. Why might a nuclear war start or be threatened? In this light, what U.S. strategic capabilities are needed for deterrence?

We sought, in short, a strategic goal that can best be termed "sufficiency."

Our review took full account of two factors that have not existed in the past.

First, the Soviets present build-up of strategic forces, together with what we know about their development and test programs, raises serious questions about where they are headed and the potential threats we and our allies face. These questions must be faced soberly and realistically.

Second, the growing strategic forces on both sides pose new and disturbing problems. Should a President, in the event of a nuclear attack, be left with the single option of ordering the mass destruction of enemy civilians, in the face of the certainty that it would be followed by the mass slaughter of Americans? Should the concept of assured destruction be narrowly defined and should it be the only measure of our ability to deter the variety of threats we may face?

Our review produced general agreement that the overriding purpose of our strategic posture is political and defensive: to deny other countries the ability to impose their will on the United States and its allies under the weight of strategic military superiority. We must ensure that all potential aggressors see unacceptable risks in contemplating a nuclear attack, or nuclear blackmail, or acts which could escalate to strategic nuclear war, such as a Soviet conventional attack on Europe.

Beyond this general statement, our primary task was to decide on the yardsticks that should be used in evaluating the adequacy of our strategic forces against the projected threats. This issue took on added importance because such yardsticks would be needed for assessing the desirability of possible strategic arms limitation agreements with the Soviet Union.

We reached general agreement within the government on four specific criteria for strategic sufficiency. These represent a significant intellectual advance. They provide for both adequacy and flexibility. They will be constantly reviewed in the light of a changing technology.

Designing Strategic Forces

Having settled on a statement of strategic purposes and criteria, we analyzed possible U.S. strategic force postures for the 1970s and beyond. We reviewed alternatives ranging from "minimum deterrence"—a posture built around ballistic missile submarines and the assured destruction doctrine narrowly interpreted—to attempts at recapturing numerical superiority through accelerated U.S. strategic deployments across the board.

There was general agreement that postures which significantly reduced or increased our strategic programs and deployments involved undesirable risks:

—*Sharp cutbacks would not permit us to satisfy our sufficiency criteria, and might provoke the opposite Soviet reaction.* If the U.S. unilaterally dropped out of the strategic arms competition, the Soviets might well seize the opportunity to step up their programs and achieve a significant margin of strategic superiority. The vigor and breadth of their current strategic weapons programs and deployments, which clearly exceed the requirements of minimum deterrence, make such a possibility seem far from remote. This might also—paradoxically—eliminate any Soviet incentives for an agreement to limit strategic arms, and would raise serious concerns among our allies. This is particularly true for our NATO allies who view the U.S. commitment to deter Soviet aggression as being based mainly on our maintenance of a powerful strategic posture.

—*Sharp increases, on the other hand, might not have any significant political or military benefits.* Many believe that the Soviets would seek to offset our actions, at least in part, and that Soviet political positions would harden, tensions would increase, and the prospect for reaching agreements to limit strategic arms might be irreparably damaged.

What ultimately we must do in between these extremes will depend, of course, on many factors. Will the Soviets continue to expand their strategic forces? What will be their configuration? What understanding might we reach on strategic arms limitations? What weapons systems might be covered by agreements?

I recognize that decisions on shaping our strategic posture are perhaps the most complex and fateful we face. The answers to these questions will largely determine whether we will be forced into increased deployments to offset the Soviet threat to the sufficiency of our deterrent, or whether we and the Soviet Union can together move from an era of confrontation to one of negotiation, whether jointly we can pursue responsible, nonprovocative strategic arms policies based on sufficiency as a mutually shared goal or whether there will be another round of the arms race.

The Role of Ballistic Missile Defense

My decision to continue with the construction of the Safeguard anti-ballistic missile system is fully consistent with our criteria and with our goal of effective arms limitation.

I would like to recall what I said last March about the problem that led us to seek approval of the first phase of the Safeguard program: "The gravest responsibility which I bear as President of the United States is for the security of the nation. Our nuclear forces defend not only ourselves but our allies as well. The imperative that our nuclear deterrent remain secure beyond any possible doubt requires that the U.S. must take steps now to ensure that our strategic retaliatory forces will not become vulnerable to a Soviet attack."

I believed then, and I am even more convinced today, that there is a serious threat to our retaliatory capability in the form of the growing Soviet forces of ICBMs and ballistic missile submarines, their multiple warhead program for the SS-9 missile, their apparent interest in improving the accuracy of their ICBM warheads, and their development of a semiorbital nuclear weapon system. That this threat continues to be serious was confirmed by my Foreign Intelligence Advisory Board—an independent bipartisan group of senior outside advisers—which recently completed its own review of the strategic threats we face.

I pointed out in the same statement that we cannot ignore the potential Chinese threat against the U.S. population, as well as the danger of an accidental or unauthorized attack from any source. Nor can we dismiss the possibility that other countries may in the future acquire the capability to attack the U.S. with nuclear weapons. Today any nuclear attack—no matter how small; whether accidental, unauthorized, or by design, by a superpower or by a country with only a primitive nuclear delivery capability—would be a catastrophe for the U.S., no matter how devastating our ability to retaliate.

No Administration with the responsibility for the lives and security of the American people could fail to provide every possible protection against such eventualities.

Thus on March 14, 1969, I stated the objectives of the Safeguard program:

"This measured deployment is designed to fulfill three objectives:

"1. Protection of our land-based retaliatory forces against a direct attack by the Soviet Union.

"2. Defense of the American people against the kind of nuclear attack which Communist China is likely to be able to mount within the decade.

"3. Protection against the possibility of accidental attacks from any source."

I further described the system as follows: "We will provide for local defense of selected Minuteman missile sites and an area defense designed to protect our bomber bases and our command and control authorities. In addition, this new system will provide a defense of the Continental United States against an accidental attack and will provide substantial protection against the kind of attack which the Chinese Communists may be capable of launching throughout the 1970s. This deployment will not require us to place missile and radar sites close to our major cities."

Last year I promised that "each phase of the deployment will be reviewed to ensure that we are doing as much as necessary but no more than that required by the threat existing at that time." I further indicated that in strategic arms limitation talks with the Soviet Union the United States will be fully prepared to discuss limitations on defensive as well as offensive weapons systems.

The further steps I shall propose will be consistent with these pledges. The Secretary of Defense will put forward a minimum program essential for our security. It fully protects our flexibility in discussing, limitations on defensive weapons with the Soviet Union. It is my duty as President to make certain that we do no less.

GENERAL PURPOSE FORCES

When I examined the objectives established for our general purpose forces, I concluded that we must emphasize three fundamental premises of a sound defense policy:

First, while strategic forces must deter *all* threats of general war no matter what the cost, our general purpose forces must be more sensitively related to local situations and particular interests.

Second, while the possession of 95 percent of the nuclear power of the non-communist world gives us the primary responsibility for nuclear defense, the planning of general purpose forces must take into account the fact that the manpower of our friends greatly exceeds our own, as well as our heavy expenditures for strategic forces.

Third, we cannot expect U.S. military forces to cope with the entire spectrum of threats facing allies or potential allies throughout the world. This is particularly true of subversion and guerrilla warfare, or "wars of national liberation." Experience has shown that the best means of dealing with insurgencies is to preempt them through economic development and social reform and to control them with police, paramilitary, and military action by the threatened government.

We may be able to supplement local efforts with economic and military assistance. However, a direct combat role for U.S. general purpose forces arises primarily when insurgency has shaded into external aggression or when there is an overt conventional attack. In such cases we shall weigh our interests and our commitments, and we shall consider the efforts of our allies, in determining our response.

The United States has interests in defending certain land areas abroad as well as essential air and sea lines of communication. These derive from:

—The political and economic importance of our alliances;

—Our desire to prevent or contain hostilities which could lead to major conflicts and thereby endanger world peace; and

—The strategic value of the threatened area as well as its line of communications.

The military posture review I initiated the day I took office included a thorough examination of our general purpose forces. This study explored in turn our interests, the potential threats to those interests, the capabilities of our allies both with and without our assistance, and the relationship of various strategies to domestic priorities.

The National Security Council examined five different strategies for general purpose forces and related each one to the domestic programs which could be supported simultaneously. Thus, for the first time, national security and domestic priorities were considered together. In fact, two strategies were rejected because they were not considered essential to our security and because they would have thwarted vital domestic programs.

We finally decided on a strategy which represented a significant modification of the doctrine that characterized the 1960s.

The stated basis of our conventional posture in the 1960s was the so-called "2½ war" principle. According to it, U.S. forces would be maintained for a three-month conventional forward defense of NATO, a defense of Korea or Southeast Asia against a full-scale Chinese attack, and a minor contingency—all simultaneously. These force levels were never reached.

In the effort to harmonize doctrine and capability, we chose what is best described as the "1½ war" strategy. Under it we will maintain in peacetime general purpose forces adequate for simultaneously meeting a major communist attack in either Europe or Asia, assisting allies against non-Chinese threats in Asia, and contending with a contingency elsewhere.

The choice of this strategy was based on the following considerations:

—The nuclear capability of our strategic and theater nuclear forces serves as a deterrent to full-scale Soviet attack on NATO Europe or Chinese attack on our Asian allies;

—The prospects for a coordinated two-front attack on our allies by Russia and China are low both because of the risks of nuclear war and the improbability of Sino-Soviet cooperation. In any event, we do not believe that such a coordinated attack should be met primarily by U.S. conventional forces;

—The desirability of ensuring against greater than expected threats by maintaining more than the forces required to meet conventional threats in one theater—such as NATO Europe;

—Weakness on our part would be more provocative than continued U.S. strength, for it might encourage others to take dangerous risks, to resort to the illusion that military adventurism could succeed.

To meet the requirements for the strategy we adopted, we will maintain the required ground and supporting tactical air forces in Europe and Asia, together with naval and air forces. At the same time, we will retain adequate active forces in addition to a full complement of reserve forces based in the United States. These force levels will be spelled out in greater detail in the program and budget statement of the Secretary of Defense.

"We cannot expect to make everyone our friend but we can try to make no one our enemy."
—*The President's Inaugural Address*

Twenty years ago the United States and what was then the communist bloc could be resigned to the mutual hostility that flowed from deep-seated differences of ideology and national purpose. Many of those differences remain today. But the changes of two decades have brought new conditions and magnified the risks of intractable hostility.

—For us as well as our adversaries in the nuclear age the perils of using force are simply not in reasonable proportion to most of the objectives sought in many cases. The balance of nuclear power has placed a premium on negotiation rather than confrontation.

—We both have learned too that great powers may find their interests deeply involved in local conflict—risking confrontation—yet have precariously little influence over the direction taken by local forces.

—The nuclear age has also posed for the United States and the communist countries the common dangers of accidents or miscalculation. Both sides are threatened, for example, when any power seeks tactical advantage from a crisis and risks provoking a strategic response.

—Reality has proved different from expectation for both sides. The communist world in particular has had to learn that the spread of communism may magnify international tensions rather than usher in a period of reconciliation as Marx taught.

Thus, in a changing world, building peace requires patient and continuing communication. Our first task in that dialogue is fundamental—to avert war. Beyond that, the United States and the communist countries must negotiate on the issues that divide them if we are to build a durable peace. Since these issues were not caused by personal disagreements, they cannot be removed by mere atmospherics. We do not delude ourselves that a change of tone represents a change of policy. We are prepared to deal seriously, concretely, and precisely with outstanding issues.

The lessons of the postwar period in negotiations with the communist states—a record of some success, though much more of frustration—point to three clear principles which this Administration will observe in approaching negotiations in the 1970s.

First: We will deal with the communist countries on the basis of a precise understanding of what they are about in the world, and thus of what we can reasonably expect of them and ourselves. Let us make no mistake about it— leaders of the communist nations are serious and determined. Because we do take them seriously, we will not underestimate the depth of ideological disagreement or the disparity between their interests and ours. Nor will we pretend that agreement is imminent by fostering the illusion that they have already given up their beliefs or are just about to do so in the process of negotiations.

It is precisely these differences which require creation of objective conditions—negotiation by negotiation—from which peace can develop despite a history of mistrust and rivalry. We may hope that the passage of time and the emergence of a new generation in the communist countries will bring some change in communist purposes. But failing that we must seek in the most practical way to influence communist actions.

470

It will be the policy of the United States, therefore, not to employ negotiations as a forum for Cold War invective or ideological debate. We will regard our communist adversaries first and foremost as nations pursuing their own interests as *they* perceive these interests, just as we follow our own interests as we see them. We will judge them by their actions as we expect to be judged by our own. Specific agreements, and the structure of peace they help build, will come from a realistic accommodation of conflicting interests.

A second principle we shall observe in negotiating with the communist countries relates to how these negotiations should be conducted—how they should be judged by peoples on both sides anxious for an easing of tensions. All too often in the past, whether at the summit or lower levels, we have come to the conference table with more attention to psychological effect than to substance. Naïve enthusiasm and even exultation about the fact that a negotiation will be held only tends to obscure the real issues on whose resolution the success of the talks depends. Then, since the results are almost always less dramatic than expected, the false euphoria gives way to equally false hopelessness.

Negotiations must be, above all, the result of careful preparation and an authentic give-and-take on the issues which have given rise to them. They are served by neither bluff abroad nor bluster at home.

We will not become psychologically dependent on rapid or extravagant progress. Nor will we be discouraged by frustration or seeming failure. The stakes are too high, and the task too great, to judge our effort in any temporary perspective. We shall match our purpose with perseverance.

The third essential in successful negotiations is an appreciation of the context in which issues are addressed. The central fact here is the interrelationship of international events. We did not invent the interrelationship; it is not a negotiating tactic. It is a fact of life. This Administration recognizes that international developments are entwined in many complex ways: political issues relate to strategic questions, political events in one area of the world may have a far-reaching effect on political developments in other parts of the globe.

These principles emphasize a realistic approach to seeking peace through negotiations. They are a guide to a gradual and practical process of building agreement on agreement. They rest upon the basic reality which underlies this Administration's dealings with the communist states. We will not trade principles for promises, or vital interests for atmosphere. We shall always be ready to talk seriously and purposefully about the building of a stable peace.

THE SOVIET UNION

The general principles outlined above apply fully to our approach to issues between the United States and the Soviet Union.

The Soviet Union shares with other countries the overwhelming temptation to continue to base its policies at home and abroad on old and familiar concepts. But perceptions framed in the nineteenth century are hardly relevant to the new era we are now entering.

If we have had to learn the limitations of our own power, the lessons of the last decades must have left their imprint on the leadership in the Kremlin—in the recognition that Marxist ideology is not the surest guide to the problems of a changing industrial society, the worldwide decline in the appeal of ideology, and most of all in the foreign policy dilemmas repeatedly posed by the spread of communism to states which refuse to endure permanent submission to Soviet authority—a development illustrated vividly by the Soviet schism with China.

The central problem of Soviet-American relations, then, is whether our two countries can transcend the past and work together to build a lasting peace.

In 1969 we made a good beginning. In this first year of my Administration we ratified the Non-Proliferation Treaty; we made progress in negotiating arms control on the seabed; we took steps to further the prospects of agreement regarding chemical and biological methods of warfare; we engaged in talks on a Middle Eastern settlement; and we began negotiations on the limitation of strategic arms—the most important arms control negotiations this country has ever entered. In concert with our allies, we have also offered to negotiate on specific issues in Europe: History has taught us that if crises arise in Europe, the world at large cannot long expect to remain unaffected.

But while certain successes have been registered in negotiations and there is cause for cautious optimism that others will follow, our overall relationship with the U.S.S.R. remains far from satisfactory. To the detriment of the cause of peace, the Soviet leadership has failed to exert a helpful influence on the North Vietnamese in Paris. The overwhelming majority of the war matériel that reaches North Vietnam comes from the U.S.S.R., which thereby bears a heavy responsibility for the continuation of the war. This cannot but cloud the rest of our relationship with the Soviet Union.

In the Middle East talks, too, we have not seen on the Soviet side that practical and constructive flexibility which is necessary for a successful outcome, and without which the responsibility of the great powers in the search for a settlement cannot be met. We see evidence, moreover, that the Soviet Union seeks a position in the area as a whole which would make great power rivalry more likely.

We hope that the coming year will bring evidence that the Soviets have decided to seek a durable peace rather than continue along the roads of the past.

It will not be the sincerity or purpose of the Soviet leadership that will be at issue. The tensions between us are not generated by personal misunderstandings, and neither side does anyone a service by so suggesting. Peace does not come simply with statesmen's smiles. At issue are basic questions of long conflicting purposes in a world where no one's interests are furthered by conflict. Only a straightforward recognition of that reality—and an equally direct effort to deal with it—will bring us to the genuine cooperation which we seek and which the peace of the world requires.

EASTERN EUROPE

The nations of Eastern Europe have a history with many tragic aspects. Astride the traditional invasion routes of the Continent, they have suffered long periods of foreign occupation and cultural suppression. And even when they gained independence—many of them following World War I—they remained the prey of powerful neighbors.

We are aware that the Soviet Union sees its own security as directly affected by developments in this region. Several times, over the centuries, Russia has been invaded through Central Europe; so this sensitivity is not novel, or purely the product of communist dogma.

It is not the intention of the United States to undermine the legitimate security interests of the Soviet Union. The time is certainly past, with the development of modern technology, when any power would seek to exploit Eastern Europe to obtain strategic advantage against the Soviet Union. It is clearly no part of our policy. Our pursuit of negotiation and détente is meant to reduce existing tensions, not to stir up new ones.

By the same token, the United States views the countries of Eastern Europe as sovereign, not as parts of a monolith. And we can accept no doctrine that abridges their right to seek reciprocal improvement of relations with us or others.

We are prepared to enter into negotiations with the nations of Eastern Europe, looking to a gradual normalization of relations. We will adjust ourselves to whatever pace and extent of normalization these countries are willing to sustain.

Progress in this direction has already been achieved in our relations with Romania. My visit to that country last summer—which will remain unforgettable for me in human terms—set in motion a series of cooperative programs in the economic, technical, scientific, and cultural fields. We intend to pursue these with vigor. My talks with President Ceausescu also began the process of exchanging views on broader questions of mutual concern which, in our view, will contribute to a general improvement of the communication between West and East. A similar relationship is open to any communist country that wishes to enter it.

Stability and peace in Europe will be enhanced once its division is healed. The United States, and the nations of Western Europe, have historic ties with the peoples and nations of Eastern Europe, which we wish to maintain and renew.

As I said in my toast to President Ceausescu during my visit to Romania last August: "We seek, in sum, a peace not of hegemonies, and not of artificial uniformity, but a peace in which the legitimate interests of each are respected and all are safeguarded."

COMMUNIST CHINA

The Chinese are a great and vital people who should not remain isolated from the international community. In the long run, no stable and enduring international order is conceivable without the contribution of this nation of more than 700 million people.

Chinese foreign policy reflects the complexity of China's historical relationships with the outside world. While China has the longest unbroken history of self-government in the world, it has had little experience in dealing with other nations on a basis of equal sovereignty. Predominant in Asia for many centuries, these gifted and cultured people saw their society as the center of the world. Their tradition of self-imposed cultural isolation ended abrupty in the nineteenth century, however, when an internally weak China fell prey to exploitation by technologically superior foreign powers.

The history inherited by the Chinese Communists, therefore, was a complicated mixture of isolation and incursion, of pride and humiliation. We must recall this unique past when we attempt to define a new relationship for the future.

Nor can we underestimate the gulf of ideology between us, or the apparent differences in interests and how we interpret world events. While America has historic ties of friendship with the Chinese people, and many of our basic interests are not in conflict, we must recognize the profound gulf of suspicion and ideology.

The principles underlying our relations with Communist China are similar to those governing our policies toward the U.S.S.R. United States policy is not likely soon to have much impact on China's behavior, let alone its ideological outlook. But it is certainly in our interest, and in the interest of peace and stability in Asia and the world, that we take what steps we can toward improved practical relations with Peking.

The key to our relations will be the actions each side takes regarding the other and its allies. We will not ignore hostile acts. We intend to maintain our treaty commitment to the defense of the Republic of China. But we will seek to promote understandings which can establish a new pattern of mutually beneficial actions.

I made these points to the leaders I met throughout my trip to Asia, and they were welcomed as constructive and realistic.

We have avoided dramatic gestures which might invite dramatic rebuffs. We have taken specific steps that did not require Chinese agreement but which underlined our willingness to have a more normal and constructive relationship. During the year, we have:

—Made it possible for American tourists, museums, and others to make non-commercial purchases of Chinese goods without special authorization;

—Broadened the categories of Americans whose passports may be automatically validated for travel in Communist China, to include members of Congress, journalists, teachers, postgraduate scholars and college students, scientists, medical doctors, and representatives of the American Red Cross;

—Permitted subsidiaries of American firms abroad to engage in commerce between Communist China and third countries.

The resumption of talks with the Chinese in Warsaw may indicate that our approach will prove useful. These first steps may not lead to major results at once, but sooner or later Communist China will be ready to re-enter the international community.

Our desire for improved relations is not a tactical means of exploiting the clash between China and the Soviet Union. We see no benefit to us in the intensification of that conflict, and we have no intention of taking sides. Nor is the United States interested in joining any condominium or hostile coalition of great powers against either of the large communist countries. Our attitude is clear-cut—a lasting peace will be impossible so long as some nations consider themselves the permanent enemies of others.

ARMS CONTROL

There is no area in which we and the Soviet Union—as well as others —have a greater common interest than in reaching agreement with regard to arms control.

The traditional course of seeking security primarily through military strength raises several problems in a world of multiplying strategic weapons.

—Modern technology makes any balance precarious and prompts new efforts at ever higher levels of complexity.

—Such an arms race absorbs resources, talents, and energies.

—The more intense the competition, the greater the uncertainty about the other sides's inten'ions.

—The higher the level of armaments, the greater the violence and devastation should deterrence fail.

For these reasons I decided early in the Administration that we should seek to maintain our security whenever possible through cooperative efforts with other nations at the lowest possible level of uncertainty, cost, and potential violence.

Our careful preparations for the Strategic Arms Limitation Talks (SALT) with the Soviet Union were designed to achieve this objective.

Preparations for SALT

Our immediate problem was to determine what measures would be most practical in slowing the momentum of armament and working out a procedure most likely to yield useful discussions.

In preparing for these negotiations, we were tempted to follow the traditional pattern of settling on one agreed position and launching discussions with the other side on this basis. We could have adopted the specific package proposal developed by the previous Administration or we could have quickly formulated an alternative plan. In my judgment there were two major problems with this approach.

First, I was convinced that we lacked the comprehensive and detailed body of facts and analyses to take account of the most recent developments in Soviet and U.S. strategic programs.

Second, we would have been engaged in a negotiating process—with the inevitable investment of prestige—before either side had defined its purposes. There was a danger of turning SALT into a tactical exercise or even more the kind of propaganda battle characteristic of some previous disarmament conferences.

Too much depended on these talks, for our nation and all mankind, to rush into them partially prepared. We decided that a clarification of objectives and factual data would allow us to discuss proposals in a coherent framework, and ultimately speed up negotiations. We assumed further that if the other side had a serious interest in exploring the possibilities of strategic arms limitations, they would have a joint interest with us to analyze the issues which would have to be resolved before a satisfactory agreement could be reached. For an agreement to limit strategic arms can be lasting only if it enhances the sense of security of *both* sides. It is in the mutual interest therefore to clarify each other's intentions.

Therefore, instead of attempting to hammer out an agreed government position or a simple proposal, we chose a different course.

We first laid out preliminary models of possible strategic arms limitation agreements. We compared these both with each other and with the situation most likely to prevail in the absence of an agreement. This process greatly improved our understanding of the types of agreements we should consider and pointed up some of the fundamental issues. In order to resolve these issues, I directed the formation of a Verification Panel to examine the verification aspects and strategic implications of curbs on individual weapons systems and then combinations of them.

The Panel took each strategic weapons system in isolation (e.g., ICBMs or ABMs) and explored all the issues that would be involved in its limitation. We knew that any agreement had to be verified and we knew too the reluctance of the Soviet Union to accept on-site inspection. The Verification Panel therefore analyzed in detail what we could do unilaterally. Specifically, it surveyed our intelligence capability to monitor the other side's compliance with a curb for each weapon system; the precise activities that would have to be restricted to ensure confidence in the effectiveness of the limitation; and the impact of the limitation on U.S. and Soviet strategic weapons programs.

The analysis of our capability to verify individual weapons systems provided the building blocks for analyzing various combinations of limitations. These building blocks were combined in various positions which can be grouped in three general categories. This will enable us to respond to a broad range of Soviet proposals. These categories are:

1. *Limitations on numbers of missiles.* A ceiling would be placed on numbers of missiles without an attempt to restrain qualitative improvements like MIRV (multiple independently targeted re-entry vehicles). In general, these options would stop the growth of some or all strategic missile forces. They would not change the qualitative race.

2. *Limitations on numbers and capabilities of missiles.* These options would not only limit the numbers of missiles but also their capabilities, including qualitative controls over such weapons as MIRVs. The hard issues here center around verification since the determination of quality requires a more intensive inspection than quantity.

3. *Reduce offensive forces.* This approach would attempt to reduce the number of offensive forces without qualitative restrictions on the theory that at fixed and lower levels of armaments the risks of technological surprise would be reduced.

Each of these options was analyzed in relation to various levels of strategic defensive missiles, ABMs.

The manner in which these studies were carried out contributed to their scope and their success. Discussions explored substantive issues rather than exchanging rigidly defined bureaucratic positions. Consistent with the overall philosophy of the NSC system, we focused on comprehensive assessments of the issues and alternatives rather than on attainable compromises. This presented me with clear choices, clear disagreements, and clear rationales. In the process we established a comprehensive inventory of the possibilities of a wide range of limitations. This should greatly enhance our flexibility in the forthcoming negotiations.

The SALT negotiations involve fundamental security issues for our NATO allies, as well as Japan. We have fully consulted them, engaging their views and expertise at every stage of the process. In July we discussed in great detail the relationship of SALT to the overall strategic balance with our allies and we presented the various options as we saw them then. In early November we consulted in greater detail on our approach to the first phase of SALT. We intend to continue to work closely with our allies as the negotiations continue. We consider our security inseparable from theirs.

This process involved the most intensive study of strategic arms problems ever made by this or any other government. And this process had several advantages. We were not tied to a single position; instead we had building blocks for several different positions depending on our decisions and what might prove negotiable. Opening talks with the Soviets could concentrate on the principles and objectives underlying *any* type of strategic arms agreement.

Preliminary talks in Helsinki opened November 17 and continued until December 22. Our experience there confirmed the validity of our approach. The discussions were serious and businesslike. The Soviet representatives demonstrated considerable preparation. They also seemed to welcome the "building block" approach. We were able to develop an agreed work program for further discussions without acrimony and in full awareness of the likely nature of such discussions. Above all, we could explore each other's purposes without getting bogged down in negotiating details.

From a discussion of basic principles and objectives we plan to move in April in Vienna to more specific positions. We enter this next phase with a well-developed body of technical analysis and evaluations which is being continuously expanded and improved by the Verification Panel and the NSC process. And we will make a determined effort throughout these negotiations to reach agreements that will not only protect our national security but actually enhance it.

Chemical and Biological Weapons

We are prepared to take any unilateral arms control action that will not compromise our security and will minimize the danger that certain weapons will ever be developed or used by any nation. A good example is the field of chemical and biological weapons. After extensive study, I determined that a new American policy would strengthen ongoing multilateral efforts to restrict the use of these weapons by international law. We hope that other nations will follow our example and restrict their own programs unilaterally.

When I took office, the chemical and biological defense programs of the United States had gone unexamined and unanalyzed by policy makers for fifteen years. I directed a comprehensive NSC system review of the premises, issues, and technical details involved. This major six-month study was the first thorough reassessment of this subject that had ever taken place at the Presidential level. After a National Security Council meeting in early November, I announced my specific decisions on November 25:

—*Chemical Warfare.* First, I reaffirmed the long-standing policy that the United States will never be the first to use lethal chemicals in any conflict.

Second, I extended this policy to include incapacitating chemical weapons. Third, I am submitting the 1925 Geneva Protocol—which prohibits the use of chemical and biological weapons in warfare—to the Senate for its advice and consent to ratification.

—*Biological Research.* I declared that the United States is renouncing biological warfare, since biological warfare would have massive, unpredictable, and potentially uncontrollable consequences. The United States will not engage in the development, procurement, or stockpiling of biological weapons. We shall restrict our biological program to research for defensive purposes, strictly defined—such as techniques of immunization, safety measures, and the control and prevention of the spread of disease. The United States has associated itself with the objectives of the United Kingdom draft convention banning the use of biological weapons, submitted to the Conference of the Committee on Disarmament at Geneva in 1969.

In addition, on February 14, 1970, the United States renounced offensive preparations for the use of toxins as a method of warfare. We declared that we will confine our military programs for toxins to research for defensive purposes only, and announced that all existing toxin weapons and stocks of toxins which are not required for this research would be destroyed. Although the UN Secretary General and World Health Organization have declared that toxins are chemicals, they produce effects commonly described as disease, and are produced by facilities similar to those needed for the production of biological agents. Hence we decided to remove any ambiguity in the interest of progress toward arms control.

As I stated on November 25, "Mankind already carries in its own hands too many of the seeds of its own destruction." By the examples we set, we hope to lead the way toward the day when other nations adopt the same principles.

Seabeds—Multilateral Arms Control

The responsibility for the control of armaments is multilateral as well as bilateral. The spread of technological skills knows no national boundaries; and innovation in weaponry is no monopoly of the superpowers. The danger of competitive armament is universal. Without international constraints the planet would be menaced by the spread of weapons of mass destruction to regions newly explored.

Collaborative efforts to avert these dangers have already produced a series of international agreements:

—To prohibit the testing of nuclear weapons in the atmosphere, in outer space, and underwater.

—To prohibit the proliferation of nuclear weaponry.

—To prohibit the use of Antarctica, or of outer space and its celestial bodies, for military purposes.

The United States has supported the efforts of the Conference of the Committee on Disarmament at Geneva to reach an international agreement prohibiting the emplacement of weapons of mass destruction on the bed of the sea. It is to the advantage of all to bring arms control, instead of strategic arms, to the ocean floor. The spread of weapons of mass destruction to this new realm would complicate the security problem of all nations, and would be to no nation's advantage.

Conclusion

The first year of this Administration saw significant progress in three areas of arms control.

—Unilaterally, we announced the comprehensive chemical and biological policy designed to set an example and encourage multilateral arms control in this field.

—Bilaterally, with the Soviet Union, we launched what could be the most important arms control discussions ever undertaken.

—Multilaterally, we made substantial progress toward reserving the vast ocean floors for peaceful purposes.

In all three instances we see our actions as protecting America's strength and enhancing her security. It is the biggest responsibility of this generation to avoid becoming the victim of its own technology.

ISSUES FOR THE FUTURE

The issues before us are ample proof of the challenge we face. The agenda requires not only fateful re-examinations of some of our old positions but also judgments about trends in the communist world and the effect of our negotiations on our relationship with our friends. These questions include:

1. Strategic Arms Limitations

—Our approach to these negotiations has been described in detail above.

2. Limiting the Flow of Weapons to Regions in Conflict

—When peace is in everyone's interest, we must find a way to control conflict everywhere. We must not be drawn into conflicts by local rivalries. The great powers should try to damp down rather than fan local passions by showing restraint in their sale of arms to regions in conflict. We stand ready to discuss practical arrangements to this end.

3. Resolve the Great East-West Political Issues

—We continue to be prepared to discuss the issues that divide us from the communist countries. Whether in addressing the cruel division of Europe or the future security of Asia we shall try to deepen the dialogue with the communist powers. But we will not permit negotiations to be used to sacrifice the interests of our friends. We are committed to the closest consultation with our NATO allies, and we will maintain the closest contact with our friends and allies in Asia.

4. *Closer Cooperation in Potential Crises*

—We must give practical expression to the common interest we have with the Soviet Union in identifying or limiting conflict in various areas of the world. Our choice is to find a way to share more information with our adversaries to head off conflict *without* affecting either our own security interests or those of our friends.

These are all difficult choices. Our careful consideration of the issues involved in negotiations with the communist world will take full account of them, as we proceed to build a lasting peace without sacrificing the interests of our allies and friends.

CONCLUSION: A NEW DEFINITION OF PEACE

Few ideas have been so often or so loosely invoked as that of "Peace." But if peace is among the most overworked and often abused staples of mankind's vocabulary, one of the reasons is that it is embedded so deeply in man's aspirations.

Skeptical and estranged, many of our young people today look out on a world they never made. They survey its conflicts with apprehension. Graduated into the impersonal routine of a bureaucratic, technological society, many of them see life as lonely conformity lacking the lift of a driving dream.

Yet there is no greater idealism, no higher adventure than taking a realistic road for peace. It is an adventure realized not in the exhilaration of a single moment, but in the lasting rewards of patient, detailed, and specific efforts—a step at a time.

—Peace requires confidence—it needs the cement of trust among friends.

—Peace requires partnership—or else we will exhaust our resources, both physical and moral, in a futile effort to dominate our friends and forever isolate our enemies.

—Peace must be just. It must answer man's dream of human dignity.

—Peace requires strength. It cannot be based on good will alone.

—Peace must be generous. No issue can be truly settled unless the the solution brings mutual advantage.

—Peace must be shared. Other nations must feel that it is *their* peace just as we must feel that it is *ours*.

—And peace must be practical. It can only be found when nations resolve real issues, and accommodate each other's real interests. This requires not high rhetoric, but hard work.

These principles apply to our opponents as well as to our allies, to the less developed as well as the economically advanced nations. The peace we seek must be the work of all nations.

For peace will endure only when every nation has a greater stake in preserving than in breaking it.

I expressed these thoughts in my toast to the Acting President of India at New Delhi on July 31, 1969. I repeat it now:

"The concept of peace is as old as civilization, but the requirements of peace change with a changing world. Today we need a new definition of peace, one which recognizes not only the many threats to peace but also the many dimensions of peace.

"Peace is much more than the absence of war; and as Gandhi's life reminds us, peace is not the absence of change. Gandhi was a disciple of peace. He also was an architect of profound and far-reaching change. He stood for the achievement of change through peaceful methods, for belief in the power of conscience, for faith in the dignity and grace of the human spirit and in the rights of man.

"In today's rapidly changing world there is no such thing as a static peace or a stagnant order. To stand still is to build pressures that are bound to explode the peace; and more fundamentally, to stand still is to deny the universal aspirations of mankind. Peace today must be a creative force, a dynamic process, that embraces both the satisfaction of man's material needs and the fulfillment of his spiritual needs.

"The pursuit of peace means building a structure of stability within which the rights of each nation are respected: the rights of national independence, of self-determination, the right to be secure within its own borders and to be free from intimidation.

"This structure of stability can take many forms. Some may choose to join in formal alliances; some may choose to go their own independent way. We respect India's policy of nonalignment and its determination to play its role in the search for peace in its own way. What matters is not how peace is preserved, but that it be preserved; not the formal structure of treaties, but the informal network of common ideals and common purposes that together become a fabric of peace. What matters is not whether the principles of international behavior these represent are written or unwritten principles, but rather that they are accepted principles.

"Peace demands restraint. The truest peace expresses itself in self-restraint, in the voluntary acceptance, whether by men or by nations, of those basic rules of behavior that are rooted in mutual respect and demonstrated in mutual forbearance.

"When one nation claims the right to dictate the internal affairs of another, there is no peace.

"When nations arm for the purpose of threatening their weaker neighbors, there is no peace.

"There is true peace only when the weak are as safe as the strong, only when the poor can share the benefits of progress with the rich, and only when those who cherish freedom can exercise freedom.

"Gandhi touched something deep in the spirit of man. He forced the world to confront its conscience, and the world is better for having done so. Yet we still hear other cries, other appeals to our collective conscience as a community of man.

"The process of peace is one of answering those cries, yet doing so in a manner that preserves the right of each people to seek its own destiny in its own way and strengthens the principles of national sovereignity and national integrity, on which the structure of peace among nations depends.

"However fervently we believe in our own ideals, we cannot impose those ideals on others and still call ourselves men of peace. But we can assist others who share those ideals and who seek to give them life. As fellow members of the world community, we can assist the people of India in their heroic struggle to make the world's most populous democracy a model of orderly development and progress.

"There is a relationship between peace and freedom. Because man yearns for peace, when the people are free to choose their choice is more likely to be peace among nations; and because many yearn for freedom, when peace is secure the thrust of social evolution is toward greater freedom within nations.

"Essentially, peace is rooted in a sense of community: in a recognition of the common destiny of mankind, in a respect for the common dignity of mankind, and in the patterns of cooperation that make common enterprises possible. This is why the new patterns of regional cooperation emerging in Asia can be bulwarks of peace.

"In the final analysis, however, peace is a spiritual condition. All religions pray for it. Man must build it by reason and patience.

"On the moon, now, is a plaque bearing these simple words: 'We came in peace for all mankind.'

"Mahatma Gandhi came in peace to all mankind.

"In this spirit, then, let us all together commit ourselves to a new concept of peace:

—A concept that combines continuity and change, stability and progress, tradition and innovation;

—A peace that turns the wonders of science to the service of man;

—A peace that is both a condition and a process, a state of being and a pattern of change, a renunciation of war and a constructive alternative to revolution;

—A peace that values diversity and respects the right of different peoples to live by different systems—and freely to choose the systems they live by;

—A peace that rests on the determination of those who value it to preserve it but that looks forward to the reduction of arms and the ascendancy of reason;

—A peace responsive to the human spirit, respectful of the divinely inspired dignity of man, one that lifts the eyes of all to what man in brotherhood can accomplish and that now, as man crosses the threshold of the heavens, is more necessary than ever."

Index

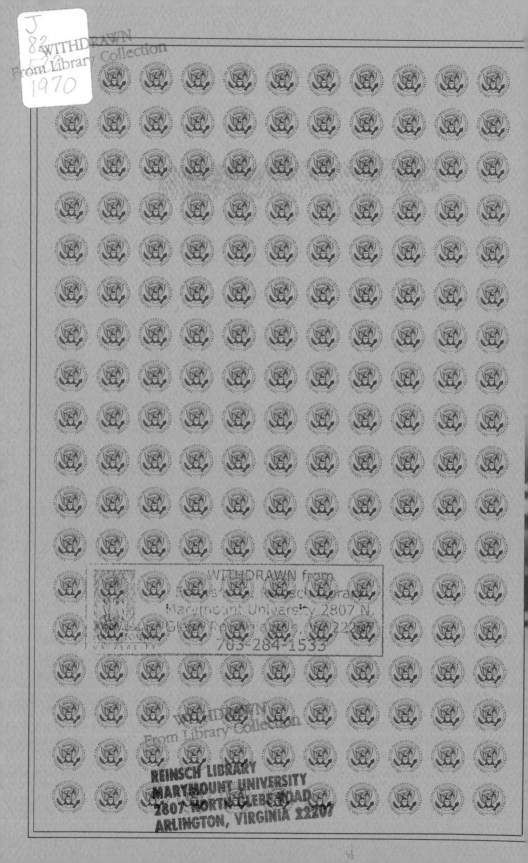